NEW HORIZONS?
THIRD WORLD INDUSTRIALIZATION
IN AN
INTERNATIONAL FRAMEWORK

ROBERT N. GWYNNE
SCHOOL OF GEOGRAPHY
UNIVERSITY OF BIRMINGHAM

Copublished in the United States with
John Wiley & Sons, Inc., New York.

Longman Scientific & Technical,
Longman Group UK Ltd,
Longman House, Burnt Mill, Harlow,
Essex CM20 2JE, England
and Associated Companies throughout the world.

Copublished in the United States with
John Wiley & Sons, Inc., 605 Third Avenue, New York, NY 10158

First published 1990

British Library Cataloguing in Publication Data
Gwynne, R. N.
New horizons? : third world industrialisation in an
international framework.
1. Developing countries. Industrial development
I. Title
338.09172′4

ISBN 0-582-02519-2

Library of Congress Cataloging-in-Publication Data
Gwynne, Robert N.
New horizons?: Third World industrialization in an
international framework / Robert N. Gwynne.
p.   cm.
Includes bibliograhical references.
ISBN 0-470-21642-5 (Wiley)
1. Developing countries – Economic policy. 2. Developing
countries – Industries. 3. International economic relations.
I. Title.
HC59.7.G88   1990
338.9′009172′4 – dc20   89–13785
                                                              CIP

Set in 10/12 pt Baskerville.
Produced by Longman Group (FE) Limited
Printed in Hong Kong.

FOR MARUJA

CONTENTS

PREFACE

The purpose of this book is not to present original ideas on the subject of industrialization in the world's developing countries, but to try to provide an appropriate framework for studying industrial development in the large number of varied countries that make up the developing world. The theme of industrial development in the Third World has been one of my major topics of concern since starting my doctorate. In my last book, I focused on the process of industrialization in Latin America and examined the structural and spatial legacy of import substitution industrialization and the relationship with the pattern and process of urbanization. In this book, however, the argument is extended in a different way.

The aim has been to compare the nature of Latin American industrialization with that of other Third World regions, most notably East Asia. For whereas the orientation of Latin American manufacturing has been undoubtedly inward looking for most of the twentieth century, the record of industrialization in East Asia can provide many examples of outward orientation in manufacturing.

The contrast in orientation introduces the question of involvement in the global economy. The Latin American strategy has been to reduce involvement in the global economy (as far as that is possible), and stimulate industrial growth towards domestic markets. This is very much the legacy of the world trade crisis of 1929–33, which provided the main stimulus to inward-oriented manufacturing in Latin America. In contrast, the global depression of 1929–33 had a relatively small impact on industrial strategies in East Asia, partly because of the colonial status of most countries and the already well-established outward orientation of Japanese industrialization.

The contrasting orientation of manufacturing growth in Latin America and East Asia calls into question the nature of the world economy for developing countries. Does it constitute a threat to national economic development, thus requiring the governments of less developed countries to protect their nascent economies and infant industries? Or does the global economy provide the context for limitless opportunity to the manufacturers of developing countries, thus encouraging governments of less developed countries to persuade manufacturers to think in terms of international rather than simply national markets?

The debate is a never-ending one in economic theory, but, in order to understand better the background and implications of the debate, the first part of the book sets out an international framework for the argument. In Chapter 2, the evolution of the global economy in the nineteenth and twentieth centuries is examined, with particular attention given to the problems of economic cycles and their impact – mainly because the existence of economic cycles in the global economy provides one major source of uncertainty to the governments of the developing countries.

It has been forcibly argued since the late eighteenth century that international trade can benefit even the poorest of countries. Chapter 3 examines the theoretical basis for this contention, and examines the value of international trade for developing countries that are relying on the export of primary rather than manufactured goods. Trade, however, is not the only form of economic interaction between a developing country and the global economy. Technology transfer, foreign investment and capital flow are three other areas of interaction. In Latin America, the crisis of capital flow has been particularly dramatic during the 1980s and worthy of special attention (Ch. 4).

It is hoped that Part I of the book gives an indication of both the opportunities and threats that the world economy can imply for developing countries. The basic conclusion (and argument of the book) is that the opportunities are increased and the threats reduced if developing countries can manage to industrialize.

The factors which determine industrial growth are very numerous, and each has its own set of theories. Chapter 5 introduces some of the economic and socio-cultural theories that have specifically looked at the question of industrial development and evaluates the institutional role of government within the industrializing process. The remaining chapters of Part II examine how developing countries themselves can best take advantage of their relationships with the global economy through trade, technology transfer and foreign investment from multinational corporations.

In particular, the aim has been to compare the success of trade in manufactured exports (Ch. 6) and domestic technological generation (Ch. 8) between countries that have adopted on the one hand an outward-oriented economic framework versus an inward-oriented structure on the other. This pursues one basic theme of the book by assessing how best developing countries can take advantage of the opportunities provided by the global economy. The opportunities and threats offered by the world economy to developing economies are further analysed in Chapter 7 by the respective examination of the product life cycle and protectionism in developed countries. Foreign investment too has been seen as both

spectre and spearhead of development in Third World countries, and Chapter 9 attempts to balance the various debates from the contrasting sides of the spectrum.

The themes of manufactured exports, technology transfer, the generation of domestic technology and the role of foreign investment in industrial development are returned to in the major sectoral case study of the book in Chapter 10, the motor car industry in the Third World. In this part, I decided to explore one case study in considerable detail rather than a number of case studies in lesser detail.

I have long perceived a major 'continental' contrast in industrialization between Latin America and East Asia. Part IV has the task of pursuing this theme. So many factors are relevant in studying industrial growth in these two 'continental' regions that it is easy to be lost unless one has a general perspective on the subject. The perspective taken in the Latin American continent (Ch. 11) is to explore the structural and spatial heritage of inward-oriented industrialization. Meanwhile, in East Asia (Ch. 12), the task has been to understand the institutional background to the outward orientation of industry and to assess both present and future implications. By necessity the scale of such treatment is large and wide ranging. The relevance of the comparison between the Latin American and East Asian experience is returned to in the final chapter, as the present and future role of industrialization in other Third World regions is discussed. However, I conclude by emphasizing another geographical point of a global scale – the present and future locational shift of manufacturing industry to what has come to be called the Pacific rim. Indeed, it should be pointed out at the outset that the great majority of regional examples used in the book come from the Pacific rim (East Asia and Latin America) rather than from Africa and South Asia.

I have had generous treatment from many friends and acquaintances in Latin America, particularly in Chile. Those who have taken time off to show me what they were doing, to exchange ideas, and to entertain me hospitably, are so numerous that I cannot even begin to recite their names. I would like to thank all colleagues and students of the School of Geography in the

University of Birmingham for providing an encouraging yet questioning environment within which to teach and write. I would specifically like to thank Tim Grogan and Kevin Burkhill for their competent assistance with the various figures and maps.

Technology and its application has figured prominently within this book and so I must pay tribute to the piece of technology that has greatly 'evolutionized' my personal writing habits; the word processor. However, the major thanks must go to Maruja, Daniel and Catherine for keeping me sane during the long bouts of time spent 'evolutionizing'!

ACKNOWLEDGEMENTS

We are grateful to the following for permission to reproduce copyright material:

The Editor of *Economic Geography* for fig. 3.2 from fig. 3.1, Vol. 40:1; Swanston Publishing for figs. 3.3 & 3.4 from maps 2 & 18 in *The New State of the World Atlas*, 2nd. ed., by Michael Kidron & Ronald Segal (A Pluto Project. Heinemann Educational Books/Pan Books, 1984); the author, Dr. A Wood for fig. 3.6 from a figure on p. 19 of *Geographical Magazine* 56:1 (1984); The World Bank for fig. 1.1 from fig. 3.7, fig. 3.5 from fig. 2.3, fig. 6.1 from fig. 5.2 (part), fig. 6.3 from box 6.1 (part) and tables 1.6 & 1.7 from tables 3.1 & 3.2, table 4.3 from table 2.4, table 6.1 from fig. 5.1, table 6.2 from table 5.1, tables 7.2, 7.3, 7.4 & 7.5 from tables 8.2 (part), 8.9, 8.3 & 8.7 of *World Development Report 1987*, fig. 3.7 from fig. 2.4 of *World Development Report 1983*, fig. 7.1 from a table on p. 23 of *World Development Report 1981*, Maria Gwynne for supplying the artwork for the frontispiece.

— 1 —

THIRD WORLD INDUSTRIALIZATION: INTRODUCTION AND CLASSIFICATION

the context is the economic system which links all parts of the world into a single functioning unit and which contains the dynamo for all societal activity. This is not economic determinism, however, for the operating of that dynamo is not a disembodied mechanistic process. Economic, political, social and cultural activities are all inter-related in a world-system whose trajectory is guided through decisions made by knowing individuals, constrained but not determined by their context, and enabled by their knowledge to make decisions that will restructure that context. Geography is about local variability within a general context. (Johnston 1984: 443–4)

The spatial development of economies and industries needs increasingly to be examined in the widest context of a world economy framework. At the same time, the relationships between the world economy framework and economic development at the local and national level can often be difficult to define. The world economic system, as it is sometimes called, is certainly not all encompassing. Local and national decisions can radically affect the nature of economic activity at their respective geographical scales. However, it can also be argued that the world economy imposes constraints upon the context of those local and national decisions. Furthermore, these constraints are constantly changing, perhaps favouring one group of countries in one period of time, only to be seen to discriminate against them in a subsequent period.

It is the argument of this book that the changing impact and constraints of the external world economy upon national and regional economies can be best adapted to in countries that industrialize with due regard to the exigencies and ever-changing nature of that external world economy. This normally indicates an international perspective in the running of national economies and a relative openness in terms of external trade, the transfer of technology and foreign investment. Outward orientation of national economies (in terms of international trade, technology transfer and investment) is to be preferred to inward orientation. This is simply because outward orientation gives national and local economies greater information and normally concomitant understanding of the changing nature of the world economy and how to turn those changes to the advantage of the local or national economy – for example, in terms of new international marketing opportunities, easier access to new technologies, greater flexibility in international capital markets, and more bargaining potential in relation to foreign investment.

More specifically, however, this book wishes to examine the crucial development issue of Third World industrialization within this international perspective. However, the approach is distinctly geographical in the sense that it constantly seeks to identify and explore the 'local variabilities' within the general context, reducing the geographical scale of analysis from the global to the continental, national, regional and local levels. I would also argue that the approach is geographical because of an interdisciplinary perspective that attempts to combine a range of factors beyond the economic – institutional, social and cultural factors, for example.

Third World industrialization, however, has been a topic largely ignored by geographers. For example, there has been no major integrating text on the subject since Mountjoy (1962). While there are large numbers of industrial geographers studying industrial location in the United States, United Kingdom, Canada and Australia, there is but a handful of geographers studying locational issues in regions where industrialization can be seen as truly crucial. The crucial nature of industrialization for Third World countries has never been so much in evidence as during the decade of the 1980s.

For the majority of countries of the Third World, the decade of the 1980s has been bad in terms of economic growth and development. For some of the poorest countries in the world, in sub-Saharan Africa, the spectres of drought and famine have contributed to economic stagnation – a zero growth in GDP in six years (1980–86) alongside annual population growth of 3.1 per cent. The mythical average person of sub-Saharan Africa has thus been getting poorer at an alarming rate during the 1980s – whereas in the previous fifteen years, the region had recorded annual growth rates of 5.6 per cent for the economy as opposed to 2.7 per cent for population (see Table 1.1).

For the more wealthy countries of the Third World that had tried to borrow their way out of economic stagnation in the 1970s, what the World Bank refers to as the highly indebted countries, the spectres of high world interest rates and stagnant world trade have been instrumental in creating a similar pattern – an economic growth rate (0.7 per cent per annum) considerably lower than that of population (2.4 per cent per annum – see Table 1.1). Even the group of developing economies that received the bonanza of high oil prices during the 1970s have performed poorly in the 1980s with again production increases (1.7 per cent per annum) lower than population growth (2.7 per cent per annum). The problem of oil has been that of declining prices (from US$40 a barrel in 1980 to US$11 dollars a barrel by the end of 1988). However, the problem of declining prices has been shared by most other commodities during the 1980s. Thus the large number of Third World countries relying on the export of primary products as their major source of income have been severely constrained during most of the 1980s.

For these three large blocs of Third World countries, then, the 1980s have brought a declining income for the average inhabitant. Furthermore, the gap between their development and that of the developed world as a whole has widened – the 1980s have brought relatively modest annual increases in GDP to the developed countries (2.5 per cent), but increases that are nevertheless significantly higher than those of oil exporters, highly indebted countries and sub-Saharan Africa.

Indeed, during the 1980s, only one group of

Table 1.1 Economic and population growth in the 1980s by world region

	Average annual growth of production (%)		Average annual growth of population (%)	
	1980–86	1965–80	1980–86	1965–80
Developing economies				
Oil exporters	1.7	7.1	2.7	2.7
Highly indebted countries	0.7	6.6	2.4	2.5
Sub-Saharan Africa	0.0	5.6	3.1	2.7
Exporters of manufactures	6.2	6.6	1.6	2.2
Developed economies	2.5	3.6	0.6	0.8

(*Source*: World Bank 1988: 225, 275)

Third World countries has proceeded to close the development gap between them and the developed world – outward-oriented industrializing countries (classified as exporters of manufactured products). Their economic growth rate between 1980 and 1986 (6.2 per cent per annum) has been over seven times that of the other developing economies and 2.5 times that of the developed world. Furthermore, the economic growth rate for this aggregation of developing countries was remarkably similar during the 1965–80 period (see Table 1.1), implying a reasonably consistent economic trajectory for them over more than two decades. With average population growth rates of 2.2 per cent between 1965 and 1980 and 1.6 per cent between 1980 and 1986, the average inhabitant of those developing countries classified as exporters of manufactures has also enjoyed two decades of steadily improving living conditions.

The evidence thus provided is distinctly general and aggregated. But it does show one indisputable fact – that during the difficult development decade of the 1980s, the economies of those developing countries that have promoted the production and export of manufactured goods have performed particularly well. It is the intention of this book to pursue the reasons behind this phenomenon and to explore its implications. The book specifically adheres not only to the importance of industrialization as a development strategy within less developed countries but also to the significance of an outward-oriented approach – relying on export growth as much as the development of the internal market.

However, it must be noted that the developing countries of today are industrializing within a very different world framework from that which faced 'earlier industrializers'. One important difference must concern the nature of the global economy and the increasingly closer connectivities that occur within it. For this reason, I think it important to introduce some of the more relevant points concerning the evolution of the modern world economy in Chapter 2. Such an analysis leads to the idea that the economic development of developing countries is presently constrained by at least two components of the global economy – the pattern and practice of trade

and access to capital. Chapters 3 and 4, respectively, examine international trading and capital constraints on Third World development.

As the Third World industrializes, it is apparent that no one overarching theory has been able to explore suitably the complex relationship between industrialization and development. Nevertheless, a number of theories have been put forward that attempt to develop generalizations concerning not only the role of industrialization in development but also what are the theoretical attributes for a successful process of industrialization. In Chapter 5, reference is made to some of the more significant theories that have attempted to explain industrial success through economic, social and cultural factors. Some wider theoretical issues are also addressed and particular reference is made to the crucial role of government in industrial development.

The complex relationships between trade and industrialization are explored in Chapters 6 and 7, with specific reference to trade policy, trade liberalization, the product life cycle and protectionism in the developed world. The issues of technological change and foreign investment in less developed countries are examined in Chapters 8 and 9 respectively, followed in Chapter 10 by the major sectoral case study of the world motor car industry. The spatial perspectives of Third World industrialization are investigated in the final three chapters, with particular reference to the industrialization of Latin America and East Asia. Before the wider issues of world economy and Third World industrialization are explored, however, it is necessary to examine them within some form of typology, due to the great variations in industrial experience and economic development within the more than one hundred countries that constitute the Third World.

TOWARDS A TYPOLOGY OF THIRD WORLD INDUSTRIALIZATION

It is a common misconception that the phenomenon of Third World industrialization is spatially restricted to a small number of countries, commonly referred to as the newly industrializing countries (NICs). This section seeks to dispel this misconception by pointing to the variety of industrial development types in the Third World and by seeing some form of industrialization occurring in all Third World countries rather than in just a select band of them.

A word about terminology here. I regard the descriptive terms 'Third World', 'less developed', 'underdeveloped' and 'developing' as broadly synonymous. As a result, these four terms are freely used to describe the same set of countries that are classified into five categories in the typology below. The adjectival terms are used interchangeably so that one term is not unduly repetitive. Newly industrializing countries (NICs) refer to a subset of Third World countries that have already made and continue to make great strides in industrial expansion.

With the aim of attempting to examine the industrial development of all Third World countries, there comes the difficult task of classification. This section is, therefore, an attempt at producing a typology of industrialization in Third World countries – unfortunately, only a rudimentary one, but at least one that goes beyond seeing Third World industrialization as spatially restricted. As with most simple classifications, many points are debatable due to the large number of variables behind the industrial process, but the purpose of the typology is to extend the argument and point to the complexities within Third World industrialization rather than produce any strict rules.

The trading constraints that primary producers have suffered since 1930 (see Ch. 3) were instrumental in making many less developed countries turn towards policies of industrialization – Latin American countries during the 1930s and 1940s and those countries emerging from colonialism during the 1950s and 1960s. The major trading constraint perceived by less developed countries was that of the declining terms of trade between primary product exports on the one hand, and manufactured imports on the other. As a result, industrial strategies tended to emphasize import substitution behind high tariff walls and with other elements of government protection. Countries pursuing the import substitution strategy typically started by producing final manufactures to replace imports. Many enjoyed initial bursts in the growth of manufacturing. But since production usually required imported intermediate and capital goods, sustained industrial growth depended on the expansion of developing country exports in order to provide the necessary foreign exchange for purchasing imported materials (such as steel), parts and machinery.

But, as Chenery (1977) noted, policies of import substitution had a differential impact on large and small countries. At low levels of *per capita* income, countries with large populations could promote a substantial industrial process oriented towards supplying the domestic market. Only after moderate levels of *per capita* income had been achieved through industrialization, was it necessary to export in order to carry on the process of industrial growth. The supreme example of this category has been Brazil, with a 1985 population of 136 million. Such a large domestic market had allowed high average growth rates of 11.2 per cent between 1965 and 1973 for a manufacturing sector primarily oriented towards fulfilling the demands of the domestic market. However, during the mid-1970s, the Brazilian government introduced a whole range of schemes to boost manufactured exports and their subsequent expansion was instrumental in maintaining average manufacturing growth rates of 4.2 per cent between 1973 and 1983 (World Bank 1985), and in causing manufactured exports as a percentage of total exports to increase from less than 10 per cent to approximately 50 per cent.

Meanwhile, it has been noted that small countries need to make an early transition to export expansion. Even at low levels of *per capita* income, small less developed countries (LDCs) need to export in certain specialized sectors and particularly labour-intensive sectors such as those of textiles, clothing and shoes. In small LDCs, increasing industrial growth and its beneficial ramifications would have to be closely linked to export expansion – as in the small East Asian states of Singapore, Hong Kong, Taiwan and South Korea.

Dynamic periods of industrial growth have also been enjoyed by those countries that have been able to expand rapidly their exports of primary products. However, the only commodity to sustain relatively high prices during the 1970s and early 1980s has been oil. Oil-exporting countries have therefore enjoyed periods of rapid industrial growth, but the decline and stagnation of oil prices in the mid-1980s have tended to halt these periods of growth. The previous schematic analysis of Third World industrialization leads to a possible four-fold division of LDCs in terms of their industrial record:

1. LDCs whose manufacturing growth has been primarily linked to their home market.
2. LDCs whose manufacturing growth has been strongly influenced by exports.
3. LDCs whose manufacturing growth has been linked to the investment of surplus oil revenues.
4. LDCs without large markets, without oil and whose manufactured exports constitute less than a 0.4 per cent share of the manufactured exports from developing economies.

1. LDCs whose manufacturing growth has been primarily linked to their home market

These are countries with large populations and markets, where import substitution policies have operated with some success, although differential performance between these countries has been related to their ability to gradually shift the emphasis to export markets. Section One of Table 1.2 presents data for the nine populous countries that had achieved more than a 0.5 per cent share of the manufactured exports from developing economies in 1985 (World Bank 1987: 49). In two of these countries (Brazil and Turkey) the manufacturing sector has come to be responsible for over one-quarter of GDP (USA = 20 per cent) and has enjoyed export growth of over 15 per cent per annum on average between 1973 and 1985; whereas Brazil's manufacturing growth in the 1970s was higher, Turkey has better weathered the 1980s recession. The manufacturing development of two other populous countries, Mexico and Indonesia, has been additionally affected by oil revenues boosting both national demand and in-

vestment opportunities. As a result, Indonesia achieved very high manufacturing growth rates between 1965 and 1980 and high growth in manufactured exports between 1973 and 1985; furthermore, its manufacturing sector withstood the shock of declining oil prices better than that of Mexico, although the latter has seen a significant expansion of manufactured exports to the United States between 1985 and 1989.

India and Pakistan reveal the pattern of countries whose manufacturing growth remains strongly oriented to their domestic markets. In contrast to the Latin American countries, their manufacturing growth rates during the 1980s have been significantly higher than those of the previous decade, encouraged by stronger national economic growth and increasing demand. Pakistan has had a slightly better record than India in terms of the promotion of manufactured exports, but not as good as Thailand with which it shares the critical structural characteristic of one-fifth of GDP in manufacturing. Two countries, Argentina and the Philippines, have recorded industrial decline during the 1980s, both partly due to political instability and the constraints of large external debts. However, whereas the Philippines have actively promoted manufactured exports (see Table 1.2), Argentina has effectively remained committed towards policies of import substitution. With its relatively small population and its lack of industrial growth since the mid-1970s, Argentina reflects the problems inevitably associated with gearing industrial growth to relatively small, domestic markets.

Section Two of Table 1.2 gives data for two countries with large markets but whose manufactured exports are negligible. With a population of 1 billion, this is understandable in the case of China. Its massive investments in manufacturing capacity over the last forty years is reflected in the very high ratio of manufacturing product to the gross domestic product – considerably higher than in any country in Section One of Table 1.2. Kitching (1982:125) has argued that Chinese economic growth since the Second World War must be partly understood in terms of that country's massive investment in state controlled industry. Its manufacturing growth rate between 1965 and 1985 has also been greater than any

Table 1.2 Third World countries with large domestic markets or whose manufacturing growth has been linked to their home market

Country[a]	Population (millions) mid-1985	Manuf'g as % of GDP, 1985	Average annual manufacturing growth rates (%)		Average annual growth rates (%) for manufactured exports, 1973–85
			1965–80	1980–85	
Section One					
Brazil	135.6	27[b]	9.8	0.3[c]	>15
India	765.1	17	4.4	5.6	<5
Mexico	78.8	22[b]	7.4	0.3[c]	7.5–10
Turkey	50.2	25	7.5	7.9	>15
Philippines	54.7	25	7.5	−1.2	>15
Thailand	51.7	20	10.9	5.3	10–15
Indonesia	162.2	14	12.0	6.4	>15
Pakistan	96.2	20	5.3	10.1	5–7.5
Argentina	30.5	28[b]	2.7	−1.6	<5
Section Two					
China	1,040.3	37	9.5	12.4	
Bangladesh	100.6	8	6.8	2.0	

[a] Country ranking in Section One is based on the share in manuf'd exports from LDCs, 1985.
[b] 1983 data.
[c] Refers to wider industry data.

(*Sources*: World Bank 1987: Figure 3.5; Tables 1, 2, 3)

other country in Table 1.2. Bangladesh, in contrast, with 50 per cent of its GDP corresponding to agriculture, still has a very small manufacturing sector in proportion, and rather indifferent growth figures, particularly for the 1980s.

2. LDCs whose manufacturing growth has been strongly influenced by exports

These countries are those most closely identified with the term 'newly industrializing countries' and are generally small- or medium-sized countries that have pursued an export-oriented policy from early stages in their industrialization. Table 1.3 presents data for seven relevant countries. Not all the countries mentioned are small. Korea's population of 41.1 million is 10 million greater than that of Argentina, but whereas the latter geared industrial development towards its relatively small market, Korea has recorded extraordinary success with outward-looking industrial policies – a growth rate of nearly 20 per cent per annum between 1965 and 1980, followed by growth rates of nearly 10 per

cent during the 1980s, and growth rates for manufactured exports higher than 15 per cent per annum between 1973 and 1985, making its manufactured exports equivalent to those of Sweden. Similar success has been recorded by Hong Kong and Taiwan, and by Singapore in the 1960s and 1970s (see Table 1.3). In a rather different league come the three remaining countries, although two, Malaysia and Tunisia, have recorded high industrial and export growth rates for the 1980s.

3. LDCs whose manufacturing growth has been linked to the investment of surplus oil revenues

Countries that have been able to invest in a crash programme of industrialization due to surplus oil revenues have often enjoyed rapid industrial growth rates during the 1970s and early 1980s. Sustained industrial growth into the late 1980s, however, has not normally occurred, unless the country has switched enthusiastically towards export-oriented policies, as with Mexico and Indonesia. Table 1.4 presents data for eight oil-ex-

Table 1.3 Third World countries whose manufacturing growth has been linked to exports

Country[a]	Average annual manufacturing growth rates (%)		Manuf'g as % of GDP, 1985	Manuf'd exports as % of total exports 1985	Average annual growth rates (%) for manufactured exports, 1973–85
	1965–80	1980–85			
South Korea	18.8	9.0	28	91	>15
Singapore	13.3	2.1	24	58	10–15
Hong Kong	n.d.	n.d.	24	92	10–15
Taiwan	n.d.	n.d.	33	90	>15
Malaysia	n.d.	6.1	20	27	>15
Morocco	5.9	0.7	17	40	>15
Tunisia	9.9	6.7	14	42	10–15

[a] Country ranking based on the share in manuf'd exports from LDCs, 1985.
n.d. no data.

(*Sources*: World Bank 1987: Figure 3.5; Tables 2, 3, 11)

Table 1.4 Third World countries whose manufacturing growth has been linked to the investment of surplus oil revenues

Country	GNP *per capita* (in dollars) 1985	Average annual manufacturing growth rates		Manuf'd Exports as % of total exports 1985	Manuf'g as % of GDP, 1985
		1965–80	1980–85		
United Arab Emirates	19 270	n.d.	20.2	1	10
Saudi Arabia	8 850	8.1	7.7	2	8
Libya	7 170	13.7	11.5	2	5
Trinidad	6 020	3.8	–4.8	14	7
Venezuela	3 080	5.9	1.4	5	21
Algeria	2 550	9.5	9.0	2	11
Ecuador	1 160	11.5	0.5	1	19
Nigeria	800	14.6	3.0	1	9

(*Sources*: World Bank 1987: Tables 1, 2, 3, 11)

porting countries that have invested oil revenues in capital-intensive programmes of industrialization. The first point to note is that four countries (United Arab Emirates, Saudi Arabia, Libya and Trinidad) have higher *per capita* incomes than some developed countries and therefore hold the term 'Third World country' very loosely; indeed, the World Bank categorizes the first three countries as 'high income oil exporters', along with Kuwait for which it supplies no manufacturing or industrial data. The category is further complicated by the fact that two oil exporters that have invested heavily in industrialization, Iraq and Iran, have been involved in a hugely debilitating war between 1979 and 1988. This group of industrializing countries, therefore, should include three further countries for which there are no data – Kuwait, Iraq and Iran.

Examining the data for the eight countries in Table 1.4, the category does show great variations in *per capita* income. However, in terms of the performance of the manufacturing sector, there are some distinct similarities. First, the manufacturing sector has a low weighting in the overall economy in all countries, apart from Ecuador and Venezuela. It should be pointed out that the latter country has been characterized by state investment in such a wide range of industry [electricity generation, aluminium (bauxite mining, alumina and aluminium production), steel, coal, iron ore] that the scale of its investments went considerably beyond the size of its oil revenues and involved heavy external debt, one reason for its low 1980s growth rate. Second, manufactured exports (which would include petrochemicals) remain a very low proportion of total exports in all countries; the dependence on oil has often meant **high exchange rates, high-cost manufacturing** production and an entrepreneurial orientation to the domestic market only. Third, the oil price increases of 1973 and 1979 and the concomitant expansion in local demand did create high rates of manufacturing growth during the 1970s, the highest being recorded in Nigeria. However, the downturn in oil prices during the 1980s has had a more variable effect on manufacturing performance. Four countries (Trinidad, Ecuador, Venezuela and Nigeria) have either recorded serious manufacturing decline or stagnation after 1982. Manufacturing growth in the remaining four countries has not been unduly disturbed by the oil price decline.

4. LDCs without large markets, without oil and whose manufactured exports constitute less than a 0.4 per cent share of the manufactured exports from developing economies

This category includes the great majority of less developed countries. They are the countries without the theoretical advantage of a large market (greater than 50 million inhabitants), without the advantage of large oil revenues during the 1970s and with an export record that does not make it enter the group of the top 15 LDC exporters of manufactured goods. However, considerable variations occur within this group. At one extreme, there are countries such as Egypt and Colombia, with broad industrial structures producing for their medium-sized domestic markets. At the other extreme, one has countries

Table 1.5 Third World countries whose manufacturing product is greater than their agricultural product

Country[a]	Agricultural product as % of GDP, 1985	Manufacturing product as % of GDP, 1985
Panama	9	9
South Africa	5	23
Uruguay	11	33[b]
Jordan	8	12
Chile[c]	10	20
Costa Rica	20	29[b]
Mauritius	15	20
Peru	11	20
Jamaica	6	20
Botswana	6	8
Dominican Republic	15	19
Nicaragua	23	27
Zimbabwe	13	29
Egypt	20	31[b]
Zambia	14	22

[a] Countries ranked according to 1985 *per capita* income.
[b] Refers to data for wider industrial grouping.
[c] 1983 data.

(*Source*: World Bank 1987: Table 3)

whose development priorities must be firmly set within the agricultural sector. This leads to a **simple manner of subdividing this category of** countries according to whether the manufacturing product is greater than the agricultural product. Table 1.5 gives data for those countries whose manufacturing product is proportionately greater than their agricultural product. All remaining less developed countries (which are not listed) fall into the category of having an agricultural product greater than that of manufacturing.

Such an index reflects agricultural as well as manufacturing strengths. Thus, countries with limited agriculture rather than sizeable manufacturing are included – Panama, Jordan and Botswana. Meanwhile, Colombia, a country with a relatively prosperous and diversified agriculture, is not included due to an agricultural product (20 per cent of GDP) still greater than that of manufacturing (18 per cent). However, in general, increasing development means a declining agricultural product relative to that of manufacturing and Table 1.5 generally reflects this principle. All the countries apart from Zambia are classified by the World Bank as middle-income economies. Most of these countries have embarked on policies of import substitution but due to limited markets have been unable to achieve significant growth rates. Some are now following vigorous export policies (Chile, Jordan, Mauritius), but others still appear committed primarily to their domestic markets (Peru, Nicaragua, Zimbabwe).

The above attempt at classification of Third World industrializing countries has relied on a small number of key variables – size of population and markets, export orientation of governments, significance of surplus oil revenues. However, one major assumption that underlies the classification, and should be noted, is that of the close

linkage between manufacturing and economic growth. This is reflected in the importance given throughout to the index of manufacturing as a proportion of GDP. It is interesting in this context to point to the inverted U-shaped relationship between GDP *per capita* and the share of manufacturing value added in GDP as shown in Fig. 1.1. Although the relationship is a general one, the previous typology can partially explain the position of those countries relatively distant from the best-fit line. Oil-exporting countries (Algeria and Venezuela) tend to be well below the line because of the effect of oil boosting the national economy and the performance of the manufacturing sector lagging behind. Meanwhile, countries whose manufacturing sector is expanding rapidly due to export growth (Korea, Brazil, Turkey) find themselves significantly above the line as do countries whose manufacturing sector has been strongly

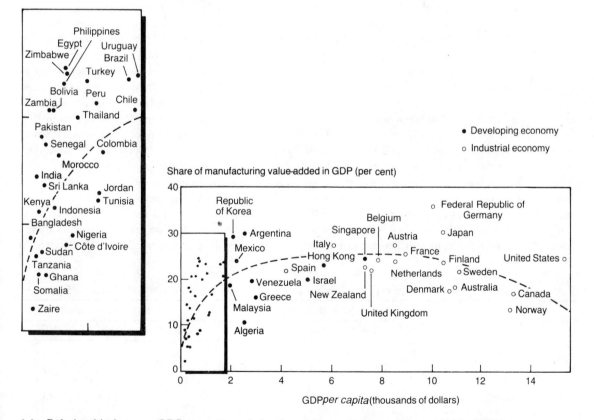

1.1 Relationship between GDP *per capita* and the share of manufacturing value-added in GDP in selected economies, 1984.
Source: World Bank *World Development Report 1987*.

oriented towards a medium-sized national market and generated few exports (Argentina, Egypt, Uruguay, Zimbabwe, Zambia and Bolivia); in this case a relatively large manufacturing sector (for the level of development of the country) has not created concomitant levels of economic growth.

THIRD WORLD COUNTRIES IN A GLOBAL MANUFACTURING SYSTEM

The attempt to produce a basic typology of Third World countries in the process of industrializing has served to show the considerable variety in the form of industrialization of these countries. The stereotype of newly industrializing countries as presented by the Gang of Four – Singapore, Hong Kong, Taiwan and Korea (Harris 1986) – can now be seen within a much wider context.

However, all Third World countries are industrializing within a global manufacturing system where tremendous technological, marketing and productive power are concentrated in but a small number of countries – the developed countries. As Table 1.6 shows, the developing countries (including China) accounted for only 18.1 per cent of world production (excluding the Soviet bloc) in 1985; the nineteen countries classified as industrial market economies, meanwhile, were responsible for as much as 81.6 per cent of world production (excluding the Soviet bloc). There had been some movement in the shares of world manufacturing production and exports corresponding to developing countries between 1965 and 1985 – a rise in the share of global production from 14.5 to 18.1 per cent and a substantial rise

in export share from 7.3 to 17.4 per cent.

However, the disaggregation of the developing countries into low income and middle income reveals that almost all the increases corresponded to the latter group of countries. Low-income developing countries, including China and India and accounting for over 50 per cent of the world's population, maintained the same low share of both global manufacturing production (about 7 per cent) and exports (about 2 per cent) between 1965 and 1985. The 55 middle-income countries, which figured prominently in the previous typology, nearly doubled their share of world production and, more significantly, trebled their share of world exports.

Furthermore, as Table 1.7 reveals, these exports were becoming increasingly more diverse, complex and less labour intensive. This was particularly demonstrated in the labour-intensive textile and clothing sector; its share of the manufactured exports from developing countries declined from 31.3 to 24.8 per cent between 1970 and 1984. Meanwhile, the share of what the World Bank classes as non-traditional manufactured exports expanded to two-thirds of the total, with the transport (mainly vehicles) and machinery sectors recording export growth rates of 20 per cent a year from developing countries. Nevertheless, the countries of the developed world dominate the exports of high technology manufactures; just five countries (USA, Japan, West Germany, Britain and France) account for 77 per cent of high technology exports.

Developing countries are attempting to increase manufactured production and exports in a highly competitive global system in which two world

Table 1.6 Shares of production and exports of manufactures by country group, 1965, 1973 and 1985 (%)

Country group	Share of production			Share of exports		
	1965	1973	1985	1965	1973	1985
Industrial market economies	85.4	83.9	81.6	92.5	90.0	82.3
Developing countries	14.5	16.0	18.1	7.3	9.9	17.4
Low income	7.5	7.0	6.9	2.3	1.8	2.1
Middle income	7.0	9.0	11.2	5.0	8.1	15.3
High-income oil exporters	0.1	0.1	0.3	0.2	0.1	0.3
Total	100.0	100.0	100.0	100.0	100.0	100.0

(*Source*: World Bank 1987: Table 3.1)

Table 1.7 Structure of manufactured exports from developing countries, 1970–84

Description	Share of developing countries' manufactured exports		Growth rate 1970–84
	1970	1984	
Traditional manufactured exports			
Labour intensive			
Textiles and apparel	31.3	24.8	11.8
Footwear	1.8	2.9	18.2
Other	2.9	2.3	11.6
Total	36.0	30.0	12.4
Resource based			
Wood and cork	3.6	1.5	6.9
Paper	0.8	1.1	17.6
Other	0.8	0.9	14.5
Total	5.2	3.5	12.2
Non-traditional manufactured exports			
Electrical machinery	16.1	16.7	14.1
Chemicals	8.3	9.9	15.3
Non-electrical machinery	4.2	8.7	20.1
Transport equipment	2.6	5.2	20.0
Iron and steel	6.2	6.5	14.2
Other	21.4	19.5	12.9
Total	58.8	66.5	15.1
TOTAL	100.0	100.0	100.0

(*Source*: World Bank 1987: Table 3.3)

regions, Western Europe (mainly Germàny) and Japan, have a distinctly asymmetric trade structure, with manufactured exports much greater than imports (see Ch. 2). In contrast, one world region (Eastern Europe and the Soviet Union) is distinctly autarkic, the constituent countries producing domestically the great majority of their manufacturing requirements and trading internationally only at a very small scale. North America, responsible for 50 per cent of world manufacturing production after the Second World War, has not only seen its share of world production considerably reduced but has also seen manufactured imports rise irresistibly, so that now manufactured imports far outweigh manufactured exports. This trend has been exacerbated during the mid-1980s with Western Europe, Japan and industrializing countries of the Third World building up large trade surpluses with the United States in manufactured goods; a US$40 billion deficit on manufacturing trade in 1983 had turned into one of US$110 billion by 1985.

The three Third World regions (Latin America, Africa and Asia) also have manufactured imports outweighing exports, but in two of them (Latin America, Asia), the imbalance has been reducing at the continental level. In Latin America, the debt crisis has put a balance of payments surplus at a premium, reducing manufactured imports and stimulating manufactured exports in countries as varied as Mexico, Brazil and Chile. In Asia, the increase in manufactured exports from South Korea, Hong Kong, Singapore and Taiwan has significantly reduced the import/export imbalance at the continental level. Only in Africa are manufactured exports negligible and manufactured imports high. However, in order to appreciate fully the present position of less developed countries in the world manufacturing system, it is necessary to examine the evolution of the world economy over the last two centuries and the role of less developed countries within that global economy.

—— PART I ——

THE
INTERNATIONAL
FRAMEWORK

— 2 —

THE EVOLUTION OF AN INTERDEPENDENT WORLD

The aim of this chapter is to trace the evolution of the world economy over the last two centuries. The precise task is to demonstrate how the present Third World countries have come to be inserted into the world economy. Such a task has been the subject of large numbers of books, such as Wallerstein (1974, 1979, 1984), Anell and Nygren (1980), Fieldhouse (1971) and Ellsworth (1965). This chapter, however, will not go into the many debates concerning the nature of capitalist growth in the Third World, but will concentrate on providing a general framework for the growth of the world economy so that the more tightly focused subsequent chapters can be put into a suitably wide historical and spatial context. Finally, this chapter will examine some empirical and theoretical contributions to the question of economic fluctuations in the world economy, and briefly analyse the impact of such fluctuations on the development of Third World countries.

WORLD PRODUCTION AND TRADE IN THE NINETEENTH CENTURY

According to Anell and Nygren (1980), it was not until the end of the Napoleonic wars that mercantilism began to disappear and a true international world economy began to emerge. Indeed, the nineteenth century saw dramatic changes in the economic interaction between different parts of the globe. Throughout the hundred years which ended in 1913, world trade and the international transfer of capital increased far more quickly than population and production. At the beginning of the nineteenth century, it has been estimated that only 3 per cent of world production circulated through international trade. Most countries were self-sufficient in terms of the production of basic goods, and trade tended to be restricted to luxuries, such as sugar, tea, spices, gold and silver. However, by 1913, world trade was equivalent to about one-third of total world output.

The nineteenth century was the age of liberalism and free trade. It could be argued that the beginning of the movement had started with the publication of Adam Smith's book, *Wealth of Nations*, in 1776. In this book, he equated economic success not only with increasing division of labour and economies of scale but also with trading growth linked to free markets:

> In discussing policy, Smith stressed the natural harmony of interests of all parties from allocation of resources in free markets, and . . . advocated the case for 'laissez-faire' policies of non-intervention. In this he was a very successful advocate because his argument gradually won over British official opinion, and British influence diffused his policy message world-wide (Maddison 1982: 14–15).

Adam Smith's book formed only a part of the general climate of liberalism. This also included the influence of the Newtonian scientific revolution establishing a breakaway from the old static

concept of a designed earth and the introduction
of a belief in unlimited technical progress. The
doctrine of liberalism appealed not only to a will
to liberate individual enterprise but also to a belief
that such liberalism would lead inevitably to the
long-run betterment of all.

In terms of the emergence of the international
economy, the theoretical benefits of free trade
were expounded by another influential economist,
Ricardo, in the early nineteenth century:

> If trade is left free, each country in the long run
> tends to specialise in the production of and to
> export those commodities in which production it
> enjoys a comparative advantage in terms of real
> costs, and to obtain by importation those
> commodities which could be produced at home
> only at a comparative disadvantage in terms of
> real costs; and such specialisation is to the mutual
> advantage of the countries participating in it
> (Ricardo 1817).

Free trade was certainly to the advantage of
Britain in the early nineteenth century as the first
major industrial power. Britain was therefore able
to control (for a time almost exclusively) one vital
aspect of world trade in the nineteenth century –
the production by the machine and in the factory
of large numbers of cheap manufactured goods,
goods that during the century came to replace the
handicraft products of many regions throughout
the world. The ensuing decline in local self-sufficiency led to large-scale investments in roads,
canals and railways. The construction of these
transport networks, built for the worldwide exchange of primary goods for manufactured
products, was again an area in which Britain
could offer both the necessary expertise and capital. The period up until the First World War saw
many elaborate transport networks built in the
developing world, but perhaps the densest and
most complete network was that created by
British capital and expertise in Argentina (see
Fig. 2.1).

The rapid growth of manufacturing production
caused a greater demand for raw materials and a
worldwide system of raw material supply
developed. The demand for foodstuffs from the
growing industrial towns was met primarily by
expanding domestic production but in Britain
there soon arose a substantial need to import

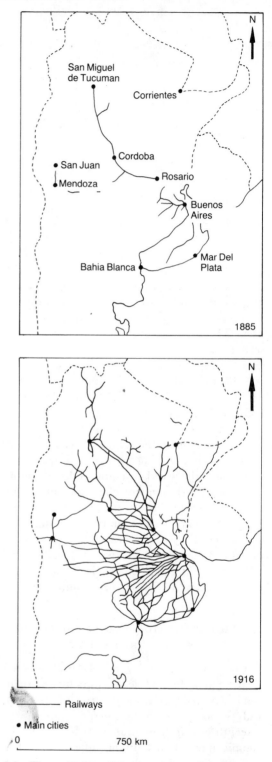

2.1   The evolution of the Argentine railway system,
1885–1916.

foodstuffs – beef from Argentina and Uruguay, wheat from Chile and North America, mutton from Argentina, New Zealand and Australia, for example. Within Britain and Europe, increases in land and labour productivity and land shortages forced a growing proportion of the population to sell their labour in the towns. The large rural–urban migrations operated to keep labour abundant and therefore cheap in the industrial towns. This occurred despite the effect of widespread international emigration, equivalent to over 10 per cent of the population of the European continent. During the period 1815 to 1913, about 43 million Europeans, out of a population which grew from 200 to 450 million, moved to North America, Australasia, Latin America and South Africa. The idea of a favourable juxtaposition of many economic circumstances lies at the heart of the industrial revolution of the nineteenth century.

The latter half of the nineteenth century very much constituted the pristine epoch of free trade. Between 1850 and 1880, the volume of world trade increased by 270 per cent and, despite an economic depression and rising tariffs, trade expanded by a further 170 per cent between 1880 and 1913. Technological conditions for the expansion of world trade were created by a rapid development of domestic and international communications. The total shipping tonnage of the world increased from 19 million tons in 1870 to 49 million tons in 1913, almost half of which consisted of steamships (Anell and Nygren 1980: 16).

From the point of view of the economic geographer, however, the most significant legacy of the nineteenth century was the dramatic reduction in the friction of distance that resulted from technological innovation in transportation. Freight rates fell by 75 per cent during the period 1820–50 and by a further 70–90 per cent between 1850 and 1914 (Anell and Nygren 1980: 16). In purely nominal terms, this meant that while it would have cost US$100 to ship x units of copper from Chile to Britain in 1820, it would have cost only US$5 nearly a century later in 1914. Such dramatic reductions in the friction of distance effect on world trade meant that factory products, made increasingly cheaper through increasing economies of scale and division of labour, were able to displace handicraft industries and upset local patterns of supply throughout the world. The lowering of the friction of distance effect during the nineteenth century began to make the world increasingly interlinked and interdependent economically. However, for an understanding of the economic development of Third World countries, their relationship with the West and the manner in which they were inserted into the world economy during the nineteenth and twentieth centuries, one must look at two other phenomena in detail – colonialism and the export of capital.

Colonialism

In his book, *The Wealth of Nations*, Adam Smith scarcely refers to the economic position of colonies, except to mention how profitable they can be for the colonists, rather than the colonial power:

> High wages of labour and high profits of stock, however, are things, perhaps, which scarce ever go together, except in the peculiar circumstances of new colonies. . . . [Colonies] have more land than they have [capital] stock to cultivate. What they have, therefore, is applied to the cultivation only of what is most fertile and most favourably situated. . . . [Capital] stock employed in the purchase and improvement of such lands must yield a very large profit, and consequently afford to pay a very large interest. Its rapid accumulation in so profitable an employment enables the planter to increase the number of his hands faster than he can find them in a new settlement. Those whom he can find, therefore, are very liberally rewarded (Skinner 1979: 194–5).

Adam Smith's seminal work was published in the same year as the beginning of the American War of Independence, a war costly for the colonial power. The attitude towards colonies changed as a result. It was argued that the benefits of free trade between countries were not adversely affected by lack of colonies. Furthermore, colonialism was now seen as an economic burden for the colonial power and during the late eighteenth and early nineteenth centuries, European states came to have little interest in expanding their colonial administration, although it must be emphasized that they kept their existing colonies and spheres of interest. Indeed, decolonization could positively assist international free trade, as occurred after the independence of the former Spanish colonies in Latin America during the second and third decades of the nineteenth century. The newly independent countries no longer had to conduct all their legal trade through the colonial power but could trade with any country with which it was profitable to do so. The early nineteenth century, its thinking deeply affected by economic liberalism, thus witnessed a general lack of interest in colonial development.

However, attitudes towards colonialism began to turn again in the latter half of the nineteenth century, although many economic historians argue that it was not until the recession of the 1870s that ideas definitely changed. Again the change can be linked to new interpretations of the economic problem and particularly to the writings of John Stuart Mill, and in particular his *Principles of Political Economy*, published in 1848. Mill and other economists argued that a country would eventually reach a stage of maturity in its national development. This stage of maturity would be characterized by a surplus of investment capital; and with capital in surplus and therefore cheap, profits would inevitably fall. During the 1870s recession, it was held that European countries had reached this stage of maturity, but that this process could be turned around by increased exports and investments abroad. The colonial question re-emerged, particularly for those who accepted part of Mill's interpretation of British economic success of the mid-nineteenth century: 'the perpetual overflow of capital into colonies or foreign countries . . . has been for many years one of the principal causes by which the decline of profits in England has been arrested' (Mill 1848).

There followed a period of territorial and colonial acquisition by the economic and political powers that were becoming prominent at the end of the nineteenth century. The continent of Africa witnessed 'the scramble' for its lands during the 1880s, as a result of which six European powers had varying degrees of colonial interest in the continent – Britain, France, Germany, Belgium, Portugal and Italy. In other world regions, the United States annexed Hawaii and Puerto Rico and took Cuba and the Philippines from Spain. Meanwhile, Russia extended its Central Asian empire towards the east and south and Japan gained control over Korea (from Russia) and Taiwan (from China).

Overall, the colonies in Asia, Australasia and Africa, and the few remaining ones in the Americas came to have a reasonably well-defined position in the emerging world economy. In the main, the colonial powers adapted or tried to adapt production in the colonies to the needs of the metropolis. The colonies were to produce raw materials for the industries of Europe, and in this way receive surplus capital investment from the metropolis. With the expansion of investment in colonial infrastructure and raw material production, the colonies would also constitute expanding markets for the manufactured products of the metropolis.

Although there were exceptions, most of the exporting countries of the non-Western world came to rely on one of three different types of economy, all closely linked to the evolving role of colonies and other developing countries in the world system of trade. The first category could be defined as the mining economy, where the country's development would be dominated by the extraction of one or two minerals, such as copper in Chile, oil in Venezuela and Iran and tin in Bolivia. Extraction, processing, transportation and distribution of the mineral would invariably be organized by a Western corporation. In this way, the mining area(s) in the developing country could constitute a type of enclave economy, a technologically advanced localized economy, highly integrated into the world economy, but with a limited degree of integration into the surrounding regional and national economy. A second type of national economy was that based around plantation agriculture, normally producing tropical or sub-tropical products such as cotton, sugar and bananas. Again Western-based corporations tended to dominate production and trade, although because of the greater spatial areas covered and the greater employment generated by plantation agriculture in relation to mining, regional multipliers would often be greater than in mining economies – for example, in labour migration and in the stimulation of regional food production through peasant agriculture. The final type of economy was one where peasant agriculture itself was expanded and organized. In this type of economy, the regional growth multipliers from the export-oriented activities could be much more extensive, although the transport, processing and trading functions would normally be in the hands of Western corporations, such as the West Africa Trading Company coordinating cocoa production in the colony known as the Gold Coast (now Ghana).

Export of capital

Finally, in examining the evolution of the world economy up until the First World War and the role of countries in Africa, Asia and Latin America in that economy, one should not forget the tremendous increases in capital flows across the world. In the first two decades of the nineteenth century, capital flows between countries were negligible. By the 1850s, they had crept up modestly – to about 2 billion dollars a year – and by the early 1870s, they were averaging 5 billion dollars a year. However, during the next forty years, the size of capital flows across the world increased by a factor of seven, to an estimated total of 35 billion dollars in 1913 (Anell and Nygren 1980: 26). Such a level of international capital flow was not seen again until the second half of the twentieth century.

The major source country of such capital outflow was undoubtedly Britain, providing nearly 50 per cent of the total for most of the period. Investments were mainly in railways, power supply and public utilities. Direct corporate investment was mainly in mines and plantation agriculture. There were three main patterns of capital flow and related investment. First, there were the attempts by the European powers to stimulate investments in newly acquired colonies. Second, the late nineteenth century saw massive increases in investment in the independent states of Latin America; British investment tended to dominate in this area with the Argentine and Uruguayan beef industry (railways, refrigeration and canning plants, refrigerated steamships), the Chilean nitrate industry in the Atacama (railways,

processing factories, water supply facilities) and the Mexican oil industry constituting outstanding examples. Finally, there were already significant cross-investments taking place between the developed countries themselves and most particularly between Europe and North America.

THE WORLD ECONOMY IN THE TWENTIETH CENTURY

The greatest epoch of world trade growth was that between the 1850s and 1914, divided up by a period of slow growth in the 1870s and 1880s. In terms of the evolution of the world economy, therefore, it is better to see 1913 as the last year of the nineteenth-century period of rapid growth in world trade. The First World War very much broke this trend, not only in the war itself but also in the aftermath, because after the First World War, protectionism 'broke out', most especially in European countries. Furthermore, two European countries, France and Britain, became locked into a complex network of debts and financial claims with Germany after the First World War. Meanwhile, some developing countries, such as Brazil, that had recorded significant industrial growth during the trading problems of the First World War, began to erect protectionist barriers around their fledgling industries after the war. This is not to say that during the 1920s significant economic growth did not occur. But where it was present, as in the United States and Japan, it was very much inward oriented, US growth being closely linked to the transport revolution consequent upon the arrival of the cheap motor car; the North American share of world car production was greater than 90 per cent throughout the 1920s.

However, while there was some regaining of world trade momentum in the 1920s, the economic depression that began at the end of the decade heralded drastic reductions in world trade. Between 1929 and 1933, world trade decreased by an astounding 65 per cent. Production fell less than trade but the fall of one-third in world industrial output between 1929 and 1932 created an unemployed mass of 30 million people in the richer countries. Industrial production in the country that had been so buoyant during the

1920s, the United States, fell by a greater amount than any other country – by approximately one-half in the first three years of the depression.

But international trade was particularly affected and the desperately slow return to free market conditions of the 1920s was halted in its tracks. Countries that had been locked into a free trading world system for nearly a century, such as Chile, saw their exports decline by as much as 75 per cent in three years; the major reason for such a decline was the radical reduction in demand for primary commodities from the industrialized countries. Their only solution was to erect high protectionist barriers around their economies and, after a century of outward-oriented growth, develop policies to promote inward-oriented growth, the most popular being that of import-substitution industrialization (substituting domestic industrial production for previously imported goods) and currency devaluations. While international trade was seriously affected, capital flows were even more so and foreign lending virtually ceased. In short, the economic depression of the early 1930s brought collapse to the international economy.

It is a curious comment on economic activity that the problems of the 1930s economic depression were not fully cast aside until the economic growth generated by the military expenditures of the Second World War. However, the Second World War also produced a radical shift in the balance of power between the world's leading industrial states, both in military and economic respects. For, in terms of the Western capitalist world, the legacy of the war was to make the United States by far the most dominant economic and military power. This was partly because the demands of the Second World War solved the US economic problems of the 1930s in expanding production and increasing government influence in the economy, mainly through the expanding defence budget. During the Second World War, the federal budget increased by a factor of ten, from US$9 billion in 1939 to US$100 billion in 1945. The unemployment problem was at last solved as 17 million jobs were created and total output doubled during the war. The contrast between the economic success of the United States, on the one hand, and the war-ravaged landscapes of Europe and Japan, on the other, meant that by the end of the war the United States accounted for as much as one-third of the world's total output. A further dramatic statistic was that by 1948, the United States controlled three-quarters of the world's monetary gold. Meanwhile, because of the tremendous growth in production in the United States during the war and its reduction elsewhere, the United States ended the war with huge trading surpluses; this kept on being a feature of world trade for many years after the Second World War.

This phenomenon of economic dominance did permit the United States and its allies to exert considerable influence in the reconstruction of the world economy after the Second World War. The grudging return to free trade after the First World War and the spectre of the 1930s depression were historical precedents that US and Allied policy makers duly noted in the Bretton Woods agreement of 1944. It is generally accepted that 'enlightened' policies emanated from Bretton Woods. First, there was the general concern to return to free trading conditions as soon as possible after the war; this was seen as particularly necessary so that the large US trading surpluses could be reduced and therefore not create a major imbalance in the post-war world economy. Secondly, there emerged from the United States a policy of generosity in defeat so that again the failings of the post-First World War reconstruction should not be repeated.

A series of 'world' institutions were set up to organize, coordinate and promote the Bretton Woods initiatives in the world economy. First of all, there was the General Agreement on Tariffs and Trade (GATT), signed in 1947, and set up to attempt to reduce tariffs in international trade (especially in trade between the major economies) and to eliminate all other measures preventing free trade. While GATT was given the task of re-establishing freer trading conditions after the war, the Marshall Aid scheme of 1948 was established in order to facilitate grants and loans to the war-ravaged countries of Europe and Japan. The United States supplied grants and loans totalling US$12.5 billion to Europe and Japan over the next four years.

Thirdly, a financial sheriff of the world

economy was established in 1947 – the International Monetary Fund (IMF). In its early years, the IMF favoured fixed exchange rates and freely convertible currencies, partly in order to facilitate the resumption of capital flows through the world economy from such capital-surplus countries as the United States. The IMF could intervene to assist economies under financial pressure, although borrowing facilities were theoretically linked to the country's economic potential. The influence of the IMF has become particularly significant during the last decade as Third World debtors have needed an IMF seal of approval on their economic policies before attracting more funds from international banks (see Ch. 4).

However, the organization specifically established to assist in the economic development of Third World countries was that of the World Bank. The World Bank was specifically designed to lend to poorer countries, and, as a result came to contain two different sorts of financial operation. The first was the International Bank for Reconstruction and Development (IBRD). The IBRD was seen as the self-financing wing of the World Bank, borrowing capital on commercial terms from the international markets and lending money to developing countries at an interest rate which would give it a small margin over its cost of funds – in order to cover administrative expenses. The other wing of the World Bank could be called its 'soft-loan window', the International Development Association (IDA). The IDA's role was to raise money from grants which came mostly from the richer industrial countries. Loans would be made to the poorest countries over long periods of time and at low annual interest rates. For example, in 1986, when 'poorest' countries were defined as those with annual average *per capita* incomes of less than US$791, loans were being made over a fifty-year time span and at an annual interest rate of only 0.75 per cent. The balance of disbursements between the two wings of the World Bank favours the IBRD by a ratio of about three to one; in 1985, for example, the IBRD gave loans worth US$8.6 billion as opposed to the IDA's US$2.5 billion.

The reconstruction of the world economy after the Second World War was very much geared to a hugely powerful US economy and a US-inspired recovery programme characterized by stimulating free trade, ordered economies and markets, and capital flows to both war-torn and impoverished countries. In dramatic contrast to the aftermath of the First World War the post-Second World War programme of reconstruction was very successful. There followed a rapid recovery in the economies of Japan and the leading European countries; during the 1950s, GDP *per capita* rose by an annual average of 3.5 per cent for the ten major European countries, double that of the United States rate. A major reactivation of international trade occurred, with world trade beginning to increase faster than world production for the first time for over forty years; during the 1960s, world trade increased by 115 per cent, world output by 70 per cent (Anell and Nygren 1980: 48). The two post-war decades also saw major increases in foreign investment and capital outflow from the United States and, subsequently, Britain and other European countries. However, the direction of such investments had changed in emphasis since the early twentieth century. By the early 1970s, over two-thirds of foreign direct investment was accounted for by the corporations of developed countries investing in other countries of the developed world. Less than one-third of total foreign direct investment now corresponded to corporations of developed countries investing in developing countries, and, within this declining relative share, the emphasis had changed, with over 50 per cent being directed towards manufacturing plant in Third World countries rather than towards mining or plantations.

The rapid recovery of the European and Japanese economies, the reactivation of international trade, the increasing world flow of capital and the growing influence of multinational corporations brought a twenty-year period (1955–75) of the most rapid industrial growth the world had ever seen (UNECLA 1979) – see Table 2.1. An average annual growth rate for Japanese industry of 12.2 per cent established the basis for Japan's subsequent industrial pre-eminence of the late 1980s. European industrial growth was less than half that of Japan, but it was nevertheless nearly double that of the United States. This twenty-year period thus saw the gradual eroding

Table 2.1   Average annual industrial growth rates,
              1955–75

	Per cent
North America	2.8
Western Europe	4.8
Eastern Europe/USSR	9.8
Japan	12.2
Latin America	6.9
Africa	6.8
Asia	7.4
Other developed countries	5.2

Other developed countries – Australia, New
Zealand, Israel, South Africa.

of the economic pre-eminence of the United States
that had been the legacy of the Second World
War. Industrial growth also proceeded apace in
the Third World, averaging about 7 per cent in
all three continents.

As the economically powerful United States
reconstructed the post-war world, there was one
notable block of developed countries that desisted
from entering GATT and the IMF, and that did
not participate in increased world trade and investment – the Soviet Union and the countries of
Eastern Europe. Stalin purposely and purpose-
fully disassociated the Soviet Union and the East
European bloc from US-financed and -inspired
world reconstruction. Subsequently, then, the
world has become characterized by two competing economic orders. Nevertheless, as Table 2.1
demonstrates, between 1955 and 1975, industrial
production increased substantially in these
countries, based on government control of industry and closed markets.

However, the dramatic post-war growth of industrial production and international trade in the
Western world was also based on another important factor, cheap oil. Industrial production and
energy consumption grew at similar rates during
the 1950s and 1960s. However, in 1973 and 1974,
oil increased from US$2 to US$11 a barrel and
by 1980, it had increased to US$40 a barrel. A
new era of slow growth had arrived, partly associated with these increased energy prices.
Whereas the OECD countries had recorded
average industrial growth of 6 per cent between
1960 and 1973, in the following decade (1973–82),

this had dropped to less than 2 per cent; the
average industrial growth rate for Europe and the
United States was less than 1 per cent. The period
contained two small recessions, one in the mid-
1970s and another between 1981 and 1982, when
international trade stagnated and declined.

It could be argued that the early-1980s recession
had two immediate effects on the world economy.
First, it presaged the fall in the price of oil as oil
supply began to outstrip demand during the
recession. Second, it was instrumental in producing a debt crisis for many of the rapidly growing
developing countries, such as Brazil and Mexico.
This will be returned to in much greater detail in
Chapter 4. It is sufficient to mention here that two
characteristics of the recession, trade stagnation
and high interest rates, brought two critical
problems for rapidly growing developing
countries – export stagnation and high interest
payments on debts contracted in the 1970s. Such
was the severity of the debt crisis that an international financial crisis seemed distinctly
possible.

However, it appears that some form of equi-
librium began to be replaced in the world
economy by US economic expansion during the
mid-1980s. United States economic growth
through the mid-1980s has been partly linked to
US government expenditure rapidly increasing
but without a concomitant raising of taxes. Such
an economic policy in Third World countries has
normally received severe reprimands from the
IMF and serious short-term implications for the
running of the economy. However, for the world's
most powerful economy, the experience of the
mid-1980s shows that other rules must apply. The
raising of US government expenditure without increasing taxes naturally caused a large US budget
deficit. This has had to be financed by overseas
borrowing. However, after the debt crisis, these
funds were readily, even eagerly, supplied.
Among the international banks, this was apparently due to their perceptions of the larger,
more dynamic, developing countries as unreliable
recipients of surplus capital, on the one hand, and
the capital-surplus positions of Europe and
Japan, on the other. In other words, surplus
world capital seemed to find a most suitable destination in the form of the US budget deficit, as

it was both profitable (offering high interest rates) and secure (located in the country at the heart of world capitalism).

The combination of increasing government expenditure and reducing taxes did create the basis for rapid growth in the US economy, and partly because of such rapid growth, the dollar kept strong. With the US dollar strong in relation to most world currencies, the US economy came to act as *the* major growth pole in the world economy, especially during 1984 and 1985. Most countries attempted and succeeded in increasing exports to the United States. The major gains were felt by Japan and the East Asian NICs, but the expanding US market proved particularly important for the indebted countries of the Third World, who now had a dynamic world market to which to direct their exports. The result for the United States, however, was a major trade deficit, that hit the awesome figure of US$170 billion in 1987. The 1980s have, therefore, witnessed a rectification in the world economy, with renewed trade growth after the 1981–82 stagnation. In many ways, this can be attributed to the continued pre-eminence of the United States in the world economy, a legacy from the Second World War, and the US growth record during the mid-1980s.

However, as the 1990s approach, a serious question mark looms. For the United States has stimulated growth through borrowed money and through a massive expansion of imports, two factors that are now seriously sapping its economic strength and pre-eminence in the world. Indeed, the United States is now the world's greatest debtor. In many ways, the crises in the world stock markets in October 1987 reflected the basic uncertainty over the future of the US economy and, thereby, the world economy, due to the continued perception of US pre-eminence in the latter.

However, the world's most successful economy is now undoubtedly that of Japan (see Ch. 12). But despite a reorientation of the Japanese economy since 1986, to a more inward-looking approach, the late 1980s have shown the difficulties associated with Japan opening up its markets to foreign goods. As a result, huge trade surpluses continue, alongside large capital reserves. Unlike US economic success, it seems that it is much more difficult to transmit Japanese growth impulses to other countries through increased trade.

What then is the nature of the question mark over the world economy? On the one hand, the United States is still the dominant world economy but its economic power is diminishing due to fiscal and trade deficits. Nevertheless, its recent growth did provide a stimulus to the rest of the world economy in the mid-1980s. On the other hand, Japan will soon be the pre-eminent economic power. However, it has proved very difficult to transmit its growth to the rest of the world economy, due to large trade surpluses that have been maintained despite three years of home-oriented growth. Japan's expansionary fiscal policy has provided little stimulus to the world economy. As the world's largest creditor nation, Japan is finding it difficult to invest its large quantities of surplus capital; this last factor is, however, having a favourable impact on the heavily indebted countries of the world as international interest rates come down (see Ch. 4).

ECONOMIC CYCLES AND THEIR IMPACT

Our highly schematic coverage of the evolution of the world economy over the last two centuries has at least shown that economic growth is not a smooth, harmonious process; rather, it has been a process characterized by considerable ups and downs. Do these ups and downs reveal a discernible pattern? Indeed, can one talk of economic cycles?

Cyclical theory is a very controversial area of economic theory. The classical economists, Smith and Ricardo, that we briefly referred to in the context of the advantages of free trade, did not perceive of cycles as such. They did, however, think that economic development was such a difficult question that economic growth itself would inevitably be halted by population expansion and resource exhaustion. Nevertheless, by the end of the nineteenth century, the neo-classical economists, such as Marshall, had a much more optimistic view of long-term economic development, and came to believe fundamentally in the gradual and harmonious nature of economic growth. They argued that the classical economists

Table 2.2   Kondratieff's long-wave chronology

	Rise	Decline
1st long wave	1780s/90s to 1810–17	1810–17 to 1844–51
2nd long wave	1844–51 to 1870–75	1870–75 to 1890–96
3rd long wave	1890–96 to 1914–20	1914–20 to (1944–51)
4th long wave	(1944–51 to 1970–75)	(1970–75 to ?)

Dates in brackets refer to author's estimates of recent long-wave chronology.

had underestimated the effect that technological progress would have on economic growth, particularly as regards being able to reduce the theoretical constraints of population expansion and resource exhaustion. Technological progress may cause temporary unemployment for a particular labour group, but the net effect of such progress would be to increase the demand for labour (Baldwin 1966: 26). They believed that technical progress would keep yielding good investment projects. Economic stagnation or decline may occur temporarily in the short term, but it was central to neo-classical analysis that such stagnation would bring a drop in the interest rate. A fall in the interest rate would make large numbers of investment projects profitable and the resulting economic growth would soon end the brief period of stagnation; short-term fluctuations in economic growth were thus envisaged but no long-term cycles or waves.

However, in the 1920s, a Russian economist, Kondratieff, studying in the Business Cycle Research Institute in Moscow, analysed past economic growth within capitalism and came to distinguish long waves of fifty years' duration (see Table 2.2). The apparent similarity of Kondratieff's long-wave chronology of the nineteenth century with what has subsequently occurred in the twentieth century seems to indicate that the distinctive pattern that he discerned continues. It should be emphasized that the statistical background of Kondratieff's work was most closely linked to price movements rather than to indicators of production.

Kondratieff's thesis was most clearly demonstrated by long-term movements in wholesale prices. He analysed wholesale price developments for France, the UK, and the USA, and it is not surprising that in these relatively open economies he found that price trends were similar in the different countries, particularly as he adjusted the price indices to eliminate the effect of exchange rate changes which gives the series greater resemblance. On this basis Kondratieff claimed his waves to be an international phenomenon (Maddison 1982: 69–70).

As with most researchers empirically analysing past economic indicators for distinctive patterns, Kondratieff had little to say about the causes behind the empirical regularity he discovered. However, one theoretical writer who did step into the breach of attempting to explain cycles and waves in economic development was Joseph Schumpeter (1934, 1939, 1943). Schumpeter disagreed with the neo-classical analysis of capitalist growth as a gradual and harmonious process, without major ups and downs. He believed that capitalist growth occurs in leaps and spurts as great new investment opportunities open up, such as the wide variety of opportunities created by the expansion of the railroads in the mid-nineteenth century. What he termed railroadization (see Table 2.3) created opportunities for direct investment in the iron and coal industries, reduced transport costs and expanded the spatial extent of markets and resource extraction. Early-twentieth-century growth, meanwhile, was closely linked to the introduction of the automobile and the considerable extension of its use in the United States.

Schumpeter thus regarded cyclical development as basic to capitalist development and rejected the gradualist, neo-classical theory of capital accumulation. According to Schumpeter, in an economy in which growth takes place in an uneven fashion, major business decisions involve a high degree of risk and uncertainty.

The neoclassical picture of businessmen carefully comparing expected yields with the interest rate may not be relevant in these circumstances. The margin of possible error in one's estimate of

Table 2.3 Schumpeter's long-wave chronology

	Prosperity	Recession	Depression	Revival
1. The Industrial Revolution Kondratieff (cotton textiles, iron, steam power)	1787–1800	1801–13	1814–27	1828–42
2. The Bourgeois Kondratieff (railroadization)	1843–57	1858–69	1870–85	1886–97
3. The Neomercantilist Kondratieff (electricity, automobiles, chemicals)	1898–1911	1912–25	(1925–49)	(1950–73)

Dates in brackets refer to author's estimates of recent long-wave chronology.

expected yield from an investment project may be so high that the particular interest-rate level is unimportant in determining the volume of investment. If it is highly uncertain whether a firm can earn 10% or 20% on a capital project, then whether the cost of funds is 6% or 5% is not likely to be crucial in the investment decision (Baldwin 1966: 35.

Schumpeter thought that most major investments that lead the economy forward are made under such conditions. Ordinary businessmen hesitate to invest in such an environment. It takes a special sort of person, the entrepreneur, to get things moving.

> The entrepreneur is motivated by much more than the standard desire to raise his income level. He has such grandiose goals as conquering others in competitive economic battles, the desire to establish a private dynasty, and the wish to create something entirely new. His drives are so strong that he is willing to undertake investment activity in a highly dynamic economy while the person with ordinary motivations will not (Baldwin 1966: 36).

So entrepreneurship was the key to economic development in Schumpeter's system. The entrepreneur's role was to innovate and to undertake new combinations of productive factors. The entrepreneur might introduce a new commodity into the market, utilize a new productive method, open up a new market area, develop a new source of raw-material supply, or completely reorganize an existing industry. The entrepreneur was neither an inventor nor a capitalist who furnished investible funds, although a particular entrepreneur might also fulfil these roles. The es-

sence of entrepreneurship was creating something new in the market place. Schumpeter believed that there was never any lack of technological improvements. What was sometimes absent was the entrepreneurial talent required to introduce these inventions into the economy. Furthermore, Schumpeter argued that each new Kondratieff wave represented a major upsurge in innovation and entrepreneurial dynamism (see Table 2.3).

Although an ingenious theory developed to explain the cyclical nature of capitalism, there are some serious weaknesses in Schumpeter's theoretical justification of long-wave theory. First, he does not explain why innovation and entrepreneurial drive should come in waves rather than in a continuous, albeit irregular, stream, which would seem a more plausible hypothesis associated with entrepreneurial activity. Second, the waves of innovation were expected to affect countries more or less simultaneously; there would seem little justification in such a position. For example, different countries have taken the lead for different innovations in the past – the United Kingdom with the railways, the United States with the automobile, and presently Japan with the application of microprocessor technology. Finally, given all the other factors that must enter the economic question, Schumpeter tends to exaggerate the importance of entrepreneurial activity as a factor of production and overemphasizes its scarcity in periods of long-wave decline.

Perhaps one reason for Schumpeter's significance as a theoretical economist was his ability to link the above ideas on entrepreneurial activity not only to long-wave chronology but also to the breakdown of capitalism itself. First, he thought he saw innovation turning from an individual activity into a routinized, depersonalized activity undertaken within the bureaucracy of big business. Next, he felt that the growth of the giant business corporation, in which control was frequently separated from ownership, was weakening the fundamental capitalist institutions of private property and freedom of contract. Furthermore, Schumpeter was concerned about the ability of businessmen and industrialists to hold their leadership in the governments of capitalist countries. In particular, he was afraid that they would not keep the allegiance of labour, trade union power would grow, and socialism would eventually emerge.

The final breakdown of capitalism could thus be seen as coinciding with the decline of a Kondratieff long wave. The lack of entrepreneurial activity, the dynamic force behind capitalism according to Schumpeter, would be the reason. Therefore, Schumpeter was pessimistic about the future of capitalism, as it seemed that it would be increasingly difficult for further Kondratieff 'rises' to occur, with entrepreneurship becoming stifled by bureaucracy, large corporations and government. In retrospect, however, Schumpeter may be seen to have overemphasized the impact of large corporations on innovation. For example, the success of Japan's industrial expansion has been partly linked to the success of continued and sustained innovation stimulated and encouraged through large multifunctional corporations. Perhaps the late twentieth century has seen a change in the nature of innovation within capitalism, from a reliance on individual entrepreneurship to the greater significance of what could be termed corporate entrepreneurship.

In any case, realistically, entrepreneurship must be seen as just one of many factors behind the long-term fluctuations in capitalism over the last two centuries. If one is persuaded to some extent by the Schumpeterian argument, one could see the success of entreprenuerial activity as a distinguishing feature of capitalism in relation to other forms of political and economic organization. But, if one accepts this argument, it still does not explain the long waves themselves and, in particular, the decline of the long wave, when entrepreneurial activity is presumed to slacken. Perhaps, one should accept a very general interpretation behind the long-wave chronology of the last two centuries. Maddison (1982: 83), for example argues that:

> it is clear that major changes in growth momentum have occurred since 1820, and some explanation is needed. In my view it can be sought not in systematic long waves, but in specific disturbances of an *ad hoc* character. Major system shocks change the momentum of capitalist development at certain points. Sometimes they are more or less accidental in origin; sometimes they occur because some inherently unstable situation can no longer be lived with but has finally broken down. I also feel that the institutional-policy mix plays a bigger role in capitalist development than do many of the long-wave theorists.

In this latter context, it could be argued that the global institutions set up after the Second World War to stimulate, coordinate and improve interaction and trade in the world economy can be seen to be significant in explaining the record of economic growth in the latter half of the twentieth century.

What impact have such cyclical patterns of the world economy had on the development of less developed countries? It should be remembered that Kondratieff noted that the impact of the downturn of the wave would adversely affect less developed and agricultural countries and regions, because of poor terms of trade for agriculture in periods of decelerated development. This argument has been emphasized and developed by Lewis, among others; in terms of trade cycles:

> The trade cycle usually affects the less developed countries more violently than it affects the industrial countries, because of greater dependence on the prices of food and raw materials, which fluctuate more violently in the cycle than do the prices of manufactured goods. In the boom prices rise sharply. There is a sharp rise in wages in the less developed economies (especially if there are strong trade unions). The rise is not confined to workers in export industries. Because of increased domestic expenditure all domestic prices rise — food, rents, services — and the resulting rise in the cost of living sends all wages, salaries and profits spiralling upwards. Government revenues rise, but

so also do government expenditures, on salaries of civil servants, as well as on providing extra services. Then comes the sharp break, as a result of which the prices of export commodities may fall by 30 to 50 per cent within twelve months. There is then a scramble to bring down the level of internal prices, wages, rents, salaries and so on. This is extremely difficult, and provokes grave dissension and civil strife, which is particularly acute if the agricultural sector is based on plantation wage labour rather than peasant production, and particularly bitter if employers and employees differ in race or religion (Lewis 1955: 289–90).

The rise and fall of trade cycles is of a shorter time span than the Kondratieff waves. However, the downturn of the Kondratieff wave in the longer term and of the trade cycle in the shorter term can be seen to bring greater problems to the less developed than to the developed country, to the agricultural or primary-producing country as opposed to the manufacturing nation. However, in order to understand the full implications behind such a statement, it is necessary to investigate more closely the nature of international trade and, in particular, the problems that face primary-producing Third World countries in achieving economic growth through export expansion.

— 3 —

INTERNATIONAL
TRADE AND
ECONOMIC GROWTH

Central to the issue of Third World industrialization is the question of international trade. As we have seen in our brief survey of the evolution of the world economy and economic cycles, the depressions and recessions in the world economy affect much more profoundly the agricultural and primary-producing countries rather than the economies where manufacturing exports predominate. The simple lesson of such recent economic experiences is that to industrialize and to promote manufacturing exports is effectively to reduce the adverse effects of recessionary movements in the international economy. We will look more closely at the precise relationship between trade policy and industrialization in Chapter 6. In this chapter, we will pursue the more general debate as to whether economic growth is best achieved through policies of trade or self-sufficiency, and whether trade policy in Third World countries should be primarily geared towards promoting exports of primary or manufacturing products. It is first useful, however, to discuss the nature of international trade theory itself.

INTERNATIONAL TRADE THEORY

International trade theory can be seen as a theory of spatial interaction, because it postulates that there are distinct advantages in regions and countries trading with each other, despite large distances between them. Referring back to Chapter 1, it is interesting to point out that in the evolution of economic geography during the late 1950s and early 1960s central place theory was preferred to international trade theory as a core model of the discipline, despite some useful empirical analyses of regional trade interaction by such as Ullman (1956) and Smith (1964).

International trade theory has a distinctly different emphasis to that of Christaller and Lösch's central place theory, which basically saw regions as non-trading entities, at least in terms of external trade. Rather, in central place theory, the location of economic activities within regions was seen as closely related only to internal factors, such as the operation of range and threshold (Lloyd and Dicken 1977). It always seems ironic that a theory which emphasized the friction of distance was preferred in economic geography just at a time when the frictional effect of distance was at its historical lowest; and that a theory that stressed the benefits of economic interaction between countries and regions despite large distances, international trade theory, was largely ignored.

For the economic geographer, one important general question to ask is what are the advantages of trading? Does world economic growth benefit from increasing trade between countries or from a system in which all countries attempt to be as self-sufficient as possible, each country producing as far as possible its own full range of requirements? Why do people trade and why have they done so throughout history? A sound geographical response to such questions would be that different areas and regions of the world produce different products and that the interchange of products between differing regions is essential. This is closely linked to the geographical reality of a heterogeneous landscape; in passing, this points to another criticism of central place models, which were based on a theoretically homogeneous landscape over which there was no need to trade.

The whole economic basis for international trade, then, rests on the fact that countries do differ, and not only in terms of their resource endowments but also in terms of their economic and social institutions and their capacities for growth and development. Within the highly diversified range of countries known as the Third World, some countries are very populous yet deficient in natural resources and human skills. Others are sparsely populated yet endowed with abundant mineral and raw material resources. Still others are small and economically weak, having neither the human nor the material resources on which to base a sustained and largely self-sufficient strategy of economic and social development. Yet, despite these contrasts, it could be argued that most less developed countries face similar issues in terms of their international trading relations with both the developed countries and each other. One of these issues refers to the theoretical benefits of international trade itself.

Upon the geographical reality of a heterogeneous landscape, people find it advantageous to develop those resources with which they are best endowed and to work in those activities for which they are best suited. They can then trade in those products in which they have a comparative advantage and can exchange any surplus of these home-produced commodities for products which other regions and people may be relatively more suited to produce. These principles of specialization and comparative advantage have long been applied by economic theorists to the exchange of goods between individual nations in the form of international trade. In answer to the questions of what determines which goods are traded and why some countries produce some things while others produce different things, economic theorists have sought the answer in terms of *international differen-ces in costs of production and prices of different products*. ×

The concept of *relative* cost and price differences is basic to the theory of international trade. It is known as the principle of comparative advantage. It asserts that a country will specialize in the export of those products which it can produce at the *lowest relative cost*. For example, let us take two countries, Japan and Chile, Japan specializing in motor vehicles and cameras, Chile in fish and vegetables. Japan may be able to produce cameras, cars *and* fish and vegetables at lower *absolute* unit costs than Chile, but since the commodity cost differences between countries are greater for the manufactured goods than for primary products, it will be to the advantage of Japan to specialize in the production of manufactured goods and exchange them for Chile's primary produce. Thus, while Japan may have an absolute cost advantage in all products, its *comparative* cost advantage lies in manufactured goods. Meanwhile, Chile may be at an *absolute* disadvantage with Japan in both secondary and primary activities because its absolute unit costs of production are higher for both types of products. Nevertheless, it can still engage in profitable trade because it has a *comparative* advantage in primary production – because its absolute cost disadvantage is less. It is this phenomenon of differences in comparative advantage that gives rise to profitable trade even among unequal partners.

One way to demonstrate the theoretical advantages of trade is to consider what would happen to a nation's production and consumption levels in its absence; the following two-country model is adapted from Todaro (1978). First, it is convenient to divide the world (or our trading system) into two countries – say, Third World and Developed World. Suppose Third World is endowed with 100 units of labour. It is capable of producing two types of goods; agricultural and manufactured goods. A unit of manufacturing output requires 5 units of labour while a unit of agricultural output may require only 1 labour unit. If these input–output relationships between labour and production are fixed by the prevailing technology, then if the entire labour supply is in manufacturing production, a total of 20 units can be produced. Alternatively, if all Third World labour were to engage in agriculture, a total of 100 units of output can be produced (see Fig. 3.1*a*). However, presumably Third World would wish to produce both agricultural and manufactured goods. Figure 3.1*a* shows all the various combinations possible between the two extremes. However, for purposes of comparing Third World consumption before and after trade, we will say that before trade Third World manages to produce 50 units of agricultural goods and 10 units of manufactured goods (point P in Fig. 3.1*a*).

Now we can open up the possibility of trade by introducing another country, Developed World. We will assume that in Developed World there is the same availability of labour – 100 labour units. However, there is one crucial difference in that instead of requiring 5 units of labour to produce 1 unit of manufactured output (as in Third World), Developed World requires only 2 labour input units. Developed World is thus a more efficient (lower cost) producer of manufactured goods

than is Third World. We will, however, assume that agriculture requires the same 1 labour input per unit of output as in Third World, so that both countries are equally efficient in food production, having the same real labour costs per unit of output. Therefore, if Developed World's labour resources are fully employed, it is capable of producing, at the extremes, 50 units of manufacturing output and no agriculture or 100 units of agriculture and no manufacturing. However, it is more likely to produce a combination of both, and the various possible combinations are reflected in Fig. 3.1*b*. For the purpose of comparing Developed World's consumption before and after trade, we will assume that before trade Developed World produces 50 units of agricultural goods and 25 units of manufacturing goods (point P in Fig. 3.1*b*).

Now we can start to see what happens when Third World is allowed to trade with Developed World. Their differing cost and price structures make it potentially profitable to trade. For al-

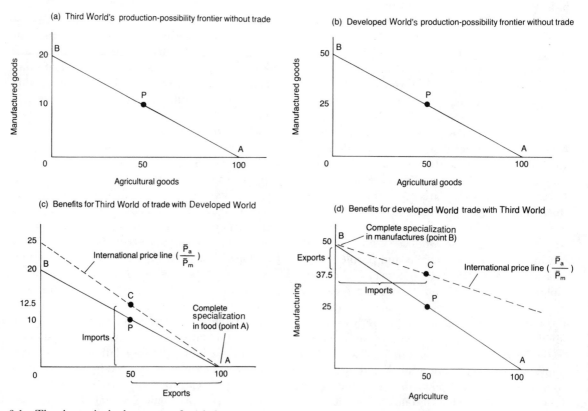

3.1   The theoretical advantages of trade between Third World and Developed World.

though Developed World is just as efficient as Third World in agriculture, it is much more efficient in manufacturing, where it requires only two-fifths as much labour to produce a unit of output. Developed World, therefore, has a *comparative advantage* in the production of manufactured goods. Meanwhile, although Third World does not have an absolute productivity and cost advantage in either commodity, in relative terms it does have a *comparative advantage* in agricultural production *vis-à-vis* Developed World. In terms of this simplistic model, therefore, Third World should specialize in food production and export the excess over its domestic consumption requirements in exchange for Developed World's manufactured goods.

The opportunity for trade between Third World and Developed World will create one market for goods with a single common price ratio. This price ratio will depend on relative demand conditions in both regions for both commodities. It will have to settle somewhere between the two extremes of 1:5 in Third World and 1:2 in Developed World in order for profitable trade to occur for both. Let us assume that the price ratio settles down at 1:4, that is one unit of manufactured goods trades for four units of agriculture. Third World could now completely specialize in food production by producing 100 units. At the international price of one to four, it could then exchange 50 units of its food for 12.5 units of Developed World's manufactured goods. In this case, Third World's final consumption combination after trade would be 50 units of food and 12.5 units of manufactured goods (point C in Fig. 3.1c). Similarly, Developed World could specialize completely in the production of manufactures by producing 50 units of manufactured goods and trading 12.5 of these to Third World in return for 50 units of food products. Developed World's consumption combination after trade would now be 37.5 units of manufactured goods and 50 units of agricultural goods (point C in Fig. 3.1d).

As with most models, this model of the benefits of international trade suffers from a distinctive lack of reality, and we will come on to some of the complicating and real issues of international trade in the next section. Meanwhile, it is worth emphasizing that the above model (see Fig. 3.1), despite its simplistic form, does demonstrate three underlying features of the benefits of trade and the distribution of those benefits. The first is that trade enables all countries to escape from the confines of their resource endowments and consume products in greater proportions than if they did not participate in trade. This is fully demonstrated in Fig. 3.1. By specializing in food production and engaging in trade, Third World is able to consume the same amount of food as before (50 units) but 25 per cent more manufactured goods (12.5 in Fig. 3.1c compared with 10 in Fig. 3.1a). Similarly, Developed World, by specializing completely in the production of manufactured goods and trading manufacturing surpluses for Third World food, is able to consume the same quantity of food as before (50 units) but 50 per cent more of its own manufactured goods (37.5 in Fig. 3.1d compared with 25 in Fig. 3.1b).

This leads us immediately to a second important theoretical point of free trade. For although free trade will benefit all nations of the world, the benefits will be unevenly distributed depending on world demand conditions and cost differences for different commodities in different countries. Figure 3.1c shows that Third World consumption of manufactured goods increased by 25 per cent *after trade*, but Fig. 3.1d reveals that Developed World consumption of manufactured goods increased by 50 per cent *after trade*. Both countries benefited from trade, therefore, but Developed World considerably more than Third World.

The third major implication of the classical theory of international trade is that free trade will maximize global output by permitting every country to specialize in the production of those goods in which it has a comparative advantage. In Fig. 3.1a and 3.1b, production before trade amounted to 100 agricultural and 35 manufactured units. Production after trade (Fig. 3.1c and 3.1d) amounted to 100 agricultural and now 50 manufactured units − an increase of over 40 per cent as regards world manufacturing production.

I mentioned at the beginning of the chapter that the quantitative and philosophical changes in economic geography during the late 1950s and early 1960s ignored international and regional trade analysis. One interesting exception was that of Smith (1964), although his analysis (see Fig. 3.2) was restricted to the United States. However, by using the technique of complementarity indices, he was able to show that the frictional effect of distance was low in terms of cross-continental trade and that the concept of comparative advantage was much more significant. Complementarity indices are simply ratios of actual flow to expected flow, the expected flow being calculated through a gravity model with a friction of distance function. The higher the complementarity index, the higher the actual trade compared with expected trade. Smith calculated the complementarity indices for shipments of agricultural commodities to the six states of New England from thirty-four other states. Most states near to New England had very low complementarity indices, that is their actual trade was much lower than expected trade. Conversely, two states stand out with very high complementarity indices – Illinois exporting grain

products, and California, the mainland state furthest away from New England, exporting largely fruit. Figure 3.2, although now distinctly historical, is nevertheless an excellent example of the principle of comparative advantage being a stronger spatial force than the friction of distance.

According to basic theory, then, the promotion of free international trade both maximizes global output and allows countries to escape from the confines of their resource endowments. In a continental setting, such as that of the United States, the principle of comparative advantage can generate significant trading interaction between regions very far apart. Indeed, during the last two centuries, the continued reduction of the frictional effect of distance could well make the principle of comparative advantage the major spatial process in economic interaction between different countries, regions and places of the world. However, at the same time, our discussion of international trade theory has noted that, although free trade brings benefits to all countries,

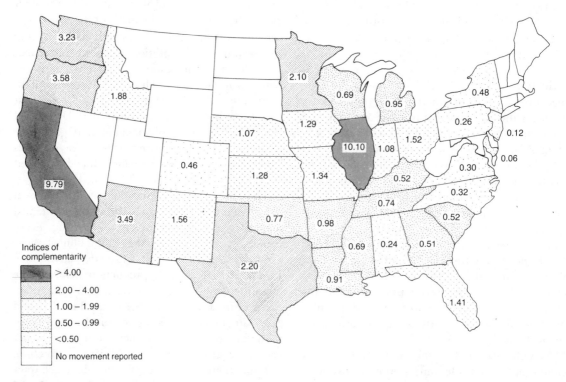

3.2   Comparative advantage versus the friction of distance: complementarity indices for shipments of agricultural commodities to New England, 1959.
Source: Smith R H T 1964.

these benefits are unevenly distributed. This becomes a very significant aspect to explore when one turns to the question of international trade and the Third World.

INTERNATIONAL TRADE AND THE THIRD WORLD

It is undoubtedly true that the two centuries of international trading growth that were chronicled in Chapter 2 have brought not only significant economic growth to the world but also very large inequalities in living standards between different parts of the world. In aggregate terms, this can best be understood by envisaging the benefits of international trade as being very much associated with and concentrated in the countries where trade developed early – Britain, the United States and Germany, for example. Broad statistics can indicate the levels of inequality that have been generated on a world scale since the early nineteenth century. Anell and Nygren (1980) estimate that in 1820 the average British citizen was only two to three times better off than the average inhabitant of Asia and Africa. By 1985, World Bank data show that the average UK citizen had a *per capita* income 35 times greater than that of the average inhabitant of Asia and Africa, where 50 per cent of the world's population resides.

Two centuries of free trade have therefore acted to concentrate spatially what could be termed trade power in the world – which effectively means that the *benefits* of free trade have been heavily concentrated over the period. Figures 3.3 and 3.4 demonstrate dramatically in diagrammatic terms the extent of the present mismatch between the distribution of world population and the world distribution of trade power. The visual impression of Fig. 3.3, demonstrating in diagrammatic form the distribution of population, is of a world dominated by Asia, with such populous countries as China, India, Indonesia, the USSR, Bangladesh and Pakistan. The continents of the Americas, Africa, Europe and Australasia look modest or even puny in comparison. However, Figure 3.4, which attempts to represent trade power in the world, seems to describe a totally different world. The pre-eminence of Asia vanishes and, within Asia, totally different states

achieve significance – Japan, Taiwan and Singapore for example. The modest proportions of Central and South America and Africa also diminish. Instead, the world seems dominated by the countries of Europe; only the United States and Japan seem to compare. To a certain extent, this is a question of scale. The twelve countries of the European Economic Community (EEC) account for more than one-third of world trade, but much of this is accounted for by trade between the various European countries. If the countries of the EEC were represented in the same way as the states of the United States, the contrast between the United States and Europe would be significantly less. The biggest contrast in trade power, however, is between the developed world (USA, Europe, Japan) and the Third World; within the Third World, there is the contrast between oil-exporting countries and newly industrializing countries on the one hand, and the rest of less developed countries on the other.

In the theoretical example of the previous section, the assumptions were such that trade benefited the industrialized country more than the agricultural country. Such an asymmetry of benefits between countries exporting primarily manufactured versus agricultural goods was intentional as the recent history of international trade has undoubtedly granted more benefits to the industrialized than the primary-producing country. This can be linked to the general economic proposition that economic development through time must be associated with the gradual shifting of the economy from a reliance on primary activity (agriculture, fishing, forestry, mining) through to a greater emphasis on secondary activity (processing of primary products, manufacturing and construction) and, finally, tertiary activity (the whole range of public and private services).

Table 3.1 gives a broad picture of sectoral patterns for the early 1980s. Unfortunately, in the World Bank classification upon which these data are based, mining is included as a secondary activity under the 'Industry' sector. Nevertheless, the relationship between primary activity (basically agriculture) and economic development is a clear one. For in sixteen developed countries, the primary sector accounts for an average of only 3

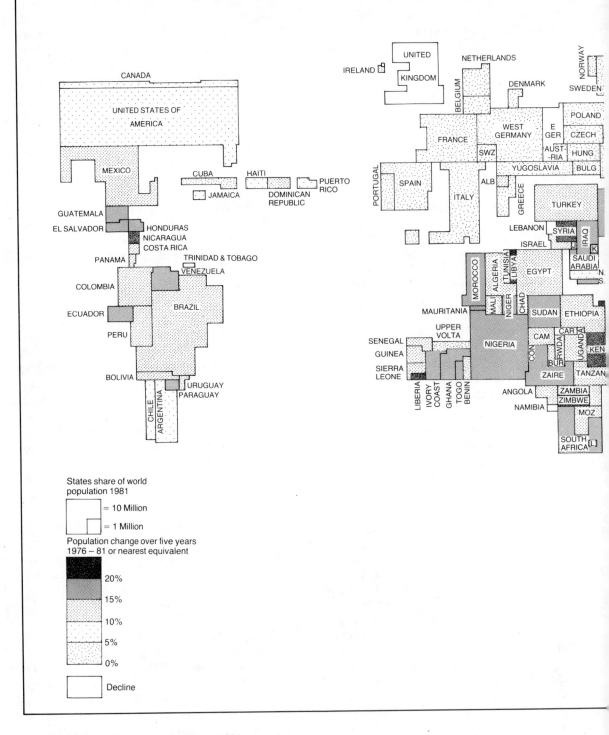

3.3   Distribution of global population, 1981.
Source: Kidron M and Segal R 1984.

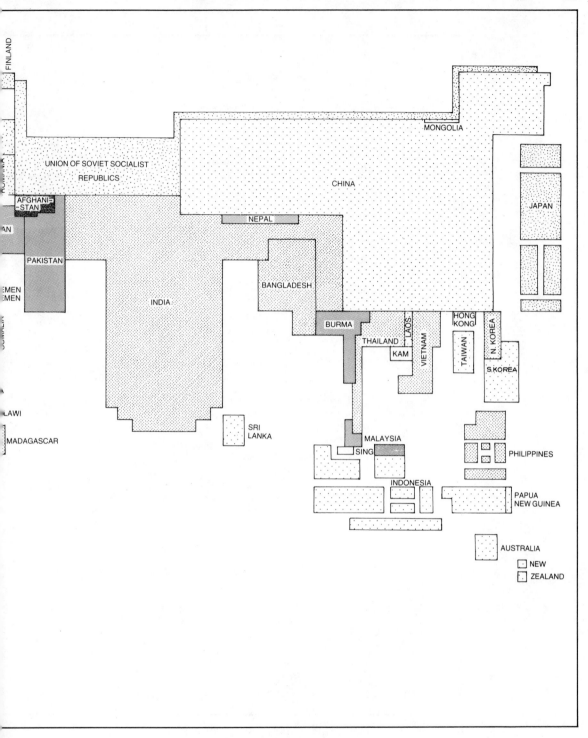

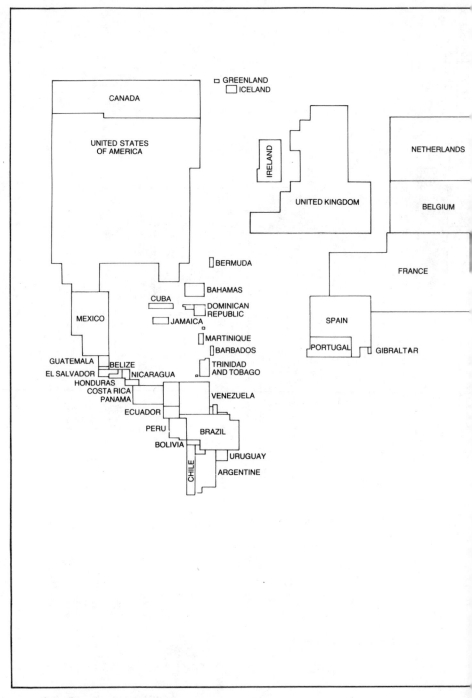

3.4   Distribution of global trade power, 1981.
Source: Kidron M and Segal R 1984.

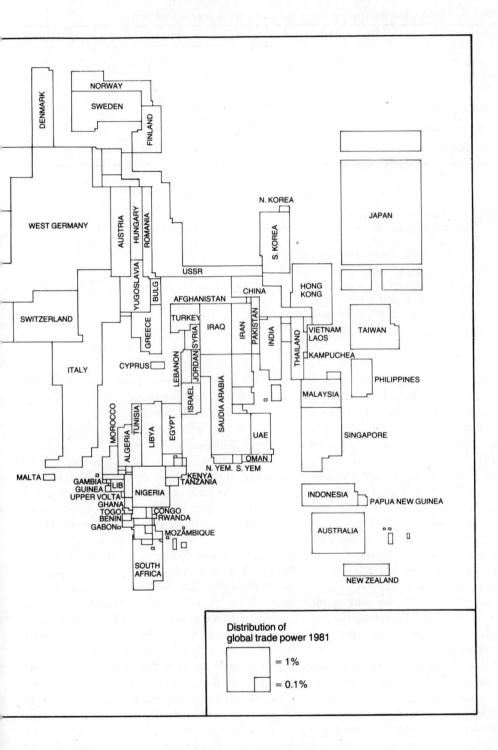

Distribution of
global trade power 1981

☐ = 1%

☐ = 0.1%

Table 3.1   1985 Distribution of gross domestic product by World Bank region (per cent)

World Bank region	Agriculture	Industry	(Manufacturing)	Services
Low-income economies	32	33	26	35
China and India	31	37	29	32
Other low income	36	19	12	45
Lower-middle-income economies	22	32	17	47
Upper-middle-income economies	10	35	25[a]	54
Industrial market economies	3	36	23	61

[a] 1984 average.

Definitions:

Sectors – Agriculture = agriculture; forestry; fishing.

      Industry = mining; manufacturing (data provided separately); construction; electricity, water and gas.

      Services = all other branches of economic activity.

World Bank regions – economies described as:

    Low income = less than US$400 *per capita* income.

    Lower-middle income = between US$400 and US$1600 *per capita* income.

    Upper-middle income = over US$1600 *per capita* income.

(*Source*: Developed from World Bank 1987: 206–7)

per cent of economic production, whereas in twenty-eight low-income countries, it corresponds to an average of as much as 36 per cent; in seven reporting countries (Somalia, Tanzania, Burundi, Nepal, Bhutan, Mali and Bangladesh), the agricultural sector still constitutes the major proportion of the economy. In between the low-income and industrialized economies, the primary sector's contribution to the overall economy declines in a regular fashion (see Table 3.1). As the role of the primary sector tends to decline with economic development, the role of the tertiary sector increases – again in more or less a regular way, from a 35 per cent participation in low-income economies to one of 61 per cent in the industrial market economies. The relationship of the manufacturing sector itself to economic development generally shows a trend of increasing significance in less developed countries – from a share of only 12 per cent in low-income economies (excluding China and India) to 25 per cent in upper-middle-income economies; data for the low-income economies emphasize the importance of manufacturing in China. However, Table 3.1 also demonstrates that the industrial market economies now have a manufacturing share lower than that of the upper-middle-income economies, presumably as post-industrial, service expansion comes to characterize those economies.

With the exception of China, most low-income and low-middle-income countries have a primary sector that outweighs the secondary sector. Furthermore, their contributions to world trade are mainly in the form of primary-good exports. For example, between 1960 and 1972, receipts from commodity exports amounted to almost 80 per cent of the total balance-of-payments receipts of all Third World countries (Todaro 1978: 273). Why can such reliance on primary-good exports be problematic? The first point to make is that most Third World countries do not rely on a variety of primary-good exports but on just one or two. Kidron and Segal (1984) point out that sixty Third World countries depend essentially on a single product for their export income; for more than one-third of them that product is oil. Overall, nearly half of Third World countries earn over 50 per cent of their export receipts from a single primary commodity; about 75 per cent of these nations earn 60 per cent or more of their foreign exchange receipts from no more than three primary products (Todaro 1978: 277)

If many Third World countries rely on the export of just one or two primary products, one fundamental question to be asked is: what has been the behaviour of prices for primary products during the twentieth century? A second and related question of central importance to this book would be: what have been the terms of trade between primary goods and manufactured goods during the twentieth century? Unfortunately for the poorer countries of the world, the answer to both these questions has been negative for much of the twentieth century. However, we will spend the rest of the chapter investigating these issues of primary product price behaviour and terms of trade in more detail.

PRICE BEHAVIOUR OF PRIMARY PRODUCTS

Since the early twentieth century, prices for primary products have not been buoyant. After the First World war, the lack of economic growth in Europe kept the growth in demand for primary products and, therefore, prices low. The Depression severely exacerbated the trend. The evolution of commodity prices since the Second World War (apart from oil) can be seen from Fig. 3.5. This figure also has the advantage of splitting up primary products into three sectors – non-food agricultural commodities (for example, cotton,

sisal, wool), metals and minerals (for example copper, iron ore, tin) and foods (for example, wheat, sugar, bananas). The overall impression is of a near-continuous fall in real prices since 1950s, interrupted only by small, short-term increases in the mid-1950s and the 1973–75 period. By far the worst price performance since the Second World War has been in terms of non-food agricultural commodities. The 1979/80 price for these commodities was only about one-third of the 1951 price, and the 1986 price was only about one-half of the 1979/80 price. According to Fig. 3.5, prices for metals and minerals were maintained much better between 1950 and 1979/80, with positive price fluctuations in the mid-1950s, mid-1960s and between 1973 and 1975. However, between 1974 and 1986, prices for metals more than halved in value. The impact of this can be seen in terms of the behaviour of the real copper price since 1966; the 1986 copper price was only 29 per cent of the copper price twenty years earlier (Table 3.2). A similar evolution of prices has occurred in the food sector, where the 1977 aggregate price was similar to that of the early 1950s. However, in the following nine years, the real price of food commodities again nearly halved in value. Although Fig. 3.5 does not include oil, the price behaviour of oil has not been dissimilar to that of other commodities, declining in terms of its nominal price from US$40 a barrel in 1980 to US$10 a barrel in 1986.

Such an analysis of recent price patterns leads to a very important question. Why have primary product prices declined in such an exaggerated fashion since the mid-1970s? Several reasons can be given. First, the demand for commodities in the industrial countries has been weak, especially for non-food agricultural commodities and metals. This latter is reflected in the fact that there has been a significant change in the ratio between

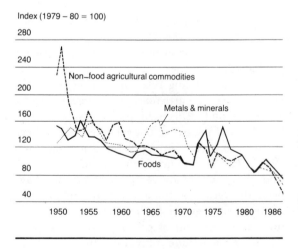

Index (1979 – 80 = 100)

3.5   The evolution of commodity prices since the Second World War (excluding oil).
Source: World Bank *World Development Report 1987*.

Table 3.2   Average annual real price of copper, 1966–87 (1987 dollars)

1966	US$2.16 per pound
1969	US$1.94 per pound
1973/4	US$1.84 per pound
1986	US$0.63 per pound
1987	US$0.81 per pound

(*Source*: *El Mercurio* 7/1/88)

consumption of metals and gross domestic product (GDP) in the developed OECD countries. For example, since 1973, there has been a 30 per cent fall in nickel used per unit of GDP, a 20 per cent fall in copper and a 40 per cent fall in tin (*The Economist* 11/8/84: 61). According to Manners (1986), the task of the 1980s has been the balancing of supply and demand along lines of price and quality within a framework of world overproduction. Such a framework, however, has led to low world commodity prices and low levels of investment in new mines in Third World countries.

A second reason goes some way to explaining the reasons for such overproduction. The high prices of the mid-1970s led to a subsequent over expansion of supply in several important raw materials, especially in oil and metals. In metal mining, for example, there was a strong lag effect felt by those investments generated after the 1973/74 commodity boom. This is because many mineral resource projects operate on a time horizon of ten to fifteen years between conception and production. After the 1973/74 commodity price rise, many investments were planned in new mines, some of which did not come on stream until the early- to mid-1980s. At the same time, those high prices of the mid-1970s encouraged greater economy in the use of such commodities. For example, in aluminium production, the 1980s has witnessed a greater use of scrap; one-quarter of all aluminium supplied to the American market now comes from recycled scrap (*Economist* 11/8/84: 61). High prices in the mid-1970s also promoted the development of cheaper synthetic alternatives. While investment in metal mining has fallen in real terms since the mid-1970s, investment in plastics has risen. Furthermore, changes in tastes, increased use of synthetic substitutes (fibre optics replacing copper for example), and the adoption of production processes that are less intensive in raw materials have all depressed demand for commodities in the 1980s.

Third, the markets of some commodities have been disrupted by the agricultural policies of the industrial countries. Domestic price support programmes in industrial countries have caused large surpluses of production. In order to 'solve' the short-term problem of such huge surpluses, the governments of developed countries have frequently sold these surpluses at a fraction of their domestic prices on world markets. As a result, a pattern of world trade has evolved that contradicts the principles of comparative advantage. Most of the world's food exports are now grown in industrial countries, where the costs of food production are high, and consumed in developing countries, where the costs are lower.

Between 1961–63 and 1982–84, the industrial countries' share of world food exports increased from 46 to 63 per cent, while the share of the developing countries fell from 45 to 34 per cent (World Bank 1986: 10). The World Bank's verdict in 1986 was as follows:

> The industrial countries have erected high barriers to imports of temperate-zone products from developing countries and then have subsidised their own exports. The special trade preference schemes they have extended to many developing countries have not been a significant offset to their trade restrictions. . . . Policies in industrial countries affect the level, direction and stability of world prices. The fact that both industrial and developing countries insulate domestic prices from world markets makes world prices more volatile than they would be otherwise (World Bank 1986: 11–12).

During the 1980s, such price volatility has been mainly in a downward direction.

With the exception of oil producers, primary-producing countries have fared poorly in international trading relations during the twentieth century. In particular, they have fared badly since the mid-1970s. Oil producers seemed to have bucked the trend, but even here prices have fallen dramatically in real terms since the early 1980s. However, one further crucial question from the point of view of this book is: what have been the terms of trade between primary and manufactured goods during the twentieth century? Can one unit of primary product exports buy the same amount of manufactured good imports today as happened ten, twenty or thirty years ago?

TERMS OF TRADE

The deteriorating terms of trade between primary products, on the one hand, and manufactured goods, on the other, for the first half of the twentieth century was 'shown statistically' by Prebisch and the United Nations Economic Commission for Latin America (UNECLA) during the 1950s. Not only did they provide statistical evidence but they also gave an explanation for such deterioration, an explanation incidentally that ties in with the cyclical theory discussed in the previous chapter. The statistical work of Prebisch and UNECLA has since been criticized widely. One serious drawback in the statistical analysis of changing terms of trade is the inability to account adequately for quality improvements in the traded items. There is little doubt that the manufactured goods imported into the developing countries have improved much more during the twentieth century than has the quality of the primary products exported from these countries. Nevertheless, the explanation offered by UNECLA economists behind deteriorating terms of trade remains of some interest.

Their argument of the declining terms of trade between the primary producers of the Third World and the manufacturing exporters of the developed world could be briefly synthesized as follows. During the recessionary period of economic cycles, the large-scale manufacturers in the developed countries reduced production rather than prices. In prosperous periods of economic cycles, however, they not only increased output but also raised wages and thus prices under the bargaining pressures of well-organized labour unions. Unfortunately, neither producers nor workers in the primary-producing developing countries possessed the power to influence the world prices of their products. In direct response to world demand, the prices of their primary products fell in recessionary periods and rose again in the more prosperous phase of the economic cycle. The net long-term result of these trends has been to increase the prices of manufactured items relative to the prices of primary products. Thus the imports of the developing countries (manufactured goods) have increased

relative to the primary-product exports of those countries. This, in turn, meant that the developing countries were able to purchase fewer and fewer capital goods with a given quantity of primary-product exports. As a result, investment and purchasing power suffered, and the growth impulses generated by the export sector for the local economy were less.

Such an argument remains of interest, but its applicability remains very much rooted in the first half of the twentieth century when there was more evidence of large, oligopolistic manufacturing firms in Europe and the United States reducing production rather than prices during recessionary periods. In the latter half of the twentieth century, with serious competition between a whole range of US, European and Japanese firms in any particular industrial sector, recessionary periods also bring reductions in price; this has undoubtedly been the lesson of the early 1980s recession. For the latter half of the twentieth century, perhaps more simple arguments need to be emphasized, such as the phenomenon of world overproduction bringing down the prices of primary products to such an extent that they even outweigh reductions in the real price of manufactured goods consequent upon increased competition and improved process technology.

Nevertheless, despite the need for changing explanations, the actual phenomenon of adverse terms of trade for primary-producing countries can still have an enormously negative impact on economic growth and development. It constituted a problem in the late 1950s and early 1960s as the world saw declining prices of commodities relative to prices for industrial goods. Between 1954 and 1962, the terms of trade between primary commodities (including oil) and manufactured products deteriorated by between 10 and 15 per cent. This happened at a time when 70–90 per cent of exports of virtually all developing countries were primary commodities and when 50–60 per cent of imports were manufactured goods.

However, it could be argued that for non-oil-producing countries in the Third World, terms of trade have become even worse since the early 1970s. Table 3.3 reveals that the terms of trade

Table 3.3 Terms of trade by World Bank region, 1975–81

	Terms of trade
Low-income economies (less than US$400 *per capita* income, 1981)	87
Middle-income economies – oil exporters	133
– oil importers	73
High-income oil exporters	208
Industrial market economies	90

(*Source*: Developed from World Bank 1983: 164–5)

of low-income economies worsened by 13 per cent between 1975 and 1981 and for oil-importing middle-income economies by 27 per cent – mainly due to the rise in the oil price and the reduction of other commodity prices. Such price movements had a dramatic impact on economies such as that of Zambia between 1970 and 1982 (see Fig. 3.6). We have already drawn attention to the drastic reduction in the real price of copper between the mid-1970s and the mid-1980s. As copper constitutes over 90 per cent of Zambia's exports, the effects on that country's international trading relations have been little short of disastrous, given the rise in the price of oil and capital goods during the 1970s and early 1980s. By 1982, one unit of Zambia's copper exports was able to import *only 25 per cent* of what it had been able to import in 1970 (see Fig. 3.6). The implications for the Zambian economy were graphically described by Wood (1984: 18–19) as follows:

> The movement of the international terms of trade against Zambia has led to a major decline in foreign exchange earnings. This has strangled the country. The mines consume much of the foreign exchange they earn to purchase machinery and lubricants, and to pay expatriates. With the collapse of the copper price the foreign exchange earned by the mines, which is available for the use of the rest of the nation, has fallen precipitously. World inflation, and especially oil price increases, have increased pressure upon the foreign exchange reserves. This has led to an almost continual balance of payments crisis since 1975 which necessitated IMF loans in both 1978 and 1981. Conditions for these loans requiring reduced

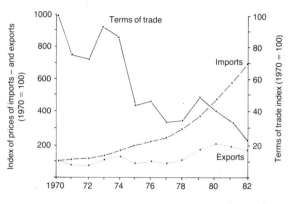

3.6   Changes in Zambia's terms of trade, 1970–82.
Source: Wood A 1984.
Source: World Bank *World Development Report 1983*.

budget deficits have placed additional constraints upon government spending.

Because of these problems *per capita* GDP declined by 23 per cent between 1970 and 1982. When the changing terms of trade are also considered the decline is over 50 per cent, bringing real *per capita* income to a level below that at independence. Reduced government spending, especially on construction and delayed imports, has led to a decline in economic activity, especially in the urban areas. The manufacturing sector is producing 10 per cent less than in 1974, while the construction industry is operating at only three-quarters of its 1974 level.

Between 1982 and 1985, Zambia's terms of trade fluctuated but did not improve, although some modest improvements occurred in 1986 (with the reduction in the price of oil) and 1987–88 (with increased copper prices). As a result between 1982 and 1985, Zambia's *per capita* income (in purely nominal terms) declined further from 640 to 390 dollars. Between 1965 and 1985, Zambia's *per capita* income had declined in real terms by the unenviable average rate of 1 per cent every year (World Bank 1987: 202).

Adverse terms of trade thus continue to affect primary-producing countries. The precise impact very much depends on the international price movements of the major commodity in question and the extent of export dependence of the country on that commodity. Zambia can be seen as an extreme case because of its near total reliance on copper exports (still 84 per cent in

Table 3.4 Evolution of terms of trade for selected countries classified by major primary export, 1980–85

Figure by each country shows 1985 terms of trade index in relation to index of 100 for 1980; figure below 100 denotes worsening terms of trade, while figure above implies improving terms of trade.

Bauxite/alumina producer (bauxite 78 per cent of exports, 1980)
Jamaica   95

Cocoa producer (cocoa 74 per cent of exports, 1980)
Ghana   91

Coffee producers (coffee greater than 60 per cent of exports, 1980)
Burundi   99
Colombia   97
Uganda   96

Copper producers (copper greater than 50 per cent of exports, 1980)
Chile   79
Zambia   72

Cotton producers (cotton greater than 47 per cent of exports, 1980)
Paraguay   83
Sudan   87

Iron ore producers (iron ore greater than 52 per cent of exports, 1980)
Liberia   91
Mauritania   96

Oil producers (oil greater than 60 per cent of exports, 1980)
Congo   95
Mexico   98
Nigeria   95
Venezuela   94

Sugar producers (sugar greater than 76 per cent of exports, 1980)
Mauritius   78

Countries whose principal exports are temperate agricultural products
Argentina   88
Uruguay   85

Newly industrializing countries; exports dominated by manufactures
Hong Kong   110
Korea   105
Singapore   101

(*Sources*: World Bank 1987: 220–1; Lloyds Bank Country Reports)

1985) and the very poor price performance of copper since the mid-1970s. Indeed, in Table 3.4, which traces the evolution of terms of trade in a number of countries whose exports are dominated by different products, Zambia records the most adverse index between 1980 and 1985.

The figures in Table 3.4 are illustrative of the problems of terms of trade for primary producers. They reveal that those countries whose exports are dominated by copper, cotton, sugar and cereals have suffered more from adverse terms of trade than producers of bauxite, cocoa, coffee,

iron ore and oil during the 1980s. However, the most interesting point to be emphasized from the table and one that is crucial to the argument in this book refers to the performance of the newly industrializing countries. In these countries, where industrialization has been strongly oriented towards international markets, terms of trade have been distinctly positive during the 1980s. In Korea, there was a 10 per cent improvement in terms of trade between 1980 and 1985; this compares favourably with Japan's increase of 13 per cent for the period. The fundamental conclusion from such figures is that the process of industrialization not only reduces the impact of adverse terms of trade but provides for a distinct improvement.

We can now turn to the question posed at the beginning of the chapter: should trade policy in Third World countries be primarily geared towards promoting exports of primary or manufactured products? On the basis of the above evidence and analysis, the answer should stress the importance of promoting and expanding manufactured exports as opposed to primary exports. To a certain extent, this has occurred in recent years. Figure 3.7 demonstrates that as export earnings of developing countries have increased from US$44 billion in 1965 to US$498 billion in 1980, the proportion of manufactured exports rose from 16 to 26 per cent. However, despite reductions in the share of agricultural exports from 43 to 20 per cent and in metal and mineral exports from 10 to 6 per cent, fuel exports

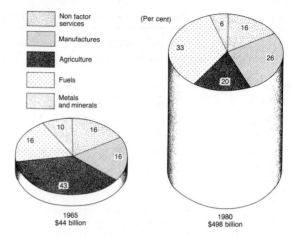

3.7   Changes in the structure of export earnings

have increased from 16 to 33 per cent of the total. As a result, primary-product exports are still equivalent to 59 per cent of total export earnings and therefore continue to predominate in the trading structure of most Third World countries.

— 4 —

CAPITAL
CONSTRAINTS ON
THIRD WORLD
DEVELOPMENT

This chapter continues to analyse the constraints on the economic development of Third World countries that are generated by the present character of the world economy. In particular, this chapter looks at another aspect of vital importance to industrialization: the provision of capital to Third World countries. The latter half of the twentieth century has witnessed dramatic changes in the worldwide flow of capital, both in terms of quantity and speed. However, such transformation in the quantity and quality of world capital flows has had little impact on the great majority of Third World countries. Furthermore, for those few Third World countries variously classified as intermediately developed or

middle income that have managed to attract large amounts of capital, such 'success' in attracting capital can normally be seen as a double-edged sword – useful in one period of time but tremendously burdensome in another.

Table 4.1 gives a broad idea of both the change in magnitude and direction of net capital flows since the late 1960s. At that time, the pattern of net capital flows between world regions could be termed 'traditional' with the developed countries of the OECD (Organization for Economic Cooperation and Development) providing the major source area for capital for Third World countries. However, the scale of net capital flow around the world was small relative to the years

Table 4.1 Changing patterns of net global capital flows ($ billion)

	Annual averages		1980	1984	
	1967–73	1974–77			
OECD countries & Switzerland	−8.25	− 0.25	+51.5	US Other OECD	+93.4 −53.2
Smaller developed countries	+1.5	+17.75	+22.0	−6.0	
Non-oil, less developed countries	+6.0	+21.0	+51.0	+35.6	
Oil-exporting countries	−1.25	−38.0	−116.0	+6.0	

+ = Net capital flows *in*
− = Net capital flows *out*

(*Sources*: Adapted from Griffith-Jones 1982; World Bank 1986)

after the oil price increases of 1973 and 1979. These oil price increases suddenly created a select band of capital-surplus countries – the oil-exporting countries, mainly those belonging to the cartel known as the Organization of Petroleum Exporting Countries (OPEC). During the mid-1970s, these countries provided the major source of capital, and the non-oil, less developed countries and the smaller (non-OECD) developed countries became the major recipients of rapidly increasing capital flows between world regions. The developed countries as a group lost their role as major net contributors to the world system of capital supply: indeed, by 1980, they had become a most significant target for surplus capital from the oil-exporting countries. Net capital flows between world regions were now at a very high level indeed, with smaller developed countries and Third World countries also reporting major increases in capital inflow.

By the mid-1980s, however, the major flow of capital was no longer between world regions but within them and particularly between the OECD countries. The United States became the major recipient of capital at the world scale as a result of its expanding budget and trade deficit; much of this capital was provided by other OECD countries with the smaller developed countries also being net contributors to the world system of capital supply. In contrast, the oil-exporting countries as a group had now become net importers of capital, partly due to the fall in oil prices during the 1980s. The pattern for Third World countries, however, had not changed; they still remained substantial net importers of capital.

Table 4.1 shows that net capital inflow into non-oil, less developed countries more than trebled between the late 1960s and mid-1970s, and then doubled again between the mid-1970s and early 1980s. What has been the impact of this apparent boom in capital inflow into Third World countries? Has its impact been beneficial or has it produced a new set of constraints for Third World development? From the point of view of this book's focus, what have been the implications for Third World industrialization? In order to answer these questions, it is first useful to concentrate on examining the history of capital flows into one continent of the Third World. In this chapter, we will attempt to trace in some detail the evolution of capital inflow into the continent of Latin America since the Second World War. Since then, capital flows between developed countries have expanded dramatically, due to a whole variety of technological and commercial reasons. Meanwhile, capital flows into the Third World continents have grown much less dramatically. However, within the Third World, capital flows into Latin America have been much greater than into other Third World continents. It is thus useful to examine closely the recent history of capital flow into Latin America, while making occasional reference to broader issues of Third World capital flows.

CAPITAL FLOWS INTO LATIN AMERICA SINCE THE SECOND WORLD WAR

In the forty-odd years since the Second World War, the nature of capital flows into Latin America has dramatically changed. In retrospect, it could be argued that the period can best be divided into three distinct phases: a period of modest increases in capital inflow from a variety of sources (1945–73); an era noted by an extraordinary rise in commercial bank lending (1973–82); and the beginning and subsequent continuation of what has been described as Latin America's debt crisis (since 1982).

Early increases in capital inflow (1945–73)

As was noted in Chapter 2, the reconstruction of the capitalist world economy after the Second World War was very much controlled by the United States. Due to the lack of war damage, the United States saw no reason for an extension of Marshall Aid to the Latin American continent. Rather the United States policy could be described as one in which US company investment in Latin America was favoured, and such a policy could be enhanced if Latin American governments made it attractive for US companies to invest. As a result, between 1946 and 1961, the major type of capital flow into Latin America was that of direct foreign investment, with US multinationals investing in a wide range of productive activities in agriculture, mining and manufacturing. However, aggregate capital inflow into the continent was kept at a relatively small scale, with only US$690 million flowing into the region during 1960, for example.

The type if not the scale of capital inflow changed during the 1960s as the US government reacted to the Cuban Revolution by providing financial assistance to Latin American governments through the Alliance for Progress, a scheme designed to stimulate structural reform, such as that of the agrarian sector. In many ways, this became the Latin American version of Marshall Aid as between 1960 and 1969 over 10 billion dollars were channelled into Latin America by the US government (Griffith-Jones 1982); such funding was responsible for over 60 per cent of foreign capital inflow into Latin America during the 1960s. However, in the late 1960s, such funding came to a halt under the Nixon administration.

By the late 1960s and early 1970s, many Latin American countries that had encouraged industrialization during the 1950s and 1960s found that their access to financial resources fell short of requirements. The net inflow of external credit between 1966 and 1970 averaged only US$2.6 billion a year. Credit was, however, coming from a variety of sources – one-third in the form of direct corporate investment, one-quarter in US government funding and one-sixth from official international agencies such as the IMF and World Bank. In terms of the subsequent evolution of capital inflow, it is worth noting that at this time international banks accounted for less than 10 per cent of total capital inflow.

The rise of commercial bank lending, 1973–82

During the mid-1970s, the nature of capital inflow into Latin America dramatically changed. First, the size of capital inflow substantially increased, to US$21.8 billion in 1978, a ten-fold increase in less than ten years. Secondly, the origin of the funds changed. In relative terms, the influence of direct investment and US bilateral aid substantially declined. Multinational banks came to account for the majority of foreign credit – 57 per cent in 1978.

The big surge in bank lending to Latin America can be traced to the oil price rises of 1973 and the consequent surpluses of capital accruing to some OPEC countries, such as Saudi Arabia and Kuwait. These surpluses began to be recycled through the 'Eurodollar' currency markets, where US dollars were traded in European currency markets. The scale of the oil-derived surplus available to the 'Eurodollar' currency markets between 1973 and 1974 has been calculated at over US$60 billion. However, Eurodollar currency loans were already far in excess of such oil-derived surpluses, totalling US$250 billion in 1973 alone. Their expansion during the 1970s was phenomenal; ten years later in 1983, Eurodollar currency loans had risen to about US$2000 billion. During the 1970s the banks involved in the Eurodollar markets extended 60 per cent or more of their Eurocurrency credits to less developed countries and particularly to Latin American countries. Furthermore, the 1970s decade saw more and more banks become involved in the profitable Eurocurrency markets; early on in the lending boom, North American banks were particularly prominent but later they were joined by banks from Europe, Japan and the Middle East.

The rapidly expanding number of international banks thus found themselves with a new role in world capital markets during the 1970s. International banks found that the credit demand of traditional clients in the developed world had slowed down as a result of recession, while deposits from oil exporters were growing very fast. This prompted the banks to lend to borrowers previously considered as marginal, such as both private and public organizations in Latin America. Meanwhile, the latter were keen to borrow, particularly in the light of the relative stagnation in capital inflow during the late 1960s and early 1970s. Indeed, Latin American governments began to prefer private bank loans to loans from foreign governments or international organizations such as the IMF. Conditions tended to be much easier, loans could be made effective more quickly and employed in a greater variety of ways, and loans could be given without reference to the management of the national economy; the IMF, for example, would pass comment on government management of the national economy and make decisions on the granting of loans accordingly. Furthermore, many Latin American governments seemed to prefer foreign private loans from international banks to foreign direct investment from multinational corporations, because the former were perceived as having fewer ties and allowed greater autonomy for national development. Finally, demand for foreign loans from international banks rapidly increased among oil-deficit countries, where they were utilized to pay for the oil, that is they were used to balance trading and current account deficits that were produced as a result of the rise in the cost of importing oil.

An international system of capital flows had suddenly developed that seemed to benefit all parties. The OPEC countries approved of the system. Their huge surplus funds were being safely invested by a wide variety of international banks from Western Europe and the United States; they were thus able to interpose Western commercial banks as a buffer between themselves and the 'high-risk' borrowers of Latin America and elsewhere. Many Latin American and some other Third World countries benefited. They were receiving large inflows of capital which in the mid-1970s, with high world inflation and low interest rates, were very cheap in real terms. Industrial nations also benefited because increased demand for capital equipment and machinery came from the borrowing nations. Finally, the international banks were contented with the arrangements. Their assets, turnover and profits rapidly increased, and they developed two new operational techniques which diminished their risks. Firstly, for large loans with long maturities, the type of credit required by Latin American countries, they devised the roll-over credit. Although the loan to the Latin American country may have had a long maturity (e.g. ten years), the interest rate would be changed every time the credit was rolled over – usually every three or six months. This floating interest rate effectively passed the risks of the market to the borrower for it was the borrower who had to bear the risks of long-term changes in the market. The second technique developed by the banking fraternity was the syndicated loan. Syndicated loans were simply credits shared by a large number of banks. In this way, the risks of default on large loans were spread over a number of banks.

It should be remembered, however, that the number of borrowing countries was limited. The great majority of the poorer countries of Africa and Asia received virtually no syndicated loan. In Latin America, countries like El Salvador, Guatemala, Paraguay, Colombia and Surinam were avoided or parsimoniously treated by the international banks. In 1983, it was calculated that just twenty-one countries accounted for 84 per cent of external debt owed to banks by borrowers in less developed countries: eleven of these were in Latin America and can be said to have been benefiting from the international system of the 1970s. However, in retrospect, the international system relied on two vital ingredients – low real interest rates and a healthy growth in the value of exports from the borrowing countries. During the early 1980s, these ingredients were singularly lacking.

The Latin American debt crisis

International economic conditions began to change dramatically in 1980, the year after the second major rise in OPEC oil prices. The reaction of the international banks was to continue the recycling of the surplus petrodollars. But the early 1980s saw the application of monetarist economic principles in two key Western countries: the United States and the United Kingdom. While the major objective of bringing down inflation to less than 5 per cent was achieved in both countries, rising unemployment and a reduction in the level of economic activity resulted. Further, when the Reagan administration reduced taxation without a concomitant reduction in expenditure, large public sector deficits were created which needed to be financed. With strict monetary control in force at the Federal Reserve Bank, the US budget deficit had suddenly to be financed by large-scale borrowing on international capital markets. Such borrowing substantially increased the world demand for dollars and as a result interest rates rose, at one time up and beyond the 20 per cent level. Due to the influence of the United States in the world economy, high real interest rates became a worldwide phenomenon.

The net effect of such events in the world economy was to reduce the level of economic activity in the industrialized countries. This in turn caused the stagnation of world trade in 1981, followed by a 2 per cent decline in 1982. The knock-on effect in Latin America was a reduction in both the volume and value of exports. In this way, an international financial system that benefited many Latin American countries in the 1970s became an enormous burden in the 1980s. In the 1970s, big Latin American borrowers such as Brazil and Mexico had financed rapidly increasing capital inflows through a rapid expansion of exports alongside low interest rates. However, with exports stagnant and interest rates high, the massive capital borrowing suddenly became transformed into a huge deadweight on the economy.

This deadweight of debt has continued to exercise an overpowering influence on the economies of most Latin American countries for most of the 1980s. How can its duration be explained? In general terms, it can be argued that two interlocking processes have become evident during the 1980s. The first refers to the lack of real power that the international creditor banks have over the debtor countries in being able to extract money or reparations from them. Indeed, even the international banks' policy of favouring the so-called 'model debtors' (those countries whose governments have seriously attempted to restructure economies in line with new realities) has not been successful as the 'bad debtors' have often negotiated as good a deal as the 'model debtors'.

The second process refers to the lumping together of both private and public debt in Latin America. First, it should be pointed out that public debt has been a major component of total national debt in Latin America over the last two decades. Congdon (1988: 113) makes the point that much of international bank lending to Latin American countries in the 1970s took the form of 'sovereign lending', that is loans to governments or to public sector bodies with government or central bank guarantees. In this way international banks 'did not have to assess in detail the viability of the investments being financed with their money or even have to check that the money was being invested'. However, the sovereign character of bank lending gave opportunities for misappropriation:

The involvement of the state lulled the banks into a false sense of security, because they did not doubt a government's preparedness to honour its financial commitments and they did not have to worry about the particular uses to which loan proceeds were put. In fact, the loan proceeds were not infrequently channelled to the personal benefit of a small number of well-connected individuals . . . . A depressingly high proportion of the so-called 'capital inflows' into Latin America were destined to become capital outflows into developed countries, with bank accounts and real estate in Florida being the favorite final resting place. Perhaps the most sickening aspect of the whole business is that the fly-by-night rascals who effectively stole the proceeds of syndicated loans did not have to carry the burden of debt service. Some time after the departure of their managements from Mexico, Argentina or Venezuela the self-styled 'banks' would be declared insolvent. They were therefore unable to repay the syndicated credits which had made their transgressions possible. But part of the original arrangement was that the loans were guaranteed by the government or central bank of the country concerned (Congdon 1988: 123–4).

Therefore, much public debt was in fact diverted into private banks, but banks of a dubious nature. On-lending from these banks was either fictitious or in highly speculative areas, such as property development. However, after these dubious national banks were declared bankrupt, the government had to continue to service the debts.

Thus, in the original evolution of international lending, public and private loans were effectively being lumped together. But even when public and private lending was separate, international banks clamoured for government guarantees on private loans, even if they had not been originally present. For example, the Chilean government refused in 1980 and 1981 to give guarantees on foreign loans to its financial institutions.

However, when these institutions were unable to service their debts properly in late 1982, the state was forced – by the international banks – to assume responsibility for them. As the potential sanctions against a small country with an internationally much disliked military government would have been difficult to resist, the Chilean government did accept responsibility, even though this was contrary to the original terms of the contracts. This is perhaps one of the most dishonourable episodes in modern banking (Congdon 1988: 227).

Debt has thus become as much a political as an economic issue in Latin America. Another commentator on the Latin American debt crisis (Whitehead 1987) has put this down to the difference between US and Latin American perceptions of debt. When the debt crisis broke, it was considered quite natural for the central banks in almost all Latin American countries to take over the responsibility for the external debt obligations of troubled private firms – to 'socialize' bad private debts, even of highly dubious firms. In contrast, the response in the United States would have been to declare bad private debtors bankrupt and to suffer any reverberations that might occur through the banking system. As we have seen, the Chilean government did attempt to follow the US model towards debt, but was prevented from doing so by the international banks and external political pressure. Furthermore, when Chile's two largest private corporations were declared bankrupt in January 1983, the Chilean government was forced to intervene and effectively 'socialize' their bad private debts. The negative reverberations of the bankruptcy of Chile's two largest corporations *without* consequent government intervention would have been so widespread in terms of further bankruptcies, closures, productive decline and economic instability, that government intervention in the running of the two corporations and the declaration of public responsibility for private debt were seen as essential.

Whitehead (1987: 22–3) makes an interesting point when he transfers such Latin American attitudes to private and public debt at the national level to the international scale of analysis:

> there is usually also an operating assumption that the Central Bank will be obliged to bail out any subordinate financial intermediaries that run into severe difficulties, at least unless there is a political decision to the contrary. . . . Since this is how the domestic financial system operates in the typical Latin American republic, it is almost inevitable that such experiences will be reflected in popular (and even some elite) assumptions about the

international financial system. One such assumption would be that America's most loyal allies (most reliable clients) are entitled to a degree of protection from Washington when the international economy turns sour.

Such intervention by the US government in the Latin American debt crisis has not materialized. Washington has made no serious attempt to create a special fund to bail out the Latin American debtors. This leaves little scope for manoeuvre between the international creditor banks on the one hand, and the governments of the debtor countries on the other.

> The critical sticking point appears to be that neither private nor public international creditors, can allow themselves to be seen lending to distressed debtors at less than their own 'cost of funds'. To do so, they maintain, would undermine the entire rationale of commercial banking practice, and would destroy the confidence of their depositors. Only a formal guarantee [from the US government], or subsidy, backed by taxpayers' funds, would enable them to give ground on this point (Whitehead 1987: 23–4).

However, the serious fiscal problems of the US government during the late 1980s would seem to preclude any such remedies.

Meanwhile, the international creditor banks seemed to have arrived at their point of maximum concessions in early 1987 (see Table 4.2). Since 1982, international banks have given more and more concessions to debtor countries. As Table 4.2 demonstrates, in 1982/83, loans to public and private debtors in Latin America were still potentially very profitable, the interest rate being charged on average at $2\frac{1}{4}$ per cent above the London Interbank Offered Rate (LIBOR), one of the major markers for international capital transactions. By 1987, however, the average interest rate

Table 4.2 Terms of Latin American debt renegotiations, 1982–87

Year	Margin over LIBOR (average)	Repayment Period (years)	Grace Period (years)
1982/3	$2\frac{1}{4}$%	8	3
1984/5	$1\frac{3}{8}$%	12	4
1986/7	$\frac{7}{8}$%	16	6

Table 4.3 The evolution of debt indicators for developing countries since the 1982 debt crisis (per cent unless stated)

Indicator	1982	1983	1984	1985	1986
Ratio of debt to GNP	26.3	31.4	33.0	35.8	35.4
Ratio of debt to exports	117.6	134.8	121.2	143.7	144.5
Debt service ratio	20.6	19.4	19.5	21.4	22.3
Ratio of debt service to GNP	4.6	4.5	4.9	5.3	5.5
Ratio of interest service to exports	10.4	10.1	10.3	10.8	10.7
Total debt outstanding and disbursed (billions of dollars)	551.1	631.5	673.2	727.7	753.4

GNP – gross national product.
Debt service – the (annual) sum of interest payments and repayments of principal on external debt.
Debt service ratio – total debt service divided by exports of goods and services.

(*Source*: Adapted from World Bank 1987: 18)

charged on Latin American debt was down to only $\frac{7}{8}$ per cent over LIBOR, a rate that the international banks argue reflects merely 'the cost of the funds'. This is because, added to the administrative overheads, not all banks can acquire money as low as the LIBOR rate and most are forced to carry on 'involuntary lending' to debtor countries so that the latter can be recorded as current in their interest payments. Alongside the concession of declining margins over LIBOR, international creditor banks have extended the average repayment period for loans (doubling from 8 to 16 years in four years) and the average grace period during which no repayment of principal is requested (see Table 4.2). There has also been a softening of the macro-policy conditions required by the public agencies that are a part of most reschedulings. With these changes, international banks now argue that not only has the 'bottom line' been reached in terms of concessions but also that the former profitability of lending to Latin American debtors has totally disappeared and, as we will see later, major losses are being recorded.

The last half of the 1980s has seen the world economy ameliorating slightly for the debtor countries in that international interest rates have declined since their early 1980s peak (the LIBOR rate declined from an average of 16 per cent in 1981 to 7 per cent in 1986) and world trade has begun to grow again after its stagnation between 1981 and 1983, stimulated in particular by the growth of US imports. Reductions in world interest rates and prospects for export growth have loosened the external constraints on Latin American economies.

Nevertheless, there still remains little room for optimism on the central issue of debt. For as the efforts of international banks, the IMF and the World Bank for easing the financial burdens faced by Latin American countries near their limits, the difficulties of debt servicing remain as intractable as ever. Since the Third World debt crisis emerged in 1982, all leading indicators of debt have been getting worse. Taking the World Bank survey of ninety developing countries (World Bank 1987: 18), all indicators show a continued worsening of the debt problem at the aggregate level since 1982 (see Table 4.3). Despite the restrictions on increased Third World lending by international banks, total debt has increased by over one-third since 1982 and the ratio of debt to GNP has increased from one-quarter to one-third; even the critical debt service ratio has crept up further.

It is difficult to transfer simple debt figures into an understanding of the burden they now hold for each country's economy. Other variables such as export performance, population totals and *per capita* income come into play. For example, if population is taken into account, an index of *per capita* debt can be calculated (see Table 4.4). According to this criterion, the big debtors in absolute terms (Brazil and Mexico) have economies less constrained than some smaller debtors such as Venezuela and Argentina. If *per capita* debt is

Table 4.4   *Per capita* dollar debt for selected Latin American countries, 1987

Country	Total debt ($ billion)	Population (millions)	*Per capita* dollar debt
Brazil	116.9	140.5	832 (764)
Mexico	105.6	82.3	1283 (1267)
Argentina	54.5	31.2	1747 (1428)
Venezuela	32.2	18.2	1769 (2207)
Chile	19.1	12.4	1540 (1642)
Peru	15.3	19.3	793 (672)

Per capita dollar debt figures in brackets refer to 1983 figures.

(*Sources*: *Financial Times* 1988: 15/3/88, 6; Gwynne 1985: 13)

then compared to *per capita* income, an even more dramatic indication of the burden of debt on some Latin American economies can be appreciated (see Fig. 4.1). For two of the poorer Latin American countries, Nicaragua and Bolivia, *per capita* debt is respectively 2.2 and 1.3 times greater than *per capita* income. For two countries that international banks decided to lend to in great quantities (relative to their size) during the late 1970s and early 1980s (Chile and Costa Rica), *per capita* debt was also greater than *per capita* income in 1985. Chile seems to have achieved a *per capita* income slightly higher than *per capita* debt during 1988, but its economy remains heavily constrained in terms of external financing – as are those of Ecuador, Honduras, Uruguay, Argentina and Peru, where *per capita* income only slightly exceeds *per capita* debt. For these countries, located in a potentially dangerous macroeconomic framework of high relative debt, it becomes important, indeed essential, to develop judicious, careful policies, stimulating local saving, reducing inflation and promoting export growth. If such policies are seriously and successfully pursued, as occurred in Chile between 1985 and 1988, the economy can gradually grow out of such indebtedness. However, if such policies are not followed national economies can fall into a vicious circle marked by low export growth, low generation of domestic savings, continued reliance on foreign financing and increasing debt; in the case of Argentina, this led in 1987 to a mas-

sive current account deficit (US$4 billion), low export growth and a concomitant high ratio of debt interest payments to exports (56 per cent), high inflation (178 per cent) and generally low economic growth (2 per cent) (*Financial Times* 1988: 15/3/88).

It is worth noting that it is beyond these nine Latin American countries where *per capita* debt is similar to or greater than *per capita* income (see Fig. 4.1) that one finds those countries whose debt problems tend to be headline news in the international media. In fact, in terms of the *per capita* income/debt index used, both Brazil and Mexico have economies theoretically less constrained by debt than ten other Latin American countries. This is partly because the large debts that built up during the 1970s and early 1980s were matched by large populations (see Table 4.4) and expanding economies. However, it is the sheer size of their debt that is identified as the problem by international banks. From Fig. 4.1, it is evident that only three Latin American countries have escaped the full severity of the debt crisis – El Salvador, Colombia and Guatemala. This can be partly attributed to the lack of interest of international banks in these economies during the 1970s.

One indication of the worsening of the debt crisis for Latin America as a whole can be seen in the evolution of the secondary market for debt. The secondary market for debt provides the possibility for international banks to sell off their country debt to other banks or institutions. However, in order to do this, they have to sell off their debt at large discounts, and the size of the discount tends to reflect the international markets' opinion of the management of each country's economy (see Table 4.5); for example, international banks have to provide much larger discounts to sell off Peruvian (over 90 per cent) rather than Colombian (about 25 per cent) debt. However, the experience of 1987 and 1988 is that the resale value of the debt of all Latin American countries has been declining. This is creating a major problem in terms of further 'involuntary lending' by international banks due to the increasing difference between loans and their secondary market values.

The international debt crisis in general and that

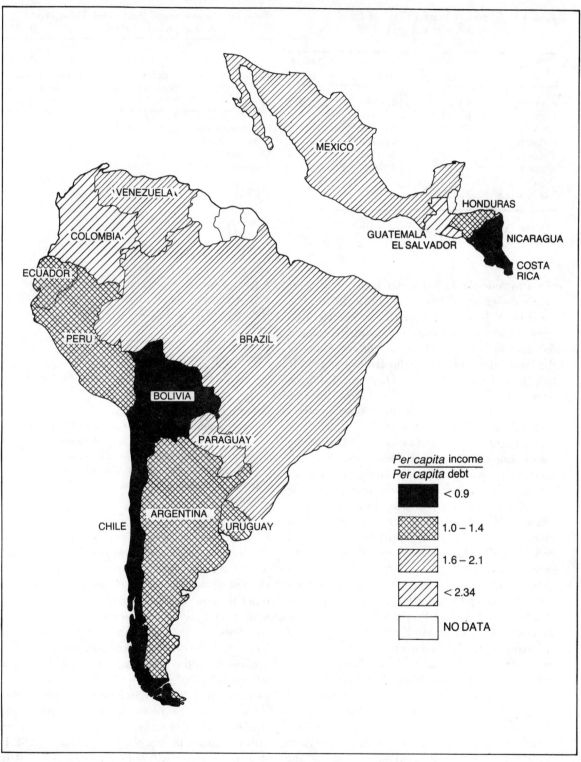

Per capita income
―――――――――
Per capita debt

■ < 0.9

▨ 1.0 – 1.4

▧ 1.6 – 2.1

▨ < 2.34

□ NO DATA

4.1 Latin America: the relationship between *per capita* income and *per capita* debt, 1985.

Table 4.5 Secondary market value of Latin American external debt, 1987–88 (per cent of face value)

	May 1987	November 1987	March 1988
Argentina	58–60	33–37	28
Brazil	62–65	37–41	46
Chile	67–70	50–53	57
Colombia	85–88	72–76	
Ecuador	52–55	31–34	
Mexico	57–60	48–52	48
Peru	14–18	2–7	
Venezuela	72–74	49–53	

(*Sources*: Adapted from *Wall Street Journal*, 18/11/87; *Financial Times* 15/3/88)

Table 4.6 International banks and Third World debt exposure, 1988

Bank	Third World debts as per cent of equity	Percentage of Third World debts for which provision has been made
Commerzbank	82	35[a]
Deutsch Bank	17	70
Dresdner Bank	62	50[a]
Credit Suisse	36	45[a]
SBC	17	60[a]
UBS	24	50[a]
Barclays	63	25
Lloyds	141	30
Midland	143	27
NatWest	45	30
Chase Manhattan	228	23
J. P. Morgan	90	25
Manufacturers Hanover	329	22
Citicorp	185	26

[a] Estimates.

(*Source*: Adapted from *Financial Times*, 15/3/88: 6)

of Latin America in particular has thus exacerbated rather than improved since 1982. The commercial banks are lining up to give as little credit as possible to the debtor countries, even in terms of so-called involuntary lending. Some of the larger and more successful banks have made huge provisions for debt loss. However, Table 4.6 demonstrates that at least five banks (Lloyds, Midland, Chase Manhattan, Manufacturers Hanover and Citicorp) would be in a serious predicament in the face of any mass defaulting by Latin American countries due to the fact that their Third World debt exposure is in all cases substantially greater than their equity – in the case of Manufacturers Hanover Trust Bank three times as great. The European banks have already made large provisions for Third World debt and two British banks (NatWest and Barclays) also seem secure.

While commercial banks make huge provisions for debt loss and restrict further loans, it seems that both the IMF and World Bank only have the capacity for financing 'restructuring' and 'adjustment' in debtor countries on a relatively small scale. They certainly do not have access to sufficient funds to finance a grand plan to 'solve' the debt crisis. A new multilateral organization financed by the industrialized countries to reduce the impact of the debt crisis on Third World countries in general and Latin American countries in particular also seems out of the question:

The most obvious obstacle to any such scheme is that it would involve using substantial amounts of taxpayers' money both to help out foreign countries and to help banks. The conservative atmosphere and fiscal discipline in most industrialized countries essentially rule out such a solution (Nicoll 1988: 6).

The governments of most debtor countries believe that on present policies, the prospects confronting them are so grave that 'something will have to give'. However, the lack of success of a debtor' cartel (or any substantial unity between the debtor countries) makes it difficult to conceive of a major break between debtor countries on the one hand, and international banks and the developed countries in which they are based, on the other. Added to this the lack of success attached to both Brazil's one-year debt moratorium (1987/88) and Peru's severe restrictions on debt payments to international banks (the equivalent in value of no more than 10 per cent of exports in any one year) make it unlikely that any country will opt completely out of debt rescheduling. In the Treaty of Acapulco in

November 1987, eight Latin American countries stated that international banks should only receive prices for their loans as measured by the secondary market (*Financial Times* 30/11/87: 1). However, the precise nature of such a scheme was not clarified. Nevertheless, the use of the secondary market has produced at least three innovative methods of reducing debt, albeit marginal reductions.

The first scheme is that of debt–equity swaps. The basic idea is to change debt into investment through use of the secondary market. It is based on the fact that there are many international banks, particularly the smaller banks, that want to get rid of their foreign loans and are willing to do so at a big discount. The country that has best utilized the debt–equity swap idea is Chile. A hypothetical example can show how it works. A Canadian timber firm is interested in investing in Chile's booming timber and cellulose sector and realizes that substantial discounts can be achieved in locating a US$10 million plant there. For this purpose the firm approaches a large international bank as broker, say Citicorp. Citicorp conveniently knows of a small Mid-West bank that would like to get rid of a US$10 million Chilean loan that it has on its books. The secondary market is consulted and Chilean loans are trading at 57 per cent of their true value. The arrangement takes place. The Mid-West bank receives US$5.7 million (57 per cent of US$10 million), and the Canadian timber firm pays this plus the commission to Citicorp. The Canadian timber firm now owns US$10 million of loans. It goes to Chile's Central Bank and obtains approval for its new investment. The Central Bank then allocates the firm US$10 million worth of pesos, at the official exchange rate, in return for the US$10 million worth of loans, which are thus paid off. The Canadian timber firm begins to build its cellulose plant.

The loser in this swap is the Mid-West bank which has traded loans with a book value of US$10 million for US$5.7 million in cash; however, its Third World debt exposure has been reduced. The winners in the swap are the broker (due to the commission), the timber firm (obtains pesos at a 43 per cent discount) and Chile, which no longer has to pay interest on the US$10 mil-

lion. As the scheme also allows Chilean investors to do swaps, using foreign currency held abroad, it has also helped bring flight capital back into the country (*The Economist* 7/3/87: 87–90). Between mid-1985 and end-1987, Chile had managed to retire more than US$2 billion worth of debt due to debt–equity swaps. During 1987, external debt fell from US$19.4 billion to US$19.1 billion as a result of the scheme. The debt–equity scheme in Chile has therefore been very successful at the margin, reducing debt (by 1.5 per cent in 1987), promoting increased foreign investment and enabling the national economy to grow out of its heavy indebtedness.

A scheme that seems to have been less successful is that pioneered by Mexico, the bonds for loans scheme, again making use of the secondary market for country loans (*Financial Times* 31/12/87: 2). The basic premise is that banks agree to forgive part of their loans, taking another asset in exchange which has a lower face value but is more attractive (that is, it can be cashed in whenever the bank chooses). The Mexican scheme involved the issue of Mexican securities backed by US Treasury bonds. However, it seems that the banks have not been particularly interested in the scheme. In the first bonds-for-loans tendering in early 1988, only 139 out of more than 500 creditor banks tendered any of their exposure and only 95 of them at discounts which Mexico could accept. The response was such that Mexico accepted discounts of as little as 25 per cent, that is securities were issued at up to 75 per cent of the original value of the loan (far higher than the Mexican authorities had wished to go). The Mexican government had hoped to retire as much as US$10 billion of debt from the scheme in 1988; in the end, it managed to cancel only US1.1 billion.

It could be argued, however, that Mexico would have achieved the same result if it had simply bought back debt rather than go through its complex bond swap. The effect of its offer was that it cancelled a net $1.1 billion of debt by spending $532 million of reserves to buy zero-coupon US government bonds to be used as the collateral for its bonds. This works out to 48 cents on the dollar, which is exactly the secondary market price of Mexican debt (Nicoll 1988: 6).

The third scheme to use the secondary market value for loans is simply the buying back of commercial bank debt from the exchange reserves of debtor countries. Up to 1988, however, it had rarely been used as a way of retiring debt. This was partly due to the political problems of using valuable exchange reserves simply to retire debt in the face of demands not to honour the debt at all and partly due to legal restrictions in loan clauses. However, in March 1988, with IMF participation, Bolivia's creditor banks agreed to sell back US$308 million of debt to Bolivia at 11 per cent of its face value, the secondary market rate for Bolivian loans; Bolivia's payment of US$33.5 million was made from reserves (*Financial Times* 17/3/88: 3). In some ways, this can be seen as a special case due to IMF involvement (including the setting up of a fund for donations from industrialized countries) on the one hand and the tremendous weight of Bolivian debt in relation to that country's population and economy (see Fig. 4.1) on the other.

CAPITAL FLOWS AND THE THIRD WORLD

In retrospect, the decade of the 1970s can be seen as extraordinarily and exceptionally favourable for some Third World countries in terms of capital flows. It was a decade in which capital flowed from capital-surplus to capital-deficient countries, although the actual number of the latter that benefited was still small. In contrast, the 1980s has witnessed a complete reversal of such a worldwide tendency, the capital flowing *out* of capital-deficient countries, and particularly Latin American countries, and *into* the capital-surplus countries of the industrialized world in general and the United States in particular.

As regards the long-term development of Third World countries, the net outflow of capital is most alarming. Indeed, within the framework of such a potentially hostile world economy, there seems to be only one policy that makes sense – a policy of making capital find its market value (through interest rates) in each Third World country. In the short term, this inevitably means high interest rates and a concomitant recession, strenuously avoided by such countries as Argentina, Brazil and Peru. However, in the medium and long term, it stimulates domestic saving, thus reducing the need for foreign financing. If such a policy is linked, as it has been in Chile between 1985 and 1988, to a serious policy of trade liberalization and export promotion, the export sector can provide the crucial growth stimuli to move the economy out of recession and into a period of stable outward-oriented growth.

The essential point is that within the world system of capital supply of the 1980s, Third World countries have little room for manoeuvre if their aim is one of long-term, sustained economic growth. This is particularly so for the highly indebted countries, strapped by high annual debt repayments and the need for large trade surpluses every year. Under such conditions, the economic powers of the national government must concentrate priorities on the export sector. As in Chile, increases in domestic demand, frequently seen to be associated with trade liberalization, can be avoided by policies of high interest rates, stimulating local saving as opposed to consumption. In this way, both Chile and Mexico are seen as 'model debtors' by international banks and organizations. Their 'realistic' policies have managed to achieve economic growth within the constraints of serious indebtedness. As a result, there has been a gradual lowering of the weight of external debt on the national economies.

The basic question that must be addressed in this book, however, is the role of industrialization in the development of heavily indebted countries. Do policies that favour industrial expansion assist to a greater degree than other sectoral policies in the promotion of export-oriented growth and the reduction in the debt burden? Parts of subsequent chapters will re-address this theme, but for the moment it is worth making three points. First, during the 1980s, and particularly until 1987, Third World countries specializing in primary production suffered from low prices for primary products, relative to prices for manufactured products. Therefore, because manufactured products maintained their prices much better in international trade than primary products, those Third World countries promoting industrial exports performed much better in world trade than Third World primary-producing countries. Secondly, and as a result, the newly industrializing countries (NICs) have tended to reduce the impact of their inherited debt burden more successfully than non-NICs. South Korea is a notable example in this respect, but Mexico has also achieved some success in reducing the weight of debt on the performance of its economy. It could be argued that Brazil was doing likewise until the turnabout in economic policies in 1985.

Thirdly, for those non-NICs that have nevertheless attempted export-oriented industrialization as a way out of the debt problem, some interesting results have been achieved both in terms of export expansion and debt reduction. However, we will return more specifically to the question of manufacturing exports from Third World countries in Chapters 6 and 7.

—PART II—

PERSPECTIVES ON INDUSTRIAL GROWTH IN THE THIRD WORLD

— 5 —

THEORIES OF INDUSTRIALIZATION AND THE ROLE OF GOVERNMENT

The modern discussion of how industrial development is achieved in the poor country is, in fact, an intellectual curiosity of the first order; it proceeds from almost perfect certainty as to what will serve industrialization, but there is also almost total uncertainty as to the result of any given line of action. Were the means for getting industrial development known, nearly all of the poor countries would now be on the way to industrial success (Galbraith 1979: 91–2).

As the Third World industrializes, it is apparent that no one overarching theory has been able to explore suitably the complex relationship between industrialization and development. One point that should be made from the outset is that industrialization is not always seen as an appropriate strategy for the development of Third World countries. In Kitching's (1982) excellent critique of economic populism, he points to the wide variety of modern populist thought (Nyerere; the ILO; Lipton; Schumacher) that has decried industrialization (and particularly that of a capital-intensive nature) and favoured agricultural growth as the prime strategy of development. Meanwhile, within the ranks of Marxist theorists, there have been a wide range of writers who have regarded industrialization linked to foreign capital and technology as bringing stagnation to less developed countries, rather than development (Frank 1969; Baran 1973, for example).

Nevertheless, it should also be pointed out that in some recent attempts to survey the field by Marxist geographers and economic analysts (Corbridge 1986: 128–88; Jenkins 1987b: 30–3), the so-called neo-fundamentalist or Warrenite theories of development and industrialization have been re-emphasized. The basic argument is that in the medium to long term, capitalism and industrialization are essential for the development of Third World countries; 'it is the self-sustaining momentum and rapid pace of technological change under capitalism, and especially industrial capitalism, that distinguish it from all earlier societies' (Warren 1980: 12). Furthermore, 'equality, justice, generosity, independence of spirit and mind, the spirit of inquiry and adventure, opposition to cruelty, not to mention political democracy are not late-comers to [but] . . . are either ushered in by capitalism or achieve a relative dominance unequalled by any major earlier or contemporaneous cultures' (Warren 1980: 21).

Furthermore, in modern capitalism, with competition between industrial corporations from different world regions, Corbridge (1986: 136) criticizes the Leninist idea of international capitalism being stultified by monopoly capitalism – where small numbers of global corporations carve up and control world markets, thereby enjoying monopoly profits. Corbridge (1986: 177–84) skilfully uses the modern example of Taiwanese industrialization to show how capitalism and industrialization can bring dynamic growth to Third World countries rather than stagnation and dependency. However, while the present author agrees with such an analysis, the underlying contention that successful capitalism will inevitably evolve into Marxist socialism seems much more difficult to accept. There has never been a case of an industrialized country turning to Marxist socialism or communism. Almost all cases (Russia, China, Cuba, for example) of communist countries have emerged from *unsuccessful capitalism* at an early stage in their development, when the economy tended to be dominated by agriculture and normally peasant agriculture. In short, the neo-fundamentalist framework gives a most positive framework for the role of capitalism and industrialization in transforming the societies and economies of Third World countries, but the underlying contention that such capitalist success will lead to socialism appears distinctly questionable, indeed mystifying.

However, the aim of this chapter is not to comment on the wide range of disparate theories that relate to the political economy of industrialization or the role of industrialization in development (some of these issues will, however, be returned to in Ch. 9). Rather the aim is to examine the small number of theories that have attempted to comment on the theoretical attributes that are required for a successful process of industrialization. These types of theory have tended to emerge from the field of economic history. Some represent theoretical generalizations that have emerged from analysing the experiences of countries that have followed a successful path to industrialization. This chapter will examine the work of three influential theorists (Rostow, Gerschenkron and Talcott Parsons) before making some general points about the lessons that can be drawn from the past. The crucial role of government in the industrialization process will then be examined.

THE ROSTOW MODEL

One of the most influential post-war models, at least in terms of policy making, has been that of Rostow (1960). One reason for the model's popularity among policy makers was its way of simplifying and formalizing the development process. According to Rostow, rapid development came during a period of take-off which depended for its very existence and success on the fulfilment of a series of preconditions. Rapid industrialization constituted a fundamental cornerstone of the take-off stage. The preconditions for take-off and concomitant industrial growth could be seen as a checklist or recipe and included the following ingredients:

1. A transformation in agriculture, yielding higher productivity on the land and thus freeing surplus labour, food, and raw materials for use in industry.
2. An accumulation of social overhead capital, mostly in the form of transport-related facilities (ports, docks, canals, railways) which would act to extend markets, allow supply and demand to interact quickly and efficiently, and move in raw materials at tolerable prices and move out bulky products at tolerable costs.
3. A development of the ancillary services for industry, most especially banking.
4. The presence of entrepreneurs willing to take risks in non-conventional fields.
5. The presence of sufficient skilled labour and power resources.
6. An increased exploitation of domestic raw materials or an increase in the importation of ores.

Such a list of preconditions seems to have been present or developing in the historical experiences of both the United States and Britain. However, its wider applicability even in historical terms has been severely criticized by Trebilcock (1981) who argued that if the Rostowian model is 'to lend a justified shapeliness to the analysis of industrial growth', the various prerequisites should be unique to the early industrial stage. But, reviewing nineteenth-century European industrialization, Trebilcock (1978: 6) came to the following conclusion:

Even the most casual review of nineteenth-century economic development will reveal that many of the factors described by Rostow as preconditions may occur at almost any stage of the growth process, often well after the economy has embarked upon 'take-off'. Thus in Russia, the lending of capital through an effective native banking system did not develop in advance of the industrial spurt of the 1890s, but in the 1900s, when the spurt had already begun to slow. Similarly, Russia's agricultural transformation is difficult to detect: it certainly did not precede 1890; it may have arrived with Stalin's collectivization programme of the 1930s; or, as some would argue, it may be yet to come. In Italy also, agriculture has presented a problem: here industrialization occurred against the backcloth of savage rural poverty, in the south most especially, and both the industrial achievement and the agricultural problem have persisted into the present time.

Trebilcock added that 'if the preconditions can appear in so capricious a manner, and sometimes scarcely appear at all, then clearly the descriptive accuracy of the model is placed in doubt'. In terms of Third World countries, recent experiences again show contrasting evidence – agricultural transformation occurring along with industrial growth in some such as Taiwan, but being absent in many of the oil-rich economies, most notably Nigeria. Rostow also underrated the amount of domestic savings required to finance sustained industrial growth. As a result, the preconditions of Rostow are *not* preconditions; sometimes they can be seen to operate, but at other times not. Rather they constitute a set of factors that the governments of less developed countries should bear in mind in any serious attempt at industrialization.

THE GERSCHENKRON MODEL

Gerschenkron adopted a radically different stance to Rostow with no discussion of preconditions (Gerschenkron, 1962). Rather the Gerschenkron model argued that industrial growth issues from a context of economic deprivation. The model propounded that a number of benefits are conferred on industrial latecomers that may promote a rapid leap out of backwardness into sustained economic growth. This is partly based on the observation that some industrial latecomers during both the nineteenth and twentieth centuries have grown at a faster rate than their predecessors; the rapid growth of Japanese industrialization at the

turn of the century and of Korean and Taiwanese industrialization in the 1960s and 1970s are examined in Chapter 12. The deprived-economy model concerns itself with the beginnings of industrial growth and assumes under-endowment as the starting point. Gerschenkron argued that as other countries advance and backwardness deepens, the underprivileged society will become increasingly sensitive to the contrast. As social tension increases, a vast effort is made to bridge the gap and a lunge for the benefits of industrial growth occurs.

Such growth is deemed possible as backwardness conveys a number of advantages on backward nations. The more backward the country, the more sophisticated will be the industrial equipment, technology and plant it can select for its manufacturing debut. It will be able to import the most modern machines with the concomitant advantage of enjoying the most significant economies of scale available. In theory, the costly stages of technological development may be skipped and complete industrial systems implemented. The import of new, capital-intensive technology can also compensate for an unskilled labour force.

The state, rather than the private sector, is viewed as the main agency of development, serving to coordinate and manage the industrial process. As the input needed to launch industrialization increases with backwardness, Gerschenkron argued that the process requires a correspondingly larger state response, particularly in terms of financial assistance; in this context, he placed significant emphasis on the creation of a national investment bank. Thus, the overall conclusion was that the greater the country's initial deprivation, the more coercive and comprehensive the state's action would have to be.

Meanwhile, little credence was given to Rostow's idea that certain prerequisites were necessary to be fulfilled before industrialization could take place. In particular, Gerschenkron saw agriculture as unresponsive to the dramatic economic changes wrought by industrialization, remaining inflexible and backward. Moreover, while Rostow's model demanded a supply of creative capitalists, Gerschenkron's context of backwardness made this much more unlikely, and unnecessary; the state would be the prime mover in galvanizing industrial growth.

Whereas Rostow's model seemed closely linked to the case studies of the United States and Britain, the Gerschenkron theory was strongly influenced by Eastern Europe. However, in terms of Third World industrialization, it did have the distinct advantage of recognizing that the position of present less developed countries in relation to the world market is fundamentally different from that of the advanced countries on the eve of their industrialization. As a result, Gerschenkron's ideas proved popular during the 1960s not only in the newly independent countries of Africa and Asia but also in the industrializing countries of Latin America. The subsequent industrial experience of these countries does reveal certain problems with the present-day applicability of Gerschenkron's theories.

First, there is the problem of the assumed benefits to the backward country of being able to import the latest technology. Landes (1969) argued that the burden of development has grown over time as the initial costs of technology and plant have increased due to rising capital intensity and the scale of modern production. Alongside the problems of inadequate skilled labour and insufficient technical and managerial talent, this has meant that 'the freedom of the latecomer to choose the latest and best equipment has become a myth'. This is particularly pertinent for small LDCs, which predominate in the Third World. Generally speaking, small countries have markets insufficient for the supply of goods that would emanate from new imported plant essentially geared to large economies of scale and production runs. Furthermore, it is often difficult for the Third World enterprise, whether state or private, to export surplus production in highly competitive world markets.

This is closely linked to a second problem with the applicability of the Gerschenkron model – that the straightforward import of the latest technology is not enough. The Japanese mode of industrialization (see Ch. 12) has demonstrated that industrial growth is rooted in the constant adaptation and improvement of imported technologies. Without the capacity to adapt and

improve technologies, both in terms of product and process, the imported technology of the LDC, even if it is the latest design, will soon age and become obsolescent. The LDC may have the capacity to import the latest technology and hence derive considerable initial advantages from it. But for the benefits to be long lasting, the LDC must have established a technological infrastructure that can adapt and improve these technologies. This has proved a much more difficult objective to achieve.

Thirdly, Gerschenkron's theory relies on the prominent involvement of the state during industrialization. However, the recent history of industrialization in LDCs has often demonstrated that close government involvement has not always been advantageous. The most common problem has been of a government overprotective towards industry, providing subsidies, heavily protected domestic markets and local monopoly conditions. As a result, the striving for efficiency and risk taking by private industrial firms, two vital ingredients for industrial success, can become seriously dampened as industrialists become conditioned to being extricated from problems by a benevolent state.

THE PARSONIAN APPROACH

The models of Rostow and Gerschenkron do have one aspect in common, in that economic criteria are emphasized in both. However, there are some economic criteria that, while being regarded as important at the theoretical level, can have contradictory impacts at the empirical level. The availability of natural resources would be one example. A rich endowment of natural resources, such as coal, has been important in the industrialization of some countries (USA, UK, Germany), but virtually insignificant in others (Japan, Singapore). Furthermore, there are many countries with rich and varied resources, alongside low populations, that have found it difficult to industrialize (Chile, Venezuela). If such significant economic variables as the availability of natural resources can have such varied impacts, perhaps, it is argued, social and cultural factors should be seen as the key variables explaining industrial success or failure. 'Social characteristics may exert an influence upon the course of industrialization at least as powerful as any derived from the more basic economic equipment. Mobile or fluid societies, in which the talented individual may rise by achievement irrespective of background, will provide a wider field for entrepreneurial recruitment than hierarchic or "fixed" societies' (Trebilcock 1981: 11).

Arguments of this type were put forward by the American sociologist, Talcott Parsons. According to Parsons (1951), every society possesses a set of 'role expectations', or the roles which the individuals within the society expect one another to perform. The society protects this series of role expectations by its system of rewards and retributions. Together, the 'role expectations' and the system of rewards and retributions constitute a 'social value system' which has a substantial ability to condition the activities of society's individual members. Thus, for the entrepreneurial activities of the society to be effectively developed, it is necessary that the fundamental behaviour patterns of capitalism (risk taking, profit motivation, the impersonal non-familial organization) 'should interlock smoothly with the society's prevailing value system, and should receive the "social approval" of the community' (Trebilcock 1981: 12). Considerable empirical evidence to back up Parsons's statements can be provided from such diverse cases as the United States and Japan since the 1870s.

One problem of Parsons's theory was that the concept of social approval exaggerated the cohesion displayed by societies in their attitudes to economic change. This problem was taken up in the Parsonian tradition by the Argentine sociologist, Gino Germani (1965), who saw social change under industrialization as asynchronic. Germani argued that social institutions, groups, values and attitudes change at a different pace with industrialization. Thus, social forms coexist in society which belong to different epochs and stages of transition. Some parts of society remain fairly traditional and backward coexisting with others which have already become modern. This is why the process of transition is conflictive and is lived as a crisis which divides groups and institutions. Germani's thesis is three-fold. First, in pre-industrial societies most actions are prescriptive whereas in industrial societies there is a predominance of elective actions. Secondly, Germani proposes that in traditional societies change tends to be a violation of traditional norms and therefore is abnormal and rare; in a modern society, on the contrary, change becomes a normal phenomenon. Finally, traditional societies possess an undifferentiated structure with few institutions performing many functions. In industrial societies each function tends to be performed by a specialized institution which results in a differentiated structure.

These three main changes of the transition process must also occur in the sphere of knowledge, science and technology. Instrumental rationality, separation from theology and philosophy, and increasing specialization must guide the production and development of knowledge. In the sphere of the economy, new specific and autonomous institutions must appear, operating according to principles of rationality and efficiency and with bureaucratic forms of organization. Social stratification must change from a close ascriptive system to an open system which works according to norms of achievement, performance and acquisition. This entails a shift from low levels of social mobility to high levels of social mobility. The state must be organized according to rational and bureaucratic norms and there must be an increase in the political participation of popular strata. Relating back to Parsonian theory and industrialization, Germani would therefore see the growth of industrial enterprise as asynchronic, most particularly in terms of its spatial and institutional development.

In both Parsons and Germani's approaches, entrepreneurs effectively come to constitute an integral part of their society, whether asynchronically or not. Finally, it is worth pointing out that this goes diametrically against the argument of Schumpeter (1943) who saw the entrepreneur as a figure who should not conform to any social orthodoxy, class or any other conventional restraint – a person outside the society, rather like the knights of the Middle Ages (Schumpeter 1939: 83), able to innovate, create new combinations of factors (land, labour, capital and technology) and push through new concepts. However, Schumpeter did see the role of the entrepreneur diminishing in the last half of the twentieth century as large corporations and what Galbraith (1967) termed the 'technostructure' came to be the depositories of invention, information and innovation. In this way, he saw entrepreneurial activity becoming institutionalized, which is more comparable with the Parsonian approach.

RELEVANCE FOR THIRD WORLD INDUSTRIALIZATION

These three theories certainly do not exhaust the range of theories developed with the intention of explaining industrialization, its origins and its evolution. However, all three have been influential in the post-war period. Rostow's model has been influential in many international agencies concerned with Third World development. Parsons's theory is significant as the major non-economic attempt to explain differential national success in industrialization and an important root of modernization theory. Meanwhile, Gerschenkronian theory very much tied in with the post-war policy of import substitution industrialization and the popular 1950s theory of the 'big push'.

During the 1950s, industrialization was seen as a priority by many Third World governments, including those of newly independent countries. This was closely linked to the emphasis in government policy on achieving economic growth. The idea of concentrating limited internal resources (of capital) and foreign aid/investment on a crash programme of industrialization was seen as a possible way out of the constraints that underdevelopment placed on economic growth. It was in this context that the theory of the 'big push' emerged. Its basic idea was that a massive investment in a wide range of industry should be encouraged because it would bring two interlocking benefits at the national level. First, demand would, increase, mainly through the large numbers of workers employed in the factories being built and the increase in their wages over what they would have earned in agriculture. Secondly, for many industries, and particularly those involved in energy or communications, the achievement of economies of scale would con-siderably reduce the unit price of the industrial product – for example, in electricity and steel production. The theoretical attractions from the interlocking of these two benefits were expressed by Rosenstein-Rodan (1962) as follows:

> If a hundred workers who were previously in disguised unemployment in an underdeveloped country are put into a shoe factory, their wages will constitute additional income. If the newly employed workers spend all of their additional income on the shoes they produce, the shoe factory will find a market and will succeed. In fact, however, they will not spend all of their additional income on shoes. Let us vary the example. Instead of putting a hundred previously unemployed workers in one shoe factory, let us put ten thousand workers in one hundred factories which between them will produce the bulk of the goods on which the newly employed workers will spend their wages. What is not true in the case of one single shoe factory will become true for the complementary system of one hundred factories. The new producers will be each other's customers and will [each create] . . . an additional market. The complementarity of demand will reduce the risk of not finding a market. Reducing such interdependent risks naturally increases the incentive to invest.

The case for the 'big push' thus rested on two crucial points. First, the need for significant economies of scale to be achieved in each of the manufacturing establishments, entailing considerable internal demand for each item. For this demand to be achieved, income levels must be raised over the entire economy. This led to the second factor of a massive all-out investment programme in industry and the concomitant evolution of a large industrial workforce.

Such 'big push' policies of the Gerschenkronian school were reminiscent of the policies of both Stalinist Russia and Maoist China (Kitching 1982: 124–33), albeit in a very different political context. Within most Third World countries, they were rarely followed to their logical conclusion, mainly because the required savings and foreign aid and investment were not available in sufficient quantities for such an all-out investment programme. Perhaps the only 'big push' programmes with enough finance to achieve the ambitious objectives occurred two decades later with the industrialization programmes of the oil-exporting countries or with the international commercial banks providing the quantities of capital required for a rapid expansion and diversification of the Brazilian industrial product. Between 1955 and 1976, Brazillian cement production increased seven times in magnitude, ingot steel production eight times, motor vehicle production thirty times and aluminium production 127 times (Dickenson 1978) – a sure example of an industrial process benefiting from the interlocking of greater economies of scale and increasing demand. Furthermore, it was spatially concentrated in the industrial triangle of south-east Brazil.

The 'big push' philosophy, although not adopted in its entirety by countries in the 1950s and 1960s did undoubtedly give the emphasis in economic growth to large-scale projects (such as in energy generation) and capital-intensive manufacturing growth. The theoretical advantages of economies of scale came to be more evident than those of demand increases consequent upon an expanding manufacturing labour force. Firstly, this was because modern imported plant did not, by its very nature, generate a significant amount of employment. Secondly, the amount of employment generated through a crash programme of industrialization tended to be limited in terms of the labour force as a whole. One indication of this is to calculate the present proportions of labour employed in industry. The seventy-three low-income and lower-middle-income economies of the world as defined by the World Bank, with a 1985 population of 3.11 billion (or nearly two-thirds of the world's population) have a weighted average of only 14 per cent of their labour force working in industry, as opposed to a weighted average of 67 per cent in agriculture (World Bank 1987).

What then are the lessons of theories that have attempted to explain the past in order to assist in the development of the future? First, and continuing on from a theme developed in Chapter 1, a country with a large domestic market is in a better position to establish industrial plants that take advantage of economies of scale. Certainly 'big push' industrialization has been more successful, everything else being equal, in countries with a large geographical size and a large population. Second, Third World countries may benefit temporarily from the import of the latest technology. However, for there to be permanent benefits, the country in question must develop a technological expertise from within the country that can adapt and improve both the product and process of imported technology. In turn, this requires significant government investment in education. Meanwhile, Rostow's emphasis on the national development of a transport and energy infrastructure and a stable institutional and macroeconomic environment must still remain important objectives for any industrializing country. Both Gerschenkron and Rostow gave importance and credence to these latter points of infrastructural **investment, institutional stability and education.** However, their undoubted significance in the process of industrialization introduces the wider question of government involvement in both economic and industrial growth.

THE ROLE OF GOVERNMENT

Gerschenkron saw the role of government as pivotal within the industrialization process. Rostow saw the role of government as crucial in providing the required infrastructure and general background for industrial growth. What have been the implications of government involvement in industrial development in the post-war period? The presence of government varies greatly across countries according to ideology, political structures, administrative capacity, and the level of development. This section considers some of the broad principles that govern policy choices for industrialization.

The development needs of poor societies are so urgent that tremendous pressures are placed on their governments to stimulate industrialization, as in the case of the 'big push' programmes recommended during the 1950s. Yet the human and physical resources available to developing country governments are so limited that they have great difficulty in attaining their many economic objectives, including physical infrastructure, agricultural development, health, education or the alleviation of poverty. The governments therefore have to be careful in choosing the balance of their policies towards industry. Governments can act directly in the industrial process through the provision of infrastructure and a set of economic rules governing legal, monetary and fiscal functions. Governments can also operate indirectly in the industrial process through intervening in markets.

The direct role of government

All governments take responsibility for producing a range of goods and services, called public goods, that only they are in a position to supply adequately. These include national defence, internal security, money and the provision of a legal system. In terms of industrialization, there are perhaps five public goods that can be regarded as significant.

First, a legal and institutional system which reduces the costs and risks of transactions. Property rights provide for the ownership and transfer of factors of production and goods. Every type of economy can be defined by its property rights or economic rules. The question is whether any given set is efficient and stable. 'Knowing clearly who owns what and how goods and services can be used, bought, and sold reduces uncertainty and provides the basis for the specialization and investment essential to industrialization' (World Bank 1987: 61). Unfortunately, industrial enterprises in LDCs can suffer from a wide range of institutional problems including: internal political pressures from government (e.g. to control prices); dealing with a slow and arbitrary bureaucracy; lengthy regulatory procedures; corruption; the risk of expropriation; uncertainty over whether legal and contractual rights would be upheld by the courts; uncertainty about changes in legislation, such as on tax rates; flexible interpretation of laws by governments. The less these institutional problems are permitted to affect adversely the private industrial enterprises, the greater the possibilities for industrial growth. However, Third World governments can provide not only some of the solutions to these institutional problems, but also they can often be the source of the problems themselves.

Increasing the technological knowledge and business information available to producers can be seen as a second public good. Governments have a comparative advantage in collecting and disseminating certain kinds of information, especially in developing countries, where information and its analysis is scarce. In Japan and Korea, government has played a significant role as a clearinghouse for information and in providing forecasts on domestic and foreign markets and new technologies.

The protection of consumer welfare can be seen as a third area for direct intervention by government. For example, governments have the obligation to regulate industrial enterprises in order to protect welfare by checking weights and measures, by establishing health standards for foods and drugs and clean air, by requiring product safety standards and product guarantees, and by imposing safety standards in the workplace.

Fourthly, governments should be responsible for providing education. Education assists the process of industrialization by teaching the skills of basic literacy and numeracy and the ability to think adaptively. In this context, it is interesting to point out that Korea's 11 per cent per annum growth in manufacturing between the mid-1970s and mid-1980s was founded on a 1975 educational profile in which 48 per cent of its labour force had completed secondary education and another 36 per cent had at least some primary education. Returns to investment have generally been higher in education than in physical assets. World Bank (1987: 64) research has calculated that economic rates of return to primary education in a sample of twenty-six developing countries averaged 28 per cent, compared with estimated returns on physical capital of 13 per cent. The World Bank (1987: 63) concludes that such data 'suggest that lack of education is a greater obstacle to industrialization than lack of physical assets'

The provision of infrastructure can be seen as a fifth public good. Both Gerschenkron and Rostow were in agreement on the necessity for governments to invest heavily in the provision of infrastructure in the early phase of industrialization. Two important arguments can be used for this. First, large single projects are often required (such as in power generation or water provision), partly to benefit from economies of scale. It is generally considered that in the circumstances of a less developed country, with underdeveloped capital markets, only governments can generate and organize the massive amounts of capital required. Secondly, for other infrastructural investments such as roads, user fees are difficult to collect unless at government level (petrol taxes or vehicle licence fees to cover road construction for example).

The indirect role of government

Governments can also play an indirect role in industrialization through intervention in markets. The most durable argument for intervention is based on the infant industry idea, protecting new industries so as to give them a 'breathing space' from international competition. Governments of many developing countries argue that private investors will not undertake investments which take time to come on stream or require a long learning process *without* import protection in the form of tariffs or quotas. Cases of successful infant industry protection are difficult to prove or disprove. The Japanese case study is often cited in support of infant industry protection due to the high import barriers that Japan maintained well into the 1960s. Korea has closely followed Japan's example, and, infant industry protection has been a popular policy in Latin America ever since the 1930s. However, here the evidence is contradictory. In the smaller countries, such as Chile and Peru, infant industries were unable to evolve into internationally competitive industries and indeed became notoriously high cost (Gwynne 1985: 25). Governments were left with the hard decision of either maintaining high levels of protection (and the associated problems of high prices, reduced local demand and low economies of scale) or dismantling the complex paraphernalia of protection and allowing the cold winds of international competition to potentially wither their infants. In the larger countries of Latin America and most notably Brazil, infant industries were able to evolve more competitively and governments encouraged them to become internationally competitive with the help of large export subsidies, such as in the case of the Brazillian motor vehicle industry (see Ch. 10).

Infant industry protection probably works best with a pre-arranged and credible timetable for withdrawal. In addition, selectivity is important. One sector can be protected only at the expense of others. The more widespread the protective support, the more the exchange rate becomes overvalued, the greater the discrimination against exports and the more thinly are scarce resources spread through the economy. In the 1960s, the Chilean government, in protecting the development of the electronics, electrical and vehicle industries (in which Chile enjoyed no comparative advantage), effectively reduced the resource directed towards the timber, cellulose, paper and fish processing sectors (in which it enjoyed a considerable comparative advantage). The question of selectivity is intimately linked to the debate over industrial targeting, particularly in terms of the East Asian economies of Japan, Korea and Singapore, where it is maintained that governments have intervened in the market to promote specific activities and firms with considerable success. At any one point in time, intervention has been aimed at a limited number of targets. The Japanese Ministry of International Trade and Industry (MITI) targeted steel and shipbuilding in the 1950s, motor vehicles in the 1960s and microelectronics in the 1970s. The World Bank's view of whether the East Asian experience of industrial targeting can be used as a model for other less developed countries is, however, distinctly cautious:

> Whatever the allocative effects of industrial intervention in East Asia, it has been carried out by strong and capable governments. It has also been selective and time-bound, and competition has been maintained in domestic markets. The level of intervention has been reduced over time. Central guidance becomes progressively more demanding as economies become more complex and as the opportunity for imitating more developed economies diminishes. Finally, if some East Asian governments have intervened successfully, it is not clear whether most developing countries could emulate their administrative capacity, the ability of their firms and governments to cooperate closely in pursuit of agreed economic goals, or the degree of

competition in their domestic markets (World Bank 1987: 71).

Such caution is intimately linked with the view that there are a number of problems associated with governments intervening in the industrialization process in developing countries – due to the very nature and efficacy of government itself:

> Economies in transition from traditional to modern forms of organization face special difficulties, because of problems of poor information and because of the way individuals cope with risk. Levels of education are lower than in industrial countries, investment in the machinery of communications is lower, the investigative capacity of the state and of the watchdog professions (lawyers, accountants, journalists) is lower. Risks arise from the increasing number and complexity of transactions in a modernizing economy, often between people who do not know or may not trust each other and where legal and economic rights are uncertain. So individuals steer clear of impersonal transactions in favor of the more familiar relationships of kinship, friendship, or client and patron. Because of lack of information and risk avoidance, an informal policymaking system often stands behind the formal structure.
>
> In some countries the legislative and judicial branches of government are weak and leave wide discretion for administrative decision-making. Tax rates often do not correspond to those set by law. Unauthorized and *ad hoc* concessions are common; noncompliance is rife. In other countries the legal system is well developed. But an abundance of confusing and inflexible regulations has produced a cumbersome bureaucratic process. Laws are passed, then not effectively implemented. Litigation is costly, and so few people seek legal redress (World Bank 1987: 72).

The above quotation demonstrates some of the practical problems of arguing, like Gerschenkron, that industrialization must take place within the context of strong government involvement. Government involvement is essential for industrialization but it must not be assumed to be ideal, that is with clear laws, effective enforcement and a smooth resolution to disputes. The reality is considerably far from the ideal. Nevertheless, governments must attempt to create as far as they can a clear and stable legal and institutional system within which industrial enterprises can develop. An efficient and adequate supply of infrastructural services such as transport, communications, power and education is also vital for modern industry. Furthermore, government influence on industry can be seen as crucial in terms of macroeconomic policies, particularly as regards relationships with the world economy through levels of protection for domestic firms, the nature of international competition and the promotion of exports. It is in this context that it becomes necessary to analyse the important issue of trade policy among the governments of less developed countries.

6

TRADE POLICY AND INDUSTRIALIZATION

As we saw in the last chapter, many economic theorists after the Second World War saw industrialization as an essential process in attaining rapid economic growth. However, it could be argued that some of those who favoured policies of rapid industrialization for Third World countries in the 1950s and 1960s had a rather limited perspective. Their arguments often appeared to indicate that the very fact of industrialization would bring modernization, social change and economic growth to less developed countries.

However, in retrospect, the question was much more difficult and complex than that. An emphasis on achieving industrial growth *per se* often led to massive capital spending and dramatic short-term repercussions, but without leading to a more sustained and long-term growth in industry. The real question was not how fast an economy can industrialize in the short term, but how to structure the industrial sector so that it could support sustained economic growth. Into this complex equation, the consideration of how to generate increases in manufactured exports has, in retrospect, been vital. The success of most of those countries classified as newly industrializing countries can be partly attributed to their success in generating a sustained expansion of manufactured exports. This chapter will examine the theoretical advantages of outward-oriented trade strategies for the process of industrialization before examining the political and economic problems associated with countries shifting from

an inward- to an outward-oriented trade strategy. This latter issue, furthermore, introduces important political themes into the question of Third World industrialization.

TRADE STRATEGIES AND INDUSTRIAL GROWTH

Trade strategies can be broadly divided into two groups: outward oriented and inward oriented. The World Bank (1987: 78) defines an outward-oriented strategy as one in which trade and industrial policies do not discriminate between production for the domestic market and exports, nor between purchases of domestic goods and foreign goods. In contrast, an inward-oriented strategy is one in which trade and industrial incentives are biased in favour of production for the domestic over the export market. Protection switches demand to products produced domestically. Exporting is discouraged by the increased cost of imported inputs. It is further hindered by the increased cost of domestic inputs relative to the price received by exporters, which commonly occurs through the appreciation of the exchange rate following the imposition of barriers to imports. Some countries try to get round these added costs to exporters by establishing export subsidies.

In its 1987 World Development Report, the World Bank (1987: 82–3) used its above definition to divide the forty-one developing countries for

Table 6.1 World Bank classification of forty-one developing economies by trade orientation, 1963–73 and 1973–85

Period	Outward oriented		Inward oriented	
	Strongly outward oriented	Moderately outward oriented	Moderately inward oriented	Strongly inward oriented
1963–73	Hong Kong Korea Singapore	Brazil Cameroon Colombia Costa Rica Côte d'Ivoire Guatemala Indonesia Israel Malaysia Thailand	Bolivia El Salvador Honduras Kenya Madagascar Mexico Nicaragua Nigeria Philippines Senegal Tunisia Yugoslavia	Argentina Bangladesh Burundi Chile Dominican Republic Ethiopia Ghana India Pakistan Peru Sri Lanka Sudan Tanzania Turkey Uruguay Zambia
1973–85	Hong Kong Korea Singapore	Brazil Chile Israel Malaysia Thailand Tunisia Turkey Uruguay	Cameroon Colombia Costa Rica Côte d'Ivoire El Salvador Guatemala Honduras Indonesia Kenya Mexico Nicaragua Pakistan Philippines Senegal Sri Lanka Yugoslavia	Argentina Bangladesh Bolivia Burundi Dominican Republic Ethiopia Ghana India Madagascar Nigeria Peru Sudan Tanzania Zambia

(*Source*: World Bank 1987: 83)

which it had data into outward and inward oriented for two time periods: 1963–73 and 1973–85 (see Table 6.1). these two classifications were further subdivided in terms of their relative strength. Four categories of countries were thus distinguished for the two time periods as follows:

1. *Strongly outward oriented* Trade controls are either non-existent or very low in the sense that any disincentives to export resulting from import barriers are more or less counterbalanced by export incentives. There is little or no use of direct controls and licensing arrangements, and the exchange rate is maintained so that the effective exchange rates for importables and exportables are roughly equal.

2. *Moderately outward oriented* The overall incentive structure is biased towards production for domestic rather than export markets. But the average rate of effective protection for the home markets is relatively low and the range of effective protecting rates relatively narrow. The use of direct controls and licensing arrangements is limited, and although some direct incentives to

export may be provided, these do not offset protection against imports. The effective exchange rate is higher for imports than for exports, but only slightly.

3. *Moderately inward oriented* The overall incentive structure distinctly favours production for the domestic market. The average rate of effective protection for home markets is relatively high and the range of effective protection rates relatively wide. The use of direct import controls and licensing is extensive, and although some direct incentives to export may be provided, there is a distinct bias against exports, and the exchange rate is clearly overvalued.

4. *Strongly inward oriented* The overall incentive structure strongly favours production for the domestic market. The average rate of effective protection for home markets is high and the range of effective protection rates relatively wide. Direct controls and licensing disincentives to the traditional export sector are pervasive, positive incentives to non-traditional exportables are few or non-existent, and the exchange rate is significantly overvalued.

The World Bank went on to trace the links between trade strategy and macroeconomic performance (see Fig. 6.1). Growth rates of GDP show a broad descending pattern from the strongly outward-oriented to the strongly inward-oriented economies. For the period 1973–85, seriously affected by two world recessions, the three strongly outward-oriented countries recorded an annual average growth of 7.7 per cent, three times that of the fourteen strongly inward-oriented countries (2.5 per cent). The record of the sixteen moderately inward-oriented countries, however, was broadly similar to that of the eight moderately outward-oriented economies. A similar pattern occurred with *per capita* income. In the strongly outward-oriented economies, *per capita* income grew by an annual average of 5.9 per cent between 1973 and 1985, whereas it declined in the strongly inward-oriented countries. The moderately defined countries, meanwhile, recorded similar rates of modest growth in *per capita* income.

The rate of economic growth can be affected both by the level of savings and by the efficiency of investment. In terms of savings, the World Bank classification provided an interesting pattern. The average ratio of gross domestic savings to GDP of the strongly outward-oriented economies was exceeded by all other groups in 1963, registering only 13.0 per cent. By 1985, however, the strongly outward-oriented economies had more than doubled their savings ratio to 31.4 per cent, whereas the savings ratios of the other three groups grew only slightly; the reasons behind this phenomenon will be examined in the next section. Meanwhile, efficiency in the use of additional capital resources in an economy can be reflected in the economy's incremental capital–output ratio – the ratio of gross investment to the increase in GDP. Lower values suggest more productive investment. For both periods, there is a clear association between lower incremental capital–output ratios and increased outward orientation (see Fig. 6.1).

From the criteria used by the World Bank in its classification, one would expect the outward-oriented economies to be more successful in terms of increasing their manufactured exports. Indeed Fig. 6.1 shows this to be the major contrast between the two sets of countries. Between 1965 and 1973 the manufactured exports of the two outward-oriented groups grew by an annual average of 14.8 and 16.1 per cent, compared with 10.3 and 5.7 per cent for the inward-oriented groups. Between 1973 and 1985 the differential performance of the two groups intensified with growth rates of 14.2 and 14.5 per cent versus 8.5 and 3.7 per cent.

The World Bank went on to trace the links between industrialization and trade strategy (see Table 6.2). Again the major contrasts to be noticed are those between the strongly outward and strongly inward economies, particularly in terms of growth in manufacturing value-added, the share of manufacturing value-added in GDP, the share of the labour force in industry and employment growth in manufacturing (see Table 6.2). However, the differences in the industrial performance indicators of the moderately outward and inward countries are much less clear, except in terms of the share of manufacturing value-added in GDP.

As with all classifications, there are problems

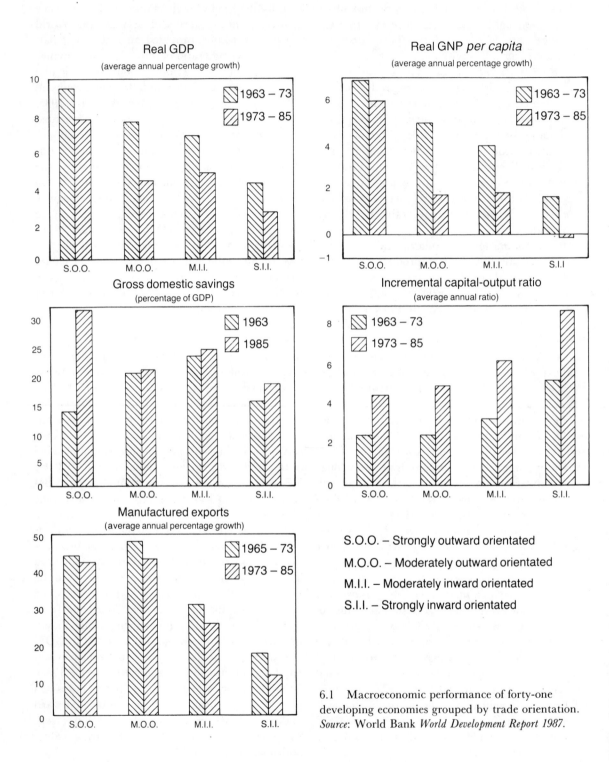

6.1   Macroeconomic performance of forty-one
developing economies grouped by trade orientation.
Source: World Bank *World Development Report 1987*.

Table 6.2 Characteristics of industrialization for forty-one developing economies grouped by trade orientation

Trade strategy	Average annual growth of real manufacturing value-added		Average share of manufacturing value-added in GDP		Average share of labour force in industry		Average annual growth of employment in manufacturing	
	1963–73	1973–85	1963	1985	1963	1980	1963–73	1973–84
Strongly outward oriented	15.6	10.0	17.1	26.3	17.5	30.0	10.6	5.1
Moderately outward oriented	9.4	4.0	20.5	21.9	12.7	21.7	4.6	4.9
Moderately inward oriented	9.6	5.1	10.4	15.8	15.2	23.0	4.4	4.4
Strongly inward oriented	5.3	3.1	17.6	15.9	12.1	12.6	3.0	4.0

(*Source*: World Bank 1987: 87)

to point out. The key strongly outward-oriented group is based on the performance of only three countries (Hong Kong, Korea and Singapore); Taiwan is not a World Bank member. Care should be taken not to see the classification as a dichotomy but as a continuum, in which the most significant contrasts in performance are between the two extremes. Contrasts between the moderately defined countries appear to be much less extreme and should not be overemphasized. However, it should be pointed out that three of the eight countries classified as moderately outward oriented for the 1973–85 period (Chile, Turkey and Uruguay) were regarded by the World Bank as strongly inward oriented during the 1963–73 period. They, therefore, had to undergo radical changes in trade policy during the period along with a concomitant restructuring of the economy. It could be argued that the long-term benefits of outward orientation have not yet been enjoyed by these countries. I return later in the chapter to analyse closely the trade policy reform and economic restructuring of one of these countries, Chile.

The case for outward orientation

Chapter 3 examined the problems of primary-producing countries as regards the declining terms of trade for primary commodities in relation to manufactured goods. The overall conclusion of the chapter was of the need for less developed countries to increase manufacturing production. The basic question then, however, is whether the strategy should be inward or outward looking. In the 1950s, inward-oriented, import-substituting strategies were commonly supported and, despite the industrial success generated by the outward orientation of some East Asian countries, new arguments have been levelled against export promotion.

The major one is the argument that if all developing countries followed an export-promoting strategy based on the newly industrializing countries (NICs) of East Asia, industrial countries would refuse to absorb the resulting volume of imports. However, there are at least three points to make against this pessimistic argument concerning the future growth of Third World manufacturing exports. First, the capacity of industrial nations to absorb new imports from developing countries should not be underestimated given that developing country exports currently account for only 2.3 per cent of the markets for manufactures in the industrial economies. Second, the resources of the developing countries are so varied that a wide variety of different products can be produced for export to the industrial countries. Furthermore, these countries do not need to have such a high export-to-GDP ratio for manufactures as the East Asian NICs in order to sustain long-term industrial and economic growth. Finally, the first wave of NICs is already providing markets for the labour-intensive products of the countries that are following.

Inward-oriented economies are generally characterized by high levels of protection for manufacturing, direct controls on imports and investments, and overvalued exchange rates. In contrast, outward orientation links the domestic economy to the world economy. However, outward orientation does not necessarily mean less government intervention. Some countries have pursued outward orientation at a leisurely pace, promoting exports while only slowly dismantling import barriers. The World Bank (1987: 90) argues that 'the advantage of an outward-oriented strategy over an inward-oriented strategy is that it promotes the efficient use of resources'. The major source of these advantages seems to be that countries do not experience the costs of protection. These costs of protection can be divided into consumption losses and production losses.

Consumption losses refer to the losses in real income of consumers of the protected product that occur because protection generally induces consumers to buy less of the protected product while paying a higher price. As an example one could compare the Chilean motor car market within an inwardly and outwardly oriented trade regime. In Chile's inwardly oriented trade regime of the late 1960s, small Citroën cars cost the Chilean consumer a sum equivalent to three times their internationally traded price (Gwynne 1978b). However, in the outwardly oriented trade regime of 1980/81, small Japanese cars entered the Chilean market with only a 10 per cent tariff adding to the costs of shipment and insurance – and therefore the Chilean consumer had only to pay about 25–30 per cent above the internationally traded price.

The costs of protection also refer to production losses. A production loss is involved to the extent that resources have to be drawn from other activities (including production for export) where they can be more efficiently used. For example, in the inwardly oriented period of Chile's industrialization during the 1960s, national resources were channelled into a wide range of assembly industries – motor vehicles, televisions, radios, cassette recorders, calculators. These products were mainly aimed at the national market and, because of their high production costs, export markets proved impossible. At the same time, however, Chile's export-oriented fish-

ing and forest products sectors were starved of resources and stagnated.

The costs of protection can also refer to the inefficiencies generated by domestic monopolies and those added costs that are generated by the imposition of import quotas, credit restrictions and foreign exchange controls. The World Bank (1987: 90) has argued that by dismantling the administrative system of protection, 'entrepreneurs could direct their energies away from unproductive activities, such as lobbying for changes in regulations'. The bureaucracy of protectionism can certainly generate a range of unproductive jobs, such as that of the 'despachante' in Brazil. 'The "despachante" is an intermediary who, in return for a commission or fee, purchases and fills out the multiplicity of legal forms, delivers them to the proper persons, and extracts the needed permission or document' (World Bank 1987: 73). The industrialist's need for the 'despachante' in Brazil can be overwhelming. 'Not many years ago the case was reported of an export licence that required 1470 separate legal actions and involved thirteen government ministries and fifty agencies' (World Bank 1987: 73).

The nature of foreign investment can be markedly different between an outward-oriented and inward-oriented economy. Foreign investment is attracted to inward-oriented economies for two closely related reasons. The first reason is termed that of tariff jumping; the foreign company wants to have a presence in a protected market and therefore establishes a plant. The second reason is that of oligopolistic reaction (Knickerbocker 1973; Gwynne 1979b); the foreign company sees an industrial rival invest in a plant in a protected market and decides to follow suit. Unless government monitoring of foreign firm entry is tightly controlled, this type of foreign investment can result in a multiplicity of small-scale investments geared solely to the domestic market.

Meanwhile, an outward-oriented trade strategy will not attract investment projects which depend on the retention of import barriers. This can mean less foreign investment. However, when foreign investment is attracted, it will be attracted to exporting industries or industries with the potential for export. Firms in these industries should be able to derive significant benefits from economies of scale because the size of the domestic market does not limit their output. This type of investment in outward-oriented countries can thus result in plants operating in function of world markets (not just the national market) and with the opportunity of steady expansion in those markets.

One of the most interesting insights from the previous statistical analysis of trade strategy and macroeconomic performance was that strongly outward-oriented countries have achieved spectacular growth in savings rates, much greater than that occurring in inward-oriented countries (Fig. 6.1). Why should this occur? Perhaps the major reason is that in outward-oriented countries high real interest rates have become an important incentive for personal savers. Capital markets are often highly distorted and underdeveloped in developing countries, and they tend to be more so in inward-oriented than in outward-oriented economies. Indeed, in some inward-oriented countries, capital markets have offered negative real interest rates, a powerful reason behind the lower savings ratio on these countries. In contrast, in outward-oriented countries, due to their closer links with international financial markets, more realistic interest rates prevail with concomitant increases in the generation of savings from within them.

Despite the long-term attractions of outward orientation, Table 6.1 shows that between 1973 and 1985 relatively few countries underwent policy shifts towards more outward orientation – most notably Chile, Turkey, Uruguay and Tunisia. In contrast, other countries became more inward looking, most notably Cameroon, Colombia, Costa Rica, Côte d'Ivoire, Guatemala and Indonesia. So despite the theoretical advantages of outward orientation, the tendency has been for more inward orientation over the last decade.

This apparent anomaly can be partly explained in political terms. It is politically difficult to accept the short-term hardships associated with trade policy reform and the concomitant restructuring of the economy alongside the anticipation of future, sustained growth in the long term.

Political pressures build up rapidly with short-term economic problems and hence there are many recent examples of trade reforms being halted or reversed (Pakistan, Brazil, Argentina). Therefore, it becomes important to investigate the few countries that have engineered trade policy reform and economic restructuring despite the associated political problems. Perhaps the most interesting of these cases is that of Chile, partly because it was one of only three countries to change from being strongly inward oriented during the 1963–73 period to being moderately outward oriented during the 1973–85 period and partly because 1973 conveniently coincided exactly with the change in economic policy. The Chilean case study thus provides an excellent insight into both the advantages and pitfalls of trade liberalization on the process of industrialization. Furthermore, it permits us to widen the theoretical perspective and examine political issues alongside those of economic theory.

TRADE LIBERALIZATION IN CHILE, 1973–87

The increasing evidence of the benefits of an outward orientation of trade strategies has produced increasing disenchantment with the inward-oriented approach and greater interest in trade policy reforms. However, trade policy reforms and subsequent economic restructuring bring short-term economic problems as the protected industrial sectors find it difficult to compete with international competition. Increasing bankruptcies and unemployment in these sectors are not immediately offset by expansion in exporting sectors. The ensuing political pressures have deterred many governments from pursuing policies of trade reform to their logical conclusion. One government that has resisted political opposition to radically change trade policy is that of General Pinochet in Chile, who came to power in 1973. The Chilean case study thus permits a fourteen-year analysis of the effects of trade reform on economic development in general and industrial growth in particular.

In 1973, Chile was one of the most protected countries in the world. The origins of accentuated protection date back to the 1929–32 period when the value of Chile's exports declined by 75 per cent in three years. The interpretation of such an economic calamity was that the free trade model, which had been broadly in force beforehand, no longer served the interests of the Chilean state. Within five years, a complex array of protective measures was in place – tariffs of over 100 per cent, exchange controls, multiple exchange rates and import quotas (Gwynne 1985: 197–8). These controls did not begin to be effectively dismantled until 1974. At the time of the military coup in September 1973, import tariffs averaged 105 per cent with some goods subject to nominal tariffs of more than 700 per cent (see Table 6.3). In addition to tariffs, a battery of quantitative restrictions was applied, including outright import prohibition and prior deposits of up to 10 000 per cent of the value of the goods to be imported. These protective measures were complemented with a highly distorted multiple exchange rate system consisting of fifteen different rates (Edwards and Edwards 1987: 111).

In late 1973 the first set of trade liberalization measures was taken. The maximum tariff was reduced from 700 to 220 per cent, and those duties between 50 and 220 per cent were reduced by ten percentage points. This first round of tariff reduction had little effect on relative prices and foreign competition, since the great majority of these duties were redundant and the prices of imported goods remained very high. At this point, the military government was undecided about its commitment to freer trade. However, by 1976, the monetarist Treasury Minister, Sergio de Castro, had seemingly won the argument inside the government when he announced that 'a tariff schedule ranging from 10 to 35 per cent is perfectly adequate for the Chilean economy since it provides reasonable levels of protection for the nation's industrial activity' (Mendez 1979: 209). In December 1977, he announced that the final goal was to reduce tariffs to a uniform rate of 10 per cent by mid-1979. Thus between late 1973 and mid-1979, the maximum tariff rate was reduced from 220 to 10 per cent and the average nominal tariff from 94 to 10 per cent (Ffrench-Davis 1980). All quantitative import restrictions had been removed by 1976 as had multiple exchange rates. In six years, Chile had been

Table 6.3   Changes in effective rates of protection and industrial production in Chile, 1973/4 to 1979/80

Sector	Effective rates of protection (%)		1980 industrial production
	1974	1979	(1973 = 100)
Food	161	12	103.9
Drinks	203	13	159.6
Tobacco	114	11	109.1
Textiles	239	14	38.0
Footwear	264	14	47.8
Timber	157	15	109.0
Furniture	95	11	166.7
Paper	184	17	139.8
Printing/publishing	140	12	112.2
Leather	181	13	31.5
Rubber	49	15	51.3
Chemicals	80	13	74.0
Oil/coal products	265	13	275.2
Construction materials	128	14	158.4
Metal products	147	15	72.3
Machinery	96	13	57.9

(Developed from Gwynne 1985: 224 and Edwards and Edwards 1987: 114)

transformed from one of the most protected to one of the most open economies (see Table 6.3)

What impact did this have on the industrial sector? Table 6.3 brings together data for changes in both effective rates of protection and industrial production during the 1970s. In terms of aggregate industrial production, the measures had very little impact. Industrial production in 1980 was only slightly higher than in 1973 (Gwynne 1985: 224). However, within this global figure the extent of industrial restructuring was quite remarkable. Two sectors which had enjoyed effective rates of protection greater than 235 per cent in 1974, textiles and footwear, were reduced in size by more than half between 1973 and 1980 as their effective rates of protection were cut to just 14 per cent. Equally dramatic sectoral declines were recorded in other import-substituting industries oriented towards the domestic market – leather, rubber, ceramics, glass, electrical and electronic products and motor vehicles; significant declines also occurred in the machinery, metal products, chemicals and plastics sectors.

Chile has notable resources of fish and timber, both poorly developed during the import substitution phase. The industrial sectors that processed these resources – food, timber, furniture, paper – increased the value of production by 3.9, 9.0, 66.7 and 39.8 per cent respectively. Some sectors geared mainly to the domestic market grew as a result of rapid economic growth in the late 1970s – construction materials, iron and steel, oil and coal products (also affected by the rise in the price of oil), printing and publishing, drinks, tobacco and clothing (despite a major switch to imported textiles). However, with the manufacturing sector effectively remaining static within an expanding economy, its share of total GDP fell from 29.5 per cent in 1974 to 18.9 per cent in 1982 (Banco Central de Chile 1984).

The accelerated trade reform in Chile between 1973 and 1980 thus caused a major restructuring of industry, with heavily protected sectors being heavily rationalized and export-oriented sectors recording growth. Labour productivity in manufacturing increased substantially. According to the author's figures, labour productivity in the manufacturing sector increased by 28 per cent during the period 1973 to 1980 (Gwynne 1985: 224). Meanwhile, Bardón, Carrasco and Vial (1985) calculated that average labour productivity in manufacturing increased by 41.6 per cent for the decade 1971 to 1981.

As a result of stable production and rapidly increasing productivity, manufacturing employment declined considerably, particularly in the short term. Perhaps the major short-term problem was the juxtaposition of heavy rationalization in the import-substituting sectors with sluggish investment in the export-oriented industries. 'Contrary to the simplest textbook case, physical capital is fixed in its sector of origin, which made the expansion of production in a number of the exporting sectors somewhat sluggish at first. Only as additional investment took place through time was it possible to fully increase production and employment in these expanding sectors' (Edwards and Edwards 1987: 121). Although the performance of other sectors apart from manufacturing contributed to increasing unemployment, the total unemployment rate in Chile (including work programmes)

increased from 5 per cent in 1973 to 21 per cent in 1976. Such an increase in unemployment was not rectified in the short term as the rate had only declined to 15 per cent by 1981.

The full effect of trade liberalization on Chile's industrial sector was interrupted, however, in 1980, because during that year the Treasury Minister, de Castro, began to promote an overvalued exchange rate, ostensibly to reduce inflation. In an interesting analysis, Edwards and Edwards (1987: 70) attribute part of the blame for an overvalued exchange rate to the liberalization of the capital account in April 1980 and the 'eagerness to lend money to Chile on behalf of the international financial community', both of which led to the tripling of foreign debt between 1978 and 1982. The combination of the increasing availability of foreign funds and the pegging of the exchange rate led to an accentuating overvaluation of the Chilean peso from mid-1979 to the major devaluations in the latter half of 1982. An increasingly overvalued exchange rate made it more difficult for manufacturers to export but easier for importers to import manufactured goods. Large trade deficits resulted in 1980 and 1981.

De Castro's policy of pegging the Chilean peso to the US dollar brought a financial crisis and the inevitable catastrophe of massive devaluations in 1982, resulting in a 14 per cent decline in the economy for the year. Within the crises produced by massive foreign debt, large Chilean corporations being declared bankrupt and intervention in them by government, exaggerated economic decline and unemployment increasing to levels of 35 per cent of the workforce, a coherent outward-oriented policy was not in place again until 1985. The lessons of the previous twelve years had shown that on the one hand an outward-oriented policy can bring rapid economic growth. On the other hand, however, the more open position of Chile within the world economy brought significant risks. This required some conception on the part of economic ministers of the long-term impact of changes in the world economy on Chile and a careful tailoring of Chilean economic policy to external as well as internal variables. In particular, the exchange rate must be allowed to move with market forces.

Between 1985 and 1989, the new Treasury Minister, Büchi, managed to tailor Chilean economic policy more successfully to the key external variables of the world economy while stressing the need for outward orientation. As yet, it is too early to make a detailed assessment at what could be termed Chile's second and more cautious attempt at an outward-oriented economic policy. Data on Chile's recent international trade are, however, available. Thus, in conclusion, it will be useful to examine the evolution of Chile's international trade over the fourteen years since its initial moves towards a more open economy (see Table 6.4).

The impressive record of export growth in Chile during the 1970s is well demonstrated in Table 6.4 with exports in 1980 being nearly five times greater than those of 1971. However, within this overall export growth, the most remarkable figures were recorded by the manufacturing sector, whose 1980 exports were twelve times greater than those of 1971. Some of these increases were due to the depressed level of domestic demand causing firms to seek out new foreign markets; this was particularly the case in the metal products and machinery sector. In other cases (fish meal, paper, basic metals, e.g. copper and steel), the increase in exports was partially related to a more

intensive utilization of large investments that had been undertaken prior to the military regime. The high real exchange rate made it profitable to use existing capacity more intensively and to implement investment projects that improved the quality of production and had a high marginal return. Other export increases (cellulose) were the result of completely new investments and in the 1979–82 period, new plants came on stream in most of the leading export sectors.

Unfortunately, with the rapidly appreciating Chilean peso of 1980–82, export growth became difficult. This was followed by the crises of 1982–84, when foreign capital inflows dried up and, in the aftermath of the massive devaluations of late 1982, the two leading Chilean corporations (both with significant export activities) were declared bankrupt and intervened in by the government. Most exporting companies found their financial structure distinctly shaky as a result, which effectively curtailed significant new investments until the late 1980s. Even by 1986, exports of manufactures had not recovered their 1980 levels, with exports of timber products, chemicals, basic metals and metal products being significantly down. In particular, some metal products firms, which had been able to stimulate exports under trade reform, found it impossible to survive the over-

Table 6.4 Evolution of Chilean exports, 1971–87 (millions US$)

	1971	1980	1984	1986	1987
1. Mining	813.2	2946.2	2165.7	2299.2	2745.8
(Copper)	701.8	2154.8	1584.4	1771.0	2100.5
2. Agricultural products	29.4	339.9	428.1	683.0	743.0
(Fresh fruit)	13.4	244.4	291.5	476.8	527.2
3. Manufactured goods	119.6	1427.3	1063.4	1240.1	1613.2
(Fish meal)	29.8	233.5	275.7	314.9	358.3
(Frozen/canned fish and shellfish)	n.d.	50.8	78.7	106.5	141.3
(Timber products)	7.0	286.2	116.3	137.4	151.5
(Paper & Cellulose)	32.0	297.2	259.4	272.4	364.9
(Chemicals)	11.8	163.2	124.3	119.5	103.2
(Basic metals)	9.0	147.4	60.5	77.2	87.3
(Metal products)	4.4	63.9	19.5	23.1	26.8
TOTAL (1 + 2 + 3)	962.2	4713.4	3657.2	4222.3	5102.0

(*Source*: Annual External Trade Reports of Chile's Central Bank)

valued currency and chaotic devaluations of the early 1980s. Paper and cellulose exports at least managed to keep their output levels similar, but due to declining world prices, their value declined until 1987. Only fish meal of the major manufactured exports managed to increase in terms of both tonnage and dollar value, partly due to the coming on stream of new early 1980s plant. On a smaller scale, early 1980 investments in canning and freezing plants for fish and shellfish have also proved profitable and as a result this subsector provides the only major growth area in Chile's manufactured exports during the 1980s (see Table 6.4).

IMPLICATIONS OF THE CHILEAN MODEL

Chile is one of the few examples of trade reform emerging from serious economic crises. In the early years of trade liberalization, it is possible to distinguish two economic crises. The first was provided by the aftermath of the Allende regime when inflation in excess of 600 per cent existed in spite of price controls. The gradual reduction of price controls alongside a major devaluation were the two immediate policies adopted at the end of 1973 (see Fig. 6.2). The following year saw the beginning of a multi-pronged attack on the economic crisis – besides the beginnings of trade

6.2 Major economic liberalization policies in Chile, 1973–88.

liberalization (tariff reform and the reduction of non-tariff barriers), serious attempts at reducing the massive budget deficit (Gwynne 1976) and selling off the industrial enterprises and banks nationalized under the Allende regime began.

The 1975 refusal of the industrialized countries of the Paris Club for a variety of political and economic reasons to increase credit to the now highly indebted Chile provided another crisis (*The Economist* 1975). Interestingly, the crisis was met with a renewed vigour to liberalize. In political terms, this was put over as a way of reducing Chile's dependence on foreign governments and their decisions as represented in the Paris Club. Inflation was also still running at over 300 per cent and so a 'shock' anti-inflationary programme was designed in which there was: an across-the-board reduction in government expenditure (between 15 and 25 per cent); a 10 per cent increase in income taxes; an acceleration in reducing the size of the public sector; and a tight monetary policy. For the Chilean population, the years 1975 and 1976 brought incredible austerity – a 13 per cent decline in GDP in 1975, unemployment rising to over 22 per cent of the workforce in 1976 and major reductions in purchasing power.

The political repercussions of such an austerity programme cannot be underestimated. Indeed, attempts at economic stabilization and liberalization in other Latin American countries have often failed to cross this hurdle of austerity. The question of why Chile was able to cross this hurdle while other Latin American countries have not is difficult to answer. However, two factors stand out, although commentators from different wings of the political spectrum would place contrasting emphases on them. First, the Pinochet regime exerted strong political control on all aspects of Chilean life – the media, labour organizations, political groupings; the government was therefore able to scotch or significantly reduce adverse political reactions to the programme. Secondly, the military government was able to place the blame for economic austerity on gross economic mismanagement by previous regimes and (to a lesser extent) the behaviour of foreign governments; the government was therefore able to hold out the idea of economic improvements in the long

term despite accentuated austerity in the short term.

This discussion of the relevance of the Chilean case study to other Latin American countries in particular introduces two further questions: one as background and one in terms of forecasting. Why have Latin American economies been so characterized by crises? Can a modified Chilean model promoting trade liberalization and the growth of manufacturing exports (but without the exchange rate mistakes) be applied to other Latin American countries?

The first question must be deemed as difficult because it involves generalizing about so many individual cases. However, even a brief answer to the question must mention the problem of inflation, often provoked by government deficits being financed by the creation of money. From this point of departure a generalized pattern can often be distinguished. Governments attempt to offset inflation by supporting the exchange rate – in order to hold down the domestic price of imports. But, as a result, the exchange rate becomes progressively overvalued. At the same time governments may also use price controls or subsidies to hold down prices. This approach may work in the short term, but it creates other distortions which then require new controls. Most significantly, the overvaluation of the exchange rate will reduce the supply of exports while increasing the opportunity for imports. A balance of payments crisis may result followed by the introduction of tighter direct controls on imports. The external deficit will have to be financed by extra borrowing, and so debt builds up. Meanwhile, price controls will either increase the budget deficit (if they are sustained through subsidies) or simply reduce the incentive to produce. In these extreme circumstances of crisis governments are faced with the need to act on several fronts. For the short term they need to stabilize the economy, usually through a combination of devaluation and anti-inflationary austerity programmes. For the longer term, liberalization of the economy, including trade, would be required.

Can trade liberalization occur in Latin American and other developing economies? The first point to make is that it is difficult to engineer

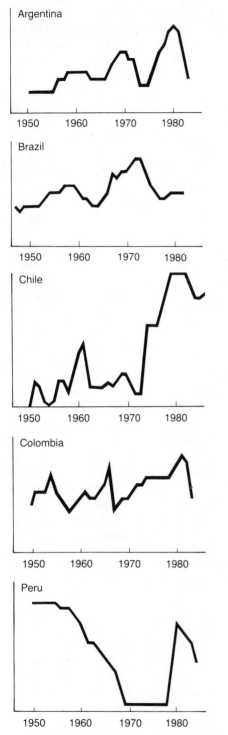

6.3 Trade liberalization indices for Argentina, Brazil, Chile, Colombia and Peru, 1946–86.
Source: World Bank *World Development Report 1987*.

trade reform in a country suffering from inflation and facing a stabilization crisis. Inflation leads to a progressive overvaluation of the exchange rate, which increases the bias against exporting. Trade liberalization could follow such a crisis, as it did in Chile, but it is not a short-term measure. One or two years of considerable austerity and economic restructuring are required with considerable political costs involved. In this sense, Chile may be seen as a special case due to its own particular political circumstances of the mid-1970s. Attempts at trade liberalization started in Colombia and Peru in the late 1970s, in Brazil in the late 1960s and in Argentina in the mid-1970s under the Economy Minister, Martinez de Hoz. However, all these attempts were subsequently reversed as the short-term economic problems and political costs mounted (see Fig. 6.3).

The Chilean case demonstrates most forcibly the importance of keeping the real exchange rate constant in any sustained attempt at export promotion. In the case of Chile or most other developing economies, it is necessary that the quantitative difference between domestic inflation and world inflation is continually allowed for in the devaluation of the domestic currency – particularly against the currencies of the major trading partners of the country in question. The disregard given to the real exchange rate by Chilean economic ministers between mid-1979 and mid-1982, when Chilean inflation was considerably higher than US inflation, constituted the single most important factor in the severe economic crisis of 1981 to 1984 and why it took seven years to regain the export levels of 1980.

The need for a continual watch of the country's real exchange rate is part of the wider lesson for export-promoting governments; and that in adopting more outward-oriented policies an understanding of the operations of the world economy and the nature of the country's links with the international economy become paramount. The essential failure of the Chilean economic ministers in the early 1980s was not to recognize that the Chilean economy could no longer sail on regardless of international pressure – as it had been able to do in its long protected phase of development. The Chilean lesson then is that although there may be considerable medium-

and long-term benefits from an outward-oriented approach, there is also increased potential for disaster unless cautious policies are adopted that have at their base a realistic assessment of the country's position in the world economy.

It has been felt necessary to dwell on the Chilean case because it more closely represents the advantages and disadvantages of developing countries liberalizing their trade than the free trading ports of Hong Kong and Singapore that have always stressed the need for free trade. However, as Table 6.1 demonstrated, the majority of developing economies have inward-oriented trade regimes. The Chilean case, giving the example of an economy switching from a strongly inward-oriented to an outward-oriented economy is more instructive for the majority of Third World countries and particularly those of Latin America. However, there are other examples of countries reforming their trade policy and switching to more outward-oriented approaches in other parts of the Third World. These will be dealt with more specifically in the continental surveys in Part IV of this book.

However, drawing upon Third World experience in general and the Chilean case study in particular, this section will conclude by discussing the mechanics of trade policy reform. The World Bank (1987: 109) stressed that 'moving from non-tariff barriers to tariffs is a move toward a more open trade policy'. Tariffs are generally less protective than quantitative restrictions and a tariff is a price instrument and not a quantity instrument. Hence, changes in foreign prices feed through more readily to the domestic economy.

> Quotas, by contrast, uncouple national economies from the world economy. For example, in India cotton is protected by quantitative restrictions, and textile producers are required to use Indian cotton. As a result, movements in the price of this crucial raw material are not always related to those of world cotton prices, which determine the cost of this input to competitors. It is therefore difficult for Indian producers to commit themselves to production for export: the conditions under which they have to compete are unpredictable (World Bank 1987: 110–11).

The shift from quotas to tariffs has normally been highly beneficial. After the government of Sri Lanka replaced most of its quantitative restrictions with tariffs in 1977, the economy rebounded with GDP growth rates of 5.7 and 6.4 per cent in 1978 and 1979, respectively. Even in the sectors where protection had been lowered, production increased as firms began to operate with fewer restrictions. This led the World Bank to conclude that 'in an economy in which trade is regulated largely by quantitative restrictions, a liberalization policy should start with a shift from the use of quotas to the use of tariffs, even if it means very high tariffs' (World Bank 1987: 110).

Although tariffs are preferable to quotas, the evolution of trade reform must also envisage the lowering of tariffs. This has two dimensions – the lowering of the average level of protection and the reduction in the average dispersion of protection, that is the dispersion between the lowest and highest tariffs. Governments have approached the task in several ways: an equiproportional cut in all tariffs, an equiproportional reduction of the excess of each tariff over some target level, higher proportional reductions of higher tariffs, or some combination of these and other methods. Chile's tariff reductions followed the concertina approach. First, all tariffs above a certain ceiling are lowered to that ceiling; next, all tariffs above a new, lower ceiling are lowered to the ceiling; and so on. The World Bank (1987: 110) suggests that 'as a rule, simple schemes widely applied work better than case-by-case and fine-tuning methods'. Chile's reforms achieved a uniform tariff of 10 per cent, although this was subsequently revised to 20 per cent.

Overall, however, trade policy reform requires a strong political commitment so that the short-term costs can be withstood for the long-term gains to be enjoyed. This has made trade reform a much more complex task for Third World countries than the simple mechanics of trade reform would suggest. In order for trade reform to be successful, it has normally had to be promoted within a wider context of liberalization – of government financing, macroeconomic policy and capital and labour markets. The process of trade reform also makes the particular economy more vulnerable, both to changes in the world economy and to mistakes in domestic government policy. However, the long-term benefits should outweigh short-term risks and setbacks, as long as the firm political commitment to reform is perceived by all concerned. Once, however, trade reform is envisaged by firms as short term and half-hearted, the benefits of reform tend to evaporate. For trade reform, although bringing several advantages to firms, also brings increasing risk. One of these risks is the attitude of the industrial countries to increasing exports of manufactured goods from developing countries and the concomitant threat of protectionism.

7

GLOBAL SHIFT?
PRODUCT LIFE
CYCLES AND
PROTECTIONISM

Chapter 6 emphasized that the trade policy of developing countries must be seen within the overall context of the dynamics of a changing world economy. The focus of the argument can now change from trade policy and reform in the developing countries themselves to the international scale. We have noted in Chapter 3 the considerable problems that face Third World countries when they rely on exports of primary products. Does the world economy grant industrializing countries of the Third World a more favourable framework in terms of the export of manufactured goods?

Some commentators have argued that it does not (Hawkins 1986: 282). They argue that the main growth areas in manufacturing trade are skill-intensive sectors such as chemicals and machinery; for example, these two sectors accounted for 70 per cent of world manufacturing growth between 1974 and 1980. Because these sectors are classified as skill intensive, they are seen as geographically concentrated in the developed countries. Meanwhile, it is the labour-intensive sectors, such as foodstuffs and clothing, which are seen as possibly developing in Third World countries. However, it is pointed out that these sectors are expanding very slowly, accounting for only 12 per cent of world manufacturing growth between 1974 and 1980. The international trade scenario for industrializing countries of the Third World does not therefore seem attractive. They have to specialize in the slow-growth in-

dustrial sectors of the world economy while the countries of the developed world concentrate on the high-growth sectors.

However, the international scenario need not be seen as so negative for the manufacturing exporters of the Third World. In this chapter, we will explore the possibility of Third World countries being able to export relatively advanced technological products. In particular, we will explore the possibilities of manufactured exports from developing countries being assisted through the intermediary of multinational corporations within the conceptual context of the product life cycle. However, the relatively optimistic framework provided by the product life cycle model relies heavily on the concept of free trade in manufactured goods between developing and developed countries. In the final section of the chapter, we examine the problems of manufactured exports from Third World countries being hindered by the threat and reality of protectionism from the industrialized countries.

THE PRODUCT LIFE CYCLE

The international context of trade in manufactured goods in general and the product life cycle in particular can best be put into perspective by a brief reference to the Hecksher–Ohlin theory of international trade. In contrast to the classical theory of international trade, the Hecksher–Ohlin model took into account the effect of differences in factor supplies (land, labour and capital) throughout the world on the international specialization of production (Todaro 1978). Their factor endowment theory can be said to rest on two crucial propositions. The first proposition states that different products require productive factors in different relative proportions. For example, within manufacturing, certain products or activities (clothing, footwear, assembly of electronic products) require relatively greater proportions of labour per unit of capital than other goods and activities (cars, chemicals, products derived from automated and robotized technology). The second proposition is that countries have different endowments of factors of production. Some countries like the United States have large amounts of capital per worker and are thus designated as 'capital-abundant' countries while others like India, Egypt or Chile have little capital and much labour. They are thus designated as 'labour-abundant' nations. In general, industrial countries are assumed to be relatively capital abundant and developing countries labour abundant. The factor endowments theory goes on to argue that capital-abundant countries should specialize in such products as cars, aircraft, telecommunications, computers and other products which utilize capital intensively in their technology of production. They should then export some of these capital-intensive products in exchange for those labour-intensive products which can best be produced by those countries that are relatively well endowed with labour, such as clothes, shoes and electronic subassemblies.

The concept of the product life cycle rests not only on the propositions of the Hecksher–Ohlin model but also on Kuznets's marketing concept of the evolution of a product. Figure 7.1 shows in diagrammatic form the three phases of the product life cycle matched against hypothetical sales volume. As can be readily appreciated, the 'new' phase represents a period of low sales and low sales growth, the 'growth' phase a period of rapid sales growth and the 'mature' phase a period of high sales with little change over time. Such an idealized product history reflects the operation of numerous variables, the balance of which will be different for each product. Generally, however, certain tendencies may be common.

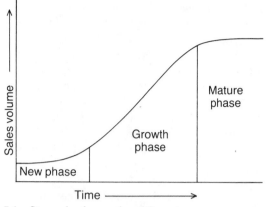

7.1   Stages in the product life cycle.

The 'new' phase constitutes the period that follows the placing on the market of a new invention or innovation. During this period, numerous technical problems will have to be resolved in product design and the production process. The product is likely to be expensive and with limited sales, but the sales strategy for the future will need to be decided upon. If the product passes through this trial period, it will enter the 'growth' phase, a period of cost reductions and increasing sales. As a mass production system is organized and economies of scale taken advantage of, costs will decline markedly, thus causing sales to increase as larger sections of the population are able to purchase the product. The phase of 'maturity' arrives when the potential for further cost reductions comes to an end and annual purchasing stabilizes as markets become saturated.

Within the context of world trade in manufactures and of multinational manufacturing corporations, the product life cycle can also be seen as a framework for the changing location of production on a world scale (Vernon 1966). The matching of the product life cycle with global shifts in production can be formalized into four stages:

1. *Initial production*   During the 1960s and 1970s, most new inventions and innovations, even if they originated elsewhere, tended to be first put on the market in the United States (Vernon 1966), due to that country's 'entrepreneurial talent, large market and large high income'

(Franko 1976). During the late 1970s and 1980s, this pattern has changed, mainly because of the increasing strength of Japanese corporations in the world markets of new consumer goods. Japanese corporations prefer to put new products on the market first in their own country, as has happened, for example, with the compact disc player and the digital audio tape (DAT) system. 'The Japanese love of gadgetry has normally meant that sales in the first and most expensive year of a product's life are high enough to justify continued support from manufacturers' (Rapoport 1987a: 48). 'Scattering new products on their home market and seeing if anyone buys is how many Japanese companies do market research. Bad product ideas can be weeded out early, and efforts concentrated on those projects offering the highest potential returns' (de Jonquieres 1987: 27).

2. *Mass production in the initial production location*   If the product catches on within the income sectors of the United States and/or Japan, the US or Japanese firm(s) involved will begin to organize the mass production of that product in the location of initial production. In terms of compact disc players, this occurred within the first year of production (1983), although mass production of DAT players was delayed longer. During this early build-up of production, US and Japanese firms export the product to all other world regions.

3. *Mass production in other industrial market economies*   During this period, other leading industrial countries start mass production of the product – including the production of Japanese products in the United States and vice versa. In Europe, for example, US or Japanese subsidiaries, European firms adopting licensing agreements and firms developing their own prototypes can begin mass production of the product. Due to lower labour costs and a newer, more rationalized production system, per unit costs may be lower than those of US plants although not necessarily lower than those of Japanese firms. During this phase, therefore, European plants take over the supply of the European market and perhaps encroach on other world markets.

It should be pointed out that in Vernon's reconsideration of the product cycle in 1979, he saw this stage as of less and less significance as the technology gap between the United States and other industrial countries greatly diminished. But in some ways, this can be seen as a curiously restricted, US-oriented view. Although innovations may now appear in *either* the United States, Japan or Western Europe, a subsequent stage of shifting production to the other developed regions of the world will follow. In other words, the pattern no longer automatically starts with the US innovation (as already noted Japanese innovation has become much more significant during the 1980s), but the subsequent diffusion of the innovation from the initial production location in one developed country to other developed countries nevertheless occurs.

4. *Mass production in the less developed countries*   As the production process and machinery become standardized, the US, Japanese or European firms may decide to locate plants in less developed countries where labour costs will be considerably lower, although perhaps not other costs. If the labour cost component in production is large, these plants may begin to produce the product for most world markets.

Such a formalized locational shift of world industry linked to the evolution of a product's sales provides an optimistic scenario for Third World industrialization. Some examples of such dramatic locational shifts have been identified. Franko (1976) gave a detailed account of the worldwide shift of the integrated circuit, the forerunner of the microchip. Invented by the British firm, Plessey, in 1957 and put on the market by the US firm, Texas Instruments, in 1958, mass production started in the United States in 1960. The mid-1960s saw mass production in Europe and Japan, and the late 1960s witnessed mass production in such developing economies as Hong Kong, Taiwan and Mexico. Important producers such as Fairchild spearheaded such a locational shift in order to minimize costs. In the late 1960s, the production of integrated circuits had a well-defined labour-intensive stage – the manual testing of each circuit. If world production of such a technologically advanced product as the integrated circuit could go through the four stages of locational shift in less than a decade, did this not herald a new phase for Third World industrialization?

The experience of Taiwan since the late 1960s has led to answers in the affirmative. Between the mid-1960s and the mid-1970s, Taiwan saw a gradual increase in two main export-oriented industries: textiles and the assembly of electronic products. The assembly of electronic products definitely fitted into the product life cycle model. As worldwide electronic firms tried to reduce their costs of production in the 1960s for basic electronic products such as transistor radios and black-and-white televisions, small assembly plants were created in Taiwan; in the mid-1960s, it was calculated that Taiwanese wage rates were less than one-twentieth of those current in the United States (Berry 1978). By 1976, the value of production of the Taiwanese electronics industry had reached US$1.4 billion. However, during the late 1970s, the worldwide electronics firms saw Taiwan as a cheap labour-cost location for the increasingly sophisticated products of the electronics industry – colour televisions, hi-fi systems, radio cassettes. Existing plants were expanded and new plants were created by US, European, Japanese and Taiwanese companies. Electronics production in Taiwan trebled in four years to US$4.2 billion in 1980. Of this 1980 production figure, US$3 billion (or 70 per cent) were exported, causing electronic products to overtake textiles as the major export category. As much as 95 per cent of these electronic exports were consumer products typical of the last stage of the product life cycle, such as radios and televisions. Further evidence of Taiwan becoming basically an assembly location for products drawing towards the end of their life cycle is that, in 1980, the research costs of the Taiwanese electronics industry amounted to only 0.4 per cent of sales; a figure of over 10 per cent of sales is recorded in the Japanese industry.

The 1980s saw another phase in the growth of the Taiwanese electronics industry as increasingly more sophisticated electronics products came to be produced in Taiwan – videotape recorders, computer terminals, mini-computers, word processors and electric typewriters. By 1984, exports of electronic goods had reached US$4.8 billion – roughly one-sixth of total exports of US$30.5 billion; this proportion was broadly maintained as total Taiwanese exports reached US$39.8 billion in 1986 (*Financial Times* 12/11/87). Taiwan's export growth has been so vertiginous that by 1987, exports accounted for nearly 50 per cent of GNP.

Firms operating in and selling to the US market, however, have begun to see Taiwan as an increasingly high-cost location. The two decades of rapid economic (and particularly manufacturing) growth since the mid-1960s have brought such major increases in employment that Taiwan has come to suffer from labour shortages. Labour shortages have meant higher wages so that by 1987 Taiwanese wage rates were one-third of those in the United States. With higher wage rates in Taiwan, it has become imperative for international firms to look for new locations with low labour costs in order to manufacture products coming towards the end of their life cycle. Two examples, that of the Mexican border and the Chinese border with Hong Kong, reveal that the Taiwanese factor can benefit other locations in the future.

The Mexican border (see Fig. 7.2) has three advantages over a Taiwanese location for firms operating in the US market. First, hourly wage rates of US$0.85 were less than one-third those of Taiwan (US$2.95) in 1986 (Gardner 1987: 14). Secondly, transport costs are distinctly lower. Third, Mexico's border industrialization programme allows for the duty-free import into Mexico of those raw materials and parts which are assembled and re-exported. When the finished goods enter the United States, duty is paid only on the added value. In 1987, there were about 1200 in-bond assembly plants or *maquiladoras* along Mexico's border generating value-added of over US$1.6 billion and employing about 300 000 workers (Gardner 1987: 14). This has meant that since the end of Mexico's oil-based spending spree in 1982 and the following debt crisis, the *maquiladoras* have come to generate Mexico's second largest flow of foreign exchange after oil. Since 1982, the number of in-bond plants has doubled, their foreign earnings have doubled and the number of workers trebled.

As in Taiwan, the electronic sector has been prominent in the boom with a wide variety of foreign corporations attracted to establish plants in the thirteen Mexican border towns (see Fig. 7.2). First of all, there are the American electrical and electronic corporations, such as General Electric, Zenith, Westinghouse, ITT and Honeywell. General Electric has fourteen in-bond manufacturing plants along the Mexican border, employing more than 15 000 (an average of over 1000 employees per plant) with products ranging from electronic ceramics to motors (Gardner 1987: 14). Even more closely following the product life cycle model, Zenith has seven television assembly and component plants along the border, employing as many as 24 000 people (an average of over 3000 employees per plant).

However, the mid-1980s have witnessed

Japanese corporations looking at Mexico's *maquila* sector in order to provide low labour-cost locations for consumer products oriented towards the US market. Between mid-1986 and the end of 1987, eighteen new plants were established, mostly in the electronic sector. Large assembly operations have been installed by Sony, Sanyo, Matsushita and Hitachi in Tijuana and by Toshiba and Seiko in Ciudad Juarez, the latter location having three small Sony, Sanyo and TDK plants before 1986 (see Fig. 7.2). European electrical and electronic corporations have been less in evidence, but nevertheless *maquiladoras* have been established by GEC, Siemens and Philips. One of the most interesting recent developments, however, has been the establishment of assembly plants by the Korean conglomerates, Samsung, Gold Star and Daewoo along the Mexican border. This development con-

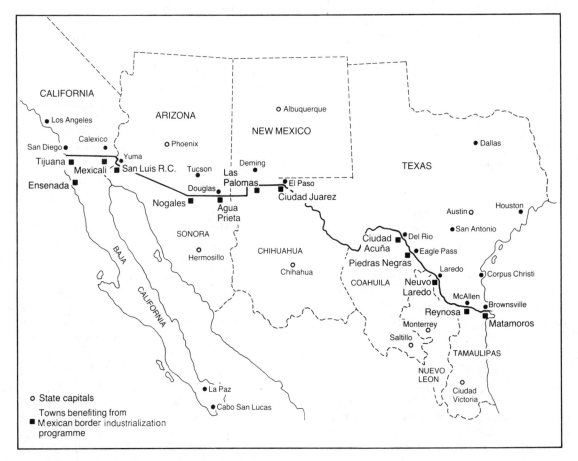

7.2   The Mexican Border Industrialization Programme.

stitutes an example of the corporations of a successful newly industrializing country locating in a less successful developing economy in order to gain access to the market of a large developed country.

Unlike Taiwan, the Mexican industrialization programme has also attracted plants in the motor vehicle sector. By 1987, General Motors had set up twenty-three in-bond manufacturing plants to produce components and is planning to have a total of fifty components plants by the end of 1990 (Gardner 1987: 14). Rockwell International, Ford and Chrysler have also established plants in the border zone. Apart from being close to the United States, these plants have the advantage of being located near to the new export-oriented plants of Mexico's motor vehicle industry. Although these plants are not in-bond, they are nevertheless growing rapidly due to certain international vehicle corporations using north Mexican assembly locations to supply the US market with small finished cars and engines; this phenomenon will be returned to in greater depth in Chapter 10.

The fact that global shifts in production linked to the product life cycle can feature manufacturing corporations of the more successful newly industrializing countries investing in less successful developing economies can also be witnessed on the Chinese border with Hong Kong. In the Chinese county of Dongguan between Hong Kong and Canton and with a population of 1.2 million, Hong Kong firms had invested in 1900 enterprises and 243 joint ventures by mid-1987, employing about 150 000 workers (Dodwell 1987a). Wage rates are less than one-third of those current in Hong Kong, one powerful reason for the large scale of Hong Kong investment in Dongguan in particular and the Pearl River delta area in general.

It is now clear that manufacturers in the British territory would have been unable to maintain price competitiveness in the world's export markets if they had not been able to exploit the cheap labour markets of places like Dongguan. . . Indeed it has become the norm for Hong Kong's textiles, electronics, toy and watch manufacturers to set up all new manufacturing operations in the territory's Chinese hinterland (Dodwell 1987a).

This brief survey of three case studies (Taiwan, Mexican border industrialization programme and the Chinese border area with Hong Kong) demonstrates that the worldwide shift of industry linked to the product life cycle can be seen to impinge upon less developed countries in the form of at least three different hierarchical relationships between spatial areas, normally activated by multinational firms.

1. The relationship between a developed industrial country and an adjacent less developed country. The most accentuated relationship in the world in this category is between the United States and Mexico, where the latter has hourly wage rates about one-tenth those pertaining north of the border. In Europe, differences in wage rates across borders are not so extreme, although the industrial growth of the South European countries (Italy, Spain, Greece and Portugal) can partly be explained by the lower labour costs they can offer to firms that have easy access to all the markets of the European Economic Community.
2. The relationship between industrial market economies in general and outward-oriented newly industrializing countries such as Korea, Taiwan, Hong Kong and Singapore.
3. The relationship between one of these successful newly industrializing countries and the adjacent area of a less developed country.

However, it should be emphasized that the optimistic framework provided by the product life cycle for global shifts in industrial production very much depends on the nature of the product in question. It would appear that for the manufacturing location of a product to be readily shifted to less developed countries, four conditions should be fulfilled. First, there must be buoyant demand for the product in order to justify new plant investment. Second, there must be a well-defined and significant labour-intensive stage in the manufacture of the product. Third, there should be a low incidence of transport costs relative to total costs in order to make long-distance trade feasible; as previously noted, an exception here could be Mexico. Fourth, the technology of the production process and product design must be more or less standardized.

Such characteristics are clearly fulfilled by the wide range of electronic consumer products (radios, televisions, cassette recorders, video recorders, hi-fi equipment, microwave ovens and so on), office machinery (word processors, electric typewriters, mini- and micro-computers) and machine tools. At a more traditional level of manufacture, it could be argued that basic clothing (shirts, trousers, jeans and so on) and footwear could be included, due to the continued significance of labour costs in their total manufacturing costs. Some unusual industries and products can also fulfil most of the conditions. The production of cargo ships and tankers that follow basic designs and use standardized technology are also characterized by an intensive use of labour and a low incidence of transport costs relative to total costs. However, there are other labour-intensive industries such as motor vehicles, often thought to have been candidates, where production has not significantly shifted away from the industrial market economies. The need for constant technological improvement and a strong domestic sales base have meant that most less developed countries, with the possible exception of Korea, Brazil and Mexico, are net importers of motor vehicles and their components (see Ch. 10).

However, a global shift of a completely different set of industries could be envisaged if Auty's (1984) argument linked to the product life cycle approach is accepted. The basic thrust of Auty's argument is that spatial variations in energy costs can be as important as those of labour in attracting industry – not now labour-intensive but capital- and energy-intensive industries. Auty (1984) examined the global petrochemical industry in the early 1980s, after the oil price rises of 1979/80. He noted that exports of low rent, intermediate products in the petrochemical industry from oil- and energy-rich countries in the Third World would replace advanced country production:

> . . . the low opportunity cost of capital in the
> oil-rich countries combined with the low
> opportunity costs of feedstock (in the form of

associated gas which must otherwise be flared) and the prospect that the net externalities from energy-intensive industrialization might be both substantial and positive encouraged resource-based petrochemical expansion (Auty 1984: 332).

The creation of a petrochemicals industry can be seen as a rational policy for oil-exporting countries in the Third World on the principle of comparative advantage alone. Indeed, since the oil price rises of 1973–74 and 1979–80, it has become a generalized phenomenon. Oil-rich producers in the Persian Gulf and elsewhere have constructed export-oriented refineries and fertilizer factories, benefiting from otherwise wasted flare gas and cheap international loans (until 1982, at least). One result has been that the new Third World producers have exacerbated the global surplus of petrochemical capacity. In just one year, 1985, Saudi Arabia brought factories with the equivalent of 5 per cent of global petrochemical capacity into production. Surplus world capacity, however, has had its greatest impact in the industrial market economies, with many large petrochemical plants closing down as a result.

Another example of the global shifting of an industry due to differential energy prices is that of aluminium. The oil shocks of 1973–74 and 1979–80 very much reversed the previous pattern of aluminium smelters being located in the developed countries. Closures of plant in the industrial market economies have coincided with the expansion of plant in energy-cheap locations in the Third World. In Japan, more than half the country's 1.2 million tons of smelting capacity has been closed, mainly due to the implications that such large smelting capacity had on oil imports. Through the oil shocks, the power costs of Japan's oil-fired smelters rose ten-fold, making them over four times that of the cost of power produced from cheap Third World sources (hydroelectricity, gas and brown coal). Meanwhile, during the 1980s new smelting capacity has been developed in Brazil, Venezuela, Indonesia and Australia, some of the major source countries of bauxite and/or with the potential for cheap power.

Perhaps the best example of a Third World aluminium complex is that which has evolved in the Guayana region of eastern Venezuela. Its development has been inextricably linked to the building of the Guri dam and hydroelectric power station in the 1960s and its considerable expansion during the late 1970s and early 1980s. The provision of cheap electricity provided the initial stimulus for the regional development body, the *Corporación Venezolana de Guayana* (CVG), to make a 50 per cent partnership with one of the six aluminium multinationals, Reynolds, to form a joint company, ALCASA, and construct an aluminium smelter at Ciudad Guayana. When Venezuela's burgeoning oil revenue was used to expand the Guri dam during the late 1970s, the CVG decided to expand aluminium smelting further through a wholly owned subsidiary, VENALUM, whose smelter had a capacity of 280 000 tons per annum when it came on stream in 1979.

VENALUM's operations fit well into the product life cycle model because its building and subsequent functioning were linked to a contract between the CVG and a Japanese syndicate to provide 140 000 tons of aluminium a year; a concrete example, therefore, of production moving from the industrial market economies to a Third World location. In order to supply both the ALCASA and VENALUM plants with alumina, the raw material for aluminium smelting, the CVG finished building a massive 1-million ton alumina plant in 1983, the manufacture of alumina from bauxite being another energy-intensive operation. The potential for the creation of the first fully integrated aluminium complex in the Third World was made possible by the late-1970s discovery of Los Pijiguaos, a huge 500 million ton deposit of high-grade bauxite, in the Guayana region; however, at present, the CVG alumina firm, INTERALUMINA, still purchases bauxite from its traditional Caribbean suppliers, Jamaica and Surinam. The aluminium complex of eastern Venezuela thus provides one concrete example of a Third World location 'taking over' production from that of developed countries due to cheaper energy costs in a capital-intensive industry.

The aluminium industry provides a good example of the energy-cost version of the product life cycle because not only are energy costs a very important component of total costs but the industry is also manufacturing a 'mature' product with large and varied world markets and using standardized process technology. Lower energy costs thus provide a great locational attraction in such a mature, competitive industry. Overall, however, the energy-cost version of the product life cycle can only apply to a limited number of developing countries, that is those well-endowed with energy resources.

In general, the product life cycle concept is optimistic about the shifting of industry from developed to developing countries based on the attractions of low labour costs for standardized products and production. Since the Second World War, this potential for global shift has not only been enhanced by further improvements in world transport systems, reducing the friction of distance, but also by an increasing standardization and routinization of productive operations within manufacturing. However, crucial changes are now taking place within process technology. Innovations in electronic control systems point toward even greater automation in the future.

> However, such automation is likely to be different from that which has prevailed in the past and which is still dominant today. With the increasing sophistication of automated processes and, especially, the new flexibility of electronically controlled technology, far-reaching changes in the process of production need not necessarily be associated with increased scale of production. Indeed, one of the major results of the new electronic and computer-aided production technology is that it permits rapid switching from one part of a process to another and allows the tailoring of production to the requirements of individual customers (Dicken 1986: 106).

Whereas previous automated systems have been geared to high-volume standardized production, the newer flexible manufacturing systems can produce goods cheaply in smaller volumes.

What impact will flexible factory automation have on global shifts in industrial production linked to the product life cycle? Two elements stand out. First, labour costs as a proportion of total costs will diminish further, thus spatial variations in labour costs will be less significant in industrial location relative to other factors. Second, the possibility of profitable small batch production will allow manufacturing production to operate at a wide variety of scales. The implications of this are difficult to judge on a global scale, but it may mean the growth and survival of more small firms alongside the large corporations. However, whereas large corporations have been at the forefront of relocating production at cheap labour-cost locations and thereby creating new plants in developing economies, smaller firms would be more likely to remain strongly attached to their domestic markets in the developed world and not spread production to Third World countries. Overall, then, it seems likely that technological change in the future may operate to dampen global shifts in manufacturing production and thereby reduce the participation of Third World countries in global industries. However, protectionist policies in the industrial market economies can be said to be reducing the participation of Third World countries in global industries already.

PROTECTIONISM

So far in this chapter, we have examined the world economy in an overtly positive light as regards the possibilities for global shifts in world industry from the developed to the Third World. However, although processes of global shift are undoubtedly at work in manufacturing industry, and particularly as conceptualized in the product life cycle, there are also considerable difficulties associated with such radical changes in the world distribution of industry. Perhaps the foremost obstacle to global shifts in world manufacturing and the industrial expansion of the Third World is the protectionist stance of the developed countries themselves. This basically serves to make it difficult for Third World countries to export manufactured products to developed countries. This can operate in a number of ways. One way is to make it easier for less developed countries to export primary goods rather than manufactured products to the markets of the developed world. This will be the theme of the following subsection. The subsequent subsections will look more generally at the question of protectionism in the industrialized countries, with particular reference to an industry that should be one of the first to benefit from global shift – the textile industry.

Problems of Shifting from Primary to Manufactured Exports

At the end of Chapter 3, we noted the importance of Third World countries promoting and expanding manufactured exports as opposed to primary exports. We have also noted the rapid growth of world trade in manufactures and the fact that the markets of industrial countries are relatively open for the import of some goods. However, for the export of processed primary products from developing countries, the markets of industrial nations still seem surprisingly difficult mainly because of the characteristic of low duties on the import of raw materials against much higher duties charged on imports of processed goods. These higher rates are, of course, intended to encourage firms in industrial countries to import raw materials and process them there. However, it is first essential to grasp the difference between nominal and effective tariffs, as some low nominal tariffs can, in reality, constitute very high effective tariffs.

In order to understand the idea that low nominal tariffs may constitute a very effective tariff protection, it is best to illustrate with a hypothetical example – say, the import of soya-bean oil into a developed country. Let us say that crude soya-bean oil can be imported duty-free into developed country A for US$1000 a ton from developing country Z. However, developing country Z can produce *processed* soya-bean oil for US$1100 per ton, but developed country A charges a duty of 5 per cent on this import – that is, US$55 (5 per cent of $1100).

The question is: what is the effective rate of protection of importing soya-bean oil from developing country Z into developed country A? Effective protection is defined as the level of protection that nominal duties place on the *value-added* component of a product. The value-added on soya-bean oil refining in the plant in developing country Z is US$100 (the difference between the price of crude and processed oil). The nominal duty on 1 ton of processed oil in developed country A is US$55. The rate of effective protection (nominal duty as a percentage of value-added) is therefore 55 per cent, a very high rate of protection indeed.

It is precisely these high rates of effective protection that face the enterprises of developing countries when they attempt to export their primary products with value-added – processed, refined, canned, frozen, packaged and so on. What seems like a relatively harmless nominal rate of 5 per cent can become in reality a crushing rate of 55 per cent when the all-important factor of value-added is taken into consideration. It basically means that a plant refining soya-bean oil in developed country A is protected by a rate of 55 per cent in relation to imports from developing country Z. As soya-bean oil has a world market price, the plant in developed country A would purchase crude soya-bean oil at the same price, and assuming broadly similar capital and labour costs, the value-added of US$100 would be approximately the same. Thus the refined oil can be sold in the developed country markets based on costs of US$1100 per ton whereas the producer in developing country Z must sell his refined oil in the same markets with an added duty of US$55, equivalent to over half his value-added.

The contrast between negligible or small tariffs on the import of raw materials and modest tariffs on processed and refined goods is common for most developed countries. In 1973, the then nine countries of the EEC had an average nominal tariff of only 0.5 per cent on imports of raw materials, but an average nominal tariff of 8.1 per cent on import of intermediate (processed and refined) goods (Anell and Nygren 1980: 61). As our previous example demonstrated, such apparently modest levels of nominal protection for the import of intermediate goods would in reality signify very high levels of *effective* protection when the value-added in the processing stage is taken into account.

The actual impact of this can be gauged from Table 7.1, which presents aggregate data for twenty-one processing chains. As in our example, nominal and effective tariffs on the import of raw materials into developed countries (Stage 1) are low. However, at the first processing stage on twenty-one commodities, whereas nominal protection remains relatively low at 8 per cent, the effective rate of protection soars to 23 per cent. Due to such high rates of protection on the import of processed goods into industrial countries, raw material imports from the developing countries are virtually double those of processed materials (column three). Further stages of processing and manufacture (Stages 3 and 4) are similarly discriminated against in terms of high rates of effective protection, although it is interesting to point out that they are less severe than that of the first stage of processing.

This particular problem of high rates of effective protection on processed primary products from Third World countries was identified at the round of multilateral trade negotiations (the Tokyo Round, 1974–79) organized by GATT. Table 7.2 reveals, however, that the subsequent advances were very modest indeed, with signi-

Table 7.1 Industrial-country tariff escalation and distribution of imports from developing countries, 1974

Level of processing[a]	Average *ad valorem* tariff		Distribution of imports from developing countries	Imports from developing countries as a percentage of total imports
	Nominal	Effective[b]		
Stage 1	3	3	54	41
Stage 2	8	23	29	26
Stage 3	9	20	9	12
Stage 4	9	15	8	23
Total			100	28

[a] Based on processing 'chains' for 21 agricultural and mineral products. For example, the chain for cotton and products is (1) raw cotton, (2) cotton yarn, (3) cotton fabrics, (4) clothing.
[b] The level of protection that nominal duties place on the value-added component of a product.

(*Source*: World Bank 1981: 23)

Table 7.2 Pre- and post-Tokyo round tariffs for six processing chains

Stage of processing	Product description	Tariff rate	
		Pre-Tokyo	Post-Tokyo
1	Fruit, fresh or dried	6.0	4.8
2	Fruit, preserved	14.5	12.2
1	Cocoa beans	4.2	2.6
2	Processed cocoa	6.7	4.3
3	Chocolate products	15.0	11.8
1	Oilseeds	2.7	2.7
2	Fixed vegetable oils	8.5	8.1
1	Rawhides and skins	1.4	0.0
2	Semi-manufactured leather	4.2	4.2
3	Travel goods, handbags	8.5	8.5
1	Semi-manufactured wood	2.6	1.8
2	Wood panels	10.8	9.2
1	Jute	4.0	2.9
2	Jute fabrics	9.1	8.3

Rates are the unweighted average of the tariffs actually facing developing country exports into 22 developed countries.

(*Source*: World Bank 1987: 138)

ficant differences being maintained in the nominal tariffs enjoyed by raw materials on the one hand and processed products on the other as they enter the markets of twenty-two developed countries. Certainly the contrast in nominal tariff between oilseeds and vegetable oils must mean the continuation of high effective tariffs on the import of vegetable oils.

The Threat of Protectionism from the Industrialized Countries

Before entering into the complex debate of the nature of protectionism in industrial countries, it is first worth putting it into the context of the broad patterns of world economic development in the twentieth century. In the first half of the century, characterized by severe protectionism as well as two world wars, the average annual growth rate of worldwide manufacturing production was 2.8 per cent; however, the average annual growth rate of worldwide manufacturing trade was much lower at only 1.7 per cent – a period then of low manufacturing growth reinforced by lower trade growth, itself a result of protectionism (UNECLA 1979).

During the next twenty-five year period (1950–75), however, characterized by increasing free trade as a result among other things of the establishment of GATT after the Second World War (see Ch. 2), the average growth rate of worldwide manufacturing production was over double that of the previous fifty years at 6.1 per cent. However, the average growth rate for worldwide manufacturing trade was over five times that recorded for the first half-century at 8.8 per cent per annum. This third quarter of the twentieth century was thus characterized by high rates of manufacturing growth reinforced by even higher trade growth, itself linked to the increasing freedom given to trade. The fourth quarter of the twentieth century has so far been characterized by decreasing rates of manufacturing growth reinforced by lower rates of trade growth, itself linked to a return to protectionism, although not yet as exaggerated as in the 1930s.

This subsection will focus on protectionism in the industrial market economies. This is not to say that developing countries are totally reliant on trading with the industrial market economies. However, only 5 per cent of developing country exports go to the centrally planned economies; the great majority of these are primary goods and most come from developing countries which have political sympathies with the Soviet Union (Cuba and Angola, for example). Another 29 per cent of total developing country exports are constituted by exports to other developing countries (World Bank 1987: 135). However, here again, primary goods and fuels predominate. As a result, the trading behaviour of the industrial market economies towards the developing countries tends to be crucial as they import 66 per cent of developing country exports and 67 per cent of their manufactured exports.

The main instrument of recent protection has been the non-tariff barrier rather than tariffs, which in the industrial market economies remain low (at least in nominal terms). In general, it could be argued that non-tariff barriers have tended to discriminate against the lowest-cost sources of imports and have proved to be unfair in that they have not treated Third World exporters equally. Often it has been the exporters with the least bargaining power whose exports have been most affected. These problems of the non-tariff barrier for both developed and developing countries can best be seen in terms of the example of world trade in textiles and clothing and the Multifibre Arrangements that have been created between developed and developing countries in order to 'manage' the trade.

Constraints on World Trade in Textiles

The manufacturing sector which has received the most persistent and detailed efforts at protection by the industrial market economies since the 1973 oil crisis has been that of textiles. In that year the first Multifibre Arrangement (MFA 1) was signed. It was aimed to establish a 'careful balance between the interests of the industrial and industrializing countries' in terms of world trade in textiles and clothing. Unlike previous agreements, MFA 1 applied to a wide variety of natural and synthetic textiles. Emerging textile and apparel producers (and particularly Hong Kong, Taiwan, South Korea and Singapore) were offered the prospect of a controlled increase in their exports of about 6 per cent per annum.

However, with world trading growth declining

after 1973, such growth rates caused Britain and France to experience a 21 per cent increase in textile imports between 1973 and 1977, which became politically linked to a 16 per cent decrease in textile employment during the same period. Both countries pushed for a more restrictive arrangement in 1977 and the resulting MFA 2 was distinctly more protectionist. It allowed the developed countries to impose more restrictive quotas and to renegotiate bilateral agreements with all major suppliers, which reduced and in some cases completely stopped the growth of imports.

MFA 2 lasted until 1981, and in that year there was considerable conflict between the developed and developing countries about the Multifibre Arrangement. The developing countries did not want any further restrictions as world trade in textiles and clothing was stagnating. The developed countries, meanwhile, wished to move away from the idea of the steady 6 per cent growth rate of textile imports from developing countries. It was also noted that MFA 2 hit the first-time exporters most, normally the poorest countries making their first attempts at manufacturing for export markets, such as Sri Lanka.

However, the resultant MFA 3 tended to discriminate against these countries by introducing a 'surge mechanism' which limited the growth of medium- and small-size exporters. Small-scale exporters would not be allowed an export surge from a low exporting base and therefore would be effectively kept to low export growth rates and small increases of exports in absolute terms. The United States and the EEC also created mechanisms to restrict imports from countries not covered by a bilateral agreement – normally first-time exporters starting from a negligible export base. The result of MFAs 2 and 3, therefore, was to discriminate severely against the poorest developing countries, which theoretically should have been providing the cheapest textile products on world markets. The small export quotas of these countries were adjusted slightly in relative terms but this proved insignificant in absolute terms. Often the industrialized countries at the forefront of the Multifibre Arrangements did not noticeably benefit.

However, two sets of countries did benefit considerably. The first group of countries that benefited from the arrangements were those developing countries that had negotiated a large market share in the first Multifibre Arrangement of 1973, most notably the industrializing countries of East Asia. By 1985, Hong Kong's exports of textiles and clothing had reached US$9.7 billion and South Korea's US$7 billion. In contrast, textile and clothing exports from Sri Lanka, one country severely affected by the restrictive conditions of both MFAs 2 and 3 for 'early' exporters, only amounted to US$280 million in 1985.

The second group of countries that benefited were those developed countries in which wage rates were lower than in other industrial market economies. This was partly because the Multifibre Arrangements broached no restrictions on textile and clothing trade between most developed countries. In 1981, Italy recorded a trade surplus in textiles and clothing of US$5.3 billion, after a doubling of textile exports to other EEC countries between 1977 and 1981. This trade surplus in textiles proved to be the world's largest of that year. Table 7.3 shows that for the first half of the 1980s, the percentage increase in US imports of textiles and clothing from the OECD countries (excluding Japan) was higher than for any developing country grouping. Although China did manage to treble its exports to the US market (due partly to political reasons), those poorer developing countries (such as Sri Lanka and Bangladesh) attempting to start up textile exports were only able

to increase exports to the US market by 68 per cent.

The essential problem of the Multifibre Arrangements, then, is that they have discriminated in favour of certain developed countries and the newly industrializing countries that were growing rapidly in 1973 and discriminated against the poorer countries that have been attempting to promote manufactured exports of textiles subsequently. This problem was recognized by the last Multifibre Arrangement (MFA 4) signed in 1986. Article 13 reads in part: 'The participating countries [are] conscious of the problems posed by restraints on exports of new entrants and small suppliers. . . .They agree that restraints shall not normally be imposed on exports from small suppliers, new entrants and the least industrial countries.'

However, if one takes the recent case of Bangladesh (World Bank 1987: 160), the reality is still very different. Bangladesh had a 1985 *per capita* income of only US$150, and was classified by the World Bank as the second poorest country in the world (of those that provided data). However, despite being such a poor country, its attempts to industrialize by concentrating on expanding textile production and exports have been fraught with difficulties.

In 1978, when it began building a textile and clothing industry with the help of the Republic of Korea, there were less than a dozen textile manufacturers in Bangladesh. By 1985 the number had grown to about 450 operational companies;

Table 7.3 US textile and clothing imports, 1980 and 1985 (billions of standard yard equivalents)

Source of imports	1980	1985	Increase 1980–85	Percentage increase 1980–85
OECD countries (excluding Japan)	546	2014	1468	269
Restricted suppliers	4339	8831	4492	104
China	325	977	652	201
East Asian NICs	2210	3784	1574	71
Japan	461	716	255	55
'New starters'	279	470	191	68
Others	1064	2886	1822	171
All exporters (total)	4884	10845	5961	122

(*Source*: World Bank 1987: 148)

these employed a total of 140 000 people and produced more than 300 million pieces a year. With 300 more companies ready to start up, Bangladesh has the potential to produce and export much more (World Bank 1987: 160).

However, Bangladesh's attempts to expand freely into world markets were restricted to the 1981–84 period when exports did increase by nearly four times. In 1984, however, France and Britain imposed quotas, followed by the United States in 1986.

> Although the industrial countries are allowed under the MFA to limit imports in the case of a sudden surge of imports and market disruption, there is no apparent justification for such limits on Bangladesh. In 1984, even after achieving spectacular growth, Bangladesh still held only 0.25 per cent of the developing country share of clothing exports to the industrial countries. The four biggest Asian NIC exporters held 60 per cent. In the United States, Bangladesh's market share was 0.32 per cent while the 'superexporters' held 66.7 per cent (World Bank 1987: 160).

The World Bank concludes that Bangladesh hardly posed a serious threat to the US industry. Yet the bilateral agreement between Bangladesh and the United States allowed only a 6 per cent annual growth rate in textile imports and was extremely detailed in terms of the quotas and categories of possible imports.

> Because of it, Bangladesh stopped expanding its textile industry and for a time had operational facilities standing idle. . .such complications create uncertainty, and the administration of the quotas absorbs scarce managerial ability and discourages investment in a subsector in which Bangladesh clearly has a comparative advantage (World Bank 1987: 160).

According to its 1973 aims, the Multifibre Arrangement was supposed to establish a careful balance between the interests of industrial and industrializing countries. However, the balance was frozen in time, and only those developing countries with well-developed textile industries in 1973 have truly benefited. Otherwise, the MFAs have proved to be a very successful constraint on the growth of textile imports from the poorer countries. In the terms of Hecksher–Ohlin's model (outlined at the beginning of the chapter),

those countries that were able to produce cheap textiles due to low wage rates, should have had a distinct comparative advantage in the production of textiles and clothing in world markets. However, the Multifibre Arrangements have prevented such theoretical benefits. It could be argued that the industrial market economies have not benefited from their protectionist stance either. By eliminating the cheapest sources of textiles, they have effectively increased the prices of textiles and clothing to their consumers. Textile imports have meanwhile increased substantially from a relatively small number of countries that have benefited from the arrangements. Although a complex protectionist mechanism in both time and space, the Multifibre Arrangements have managed to stultify the textile industry in many Third World countries without providing any obvious benefit to the developed countries that demanded it.

The Nature of Prtoectionism in the Industrialized Countries in the 1980s

Textiles and clothing represent 25 per cent of developing countries' manufactured exports, and the previous discussion has shown that the industrialized countries have mounted considerable restrictions on this trade since 1973 and most particularly during the 1980s. In a similar vein, industrialized countries have introduced non-tariff barriers against other manufactured exports of developing countries. Table 7.4 reveals how 'hard-core' non-tariff barriers have increased during the 1980s. The World Bank's definition of 'hard-core' refers to those non-tariff barriers that are most likely to have significant restrictive effects; they include import prohibitions, quantitative restrictions (as with the Multifibre Arrangement), voluntary export restraints, variable levies and non-automatic licensing of imports. The table reveals that of the industrialized countries, Japan's non-tariff barriers covered a much wider range of manufactured imports from industrial countries, although in terms of developing countries the percentage of imports covered was similar to that of the European Community.

In terms of changes during the 1980s, the most

Table 7.4 Industrial-country imports subject to 'hard-core' non-tariff barriers, 1981 and 1986 (per cent)

Importer	Source of imports			
	Industrial countries		Developing countries	
	1981	1986	1981	1986
European Community	10	13	22	23
Japan	29	29	22	22
United States	9	15	14	17
All industrial countries	13	16	19	21

'Hard-core' non-tariff barriers include import prohibitions, quantitative restrictions, voluntary export restraints, variable levies, MFA restrictions and non-automatic licensing.

(*Source*: World Bank 1987: 142)

marked increase in protectionism against imports from developing countries is provided by the United States. This was partly as a result of the serious trade deficit that began to emerge after 1982. For example in 1984, there was a tremendous growth of manufactured imports into the United States, from the developing countries. From the Asian NICs, machinery and transport exports to the United States increased by 49.2 per cent (over 1983), chemical exports by 48.3 per cent and consumer good exports by 41.4 per cent. From Latin American countries, machinery and transport exports to the United States increased by 42. 6 per cent, consumer good exports by 37.2 per cent and chemical exports by 26.6 per cent. By the end of 1984, the United States had a trade deficit of US$13 billion with Taiwan, US$4 billion with Hong Kong, US$3 billion with South Korea, US$5 billion with Brazil and US$8 billion with Mexico. Most of these deficits corresponded to the import of manufactured goods, although the Mexican figure was strongly affected by oil imports. It is interesting to note in this context that with Japan and the EC constraining Third World manufactured imports in the early 1980s, as much as 85 per cent of the increase in Latin America's exports between 1982 and 1984 was destined for the United States. Such pressure on the US trade balance from imports from both industrialized and developing countries caused the

United States to increase non-tariff barriers by 1986.

Protectionism in the industrialized countries is not necessarily linked to grave trade deficits. Japan maintains a complex and varied range of non-tariff barriers despite having a very large trade surplus in the late 1980s. West Germany has also been characterized by the juxtaposition of a large trade surplus and significant non-tariff barriers (e.g. in steel) due to its membership of the European Community. Many of these non-tariff barriers are not primarily designed against the manufactured exports of developing countries but against those of fellow developed countries. The repercussions, however, are felt by developing countries as well. One interesting example of this was the policy adopted by the French government in 1982 to restrict the import of video cassette recorders from Japan by requiring all imports to pass through Poitiers, an inland town far from any port and with a very small customs team. The measure was primarily aimed at Japanese imports which had been approaching 64 000 a month before its implementation; afterwards, they were reduced to 10 000 a month. However, the measure not only affected Japanese video cassette recorders but also those imported from other European countries and the Asian NICs.

The French measure can be seen as part of a growing attitude to Japanese imports both from European countries and from the United States, as larger trade deficits with Japan in manufacturing goods emerge. By 1984, the US trade deficit with Japan hit US$35 billion, and 'voluntary' export restraints were imposed on Japan in such crucial areas as motor vehicles and semi conductors. In Europe, there are export restraints on Japanese vehicles entering the British, French and Italian markets. Two arguments are consistently used by the American and European governments to justify increasing protectionism against Japanese imports. The first argument is that protectionism is imposed on Japanese imports as a lever to open the Japanese market which most American and European firms find very difficult to penetrate. The second and politically more powerful argument is that of the need for reciprocity in bilateral trade balances. There may be trade deficits within certain sectors such as cars and consumer electronics, but overall some reciprocal balance in trade must be achieved. With large Japanese manufacturing trade deficits occurring with the United States and most European countries, this has become a powerful argument for protectionism, but primarily directed at Japan.

Sometimes developing countries can benefit from protectionist measures established by one developed country against another. After imports of Japanese cars were 'voluntarily' kept to 25 per cent of the US market by volume in the early 1980s, Japanese companies responded by importing more expensive models than previously and by increasing the profit margins on their cheaper

models. This permitted a gap at the bottom end of the US car market that has been partly filled by Volkswagen imports from Brazil. However, the company to benefit most from this market gap was Hyundai of Korea whose sales on the US market increased from nothing in 1985 to 168 882 in 1986, or 1.5 per cent of total sales; the major product was the cheap and small front-wheel drive Pony Excel, which significantly undercut in price the cheaper of the Japanese cars.

Overall, protectionism in the industrial countries, although significant, has not been an insuperable problem for developing countries (see Table 7.5). Exports of manufactured goods from developing countries to industrial countries have managed to nearly double between 1979 and 1985, from US$53 to US$97 billion, despite stag-

Table 7.5   Value and destination of exports of manufacturers by developing and industrial countries, 1963, 1973, and 1979–85 (billions of dollars)

Exporter	Importer			
	Industrial countries	Developing countries	CPEs	World
Developing countries				
1963	2	1	0	3
1973	16	7	1	24
1979	53	31	2	86
1980	63	40	3	106
1981	67	45	4	116
1982	67	43	4	114
1983	77	42	4	123
1984	96	45	6	147
1985	97	43	9	149
Industrial countries				
1963	48	17	2	67
1973	222	54	13	289
1979	552	187	38	777
1980	624	230	42	896
1981	592	251	38	881
1982	572	235	36	843
1983	585	211	37	833
1984	648	206	39	893
1985	696	197	50	943

World Bank classification based on following:
   Industrial countries – North America, Western Europe, Japan, Australia, South Africa, New Zealand.
   Developing countries – Africa (excluding South Africa), Asia (excluding CPEs), Latin America, Middle East.
   CPEs (centrally planned economies) – USSR, Eastern Europe, China, Asian CPEs.

(*Source*: World Bank 1987: 146)

nation in 1982 and 1985; furthermore, the 1979 figure was treble that of six years earlier (see Table 7.5). The growth during 1983 and 1984 was largely due to rapidly expanding exports of manufactured goods from developing countries to the United States as both the Japanese and European markets remained fairly tight during this period. Furthermore, the non-tariff barriers of the industrial countries have proved porous with the alert NICs being able to switch exports from one sector to another, depending on the nature and extent of non-tariff barriers. Perhaps the most worrying sign from Table 7.5 is that

developing country exports to *other* developing countries have remained relatively static during the first half of the 1980s, fluctuating between US$40 and US$45 billion. Protectionism in the developing countries themselves seems to be as large a problem as protectionism in industrial countries, although the debt crisis has seriously affected demand in many of the developing countries. In this respect, it is interesting to note that exports of manufactured goods from industrial countries to the developing countries have significantly declined during the 1980s.

— 8 —

TECHNOLOGICAL CHANGE

Economists like to concern themselves with variables that are measurable. In the context of industrialization, this can refer to trade flows, productivity levels, economies of scale and so on. However, at the heart of industrialization lies an issue that has defied economists' attempts at quantification – the process of technological change. Perhaps one of the most relevant generalizations about technological change in any industry and in any country is that it constitutes the accumulation of large numbers of small improvements and adaptations rather than any single breakthrough; these latter may occur but they are not always significant in explaining technological change in the wider context. In many ways, technological change can be seen as the area in which the worlds of economics and engineering overlap. There must be an economic, commercial rationale behind the generation of new technology (for example, for a new product), but at the same time, 'the industrial engineer is accustomed to the idea that every engineering design evolves and improves in time as a result of the particular circumstances in which it is used' (Katz 1982).

From our review of theories of industrialization in Chapter 5, we could conclude that there were major contrasts as regards the explanations behind the origins and nature of technological change. Rostow tended to see a country's ability to finance and promote technological change as closely correlated to that country's level of economic development and the health of the private sector within that country. In contrast, Gerschenkron thought that the lessons of technological change could be rapidly transferred from prosperous to backward countries, particularly if the governments of backward countries took an active, interventionist role. Meanwhile, the Parsonian approach was non-economic; the ability for societies to promote technological change lay in their cultural and social fabric, rather than in any economic variables.

Furthermore, although the geographical distribution of technological change can be difficult to explain, technological leadership in any one industrial sector can shift dramatically from one country to another. For example, in the motor vehicle industry (see Ch. 10), it is argued that technological leadership has shifted from Europe to the United States, back to Europe and then to Japan during the course of the twentieth century.

In this chapter, we will begin by looking at a major focus of economic analysis in explaining technological change in industry, the role of economies of scale. The relationship between economies of scale and space will then be considered before examining more specifically technological change in Third World industry. This will be achieved by first examining technological change under policies of import-substitution industrialization, with particular reference to Latin America. This will be compared with the process of technological change within countries that have adopted export-oriented policies towards industry; the major case study here will concern the machine tool industry.

ECONOMIES OF SCALE

In examining the phenomenon of technological change, many economists have tended to focus on economies of scale and the concomitant reduction in per unit costs. Their definitions of technological change have tended to go along with Salter (1960): 'the degree of technological progress from one period to another is defined and measured as the relative change in total unit cost, assuming that the technique used in each period is that which minimizes these unit costs'.

In terms of manufacturing production, the basic idea behind economies of scale is straightforward – the larger the capacity of a plant, the cheaper will be each unit product of that plant. The simplistic locational corollary would be that, in any one industry, the larger plants will survive at the expense of the smaller plants. In terms of less developed countries (and in the absence of exports), a locational premium would thus be placed on market size – the larger plants of any world industry often only being able to survive in those less developed countries with large markets able to provide the required levels of demand.

The twentieth century has witnessed impressive advances in the economies of scale of industrial ·production and the concomitant reductions in costs per unit of production have been great. At the same time, there have been dramatic reductions in the costs of transport per unit of distance. On a world scale, this allows large plants, in theory, to produce for and distribute to larger and larger spatial markets, causing the closure of smaller plants in so doing.

What are the sources of economies of scale? Traditional economic theory divides them into four: the specialization of labour; economies of large-scale purchasing; specialization in the use of equipment; and economies of massed reserves (Lloyd and Dicken, 1977). The larger the plant, the greater is the potential for the division and specialization of labour. One classic example of modern times would be the motor vehicle assembly plant. A manufacturer could have his 2000 employees all working individually on building up a car. However, this would be very costly as each worker would require considerable skills, space and time. Instead, the employment of 2000 workers has permitted the manufacturer to develop a complex division of labour where each worker or small group of workers has a small job to do in the production of each vehicle.

Such specialization of labour reduces costs because of four major factors. First, there is no need to develop complex skills in each individual worker: the worker learns a basic job, such as fixing on headlamps, a job that can be learnt quickly and soon done rapidly. A second advantage is the saving of time: with the assembly line process, the worker moves steadily from his stock of headlamps to each individual vehicle as it progresses along the assembly line. Third, there is a saving of plant space: the assembly line brings the product to the worker and the worker does not have to move. A fourth factor refers to the ease of incorporating machinery for individual processes in the labour system, the most recent example in the motor vehicle industry being computer-programmed robots welding together car bodies.

Significant economies can also result from large-scale purchasing. With large-scale production, bulk orders from suppliers are possible and these suppliers will normally give corresponding discounts due to the bulk of the order. Furthermore, with bulk orders, the costs of transport per unit of supply are reduced as transport companies give good discounts if their lorries, railway wagons or containers are filled up by one client. Discounts on bulk buying can also correspond to public utilities, with companies normally giving big discounts to volume users.

The cost savings generated by the remaining two factors have become a matter of some debate. Specialization in the use of equipment refers to the fact that the greater the production of a plant, the better the potential use of machines. However, at the same time, there can be significant cost penalties for the low utilization of large capacity machines. Economies of massed reserves benefit large plants because they facilitate the keeping of large stocks of parts at lower relative costs than in small plants. However, manufacturing companies, particularly in the motor vehicle industry, are now turning away from large parts inventories and relying on 'just-in-time' deliveries of both components and machine parts from the various suppliers.

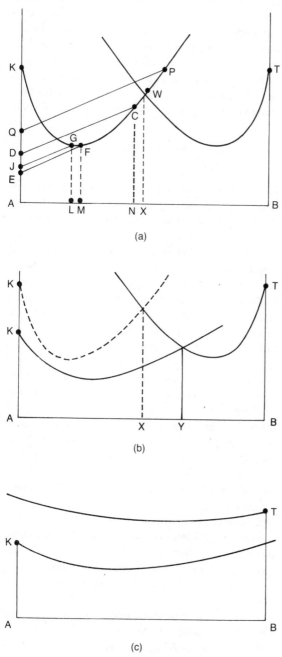

(a)

(b)

(c)

8.1 Theoretical relationships between scale of output and the spatial extent of a market.
Source: Isard W 1956.

Economies of scale and space

How do economies of scale relate to location and space? The classic theoretical insight into this relationship was provided by Isard (1956) and represented in diagrammatic form in Fig. 8.1, which can best be understood if one envisages producer A aiming to invest in new machinery and to expand both his production and the market area that he serves. Isard assumed a unilineal space economy – that is a space economy in which customers for the good produced at A are distributed along the line AB.

If only those customers located at point A want to buy the good, the cost for the producer is AK, a high cost due to low demand (only selling to consumers located at A) and consequently low economies of scale. However, if customers along the unilineal space economy AM are now willing to buy the good, then per unit costs of production will fall due to increasing demand and increasing economies of scale. Of course, in order to supply the larger spatial market, there will be additional transport costs. The slope of the line EF shows the effect of increasing transport costs above the low costs of production AE. The delivery price (both costs of production and transport costs) to the consumers at M is therefore MF.

However, given producer A's present technology and capacity of production, any expansion of the market area further than that of M will mean higher per unit costs of production (due to diseconomies of scale) and additional transport costs. For this reason, the delivery price of producer A's products will increase to CN for point N and to WX for point X. Isard called the curve that links the delivery price points (K, G, F, C, W) the margin line, simply because it reflects the delivery price at the margin of the market area. Figure 8.1a also shows a second producer of the same good, located at B, using the same technology and hence, all things being equal, enjoying the same type of margin line; the market AB is therefore divided at X where the two lines cross.

However, if increasing economies of scale are more actively pursued by one enterprise rather than the other, it is feasible for the former to start to charge a lower delivery price for a larger area.

In Fig. 8.1*b*, one assumes that producer A has invested in new technology which also signifies larger capacity. As a result, and provided he achieves a good utilization of capacity, he has been able to lower his per unit costs and, despite increasing transport costs, sell his products cheaper than producer B in the market area XY. Producer A consequently now sells to a much larger market area than producer B. Indeed, having expanded his market area successfully once, he may later be able to invest further in expanding his economies of scale – so that in spite of increasing transport costs, he can sell his products at a lower price than producer B in the whole of market area AB (Fig. 8.1*c*). Producer B will be faced with closure, a verdict on his lack of investment in new capacity.

One can see the progression of graphs represented in Fig. 8.1 as schematic of how firms in many industries compete. Those firms that build the larger plants and achieve economies of scale and lower per unit costs can first encroach on a competitor's market area and finally render the competitor uncompetitive in the whole of the market area. Such competition can be seen not only at the local and national scales of analysis, but also increasingly it can be witnessed on the international scale. Japanese industry has invested heavily in new technology and large plant ever since the late 1940s, most particularly in capacity oriented towards consumer-good production. One of the consumer-good industries that its post-war policies radically changed was that of motor cycles. By steadily expanding plant capacity, such producers as Honda were able to reduce dramatically the per unit costs and delivery price of small motor cycles – not only in Japan, but as far away as the United Kingdom, where mass market producers such as BSA were severely undercut in terms of prices and were eventually forced to close.

How relevant is Isard's model of the interaction of economies of scale with space to the industrialization of less developed countries? Can firms in less developed countries follow the example of Japanese firms and forge an industrial system based on steadily increasing the advantages of economies of scale? This question will be examined in the remainder of this chapter and

will be returned to in the regional chapters on Latin America and Asia (Chs. 11 and 12). There is one important point to make. Many observers of trends in world technology believe that the great achievements of Japanese technological expertise have been less in terms of scale economies and concomitant per unit cost reductions than in terms of assuring quality control in both product design and the production process (see Ch. 11). Suffice it to say that the Japanese experience has introduced the importance of other factors besides that of cost in the complex technological equation.

IMPORT SUBSTITUTION AND TECHNOLOGICAL CHANGE

In Chapter 6, we made the distinction between countries industrializing under outward- and inward-oriented trade regimes. In terms of government policies, one is essentially drawing the contrast between export-promotion and import-substitution policies respectively. Since the 1930s, industrialization in Latin America has been dominated by inward-looking policies of import substitution (see Ch. 11). Such an orientation has had an undoubted effect on technology generation. According to the head of the United Nations research programme into Science and Technology in Latin America, Jorge Katz (1987: 38), it has meant that 'cost reduction was not necessarily a priority of the technological search efforts undertaken by Latin American firms. Quite on the contrary, product mix diversification, quality and the more effective use of installed capacity normally appear as important objectives of the technological search efforts.' What then is the nature of technology generation in less developed countries industrializing within a framework of import substitution? The following analysis relies heavily on data and research carried out in Latin America but many of the features are common to firms in the other Third World continents.

First of all, how does one define technology? One general definition would be that of Katz who defines 'technology' as a package of technical information useful in the production of a given good or service, a factor of production it its own right (Katz 1987: 14). However, he points out that there are some peculiarities of this factor of production. First, it is not a straightforward cost or competitive factor – questions of appropriateness and applicability enter the argument. Secondly, 'rather than being exogenously given and freely and instantaneously accessible to everybody, new technical knowledge and information has to be systematically sought by manufacturing firms' (Katz 1987: 15). This implies time and cost, inasmuch as firms need to engage themselves in technological search efforts of various sorts. Such search efforts are not only highly sensitive to the micro and macro atmosphere and market regime in which firms operate, but also highly idiosyncratic to the particular enterprise which undertakes the search. Thirdly, a package of technical information is hardly ever completely specified, perfectly understood and easily replicable.

What, then, are the differences in technology generation in less developed countries (LDCs) as opposed to developed countries (DCs) especially in relation to firm search and choice of technique. The first difference between DCs and LDCs is the size of the domestic market. 'With very few exceptions industrial firms operating in LDCs are just a tiny fraction – between 1–10 per cent – of the size of their counterparts in developed nations' (Katz 1987: 25). Continuous flow and highly automated technologies, which would normally be the technology of choice for a new industrial undertaking in a developed country environment, are frequently ruled out right from the beginning by firms operating in LDCs. This is so for at least two different reasons. First, such technologies normally involve a rate of output which is well beyond the size of the local market. Second, such plants frequently embody a level of operational and maintenance complexity which cannot be adequately handled by the locally available engineering and technical skills.

As a result, manufacturing firms in LDCs usually settle for what Katz terms 'discontinuous technology', and for a much lower degree of automation than those looked for by firms in DCs. The choice of a discontinuous technology has a major impact upon such aspects as plant layout, type and cost of the equipment, organization of production, subcontracting and number of workers. Katz (1987) argues that factories using discontinuous technology frequently produce goods or services in small runs or in response to individual orders. Thus, various products can be simultaneously produced. The plant is not designed following the array of technical transformations demanded by one specific product, but rather by 'groups' of somewhat similar machines or tasks. According to Katz (1987: 27), frequent features of a manufacturing plant using discontinuous technology are:

1. The capital equipment is less expensive and of a more general nature than the one required by a continuous flow technology.
2. There is a great deal of flexibility in the way in which a given job is being performed. Given that all of the machines of a certain type can perform a particular task the actual workload is assigned to whatever machine happens to be available. Also, similar jobs can be performed with different machines.
3. Movement of raw materials, components and subassemblies between 'shops' becomes an important part of the production process. It is also a significant source of bottlenecks. The production cycle is not minimized and there is ample room for actually reducing it by carefully re-arranging the physical distribution of jobs in the space.
4. Given that the product is not highly standardized, on-the-job decision making is relatively important. 'Customer-ordered' changes are normally admitted. In this context, workers' skills in setting up the machines, in preparing tools and in actually carrying out the task, become very important indeed.

Furthermore, the use of discontinuous technology means that 'production planning is done almost every other time a given product is produced' (Katz 1987: 35). The production cycle can be reduced by limiting the amount of time in intra-plant transport for the new production run. Size of 'batch' now becomes a crucial determinant of economies of scale. Product design is also affected as 'careful attempts are made at designing some 20–30 per cent of the total number of parts and components which conform to a given product design, leaving the remaining 70–80 per cent of the total list relatively less attended' (Katz 1987: 35). Thus in a discontinuous plant there is a lot more *ad hoc* decision-making done at the shop level and, therefore, skill requirements for machine operators are significantly greater than those typically demanded in a continuous flow plant.

This section has relied heavily on the work of the UN Science and Technology Research Programme in Latin America, mainly because of the recent nature of its findings and the fact that it represents the culmination and synthesis of large amounts of empirical and theoretical studies. The empirical work was mainly carried out in four countries (Argentina, Brazil, Mexico and Peru), largely using 1960s and 1970s data. Industrialization in these countries over the time period in question generally took place behind high protective tariff barriers. The secondary importance given to forging cost reductions in the production process can largely be explained by the lack of external competition affecting these plants. When a number of domestic firms were effectively competing over the national market, Katz (1987: 42) notes that this did 'seem to induce a stronger drive in the direction of product differentiation and cost reducing'. In contrast, when firms enjoyed a monopolistic position in a protected market, their main aim was to expand their range of products rather than attempt to reduce costs. Furthermore, 'sheltered from external competition, local firms feel somewhat less compelled to improve their product's quality' (Katz 1987: 43).

The lessons of the Isard model on the importance of economies of scale and concomitant cost reductions in the adoption of new technology should, therefore, not be disregarded. The hard reality of technology change among firms in the protected markets of Latin American and most other Third World countries may be to undervalue and underemphasize the sizeable cost advantages of new technology. However, for these firms to lift their horizons from the confines of the national market to the wider world market, a change in their perceptions of new technology and its cost advantages would be necessary. Otherwise, manufacturing exports from import-substituting less developed countries will be left entirely in the hands of the multinationals – as in the case of the motor vehicle industry in Brazil and Mexico (see Ch. 10).

The Question of Subcontracting

One theoretical advantage that large- and medium-sized firms in LDCs are sometimes presumed to enjoy is that of a beneficial relationship with low-cost and labour-intensive small firms through subcontracting links. This should give them a competitive advantage over firms in DCs in terms of the cost of bought-in parts. However, Katz (1987: 29) found that large- and medium-sized manufacturing firms in LDCs make much less use of subcontracting links with small firms than their counterparts in DCs. It appears that the degree of subcontracting from the larger LDC firms does increase over time, but not at a very fast pace. The basic problem seems to be the shortage of relevant skills among the smaller firms. Indeed, subcontractors tend to grow out from the fabric of large industrial firms. Case studies carried out in different metal and textile plants show that former technicians and workers of large firms frequently settle down as independent subcontractors, sometimes on the basis of second-hand equipment and technology obtained from the same company in which they acquired their original training (Katz 1987: 28).

These broad conclusions are borne out by Schmitz's detailed empirical work on small, subcontracting firms in Brazil. In particular, he studied knitting and clothing manufacturing in Petrópolis, the hammock industry of Fortaleza and the weaving industry of Americana. 'Probably the single clearest finding which emerges in all three case studies is that the small-scale producers (owners) are not unsuccessful job seekers, but rather the contrary: they tend to be skilled workers who have left their jobs of their own accord. The respondents find that setting up their own business gives a better chance for economic and social advance than wage employment' (Schmitz 1982: 155–6). The main reasons for leaving a job in a large- or medium-sized firm were the low level of wages and an aspiration for independence. Schmitz points out that this latter can be illusory:

> By escaping factory work, many do not entirely escape wage work; unable to buy their own raw material they have to turn to larger firms and perform piece work for these firms in their own small workshops. This was most common among the subcontracted weavers of Americana; it was also frequent among the hammock producers of Fortaleza, whereas the case of the clothing producers of Petrópolis is more complicated: they buy their own raw material and yet often end up in a type of piece work arrangement with other firms on whom they depend to market their product (Schmitz 1982: 156–7).

As with the experience of small firms elsewhere, there was a high failure rate. However, the small enterprise often represents the only way for the owner and his family to increase their income. 'It is not rare for the small firm owner to accept a lower real wage (per hour), in exchange for a risky opportunity to earn a greater amount by working longer hours and incorporating the labour of his family' (Schmitz 1982: 158).

One of Schmitz's most interesting findings was to point to the relative difficulties of entrepreneurs entering the various industries that he studied. This point contradicted the results of many informal sector studies (Moser 1987; Scott 1979; Bromley and Gerry 1979) that had emphasized the ease of entry of small firms into labour-intensive industrial sectors with low levels of technology. However,

> the fact that small enterprises are in most cases set up by *skilled* workers suggests that entry into these branches is far from unrestricted. Previous knowledge of the branch seems to be a prerequisite; the minimum requirement is the ability to operate the machines, given that a good part of the work is generally carried out by the owner himself . . . Given the small scale of operation, the new producer has to master the entire production process. This requires a much wider variety of skills than work in large enterprises; the latter generally consists of a limited range of repetitive tasks which can be learned in a short time (Schmitz 1982: 161).

But perhaps Schmitz's weightiest point was his quantification of entry in terms of capital needed for machinery in the mid-1970s.

In the hammock industry this amounted to approximately US$1100 (for new equipment). In the weaving industry it came to approximately US$1900 (for second-hand equipment). In the knitting and clothing industry a complete set of new machinery would cost US$3600, but the small producers in this industry rarely begin fully equipped, and, apart from the knitting machine itself, make do with cheaper temporary solutions; thus the initial capital requirement is nearer that of the other two branches. To give these capital requirements more meaning, they can be translated into the equivalent number of monthly wages of a skilled worker in the respective branch and town. In these terms, the initial investment is in the order of between eight and fourteen months' wages (Schmitz 1982: 162).

This did not mean the new small firm entrepreneurs had saved the entire amount before starting production. Many were paying in instalments for the machinery or borrowing money. Nevertheless, the capital requirements were large for skilled workers starting from scratch and did constitute a significant entry barrier.

Schmitz's work reflects the origins and behaviour of small, subcontracting firms in the Brazilian textile sector. Entry was more difficult than global studies of the informal sector had presumed. In this sense Schmitz's work on the textile sector bears out the conclusions of Katz's research programme on the Latin American metal goods sector – that small firm entry is difficult due to capital constraints, skill shortages and often restricted markets. Sainmont (1979) found that the Chilean small firm sector, despite favourable macroeconomic circumstances, was hampered by inadequate training, poor management, indifferent financial planning, marketing and administration, a lack of quality control and a national banking system unwilling and unable to give informed advice about running a business alongside any loan that it might grant. There are, then, severe constraints on the development of small, subcontracting firms in Latin America and elsewhere in the Third World – and most particularly in countries with inward-oriented industrial policies.

What are the consequences of this lack of subcontracting? The main consequence is that a high degree of vertical integration exists within the medium- and large-sized firm in LDCs and this inevitably leads to the 'in-house' production of goods that are technologically dissimilar to the firm's major activity – a metal plant having to produce rubber or plastic components, for example. Such a pattern demands a different set of scientific, engineering and production principles for the products that are technologically dissimilar to the firm's major activity. Technological dissimilarity necessarily means lower technical specialization, underutilization of capacity and difficulties concerning production planning. Perhaps it could be argued that the inward-oriented nature of the large- and medium-sized manufacturing firms and their avoidance of international markets signifies that they do not make greater efforts to organize subcontracting links and assist smaller firms in their early development.

It is generally agreed, then, that import-substitution industrialization has not been associated with rapid technological advance, particularly as regards domestic firms. In comparison to developed countries, there has been a much greater persistence of discontinuous technology rather than continuous flow technology in the larger and medium-sized firms. These latter firms have also settled for more unwieldy strategies of vertical integration, with the associated problems of technological dissimilarity, than have similar firms in developed countries. Meanwhile, for smaller firms, there have been fewer links with major manufacturing firms than has often been imagined. Small firms have lacked the technological inputs from more sophisticated firms and as a result have remained utilizing labour-intensive and often antiquated technology.

This contrast between large, vertically integrated firms on the one hand, and small, labour-intensive, handicraft firms on the other is demonstrated in Table 8.1 for Indonesia, a country firmly committed to policies of import substitution until the 1980s. Indonesia's industrial structure in 1975 was characterized by two poles: on the one hand, 1306 large, vertically integrated firms (with an average of 485 employees per firm), mainly oriented towards the domestic market and employing 12.4 per cent of total manufacturing employment; on the other hand, nearly $1\frac{1}{4}$ million handicraft firms, utilizing basic, traditional technology, but responsible for more than three-quarters of total manufacturing employment. Small- and medium-scale industry (with between five and ninety-nine employees) is seen as a relatively unimportant firm segment, responsible for less employment than the large-scale industry (only 11.5 per cent).

TECHNOLOGY CHANGE AND EXPORT PROMOTION

We will examine the Japanese mode of industrialization in some detail in Chapter 12. However, in terms of technological change in less developed countries, it can be argued that the Japanese model has demonstrated that modern industrial success is not so much rooted in the generation of totally new technologies as in the constant adaptation and improvements of imported technological designs – first adapted to local conditions and later for export markets. In the light of our analysis so far in this chapter, the technological question for the governments of less

Table 8.1 Structure of manufacturing in Indonesia, 1975

	Size (no. employed)	No. of Establishments	Employees	
			Total	% of Total
Handicraft industries	4 or fewer	1 234 511	3 899 856	76.1
Small industries	5 to 19	48 211	319 057	6.2
Medium industries	20 to 99	5 746	273 063	5.3
Large industries	100 and over	1 306	633 581	12.4
TOTAL		1 289 774	5 125 557	100.0

(Developed from Soon 1983: 221)

developed countries attempting to industrialize could be phrased in the following way: in view of the problems of technology generation within the policy framework of import substitution, does the alternative policy of export promotion offer a significant improvement, particularly in terms of the lessons of the history of technological change in Japan?

In many ways, this question is linked to that of the product life cycle model and the associated global shifts in manufacturing production (see Ch. 7). The model gives certain insights into the global shifts of manufacturing technologies. For example, in the initial phase of a new product's design, technological development takes place in one of the leading industrialized countries. However, as the technology becomes increasingly standardized the basic model predicts a shift to less developed countries, albeit to those countries with an outward-oriented trade strategy. However, in linking the product life cycle model to the question of technological change, a more subtle interpretation is required, because technology itself is a constantly changing factor of production – that is, being continually improved and adapted to different circumstances. At this stage, it is perhaps worth looking at a relevant case study – the machine tool industry.

Technological Change in the Machine Tool Industry

The machine tool industry is a long-established industry which has undergone rapid technological change in the last thirty years. Indeed, one can tentatively talk of 'technological cycles' being observed in the recent development of the machine tool industry – each with its own product cycle evolution. Three such technological cycles can be recognized, based on fundamental changes in manufacturing technique:

1. The manually operated or standard type of machine tools represent the first 'technological cycle' and can be considered mature technically. Indeed, there have been few innovations of any significance since the early twentieth century.
2. Numerical control (NC) machine tools are the second 'technological cycle' and can be con-

sidered in the late growth stage having reached a peak in basic design standards. However, a number of innovations mainly aimed at reducing their cost or running costs remain under development.
3. Computer numerical control (CNC) machine tools represent the third 'technological cycle' which is in the early growth stages of development technically. CNC machine tools have only become standardized in certain subsectors during the 1980s and generally there is rapid innovation occurring in this sector.

The Numerical Control Cycle

In terms of recent global shifts in machine tool technology, it is most appropriate to start by examining the second 'technological cycle', that of numerical control. Numerical control (NC) is a form of automatic control in which the machine tool is controlled by a series of instructions which are encoded in the form of alpha-numeric characters on a medium such as paper tape (Tipton 1979). NC machine tools originated in the United States in the early 1950s and by the 1960s a large range of control systems had been developed together with about a dozen programming languages to assist in preparing the input data. NC control could be applied to all the traditional machines such as lathes, milling machines and drilling machines, and offered many potential advantages. It enabled the precise control of complex machining operations and reduced the time taken in setting up a machine for operation. Furthermore, it ensured repeated accuracy to tolerances of up to fifty millionths of a centimetre. These advantages reduced the need for skilled manpower and allowed an operator to control more than one machine at once.

What has been the geographical evolution of NC technology? The first NC prototype was developed in the United States in 1952 and in 1953 the first commercial NC milling machine was introduced by the American firm Giddings and Lewis. Although NC technology was first developed and utilized in the United States, Fransman (1986: 1383) details how the technology came to be transferred to Japan in the late 1950s and early 1960s:

In 1956 the Mechanical Engineering Laboratory of the Ministry of International Trade and Industry's Agency of Industrial Science and Technology began a three-year project dealing with the automation of machine tools. In 1958 the Japanese machine tool firm Makino together with the NC producer FANUC produced a prototype NC milling machine while the next year Hitachi Seiki and FANUC launched another NC milling machine. Knowledge relating to NC technology was transferred to Japan both through market-mediated as well as non-market channels . . . . From 1961 to 1964 occurred what the Japan Machine Tool Builders Association has called the 'first technological licensing boom' when 29 licenses were signed, some of which related to NC technology.

In terms of the evolution of NC technology, then, Japan tended to be very much following the innovations and initiatives emerging from the United States, particularly in the 1950s and 1960s. However, an indication of Japan's technical success in adapting and improving upon imported designs in NC machine tools can come from the export record. Japanese machine tool exports started to expand significantly in the mid-1960s, and from 1972 machine tool exports started to exceed imports, with the export–import gap steadily widening through the rest of the 1970s.

The Computer Numerical Control Cycle

By the early 1970s, however, the NC technological cycle was beginning to give way to that of computer numerical control (CNC). CNC introduced data processing and storage into the control system and enabled the programming of machines on the shop floor. CNC machine tools are therefore very flexible with the ability to carry out very complex operations with repeated accuracy. The advent of CNC, furthermore, led to the development of the multi-purpose machining centre which could combine previously separate functions, such as milling, drilling and turning, in one machine. As a result relatively finished components could be produced in a single CNC operation.

The ability of some Japanese companies such as FANUC to become technological leaders in NC machine tools by the end of the 1960s through the

adaptation and improvement of imported designs had important implications for the CNC technological cycle. Sciberras and Payne (1985) have argued that such machine tool producers as FANUC were assisted by the 'keiretsu' corporate system of Japan (see Chs. 10 and 12), in that other divisions of the 'keiretsu' provided technological expertise in microelectronics. As a result Japanese producers were in the technological vanguard of the CNC cycle, in many ways ahead of rival North American producers (from whom they had received the NC technology). One important reason behind the different performances of American and Japanese producers in the early CNC phase concerned user requirements. Watanabe (1983) argued that in the United States it was the aerospace industry which constituted the major demand for CNC machine tools. In Japan, however, it was the car components industry which was the major source of demand. Since a large number of subcontracting components' firms produced in relatively small batches to meet just-in-time deliveries to assemblers (see Ch. 10), CNC machine tools provided them with the flexibility that they required.

The consequent ability of the Japanese producers to manufacture reliable, standardized CNC machine tools for small-scale manufacturing plant, producing in small batches, meant a rapid growth of the industry, not only linked to domestic sales but increasingly to foreign markets. Machine tool exports increased ten-fold in eight years – from approximately 300 billion yen in 1973 to 3000 billion yen in 1981 (Fransman 1986: 1383). In terms of the argument being presented here, the most interesting development was the rapid increase of Japanese CNC machine tool exports to the United States.

The early development of numerically controlled machine tools gave the American industry a considerable jump on foreign competitors in international markets, but in recent years this advantage has eroded considerably, particularly in relationship to Japanese manufactured CNC units that, in the opinion of the panel, are now more advanced than those produced by the United States builders (US Academy of Sciences 1983: 25).

Machine tool technology and newly industrializing countries

After being followers in the NC phase of machine tool technology, Japanese machine tool producers became the technological vanguard of the CNC phase. Can this 'technological turnaround' be repeated in terms of the present newly industrializing countries with outward-oriented trade strategies (as defined in Ch. 6). It is worth while briefly examining Fransman's (1986: 1384–90) case study of the Taiwanese machine tool industry, in which producers have been attempting to follow Japanese CNC technology in the late 1970s and early 1980s.

Fransman's study examined the behaviour of nine Taiwanese machine tool firms and compared them with four Japanese firms in terms of technological improvement and adaptation. The overall adaptation of Taiwanese machine tool firms to CNC technology was evaluated as successful during the early 1980s:

> Significantly, none of the Taiwanese sample firms reported serious difficulties in the introduction of CNC products. Furthermore, none of them foresaw major difficulties in upgrading product quality over time in order to keep up with Japanese advances.

The anticipated capacity to keep up with technological advance in Japan was partly justified by the close links that Taiwanese machine tool firms had managed to forge with their Japanese counterparts, most particularly FANUC:

> All of the Taiwanese firms used CNC controls supplied by FANUC. Furthermore, one of the important findings of the study was that FANUC also provided some of the Taiwanese firms with assistance in introducing CNC. Assistance from FANUC took the form of FANUC sending engineers to help sort out interfacing problems and in one case the firm sent its technicians to FANUC in Japan for further instruction and training.

There was still some technological distance between FANUC and the Taiwanese firms:

> In general, however, the quality of Taiwanese-produced CNC controls was far below that of FANUC. This is reflected in the fact that all the Taiwanese firms used FANUC rather than locally-produced controls in exported machine tools, although this decision was also influenced by the highly efficient after-sales service provided by FANUC in the major export markets.

Fransman's study does, however, show that technological development within the Taiwanese machine tool firms is closely following the Japanese model of continual adaptation and improvement of imported designs.

> A senior member of one of the planning ministries in the Taiwan government argued that in sectors such as machinery, Taiwanese producers were able to make substantial improvements by using technology developed elsewhere without bearing its development costs. By following the international technology frontier rather than attempting to reach it, Taiwanese firms were able to enhance their competitive strengths (Fransman 1986: 1391).

This policy of firms towards the generation of technology is further demonstrated by comparing the responses of senior managers in Japanese and Taiwanese machine tool firms (see Table 8.2). In both sets of firms, the demand impulses of customers in foreign and domestic markets along with the products of competing firms constitute the major sources of technological improvement. In other words, technological progress in Taiwanese firms is closely linked to both the examination, understanding and adaptation of the products of rival firms as well as the specific demands of both foreign and domestic consumers. While these three factors were seen as most important in both the Japanese and Taiwanese cases, three further factors were seen as either important or fairly important in both cases – workers' suggestions (linked to the Japanese system of management and worker participation based around quality circles), suppliers of components and parts (another aspect of the Japanese model, allowing for interdependent technological advance from suppliers that emanates from the sharing of technological information between the main firm and its suppliers) and the use of professional and trade journals. As direct factors on technological advance, government incentives, consultants and links with subcontractors are seen as rather unimportant.

Table 8.2 Sources of improvements in design and selling price in machine tool manufacturers in Japan and Taiwan

Source	Four Japanese firms		Eight Taiwanese firms	
	Mean weighting*	Rank	Mean weighting*	Rank
Worker suggestions	2.75	6	2.0	4
Suppliers of components/parts	2.25	4=	3.0	6
Customers in foreign markets	1.00	1=	1.71	2
Customers in domestic markets	1.00	1=	1.88	3
Subcontractors	3.75	8	3.38	9
Consultants	3.50	7	3.25	7=
Professional or trade journals	2.25	4=	2.63	5
Products of competing firms	1.75	3	1.63	1
Government incentives/pressures	4.00	9	3.25	7=

* – Senior managers of machine tool manufacturers were asked to weight the importance of the nine sources listed above on a four-point scale as follows:

1 (very important), 2 (important), 3 (fairly important), 4 (unimportant). The mean of the responses of the Japanese and Taiwanese firms interviewed was then calculated.

(*Source*: Adapted from Fransman 1986, Tables 9A and 9B)

The low importance given by senior managers to government incentives and assistance is interesting in the light of the amount of financial help given by government and Fransman's expectation of a strong response from firms to this question.

> Apart from fiscal incentives for in-house R&D, the main form of state intervention has been through the activities of the state-owned Industrial Technology Research Laboratories (MIRL) .... By mid-1983 MIRL had 22 contracts with 18 firms, all involving the complete design of new CNC machine tools and machining centres (Fransman 1986: 1387–8).

Firms received considerable design assistance from MIRL and received hidden subsidies for their R&D efforts.

> Furthermore, the signing of a contract with MIRL usually guarantees a firm access to subsidized loans from the Bank of Communication. By mid-1983, 15 machine tool firms had borrowed a total of US$10 million. In four cases the Bank of Communication provided loans in return for a holding of 25% of the firm's total equity (Fransman 1986: 1388).

The Fransman case study is interesting for at least three reasons. First, it demonstrates that newly industrializing countries such as Taiwan are actively following the Japanese model of technological development – that is, actively copying, adapting and improving imported technological designs in relation to the demands of both domestic and foreign consumers. In a highly competitive international market in which the products of competing firms constituted the main source of improvement in both design and costs, the senior managers of eight Taiwanese firms also saw suggestions from both component suppliers and workers as important. The role of government, although considerable in financial terms, was nevertheless given less importance in relation to the concrete nature of technological advance.

Secondly, the study pointed to a very close relationship between the technological leader in CNC machine tools (FANUC of Japan) and the machine tool firms of Taiwan. This seems to point to a new system of technological transfer between firms and countries that has not been discussed in great detail up to now. Whereas North American and European countries have normally attempted to internalize technological advance, Japanese companies, such as FANUC, seem willing to externalize, at least partially, technological progress. On the one hand, an obvious problem is created by such a policy. For by giving technological assistance to rival firms in foreign countries, these firms may in the long term be able to produce products of both superior design and inferior price. On the other hand, there does seem to be a distinct advantage to such Japanese companies as FANUC. This is linked to the supply of information, in the sense that it gives such a company as FANUC both the ability to monitor closely the technological improvements of potential future competitors and the possibility of forging production/sales/technology linkages with those companies in international markets in the future.

The third point of interest that emerges from the Fransman study is the relative unimportance of government in the rapid growth and technological dynamism of the Taiwanese machine tool industry. This is borne out by Jacobsson (1984: 345):

> By all standards the Taiwanese machine tool industry has been very successful. The perhaps surprising conclusion reached when studying the role of government policy is that there has been very little directed governmental influence on the industry. The nominal tariff rate has been very low, around 10 per cent, and the effective tariff has been about the same. Some subtle import controls on machine tools exist, but are almost certainly less stringent than Korea's.

Indeed, one of the major contrasts between the recent growth of the machine tool industry in Taiwan and Korea is the greater importance of state intervention in the latter country, including financial assistance to Korean firms that buy Korean-made machine tools and import prohibition on items that can be produced locally (Jacobsson 1984: 46).

According to Jacobsson (1984: 46), the production of CNC machine tools in Korea and Taiwan is far ahead of that of other 'semi-industrialized' countries. This can be partly explained in terms of the successful following by these two countries of the Japanese model of technology generation, reliant upon the adaptation and improvement of imported designs. However, such a strategy for technological change in manufacturing industry is not without its problems, particularly in such fast-moving and internationally competitive sectors as that of CNC machine tools. What, then, are the present problems of technology generation that are being faced in these two outwardly oriented countries in such technologically advanced sectors as that of CNC machine tools?

There seem to be four problem areas that are worth noting. First, the demand-led pattern of growth in CNC machine tools in the NICs has tended to mean that scarce research and development funds are allocated on a project-by-project basis, rather than linked to a broader strategic plan; in this way, technology generation remains considerably behind that of Japan, where strategic considerations guide the direction of applied research funding. This contrast in the allocation of research funding can be seen particularly well in terms of the granting of or application for patents. In Fransman's study, he compared data for four Japanese CNC machine tool firms (6661 employees, including 869 design engineers) with eight Taiwanese CNC firms (2860 employees, including 183 design employees). The four Japanese firms registered 2130 patents (2.45 per design engineer), but the eight Taiwanese firms recorded only 15 (0.08 per design employee).

A second linked problem is that machine tool producers in both Korea and Taiwan tend to compete on price rather than quality in international markets. Fransman (1986: 1392) demonstrated that in Taiwan, eight machine tool producers levelled an average export price that was only 70 per cent of their leading international competitor, but had an average precision performance that was only 82 per cent of their respective major competitors. This reinforces the first point that there tends to be a significant technology gap between NIC producers and the best practice companies.

A third problem refers to the supply side of technologically dynamic firms in newly industrializing countries. Basically, it can be very difficult for assemblers to obtain the more sophisticated components from local suppliers. In this sense, a free-trading position can be distinctly positive. For example, the low import tariffs current in Taiwan allow for the relatively cheap import of components from more industrialized countries such as Japan. In Korea, on the other hand, high import tariffs increase the cost of imported components and make for a higher cost final product, that in turn becomes difficult to export. This is one reason for the much higher export orientation of the machine tool industry in Taiwan (73 per cent of production exported in 1981) than in Korea (18 per cent of production exported in 1981) (Jacobsson 1984: 45).

A fourth problem refers to the small size of many technologically dynamic firms in newly industrializing countries. The machine tool sector of Taiwan is still characterized by many small firms. Even in firms making complex CNC machine tools, Fransman identified four firms with 200 employees or less. As new investment and research demands are needed, such small firms find it very difficult to obtain the required funding from either their own or external sources. Theoretically, it would be ideal for a gradual process of merging to take place between the major producers. However, in Taiwan, there has been great resistance to such developments. In this case, the organizational framework of Korea, based on the large conglomerate or 'chaebol' has been more appropriate for the increasing scale of production concomitant with technological advance.

IMPORT SUBSTITUTION, EXPORT PROMOTION AND TECHNOLOGICAL CHANGE

The generation of technology is not easy to quantify and is difficult to make generalizations about, particularly in terms of Third World industrialization. Some countries, such as Brazil, have recorded significant technological advance largely within an inward-oriented framework of import substitution. In contrast, it is generally recognized that the newly industrializing countries of East Asia have managed a very fast rate of technological progress intimately linked to export-oriented policies of industrialization. Within these countries, however, there are major contrasts in government policy, with contrasts between the close involvement of government in the import and local adaptation of new technologies in Korea (Enos 1984) and the much more detached role of government in Taiwan and, even more so, Hong Kong.

Nevertheless, in the industrial development of the dynamic capitalist economies of the Third World, the ability both to gain access to new technologies and effectively utilize them is fundamental. In Chapter 5, we noted the theoretical importance of this as emphasized by Gerschenkron. It is also worth quoting Schumpeter's concise argument on the point in his book *Capitalism, Socialism and Democracy* (1943: 31–2):

> . . . new products and new methods compete with the old products and old methods not on equal terms but at a decisive advantage that may mean death to the latter. This is how 'progress' comes about in capitalist society. In order to escape being undersold, every firm is in the end compelled to follow suit, to invest in its turn and, in order to be able to do so, to plough back part of its profits, i.e. to accumulate.

If firms do not invest in new products, as we previously noted in terms of Isard's model, their market areas are cut and they will eventually be forced out of business. It can be suggested that one cornerstone of the manufacturing success of Japan and the newly industrializing countries of East Asia has been their ability to understand and come to terms with Schumpeter's maxim about capitalism, and apparently thrive as a result.

In this chapter, we have broadly compared technological development within the contrasting frameworks of import substitution and export promotion. Our treatment of technological change under import substitution was more generalized than that linked to export promotion, which relied heavily on the case study of the machine tool industry in East Asia. However, some broad conclusions comparing technological change under import substitution and export promotion can be made.

Both surveys agreed that rapid technological change was linked to competition. Outward-oriented trade strategies tend to introduce competitive pressures more successfully into the process of technological change than inward-oriented strategies. Returning to the Taiwanese machine tool industry, Fransman (1986: 1386) noted that 'firms operated under a substantial degree of competitive pressure and accordingly were compelled to pay close attention to the products and production methods of competitors'. In contrast, under the framework of import substitution,

Katz (1987: 43) pointed out that, 'sheltered from external competition, local firms feel somewhat less compelled to improve their product's quality', while the forging of cost reductions in the production process was given secondary importance.

Perhaps the central problem for less developed countries is that, with some exceptions, they have only small domestic markets. As technological change during the nineteenth and twentieth centuries has twinned increasing economies of scale with rapid reductions in per unit costs, this structural problem of the size of the domestic market can prove critical; domestic markets on their own can often not provide the necessary marketing capacity for technologically advanced plant. Meanwhile, if the domestic market can absorb the capacity of a technologically advanced plant, a monopolistic form of development may occur, which can reduce outside competitive pressures on the firm and smother future progress. It appears that the problem is best overcome by operating as far as possible on an international rather than a national scale and that this is best achieved by reducing tariffs and other impediments to trade in manufactured goods.

Operating in terms of international markets allows for increasing the economies of scale of production and introducing continuous flow technology and automation. Perhaps this is the biggest contrast between national manufacturing firms in inward- and outward-oriented trade regimes at the moment. In the former regimes, discontinuous technology can often prevail in medium and large manufacturing firms, whereas in the latter regimes, most of the larger and indeed medium-sized firms can operate with continuous flow technology. With such technological contrasts, it is the firm that has access to continuous flow technology that can enter the favourable spiral of lowering per unit costs, increasing sales, expanding profits and investment and can install even more sophisticated technology.

An international perspective can also link national firms into the networks of multinational corporations, whether in the form of technology transfer, supply, sales or subcontracting linkages. It is to this wider issue of the role of the multinational corporation in Third World industrialization that we now turn.

THE MULTINATIONAL CORPORATION AND THIRD WORLD INDUSTRIALIZATION

In switching from the technological to the organizational component of the internationalization of industry, one encounters a much more controversial and hotly debated topic. Indeed, when one has the task of creating a bibliography on Third World industrialization, it is difficult not to believe that the role of the multinational corporation provides the most fundamental issue, so extensive is the literature extolling the virtues, proving the conspiracies, demonstrating the exploitation or showing the benefits of the multinational corporation. In treating such a massive subject, in terms of words written, it is indeed difficult to limit oneself to one chapter. In terms of this book, the next chapter on the world motor vehicle industry will constitute the main empirical study. This chapter will attempt to come to grips with broad trends and some leading theoretical issues and perspectives.

DEFINITIONS

The very terminology of 'multinational' creates a problem. The term 'multinational corporation' became widely adopted during the 1960s and became associated with Vernon's Harvard Business School research projects; as a result, it came to have a neutral or positive significance towards multinationals and their relationship with economic development. For those wishing to signify that 'multinationals' had an adverse effect on economic development, the new adjective of 'transnational' was created in the early 1970s (Sunkel 1973). When the United Nations decided to set up a research centre in Mexico in 1974, it decided to use the latter term and the United Nations Centre on Transnational Corporations (UNCTC) was created; the term gained considerable influence by now signifying a neutral to negative approach regarding multinational involvement in Third World countries.

Size is one criterion of multinational corporations. Many corporations register turnover that is greater than the GDP of significant nation states. Table 9.1 presents turnover data for the leading twenty multinationals from only one region of the developed world, Europe, and compares them with the GDP of mainly developing countries. Royal Dutch/Shell, with 138 000 employees at end-1985, had a 1985 turnover significantly greater than that of Indonesia with an end-1985 population of 162.2 million. The leading European multinationals, however, are not just represented by oil corporations, such as Shell and BP, but by a wide variety of industrial sectors. Indeed apart from these two oil majors, the sizes of the corporations are broadly comparable (see Table 9.1). The twentieth corporation, Peugeot, had a 1985 turnover greater than the GDP of Chile, a country frequently referred to in this book. However, apart from Chile, the turnover of Peugeot, only the world's eighth largest motor vehicle corporation in 1985, was larger than the GDP of another 66 developing countries. Such

Table 9.1 Turnover of twenty leading European multinationals compared to GDP of selected countries, 1985

Company	Country of origin	Sector	Turnover ($ bn)	GDP ($ bn)	Country
Royal Dutch/Shell	Neth/UK	Oil	102.8	175.7	India
BP	UK	Oil	66.8	86.5	Indonesia
Siemens	Germany	Electronics	30.0	65.9	Argentina
Elf	France	Oil	29.7	38.2	Thailand
Philips	Neth.	Electronics	29.3	34.4	Colombia
Volkswagen	Germany	Motors	28.9	32.6	Philippines
Daimler Benz	Germany	Motors	28.8	31.3	Malaysia
Total	France	Oil	28.5	30.7	Hong Kong
Nestlé	Switz.	Food	28.0	30.6	Egypt
Unilever	Neth/UK	Food	27.2	29.1	Greece
Veba	Germany	Multiple	26.7	28.2	Pakistan
BASF	Germany	Chemicals	26.2	25.4	Libya
Bayer	Germany	Chemicals	25.3	22.1	New Zealand
BAT Industries	UK	Tobacco	24.0	20.6	Hungary
Hoechst	Germany	Chemicals	23.5	20.4	Portugal
Fiat	Italy	Motors	20.6	17.5	Singapore
Thyssen	Germany	Metals	19.1	16.8	Peru
Petrofina	Belgium	Oil	17.8	16.4	Syria
ICI	UK	Chemicals	17.5	16.1	Bangladesh
Peugeot	France	Motors	16.5	16.0	Chile

(*Sources*: *Financial Times* Top 500, 6/11/87; World Bank 1987)

data led Kindleberger to predict, in 1969, that 'the nation state is just about through as an economic unit'. Such a prediction was very premature, but it shows the impact on thinking that the sheer economic size of multinational corporations can provoke.

Another debate about the definition of multinational corporations revolves around the issue of how many countries must a corporation operate in before it is classified as multinational; for the Harvard Business School project it was six or more countries but Brooke and Remmers (1973) described any firm with a stake in more than one country as a multinational. Another issue which has been debated is whether the term should only be applied to privately owned firms or whether it should also extend to state corporations. If one describes such state corporations as Renault as multinational, does one also call the rapidly increasing number of state corporations in Third World countries as multinational and, even more difficult, the 'socialist internationals' of the USSR and Eastern Europe?

The form of ownership of foreign affiliates adds yet another dimension. The simplest, and historically most common, situation is where the parent company wholly owns a subsidiary abroad either directly or indirectly. However, more recently, the ownership chains have become so convoluted that considerable research may be required to identify the ultimate parent. This question is allied to that of control. Majority ownership of an affiliate abroad is not always needed in order to achieve control. Lall and Streeten (1977: 5) argued that 'a particular investor can exercise control with an equity share as low as 10 per cent'. This is important to bear in mind as the term direct foreign investment (DFI) implies that the investing firm acquires *control* over the firm in which it invests overseas.

CHANGING NATURE AND SPATIAL INFLUENCE OF MULTINATIONAL CORPORATIONS

The nature of investment by multinational corporations in Third World countries has changed in a quite fundamental way during the twentieth century. At the outbreak of the First World War over 60 per cent of all direct foreign investment (DFI) was located in developing countries (Dunning 1983); 55 per cent of all DFI was in the primary sector and only 15 per cent in manufacturing (Dunning 1983: 89). In terms of US direct foreign investment in less developed countries, as much as 70 per cent occurred in primary activities (39 per cent mining, 18 per cent agriculture, 13 per cent petroleum) and only 3 per cent in manufacturing. This pattern of a predominant investment in primary activities in less developed countries lasted until well after the Second World War.

The period between 1950 and 1970 very much constituted the heyday of DFI in less developed countries. United States DFI more than doubled in real terms and at the same time, considerably changed its sectoral structure, with DFI in primary activities being reduced to 35 per cent of the total by 1970 and DFI in manufacturing and service activities increasing to 65 per cent. Since 1970, however, the real rate of US DFI in less developed countries has declined, although the broad sectoral division of investment has largely stayed the same. Investment in manufacturing did correspond to as much as 37 per cent of total US DFI in 1984, a fact reflecting significant investments by US firms in manufacturing plant in such newly industrializing countries as Brazil, Taiwan, Mexico and Korea. The declining significance of US DFI in the Third World since the early 1970s can be attributed to a variety of reasons. One factor was the spate of nationalizations of multinational assets during the 1970s, and particularly in the mining sector (oil, iron ore and copper in particular). Secondly, the increasing rate of nationalization in Third World countries caused more cautious overseas investment strategies by the US multinationals. Thirdly, and as we noted in Chapter 4, the 1970s witnessed a substantial growth of non-equity sources of finance for Third World countries, such as those provided by the Eurocurrency markets.

As the governments of less developed countries have increasingly restricted multinational involvement in strategic mineral and petroleum activities, manufacturing and services have become the major growth areas. However, within the manufacturing sector, multinational corporations have tended to concentrate on those activities where technology is advanced and where capital requirements are high in relation to labour (motor vehicles, computers, telecommunications, chemicals). This has led to the multinationals playing a significant role in the technological advance of less developed countries. Some writers (Poznanski 1986) see this free flow of Western technology between the leading industrial countries and less developed countries (and particularly the NICs) as positive for export expansion and economic growth. Other writers (Sunkel 1973) see such a relationship as increasing the dependence of less developed countries on the leading Western countries.

The geographical patterns of home and host countries of multinational enterprises have also undergone major changes during the past eighty years. There has been a major relative decline in the importance of the West European colonial states (United Kingdom, France, Belgium, Italy, Netherlands) from about 70 per cent of total DFI in 1914 (Hamilton 1986: 8) to only 25 per cent by the early 1980s. Meanwhile, DFI from US firms rose from approximately 18 per cent of total DFI in 1914, peaking around 55 per cent in the mid-1960s and subsequently declining to around 40 per cent by the early 1980s.

This contrasts with the recent expansion of foreign investment by West German and Japanese multinationals, each country increasing its share of total DFI from around 1 per cent in 1960 to around 10 per cent by the early 1980s; subsequently, Japanese DFI has grown at a still faster rate. As one would expect, the developing countries have emerged as very modest centres of multinational enterprise, the entire Third World registering a rise from around 1 per cent of total DFI in 1960 to about 3 per cent by the early 1980s (Hamilton 1986: 8). In absolute terms, direct foreign investment increased from an average of US$6.6 billion between 1965 and 1969 to an average of US$49.4 billion between 1980 and 1983 (World Bank 1985: 126). The declining significance of DFI emanating from the United States has, therefore, been more than compensated by DFI emerging from other world regions.

The key feature of the global pattern of the location of multinational investments since the Second World War has been their spatial concentration in the developed countries and the concomitant relative decline in the importance of investments in the developing countries. By the late 1960s and early 1970s, over 80 per cent of total world DFI was being invested in the industrial countries (World Bank 1985: 126). If one looks at DFI in terms of just the industrial and developing countries, one does perceive that in the following nine-year period (1975–83), the developing country share of DFI did increase on average to between 26 and 30 per cent (the industrial countries' share thereby going down to between 70 and 74 per cent). However, the overall spatial concentration of DFI in the industrial countries has been maintained. A prominent feature of increasing DFI in the industrialized countries has been the 'two-way' or 'cross-investments' by multinational firms of the major developed countries. In this way, US multinationals have invested in Western Europe, particularly during the 1950s and 1960s, West European and Japanese multinationals in the United States, notably during the 1970s and 1980s, and Japanese multinationals in Western Europe, especially during the 1980s. In comparison, there has been relatively little investment by European and US multinationals in Japan, although this may be a feature of the 1990s as Japanese restraints on inward investment are reduced.

Post-war DFI has consistently been attracted to two other developed countries, Canada and Australia. During the 1960s, Canada actually received nearly one-quarter of total world DFI, reflecting a period when according to Hamilton (1986: 9), it became the 'branch plant economy of the US'. Since the 1960s, foreign direct investment has shifted away from manufacturing and more towards resource development, as has occurred in an even more pronounced form in Australia. With the early 1970s trend of developing countries nationalizing the mining and petroleum enterprises of the multinationals, the latter responded by switching resource investments to what they regarded as 'safe' locations, of which Canada and Australia were seen as the best choices. South Africa was perceived by the multinationals as another 'safe' location for resource developments until the 1980s.

Although all areas of the Third World have had a declining share of world DFI since the Second World War, it should be noted that two Third World regions, Latin America and Southeast/East Asia have retained a fairly stable position attracting respectively about 15 and 7 per cent of global DFI; the implication is that other Third World regions have recorded the major decline in DFI. In Latin America in the 1950s and 1960s, DFI was closely linked to policies of import substitution (see Ch. 11) which attracted multinational corporations to establish small assembly plants behind high tariff walls. During this period, multinationals established large numbers of plants but with less proportionate investment than in other world regions.

The subsequent change in policy emphasis from import substitution to export orientation maintained investment levels in Latin America, but in a much more concentrated spatial form, Brazil and Mexico receiving the greatest amounts. In Brazil, the United States is the largest single source of foreign investment with about one-third of the stock of assets; West Germany is second with 13 per cent, followed by Japan with 9 per cent (World Bank 1985: 127). The fact that 75 per cent of DFI in resource-rich Brazil is in manufacturing indicates to what extent the nature of multinational involvement in Latin America has changed. Both the Latin American NICs and those of Southeast/East Asia have benefited from multinationals establishing large-scale, specialized manufacturing plants enjoying economies of scale and oriented to global markets. However, in the future, the maintenance of DFI in East Asia may also be closely linked to increasing multinational involvement through joint ventures and licensing arrangements with China.

SOME THEORETICAL PERSPECTIVES

Nevertheless, however generally one attempts to discuss multinational involvement in the Third World, one is inevitably brought into the wider theoretical and political arguments. In essence, political views about the role of multinationals in economic development constitute a continuum, ranging from the very positive to the very negative – writers discussing multinational involvement in terms of both costs and benefits and differing primarily over the degree to which state intervention is required to ensure that benefits outweigh costs. Jenkins (1987b) uses a very interesting, dichotomous typology to classify theoretical and political attitudes. It naturally oversimplifies the wide range of views (for example, there is no position for Galbraith's idiosyncratic views) but it certainly identifies the main streams of thought. Jenkins divides theoretical contributions not only in terms of general negative or positive attitudes towards multinational involvement in Third World countries, but also in terms of non-Marxist or Marxist methodological positions. The resulting four-fold classification is as follows:

1. Non-Marxist methodology and broadly positive attitude towards multinational involvement in Third World countries. Jenkins defines this as the 'neo-classical' approach, with such writers as Meier, Vernon and Rugman prominent.
2. Non-Marxist methodology but broadly negative towards multinational involvement in Third World countries. Jenkins classifies this as the 'global reach' approach and mentions such writers as Streeten, Lall, Vaitsos, Helleiner and Newfarmer.
3. Marxist methodology but broadly positive attitude towards multinational involvement in Third World countries. Jenkins defines this as the neo-fundamentalist approach, with such writers as Warren and Emmanuel prominent.
4. Marxist methodology and broadly negative attitude towards multinational involvement in Third World countries. Jenkins classifies this as the neo-imperialist approach and includes such writers as Baran, Sweezy, Sunkel and Frank.

It is worth while to outline the main arguments of each approach as well as pointing to some of the difficulties and omissions of each.

The Neo-classical Approach

Those writers who could be defined as advocates of the neo-classical approach tend to see multinationals as efficient allocators of resources internationally that provide benefits for both home and host countries. Lewis (1955: 258) saw that capital inflow from multinationals brought far-reaching and generally positive benefits for developing countries through providing foreign exchange, raising domestic income and increasing the labour and managerial skills of the host country:

> Domestic income increases because the undertaking pays wages and salaries to local people, buys local supplies, and pays local taxes; and these payments not only increase consumption, thereby stimulating local production, but also make it possible to have larger local savings, and also to spend on schools, medical services, and other permanent improvements. If the choice is between local capital and foreign capital the advantage may be with the former, but if, as is more often the case, the choice lies between foreign capital or leaving resources undeveloped, then there is little doubt that foreign investment plays a most useful role in providing income to pay for higher standards of consumption, of education, and of domestic improvement (Lewis 1955: 258).

Such a position was common among a wide range of development economists during the 1950s. According to Jenkins (1987b: 19), however, this neo-classical standpoint was based on at least two assumptions, which Jenkins implies were questionable:

1. The supplement assumption – that foreign resources supplement domestic resources and in their absence there would be no local production.
2. The competitive assumption – that markets approximate the perfectly competitive model so that profits are not excessive and that market imperfections where they do arise are largely the result of misconceived government policies.

The most significant 'misconceived government policies' were those of import substitution which considerably restricted markets and often allowed multinationals to have monopolistic or oligopolistic possibilities in small markets. As a result concentrated market structures often resulted from DFI in small countries. In terms of neoclassical argument, this was partly linked to a pattern of foreign investment known as oligopolistic reaction (Knickerbocker 1973; Gwynne 1979b).

In a loose-knit world oligopoly, such as in the motor vehicle or tyre industries, multinationals recognize their interdependence with their rivals but lack sufficient mutual understanding to coordinate their activities. They are, therefore, likely to adopt simple patterns of imitative behaviour. The price leader raises his price, and others follow; one multinational expands capacity, and the rivals imitate, so as not to be left in a disadvantageous position in some ensuing price war. However, in terms of developing countries industrializing behind high protective tariffs, oligopolistic reaction provided serious problems.

Rival A establishes a subsidiary in a highly protected market such as Brazil. Rivals B and C reflect that this investment is likely to knock out their export business to Brazil and give Rival A a first-mover advantage if the investment should prove successful. Indeed, Rival A might do so well in Brazil that it could repatriate significant profits and extend capacity in other markets at the expense of Rivals B and C. These considerations make firms B and C imitate firm A and develop their own subsidiary in Brazil. The oligopolistic firms share both the risks and potential benefits of establishing in a new country. However, the developing country has the problem of a small number of multinationals dominating the national market for that product. This is particularly problematic in small developing country markets where excess capacity is bound to occur, creating higher per unit costs. The highly protected market, however, allows this to occur.

There also emerged the need to incorporate trade theory and technology transfer into the theory of foreign investment. In the 1960s, this resulted in the product life cycle being used as an important concept not just related to trade (see Ch. 7) but more specifically to multinational expansion. The main research thrust was provided by Vernon's research project at Harvard Business School. In Chapter 7, we have already reviewed both the benefits and drawbacks of the model. However, in this context, it is worth repeating that the model could only apply to a limited number of sectors where labour-cost savings were significant and could encourage multinationals to shift standardized production to cheap labour locations in developing countries.

Neo-classical approaches since the 1970s have been more concerned with the expansion of multinational corporations overseas through processes of horizontal and vertical integration. This has been termed the 'transactional approach' by Caves (1982: 2). According to this approach, multinationals are best divided into horizontally and vertically integrated firms.

Horizontally integrated firms are those that turn out essentially the same line of goods from their plants in each geographical market – as in the case of motor cars or other consumer products. Benefits accrue to horizontally integrated multinationals due to their potential for overcoming market imperfections, particularly in such intangible assets as knowledge, technology or marketing skills:

> . . . there is a special reason for believing that internalisation of the knowledge market will generate a high degree of multinationality among firms. Because knowledge is a public good which is easily transmitted across national boundaries, its exploitation is logically an international operation; thus unless comparative advantage or other factors restrict production to a single country, internalisation of knowledge will require each firm to operate a network of plants on a world-wide basis (Buckley and Casson 1976: 45).

Thus it is argued that the horizontally integrated multinational, in order to maximize its rent from product innovation or some other technological advance that it has achieved, should ignore external market transactions (selling the technological package to national firms in each overseas market) and produce in all possible markets. Examples of horizontally integrated multinationals can be found in the drinks industry (Coca Cola), the manufacturing of containers and packaging and the motor vehicle industry where corporations such as General Motors and Ford have historically adopted strategies of horizontal integration (see Ch. 10).

Meanwhile, the vertically integrated multi-national is a firm in which the outputs of some of its plants serve as inputs to others of its plants. Vertically integrated multinationals are particularly notable in such international, intermediate-product markets as oil and aluminium.

> The great source of enrichment to the theory of vertical integration has been a transactional approach. Vertical integration occurs because the parties prefer it to the contracting costs and uncertainties that would mar the alternative state of arm's length transactions. The vertically integrated firm internalizes a market for an intermediate product . . . intermediate-product markets can be organized in a spectrum of ways stretching from anonymous spot market transactions through a variety of long-term contractual arrangements at arm's length to vertical integration. Switching costs and durable, specific assets discourage spot transactions and favor one of the other modes. If, in addition, the costs of negotiating and monitoring arm's-length contracts are high, the choice falls on vertical integration. These are the empirical predictions of the 'transactions' approach to vertical integration (Caves 1982: 16–17).

An interesting comparison can be made between the world aluminium and copper industries in this respect. In the former, the major world aluminium corporations (ALCAN, ALCOA, Reynolds, Kaiser, Pechiney, Alusuisse) have attempted to integrate vertically the four stages of aluminium production (mining of bauxite, transformation of bauxite to alumina through chemical processes, transformation of alumina to aluminium through smelting, and the manufacture of aluminium products and components). The aluminium corporations have effectively internalized the various transactional markets for aluminium within their structures and, probably as a result, aluminium has had considerable price stability since the Second World War. In contrast, in the world copper industry, there exists a major transactional break between the mining and refining of copper, on the one hand, and the manufacture of copper products, on the other. The spot and futures markets for copper in London and New York constitute the main locations for this transaction. In the copper industry, then, due to the importance of spot market transactions and various contractual arrangements between suppliers and consumers, the market for copper is externalized and outside the control of multinational corporations. In contrast to aluminium, copper prices since the Second World War have been highly volatile, and particularly during the 1980s, with the lowest post-war prices of 1986 being followed by rapid price increases in the following two years.

Jenkins (1987b: 21–2) makes the point that a critical assumption of the transactional approach is that market imperfections are regarded as exogenous, either 'natural' or government induced and that the multinationals do not themselves generate such imperfections. This assumption marks the major difference between this approach and those who regard multinational involvement in economic development in a negative manner (see below). Indeed, the neo-classical approach favours the removal of government-induced distortions on industrial development, such as high protective tariffs. Furthermore, it emphasizes that host countries in the Third World benefit from direct foreign investment, whether through inflows of capital, technology or through a more efficient allocation of resources. In conclusion, it can be stated that the neo-classical approach is most fundamentally concerned with the efficient allocation of resources, not just at the country level, but at the global level. The activity of the multinationals, it is argued, makes both goods and financial markets more efficient than they would otherwise be (Rugman 1981: 36).

The 'Global Reach' Approach

A common thread of this approach is the view that foreign investment should be seen as part of the strategy of oligopolistic firms. However, in contrast to the neo-classical position of envisaging firms in an oligopoly of being wary of one another, the 'global reach' approach prefers to see them as acting in collusion, 'in order to remove competition between the firms concerned and to eliminate conflict' (Jenkins 1987b: 23). Large multinationals in an oligopolistic framework act together, it is argued, to restrain competition and make life easier for themselves. There is no question of their seeking to allocate resources more efficiently as the 'neo-classical' approach argues. As a result, multinationals themselves are instrumental in creating the market imperfections that characterize developing countries.

> Whereas for neo-classical writers on the transnationals, particularly internalization theorists, market imperfections are exogenous, arising from government intervention or the nature of certain products such as technology, for the Global Reach view the transnationals are themselves major factors creating imperfect markets. Far from transnationals increasing global efficiency through overcoming market failure, they reduce efficiency by making markets less perfect as a result of their oligopolistic strategies (Jenkins 1987b: 24).

Furthermore, in terms of the distribution of benefits that accrue from multinational investments in Third World countries, the great majority go to the multinational corporation, it is argued. Multinationals 'not only impede national accumulation, but they also foster an inequitable international distribution of income by shifting capital from developing to developed countries through profit repatriation, payments for technology and sales of parts and equipment' (Bennett and Sharpe 1985: 7).

The problem of this approach in relation to the 'neo-classical' approach is that it has continually suffered from a lack of hard empirical research. A small number of empirical studies have had to be relied upon to back up these theories of oligopolistic collusion, and perhaps the most notable was that of Vaitsos (1974) on the pharmaceutical industry in Colombia. Vaitsos demonstrated that the multinational drug companies charged unusually high prices on products sold to their Colombian affiliates and licensees. This provided a clear example of oligopolies charging monopoly rents. Thus Vaitsos argued that the technological monopoly that the pharmaceutical corporations enjoyed in the world was transformed into an institutional monopoly, and that Vernon's product cycle theory should be seen as a theory of monopoly cycles. Vernon (1977: 155) responded:

> The reasons for the unusual Colombian results emerged slowly. At the time, Colombia had placed a ceiling on the remission of profits by foreign companies, a practice that had not yet grown common among developing countries. Moreover, the ceiling was couched in terms that fell with particularly heavy weight on the drug companies. Stated in terms of a return on local investment, the ceiling made no allowances for the drug companies' investment in product development and trade names. Colombia also set price ceilings on the local resale of drugs, using a formula that took into account the imported cost of the product. In these special circumstances, the multinational drug companies had unusually strong incentives to set high prices on products sold to their Colombian affiliates and licensees.

The above quotation can be seen as providing the response of an adherent of the 'neo-classical' approach to the most celebrated empirical study of the 'global reach' approach. It is implied that the real culpability for high transfer prices lay in misguided government policies rather than in collusion between oligopolist firms. Such a pithy critique had little impact on the 'global reach' protagonists. For them, the Vaitsos study showed up the five major hypotheses of the 'global reach' approach (Jenkins 1987b: 24–5):

1. *Market structure* – that multinationals have tended to invest in oligopolistic markets in host Third World countries and have contributed to increased market concentration.
2. *Monopoly profits* – that the market power of multinationals enables them to earn monopoly profits in host countries. These profits, however, do not always appear in the tax returns of the foreign subsidiaries because of various accounting procedures and particularly transfer pricing.
3. *Abuse of market power and restrictive business practices* – multinationals restrict competition both individually and collectively. Individually they impose restrictive clauses on subsidiaries and licensees through technology contrasts. These include tying inputs of raw materials, parts and machinery to the multinational supplier and restricting exports in order to divide world markets. Collectively they form cartels or collude through market sharing agreements, pricing policies and the allocation of spheres of influence.
4. *Demand creation* – multinationals use their

market power to create demand for their products rather than responding to consumer preferences expressed through the market. This leads to 'taste transfer' through the multinational and the expansion of the market for products which are inappropriate for local conditions. The beverage, 'Coca Cola', has normally been seen as a prime example of such an inappropriate product.

5. *Factor displacements* – the package nature of DFI and the monopoly power of the multinationals lead to situations where part of the package displaces local inputs. Imports of capital and management can also displace local capital and entrepreneurship. The extension of control by foreign subsidiaries leads to what is termed the 'denationalization' of local industry.

The major implication of this approach has been to promote policies of nationalization of strategic resources and of greater state control over multinationals in general. During the early 1970s, when this interpretation of multinational involvement in developing countries became popular with policy makers, there was a wave of nationalizations of multinationals engaged in extractive industries regarded as strategic. During the early 1970s, perhaps the most strategic resource was that of oil.

> Increasingly, host governments and/or national oil companies have come to own and control the production of oil. In 1970, for example, some 61 per cent of the world's crude oil output was in the hands of the seven largest oil multinationals, known as the 'Seven Sisters'; only 6 per cent was produced by state production companies and the remaining 33 per cent was won by smaller multinationals. By the end of that decade, however, the share of the 'Seven Sisters' had been reduced to 25 per cent, and the smaller resource companies to 20 per cent. The state production companies, on the other hand, of which there were by now more than 100, had increased their share to 55 per cent of the total (Manners 1986: 30).

Many of these nationalizations took place on relatively amicable terms, that is the oil-rich governments paying reasonable amounts for acquiring the assets of the multinationals and signing lucrative technology contracts for con-

tinued multinational support in specialized areas (Sigmund 1980: 225).

In terms of multinationals involved in less strategic economic activities, government controls were imposed. For countries industrializing through import substitution, governments already exerted significant control over the industrial process, and controls over transfer pricing and restrictive business practices could theoretically be imposed without much difficulty. Controls on multinationals became common in the early 1970s. However, there were significant variations in government response. The Brazilian emphasis was on multinationals increasing exports and investment, whereas in Chile, under Allende, the assets of all major multinationals were expropriated with minimal compensation.

In between these extremes, the commonest development was to set up complex bargaining arrangements between multinationals and governments, as in Venezuela (Sigmund 1980: 255) and Mexico (Bennett and Sharpe 1985). Within the framework of negotiations between national governments and foreign multinationals, a whole range of issues would be discussed, bargained over and agreed – local integration (the level of local purchasing by the multinationals), amount and structure of investment, pricing policy, levels of exports, profit repatriation. Two general points stand out in retrospect. First, some very good 'bargains' were achieved by developing country governments in the early 1970s, very few of which came to fruition after the world economic crises that started in 1973 and 1979. Second, the stronger the government controls on multinational investment, the less the consequent investment. This was seen in Venezuela in the period 1974–77 when foreign investment had to abide by the strict controls of the Andean Group's Decision 24; despite massive government investments, derived from oil revenues, foreign investment kept very low (Gwynne 1985: 60).

More recently, the 'global reach' approach has focused on the packaged nature of DFI and has recommended the 'unpackaging' of direct investment into its constituent elements. Rather than acquiring capital, technology, intermediate inputs, brand names and management expertise all from the same multinational, there should be an effort to obtain each component individually. Theoretically, 'this would permit each to be obtained at the lowest possible cost and for those elements for which domestic substitutes exist to be acquired locally' (Jenkins 1987b: 26).

The 'global reach' approach takes its name from the title of the 1974 best seller on multinationals by Richard Barnet and Ronald Müller. It was very much a book of its time, and it has been difficult to update the approach. The most recent attempt is that of Newfarmer (1985). The approach has suffered from two major problems during the 1980s. The first problem is that after the rush of nationalizations during the 1970s, multinational involvement in many world industries, and particularly extractive activities, has become much less significant. State corporations from developing countries, some with overseas plants and subsidiaries themselves, have become much more prominent in these sectors. Yet this approach has not been able to incorporate these new institutional developments on the world scale.

Secondly, the idea of oligopolistic corporations 'colluding' in world markets has little relevance in the 1980s. This central theme of the approach emerged from industrial organization theory in the United States, where it had been used 'almost exclusively in the analysis of industries within the geographically constrained national market of a developed country' (Bennett and Sharpe 1985: 10). Indeed, industrial organization theories were closely linked to the US anti-trust tradition. In applying these theories overseas, certain modifications were made, but the central idea was still that of US oligopolistic firms carrying on supposed practices of collusion in overseas markets as well as in the US market.

However, the 1980s no longer see US multinationals dominant in the world. West European and Japanese corporations compete with US multinationals in almost all industrial sectors and international markets. In 1962, the 100 largest US multinationals were nearly double the size of the 100 largest non-US multinationals. However, twenty years later the difference was minimal. More recent data would probably show that the 100 largest non-US multinationals (Japanese and West European in particular) were larger than the equivalent number of the largest US firms. In this wider context, competition between multinationals of differing origins and expertise becomes a much more realistic assumption for empirical and theoretical analysis.

The Neo-Imperialist Approach

The two last criticisms of the 'global reach' approach can also be applied to the Marxist neo-imperialist perspective. In this latter approach, the multinational is seen in a more negative light still, operating as the major mechanism blocking development in the Third World. The origins of this approach can be traced back to Lenin's interpretation of multinational enterprise as an agent of rival imperial powers competing for control over peripheral countries. The growth of the multinational enterprise reflected the need 'to control raw-material sources and markets in order to protect their dominant position and to secure their investment even on a relatively longer-run profit perspective' (Roxborough 1979). The neo-imperialist framework thus assumes an intimate link between the interests of the core country and the multinational corporation that has its base there.

More recent neo-imperialist commentators have seen multinational corporations as blocking development (Amin 1977) or contributing to the development of underdevelopment (Frank 1969). According to these theories, three principal mechanisms link foreign investment to underdevelopment.

1. There is a drain of surplus from the underdeveloped countries to the advanced capitalist countries. The multinationals constitute the most prominent agent in this transfer.
2. There is an extension of the monopolistic and oligopolistic structures of advanced capitalism to Third World countries:

   . . . monopolistic firms with high profit rates will tend to repatriate profits, intensifying the drain of surplus and limiting the rate of capital accumulation within the host economies. In so far as transnationals do reinvest profits locally, they are likely to expand by displacing or acquiring local competitors or moving into new areas of activity (Jenkins 1987b: 29).

Thus, there will be an increasing foreign control over the economy, and a concomitant reduction in the activities left available to local capital. The latter will be confined to the most competitive and least profitable sectors of the economy.

3. The emergence of a dependent bourgeoisie can also be perceived, incapable of playing its historical role in promoting capitalist development.

The crucial decisions on production and accumulation would be made in the light of the global interests of the parent companies of the foreign subsidiaries, and not in the interest of local economic development, a situation which local capital would be unwilling or powerless to alter (Jenkins 1987b: 29–30).

The significant development of state corporations in less developed countries and the competitive relationship between US, West European and Japanese multinationals considerably affect the modern relevance or applicability of these highly simplistic Marxist models, based on the concept of international monopolies and oligopolies. Furthermore, the development of multinationals based in less developed countries and the centrally planned economies of the Soviet Union and Eastern Europe (Hamilton 1986) make it difficult to generalize about the specifically imperialistic intentions of multinationals. It is increasingly difficult to conceive of multinationals as economic and political appendages of nation states, and certainly not in the same way as Lenin was able to do in the early twentieth century. Furthermore, the growth of state corporations and developing country multinationals make the idea of a dependent bourgeoisie as difficult to maintain.

The Neo-Fundmentalist Approach

The image of the multinational corporation as the spectre of development, carefully nurtured by the Marxist neo-imperialists, is not, however, shared by the Marxist neo-fundamentalists. This group of theorists go back to the basic fundamental

thesis of Marx that a period of capitalism is needed prior to socialism in order to develop the forces of production and provide the required material basis for that society. 'These authors trace their roots back to Marx's view (for example in some of his writings on India) that the impact of imperialism in destroying pre-capitalist structures and laying the basis for the development of capitalism was progressive' (Jenkins 1987b: 31).

To most non-Marxists, the basic thrust of the argument can seem odd – that a successful period of capitalism needs to predate socialism/communism and that, therefore, in terms of developing countries, capitalism should be strongly encouraged, including its institutions such as the multinational corporation. Incidentally, such a view goes against historical precedent, as virtually all existing socialist and communist states either emerged directly from pre-capitalist forms of production or from an unsuccessful period of early capitalist development.

The neo-fundamentalist view is most clearly presented by the writings of Bill Warren (1973, 1980). He attributed the negative perception of capitalism as an economic force by the neo-imperialist Marxists specifically to Lenin:

The traditional Marxist view of imperialism as progressive was reversed primarily by Lenin. . . In effectively overturning Marx and Engel's view of the character of imperialist expansion, Lenin set in motion an ideological process that erased from Marxism any trace of the view that capitalism could be an instrument of social progress even in pre-capitalist societies (Warren 1980: 48).

The central argument of both the 'global reach' and neo-imperialist schools of thought concerned the role of multinationals as oligopolists, colluding over markets, establishing imperfect markets and draining the surplus of less developed countries. Warren presents a very different interpretation, nearer to that of the neo-classical approach as presented by Knickerbocker (1973):

The rise of oligopolistic market structures – or monopoly firms as they are popularly called – has not reduced competition but on the contrary has intensified it. The development of oligopoly and various forms of association and combination (in individual economies) has been associated with the disappearance of monopoly on a world scale and its replacement by competition. These two phenomena – growth of monopolistic, cartelized firms and industries, and intensification of competition internationally – were closely connected; indeed it was the latter that generated the former (along with technical factors, themselves connected to increased competition, which tended to increase the size of the individual unit). The development of large monopolistic firms also permitted major advances in efficiency, primarily through economies of scale and the systematic application of science and new organizational methods to production (Warren 1980: 79).

In this argument, then, multinationals have responded to competition in the world economy and been prime movers in technological advance, increasing efficiency and a more efficient allocation of resources at a world scale. Certainly such a framework seems much more applicable to the late twentieth century with multinationals from different world regions vigorously competing with each other in terms of price (itself affected by economies of scale and the organization of the production process through cost reductions and increasing productivity) and the technology of both product and production process.

Within economic geography, the most notable Warrenite contribution has been that of Corbridge (1986: 128). As with Warren, Corbridge attacks the writings and approach of such neo-imperialist writers as Frank. Furthermore, he focuses on the neo-imperialist attack on the multinationals and identifies four of their key criticisms: the size and power of multinationals; their fiscal impact on Third World countries; their technological and cultural implications; and their capacity to generate linkages and true economic development. He carefully elaborates the neo-imperialist case in each of these four areas and puts forward an alternative perspective;

Nevertheless, there is another side to the story. One need not hold any brief for the transnationals to realise that their critics are trying to have it every which way and the other. On the one hand they want to argue that the transnationals are the new agents of Western imperialism and the false industrialisation of the Third World. On the other hand the transnationals are blamed for the

deindustrialisation of the old world, and for being the standard bearers of a global capital which knows no home and which owes no allegiance (Corbridge 1986: 168).

In terms of the size and power of multinationals, Corbridge notes that 'the assumption tends to be that giantism alone is indicative of monopoly and thus of inefficiency, a double leap of logic which is surely open to question' (Corbridge 1986: 169). In terms of the presumed preference of multinationals for authoritarian regimes, Corbridge quotes Becker's (1984: 422–3) work which found that in Latin America there was a positive 'correlation between direct foreign investment and the potential for capitalist democracy', the opposite of the neo-imperialist prediction. As regards fiscal effects, most notably transfer pricing, Corbridge is suitably sceptical of the findings, restricted primarily, as we have already noted, to the pharmaceutical industry. In terms of the bauxite industry of the Caribbean, for example, he supports Auty's (1983: 4) findings 'that aluminium's capital-intensive production function and cost-minimising geographical fragmentation of the production chain are prime factors accounting for low regional revenue retention, rather than multinational ownership [or] transfer pricing'. This contrasted with the neo-imperialist argument that the Caribbean bauxite industry was a classic case of 'fiscal drain', with the true value of bauxite production being concentrated in the developed world locations of aluminium production.

In terms of the third area of debate, the question of technology and product dependence, Corbridge makes three useful points against the critics of multinationals. First, in answer to the 'global reach' policy of more licensing arrangements with local firms rather than DFI, it is noted that such development may be difficult with many leading-edge technologies, where technological innovation is continuously evolving. Corbridge is also dubious about the 'global reach' proposals on the unbundling of multinational technology packages to Third World countries due to the lack of extensive educational and infrastructural capacities. Furthermore, the question of what are and what are not appropriate products for Third World counries is raised. For example, such neo-imperialists as Frank (1969: 168–9) disapprove of the motor vehicle as a luxury item, but it has proved invaluable in transmitting technologies, innovations and new products to peripheral rural areas. In could indeed be argued that advanced capitalism has proved responsive to the needs of the masses 'and has actually provided them with a range of consumer durables at which only intellectuals are prone to sneer' (Corbridge 1986: 137).

As a result, Corbridge argues that multinationals have favourable implications for both growth and development. In rather idiosyncratic style, he sees the future of theories on multinationals and world development in terms of a blend of Vernon's product life cycle (see Ch. 7) and Girvan's model of corporate versus national political power. In the empirical back-up to his neo-fundamentalist position, Corbridge takes up the example of Taiwan and takes on Frank's (1982) interpretation of that country's post-war development.

> Frank dismisses the Taiwan experience on the grounds that it is externally controlled, that it is not new, and that it is quite opposed to real, democratic development. What he fails to tell us, however, is why Taiwan, exceptionally, should have grown at the unprecedented rate of 9 per cent annually throughout the period 1953–72, and why its export growth should have averaged 17.8 per cent each year over this same period (Corbridge 1986: 181).

Corbridge provides a wider analysis in which both internal and external factors interact and in which multinationals play a broadly positive role. He concludes with a passage that would not be out of place in a neo-classical text:

> If Taiwan has a lesson for us, it is that there can be room for manoeuvre. The world economy sets many imposing constraints, but it is wrong to imply that all options are closed to all Third World countries, or that they are always predetermined by the metropolitan powers (Corbridge 1986: 187).

A BRIEF CONCLUSION

This chapter first attempted to identify broad trends in the changing nature and spatial behaviour of multinational corporations in the world economy during the twentieth century. Secondly, it has tried to synthesize briefly the main arguments of four contrasting theoretical perspectives on the role of multinational corporations in Third World industrialization and economic development.

It has been concluded that both the 'global reach' and neo-imperialist approaches tend to lack relevance in the late 1980s, at a time when competition between multinationals of contrasting origins (Japan, North America, Western Europe) and expertise has become a more appropriate generalization concerning multinational behaviour in the industrializing countries of the Third World.

At the same time, there seem to be relatively close links between the neo-classical and neo-fundamentalist interpretations of multinationals and their role in the economic development of Third World countries. These two approaches seem to share three major assumptions concerning multinational involvement in Third World industrialization. Firstly, they both agree that foreign capital can be seen as complementary to local capital rather than as displacing it. Secondly, they argue that increasing competition between multinationals (from different origins) has increased the bargaining power of Third World governments. Thirdly, they appear united in the idea that multinationals not only supplement existing local resources but also generate additional local resources or utilize resources previously unutilized (Warren 1980: 173).

These assumptions seem to be in greater harmony with the present reality of multinational involvement in the industrializing countries of Latin America and East Asia (see Ch. 11 and 12) and in the world motor car industry (see Ch. 10). Although the long-term political implications of the neo-classical and neo-fundamentalist approaches are far apart, for the short-term, there is considerable agreement:

> . . . the implicit conclusion to which Warren's analysis points is that capitalist development in the Third World should be actively supported since it is removing many of the internal obstacles to growth, and that the transnationals are playing a significant role in this process (Jenkins 1987b: 32).

— PART III —

CASE STUDY

— 10 —
THE GLOBAL CAR INDUSTRY AND THE THIRD WORLD

The motor car industry has now become a true world industry. From the perspective of newly industrializing countries and Third World countries attempting to industrialize, the major question is to what extent this global industry can be located in · their territories. Can newly industrializing countries become significant exporters of finished cars, other vehicles (lorries, vans, buses) and components as they have become significant exporters of electronic goods, machine tools, ships, clothing, textiles and footwear?

As we have already seen, the global shift of many of these sectors in which Third World production and exports have become significant can be partially explained with reference to the product life cycle model (see Ch. 7). In this model, Third World countries offer the locational attraction of cheap labour costs for mobile capital and the manufacture of products entering the mature phase of both their product design and process technology. In the context of the product life cycle model, then, a crucial theoretical question is to what extent the motor vehicle can be seen as a mature product, utilizing standardized technology. In attempting to answer this question, the present chapter will concentrate on the export potentials that Third World countries presently have in terms of the global motor car industry. This chapter will therefore not focus on those assembly industries that occur in many Third World countries and that are primarily oriented towards their own domestic markets; in

terms of the Latin American countries, these industries will be briefly examined in the following chapter.

It therefore becomes necessary to discuss the motor car industry in an international framework. In the first instance, this will be done by applying the neo-Schumpeterian framework of the early 1980s MIT study on the future of the automobile to the potential for growth of the industry in newly industrializing countries. This analysis will be followed by a brief summary of major locational shifts in global production that have subsequently occurred during the 1980s. Having established an international framework for the evolution of the motor car industry, the potential for an export-oriented industry developing in newly industrializing countries will then be discussed. In particular, it will be postulated that there seem to be only three strategies that newly industrializing countries can follow in promoting an export-oriented vehicle industry during the 1990s.

PAST TRANSFORMATIONS IN THE WORLD CAR INDUSTRY

Altshuler *et al.* (1984) argued that the spread of the industry over the world can best be seen in terms of three transformations. Each transformation is related to a new innovation in either the product or production process (or both) and, as a result, brought about an increase in domestic demand and exports. Furthermore, each stage became synonymous with a new region of the world becoming predominant in production and thus in shaping the world car industry.

Stage one was identified as the change from the custom built car involving short production runs and a great number of manufacturers to a standardized product manufactured on a moving assembly line. This was introduced by Ford in the United States, with the development of the Model T between 1902 and the 1920s and also involved the division of skills so that jobs became more routinized. These methods were later adopted and developed by General Motors and Chrysler, and resulted in the world car industry becoming dominated by these three companies. In 1923, the American share of world production was 91 per cent, and throughout the 1920s it was generally greater than 90 per cent (Altshuler *et al.* 1984: 15).

The second transformation relates to the post-1945 period through to the 1960s, when demand for motor cars had increased and shifted towards a more diversified range of products. European producers had developed separately due to differences in travel patterns, road conditions and consumer tastes. Thus, when the European market opened up, they were able to offer a wide range of models, compared with the standardized American product. Further, they came to pioneer a wide range of new product technologies such as small transverse engines and later front wheel drive hatchbacks (Jones and Graves 1986). The second stage, then, was characterized by product differentiation and an emphasis on product technology. In the early 1950s, the European producers accounted for only 13.6 per cent of world car production, compared with North America's 85.1 per cent. However, with the removal of tariff walls between the countries of Europe in the 1950s and steady economic growth, producers were able to sell their specialized products in all markets of Europe and produce in quantities which allowed increasing economies of scale to be achieved. By 1970, the West European share of world car production was 46 per cent and the North American share had been reduced to 33 per cent.

Development of the Japanese car industry brought about the third transformation. Altshuler

et al. (1984) saw this transformation as existing in a well advanced form by the early 1980s. In the Japanese-inspired transformation, change occurred in labour organization with security of employment and increased worker participation in the form of quality circles. Quality circles assisted in the production process by monitoring the standard of the product at each stage of production. The organization of the manufacturing process was also different, with the use of components direct from the supplier. The arrival of components from the supplier the same day that they would be used by the assembler invalidated the need for large component stocks which had previously been the norm.

This 'just-in-time' system, by reducing inventories, was, however, more vulnerable to error. But it was argued that in this way it was also easier to pinpoint error, particularly in component quality, a feature lacking in previous manufacturing systems based on large stocks. Furthermore, the Japanese manufacturing system provided the framework for continual and multiple improvements to vehicle design, component quality and the production process. This fine tuning of the manufacturing system enabled Japanese producers to combine high-volume output with high quality and the ability to innovate rapidly and to adapt. While production in the United States and in Western Europe stagnated during the 1970s, Japanese production more than doubled. By 1981, the West European share of world car production had fallen to 38 per cent and the North American share to 27 per cent; Japanese world market share was now equivalent to that of the whole of North America.

These three transformations in the world motor car industry have left it being dominated by a small number of multinational producers, all with powerful national bases. The home of the first transformation, the United States, still holds the world's two largest producers, General Motors and Ford, as well as Chrysler, now spatially restricting its manufacturing to the North American market (including Mexico). The region of the second transformation, Western Europe, has at least four global corporations that have generally resulted from past mergers and acquisitions (Volkswagen–Audi–Seat, Renault,

Peugeot–Citroën–Talbot, Fiat–Lancia–Alfa Romeo) as well as a variety of more specialized vehicle producers (Rover, Jaguar, Mercedes Benz, BMW, Saab, Volvo).

The strongest and most remarkable corporate growth over the last three decades has, however, been in Japan, where the major industrial groups or 'keiretsu' (see Ch. 12) have invested in motor car manufacturing. 'Keiretsu' are a collection of numerous firms producing a wide range of products and centred around a bank and trading company. Each member company owns a small proportion of the shares of the other companies. 'Keiretsu' have been able to develop motor car firms from scratch partly because of the role of the 'keiretsu' bank providing the necessary funds and partly because of the advantages of mutual ownership and cooperation in providing assistance with technological change and management systems. Nine Japanese car corporations have emerged as a result, although not all are linked to a 'keiretsu' – Toyota, Nissan, Mitsubishi (with 24 per cent Chrysler shareholding), Mazda (25% per cent Ford shareholding), Honda, Isuzu (34% GM shareholding), Suzuki (5 per cent GM shareholding), Daihatsu (important Toyota shareholding) and Subaru (important Nissan shareholding).

THE FOURTH TRANSFORMATION?

The MIT report on the future of the automobile predicted that a fourth transformation would affect the industry during the 1980s but thought that the precise nature of the change was a matter of considerable debate. However, as Jones and Womack (1985) pointed out, the nature of the change would have considerable implications for the development of the motor car industry in the Third World. According to one scenario, certain Third World countries would receive major increases in productive capacity; the other scenario gave a different interpretation. The opposing views of the future world car industry can be described as those of the 'world car' and of 'technological divergence'.

The 'World Car' Concept

Prior to the early 1980s, the prevailing view on the future of the car industry was one in which the 'world car' concept would predominate. The world car has been described as 'a vehicle which shares the same basic design and as many common or interchangeable parts as possible and which will compete successfully in the world's major automotive markets, modified and tuned to their particular requirements' (Gooding 1979).

It was argued that the large automotive multinationals would tend towards increasingly internationalized production networks. Each company would produce a pool of strategic components (engine, gearbox, suspension system) from plants established anywhere in the world, so as to produce parts at the most efficient scale possible. Other components would be bought in from outside suppliers at a low price because of the quantities required.

As a result of the uniform basic design of the 'world car', competition would be based on price and thus production technology and manufacturing location would be characterized by very large economies of scale at low labour-cost locations. In order to keep costs and prices down, a geographical shift of production from the major markets in developed countries to cheaper labour-cost locations in newly industrializing countries, such as Brazil and Korea, was envisaged. It was further predicted that by 1990, the international car market would be dominated by a maximum of ten major motor manufacturers, each making a minimum of 2 million vehicles a year.

The Model of 'Technological Divergence'

The rival view of the future, that of 'technological divergence', has been most influentially presented through the four-year, seven-nation study by the Massachusetts Institute of Technology (MIT) on the future of the automobile (Altshuler et al. 1984). The MIT report argued that the introduction of microprocessor-controlled, flexible production methods, new systems of organization for the production process and the fact that the world's car buyers demand a diverse range of vehicles would mean the survival of most firms which existed in the early 1980s but with few if any new firms entering the market. The spatial corollary of this argument was that existing automobile corporations in Western Europe, United States and Japan would not only remain intact but would also remain producing principally in their domestic markets or in the markets of other developed countries.

According to Altshuler *et al.* (1984), advances in production technology during the 1980s would enable efficiency to be maintained at lower levels of production. Final assembly plants which formerly needed to produce 240 000 cars a year of one model type on a two-shift work schedule, would be able to spread this volume over a range of models due to increasing use of flexible automation. Further, advances in computer-aided design, engineering and manufacturing would reduce the total number of units a manufacturer has to build in order to recoup development costs and investment in capital equipment. It may be necessary to maintain certain mechanical components such as engines at a large production level (500 000 units per annum), but increasingly collaborative agreements would be arranged between assemblers, such as between Honda and Rover, or Fiat and Peugeot.

Changes in the organization of the production process were also seen as important by MIT, following along the lines of Japan's 'just-in-time' system. The need for close proximity between component supplier and assembler, required in order to reduce inventories and improve quality control, led MIT to conclude that component production would be likely to become more tightly concentrated at the point of final assembly in the major markets. The type of geographical concentration of component suppliers that occurs around Toyota's four assembly plants in Toyota City (Fig. 10.1) would be the ideal model that other manufacturers would attempt to emulate.

Jones and Womack (1985) saw the production of only standardized vehicle systems (lighting, braking, suspension, steering) and minor parts taking place at low labour-cost locations in the future. Furthermore, as vehicle systems incorporate new technology in both product design and productive process, these would be increasingly manufactured near to the supplier's centralized production location. Further benefits would accrue to developed country locations from adopting the more flexible Japanese approach. Closer involvement between workforce and shop-floor management would give the potential for higher quality in production and a source of new ideas for product/component design and the productive process itself. Low inventories would mean less inactive capital, while a more involved, cooperative workforce should indicate less middle management.

Thus, MIT argued that there would be few departures of firms from the industry, because the reduced minimum efficient scale of production would enable the medium-sized and specialist producers to compete with the large multinationals. They may even have a competitive edge in some market niches. At the same time, few if any new manufacturers would emerge due to the very large initial investment required and the great difficulty of car design and manufacture.

The implications for the expansion of export-

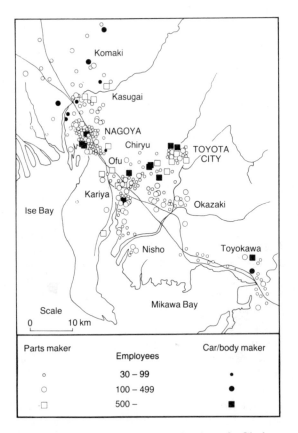

10.1   Distribution of major vehicle plants in Chukyo region, 1970.

oriented motor vehicle production in newly industrializing countries was therefore bleak. Motor vehicle production would continue being dominated by corporations that had emerged in the geographical areas associated with the first three transformations. Hence, it would be difficult for new corporations to emerge from the newly industrializing economies. Furthermore, the cost reductions that new technology had brought to the industry meant that low labour-cost locations would offer little attraction for the international vehicle corporations:

> The completely new standards of organizational efficiency established by the Japanese have pulled the rug out from under the feet of the developing countries. Between 1970 and 1981, the Japanese reduced the total number of hours needed to build a car from 250 to 130, with further improvements since then. Not only have the Japanese reduced the number of hours required to assemble a car or build an engine, but the focus of attention in seeking productivity improvements has also shifted from the cost of the factors of production to how efficiently they are combined into an integrated sequence of production operations. As a result, even the South Koreans, with a $1 an hour wage rate in 1980, cannot produce a comparable vehicle for the same costs as the Japanese with a $7 an hour wage rate. The Korean Ministry of Commerce estimated that in 1979 Hyundai's production cost for the Pony built in Korea was $3972, compared with an estimated cost of $2300 for a Toyota Corolla made in Japan (Jones and Womack 1985: 400–1).

Global shifts in car production during the 1980s

In many ways, the fourth transformation put forward by the MIT study for the 1980s can be seen as an extension of the third Japanese transformation. Certainly Japan and Japanese companies have continued to dominate the international car industry during the 1980s. The example just quoted from Jones and Womack shows that Japanese production costs were not only undercutting those of other developed countries but also those of the newly industrializing countries. The Japanese success in orienting continuous technological advance to a steady reduction in costs meant that world markets came to be dominated

by Japanese imports, leaving little potential for newly industrializing countries and their nascent industries.

The dominance of Japan in world markets during the third transformation is fully reflected in Table 10.1. Between 1974 and 1984, Japanese car exports to all world regions, except Africa, increased significantly but particularly to North America and Western Europe. By 1984, the United States recorded a $16 billion trade deficit in cars with Japan, a sectoral trade deficit that was nearly 50 per cent of the total ($35 billion). Car exports to the European Community had an even faster rate of growth.

The countries of North America and Western Europe responded to such dramatic increases in Japanese car exports with the policy of trade protection. So-called voluntary import agreements were made between Japan and most threatened countries. For example, the United States negotiated a voluntary agreement that Japanese car imports should take no more than 25 per cent of the market; in the United Kingdom, the level was 11 per cent, in France 3 per cent and in Italy imports were simply not permitted. Only West Germany seemed to allow for the relatively free entry of Japanese cars.

The protectionist reaction of the other industrial market economies to Japanese car imports has caused a definite reaction from most Japanese vehicle corporations. The reaction has been very simply one of locating plants within the protected markets. This has been particularly the case in the United States and Canada, and is occurring to a lesser extent within Europe. Table 10.2 shows that between 1982 and the end of

Table 10.1 Japanese car exports, 1974–84

Importing region	1974	1984	Rate of increase 1974–84
North America	796	1990	2.5
European Community	235	790	3.4
Other Europe	109	240	2.2
Asia	177	450	2.5
Oceania	225	230	1.0
Latin America	84	210	2.5
Africa	101	90	0.9
TOTAL	1700	4000	2.4

Table 10.2   The evolution of the production base of Japan's car companies in North America during the 1980s

Manufacturer	Location	Models	Capacity (1989)	Start-up
Honda	Marysville	Accord, Civic	320 000	Nov. 1982
Honda	Marysville, Ohio	Civic, Acura Integra	150 000	Aug. 1989
Honda	Anna, Ohio	Engines	90 000	Sep. 1986
Honda	Alliston, Ontario	Accord	80 000	Nov. 1986
Toyota/GM	Fremont, California	Chevrolet Nova Toyota FX	250 000	Dec. 1984
Toyota	Georgetown, Kentucky	Camry	200 000	Mid-1988
Toyota	Cambridge, Ontario	Corolla	50 000	Late 1988
Nissan	Smyrna, Tennessee	Pickup, Sentra	265 000	June 1983
Mazda	Flat Rock, Michigan	Mazda MX-6, Ford Probe	240 000	June 1987
Mitsubishi/Chrysler	Bloomington, Illinois	H24S Sports	240 000	Nov. 1988
Fuji/Isuzu	Lafayette, Indiana	Subaru 4WDs Isuzu 4WDs	120 000	Nov. 1989
Suzuki/GM	Ingersoll, Ontario	4WD Samurai Sprint	80 000 120 000	Apr. 1989

(*Source*: *Financial Times* Motor Industry Survey, 20/10/88)

1988, Japanese manufacturers have constructed plant with a combined annual capacity of 1 515 000 cars in the United States and of 130 000 in Canada. Figure 10.2 shows that with the exception of Mazda, most Japanese manufacturers have opted to locate away from the immediate environs of Detroit. Nevertheless, they have tended to locate their assembly plants in small towns within a one-day delivery distance of the Detroit region; the locational attraction of the Detroit region as a supplier of vehicle components can therefore still be seen to be operating, albeit in a regionally more decentralized form.

This massive plant building programme of seven Japanese manufacturers in North America constitutes the single most important shift in global car production during the 1980s. The use of Japanese process technology and organizational methods has rendered the United States a competitive location for motor car manufacturing in the late 1980s. Production of the first Japanese corporation to locate in the United States,

Honda, increased nearly six times between 1983 and 1987 (from 55 337 to 324 064). According to Nissan's head in Mexico, in 1987 production of vehicles in Mexico (with a 1987 wage rate one-tenth of that in the United States) was only 10 per cent cheaper than that in Nissan's Smyrna plant in Tennessee (Johns 1987).

THE THIRD WORLD CAR INDUSTRY: STRATEGIES FOR GROWTH

Therefore, the recent Japanese influence over the evolution of the world motor car industry has meant that costs of production have been declining due to new process technologies and organizational methods. Within this context of declining per unit costs of production, the single factor of low labour costs in less developed countries holds less and less attraction for the location of motor car assembly plants. In contrast to the recent surge of assembly plant construction in the United States, there has been no such com-

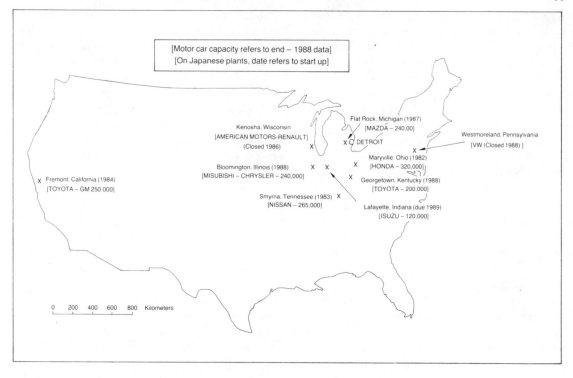

[Motor car capacity refers to end – 1988 data]
[On Japanese plants, date refers to start up]

Flat Rock, Michigan (1987)
[MAZDA – 240.00]

Kenosha, Wisconsin
[AMERICAN MOTORS-RENAULT]
(Closed 1986)

DETROIT

Westmoreland, Pennsylvania
[VW (Closed 1988)]

Maryville, Ohio (1982)
[HONDA – 320.000]

Bloomington, Illinois (1988)
[MISUBISHI – CHRYSLER – 240.000]

Georgetown, Kentucky (1988)
[TOYOTA – 200.000]

Fremont, California (1984)
[TOYOTA – GM 250 000]

Smyrna, Tennessee (1983)
[NISSAN – 265.000]

Lafayette, Indiana (due 1989)
[ISUZU – 120.000]

0   200   400   600   800   Kilometers

10.2   Japanese advance and European retreat in US car manufacturing during the 1980s.

parable growth of motor car assembly plants in the Third World. It appears that the optimistic framework that the 'world car' concept held out for the shift of motor vehicle assembly to Third World countries has been rendered obsolete by the considerable technological and organizational advances that continue to emanate from Japan. What then are the possibilities for Third World countries to establish export-oriented motor car industries?

From an examination of present trends, there seem to be three strategies that Third World countries could follow in terms of export-oriented growth:

1. A technological and financial link between a domestic corporation of a newly industrializing country and a Japanese multinational.
2. A joint venture between a domestic corporation of a newly industrializing country and a multinational vehicle corporation whose production strategies are still partially influenced by the concept of the 'world car'.
3. The granting of export incentives by Third

World governments to vehicle multinationals already operating in their territories.

Liaisons between domestic corporations and Japanese multinationals

It seems increasingly apparent that Third World car producers cannot just rely on traditional, labour-intensive assembly operations, particularly if they are to be prominent in export markets. According to Jones and Womack (1985: 405), if Third World countries are intent on developing an export-oriented motor vehicle industry: 'the objective should be to maximize the amount of wealth produced per worker using the state-of-the-art social organizational and production technology and to create jobs by expanding volume'. If this does not take place, Jones and Womack argue that the Third World countries would fall further behind in technological development and have even less chance of ever catching up. The implication of such an analysis must be that Third World motor car producers have to forge stronger links with Japanese vehicle multinationals, particularly in terms of technology transfer and new organizational methods. Because of the numbers of vehicle producers in Japan (nine), it should be possible for either private corporations in or the governments of Third World countries to negotiate such technological and organizational transfers with at least one Japanese multinational.

Third World countries can organize these technological and organizational linkages either through state-controlled corporations or through private conglomerates. The most successful private conglomerate from the Third World to organize and benefit from technological links with a Japanese multinational is undoubtedly Hyundai of Korea. Korea does have the advantage of low labour costs. In 1985, it was reported that 'an average assembly worker in South Korea earns US$2.45 an hour, less than one-fifth of a Japanese labourer's cost and one-tenth of the cost of a UAW member (in the United States)' (*The Economist* 2 March 1985). But Hyundai has not relied on this one international cost advantage only but has comprehensively invested in new process technology from Japan, mainly provided through Mitsubishi, which owns 15 per cent of the company.

Hyundai is Korea's largest private corporation with a wide variety of activities, ranging from shipbuilding.to construction. Its move into motor vehicles can almost be compared with that of the Japanese 'keiretsu'. Because of the small size of the Korean market (mid-1980s sales of 150 000 cars per annum), Hyundai has had to export in order to achieve any reasonable economies of scale. In the early 1980s it was able to export small amounts of cars to such diverse countries as Canada, Chile and the United Kingdom.

Its breakthrough as a major exporter, however, came in 1986 when it entered the US market and managed to sell as many as 168 882 cars in its first year. It should be mentioned that such unprecedented first-year car sales were closely linked to US protectionism restricting car shipments from Japan (to 25 per cent of the US market). Following the protective restrictions, the Japanese moved up market (as US quotas were fixed by reference to number of cars, not value) and thus left a gap for low-priced, small but quality cars.

Hyundai supplied its small but well-equipped front-wheel drive Pony Excel and recorded what can only be called dramatic growth in the US market; sales in the US market increased a further 56 per cent in 1987 to reach 263 000 cars. Furthermore, Hyundai has experienced considerable market growth in the Canadian market. As a result of such remarkable export growth, Hyundai's productive capacity has gone up from 150 000 in 1984 to 700 000 in 1988 (Gooding 1987).

However, it should be emphasized that such growth in production and exports has been closely linked to both the advanced product design and process technology that Hyundai has been able to employ and in which Mitsubishi has figured prominently. In particular, Mitsubishi has been of major assistance with the transfer of both engine and transmission technology. Now, in terms of quantities produced, Hyundai is nearly entering the first division of world car producers. One further indication of this has been its decision to build a 100 000-unit assembly plant near Montreal in order to become a true vehicle multinational with a productive base in North America; indeed, production started in 1989, although only the first stage of the plant has been built with an annual capacity of 30 000 vehicles.

There are certain similarities between Korea and the newest Far East exporter of motor vehicles, Malaysia. One crucial difference is that whereas Korea's growth in motor vehicle production has been mainly executed through the agency of a large private conglomerate, in Malaysia the government has taken a key role. The Malaysian motor vehicle company, Proton, is 70 per cent owned by the Malaysian government. The remaining 30 per cent contribution comes again from the Japanese multinational, Mitsubishi. Mitsubishi has been very significant in providing the technology, structuring the organization (including quality circles) and designing the production process at Proton's large assembly plant, eight miles outside Kuala Lumpur. Flexible, automated body welding has been preferred despite the supposed locational advantages of low labour costs. The cars produced are heavily based on Mitsubishi designs (most notably the Colt). The Malaysian Proton has preferential access to the markets of the South-East Asian countries that belong to ASEAN. Furthermore, the company is trying to export to both Western Europe and the United States (entry into the European market is being organized via a British distributor, based in Wythall near Birmingham).

It is too early to judge the success of the Malaysian producer, Proton, in its attempt to enter foreign markets. However, the success of Hyundai in becoming such a major exporter to the North American market in the late 1980s may set the model for any Third World vehicle corporation aiming at international markets. As a result, and linking in with the policy recommendations of the MIT report on the future of the automobile, it would appear that private and state vehicle corporations from developing countries should attempt to form technological and financial links with Japanese corporations.

Joint ventures between domestic corporations and 'world car' multinationals

Due to the popularity of the 'world car' concept in the late 1970s and early 1980s, there are at least two corporations that have forged technological and financial links with the two major proponents of the 'world car' concept, GM and Ford. They are the Korean conglomerates, Daewoo and Kia respectively. However, it should be stressed that the Korean corporations do have links with Japanese vehicle technology through their partners – GM owns 34 per cent of Isuzu and 5 per cent of Suzuki, and Ford owns 25 per cent of Mazda.

Daewoo's venture into motor vehicle production is perhaps the clearest example of the 'world car' concept boosting car production in Third World countries. Daewoo is in a 50/50 joint venture with General Motors. The joint venture is now selling a cheap Korean-made car in North America as a Pontiac Le Mans. The design is derived from the Opel Kadett produced by GM's German subsidiary with technological improvements provided by GM's Japanese affiliate, Isuzu. This particular case of a European-designed car, incorporating Japanese process technology, being built in a Third World country, primarily aimed at the North American market and all orchestrated by the world's largest vehicle corporation is the best example yet of the optimistic framework provided by the 'world car' concept for increasing vehicle production in Third World countries.

A new car production plant with an annual capacity of 167 000 vehicles is being completed in Korea in order to meet these demands. It will give Daewoo a total annual capacity of approximately 250 000 cars. GM also hopes to use the Daewoo operation to export vehicles throughout East Asia and to produce cheap mechanical parts. A deal was signed with Daewoo to make starter motors and alternators for GM's worldwide operations in 1985 (*The Economist* 1985b: 15). However, Daewoo has had considerably less marketing success in the all-important US market than Hyundai during 1988. In the first eight months of 1988, Daewoo's exports to the United States were only 46 000 against 255 000 for the same period for Hyundai despite the fact that the Pontiac Le Mans has been distributed through the extensive GM dealer network; the fact that the Pontiac Le Mans has been priced at a higher level than the Hyundai Excel may be a partial explanation (Ford 1988: 11).

Seeing General Motors expanding rapidly in Korea has brought out a classic example of oligopolistic reaction (Gwynne 1979b) from Ford. In 1986, Ford paid US$30 million for a 10 per cent shareholding in Kia 'to show how serious was its intention of drawing that company into its global strategy' and opened a Korean branch office of Ford International Business Development in order to 'develop sources for automotive components in South Korea' (Gooding 1986: 12). With Ford's new capital input and technological assistance from Mazda, Kia has expanded its annual productive capacity to 300 000 units per year. Indeed, during the first eight months of 1988, Kia exported slightly more vehicles (48 000) to the key US market than Daewoo (Ford 1988: 11).

Although Daewoo and Kia have major capital participation from GM and Ford, the importance of the respective links with Isuzu and Mazda has meant that both car assemblers have incorporated

Japanese process technology and organizational methods into their operations. Together with Hyundai, they constitute the three major Third World vehicle corporations (with 50 per cent or more local ownership). As a result of the ambitious export-oriented investment plans of these three corporations, by the end of the 1980s, Korea had the potential capacity to produce 1.2 million vehicles a year.

Furthermore, high local content agreements mean that such growth should be passed on to the diversified components sector. However, here again there is evidence of considerable technological and financial linkages between Korean companies and Japanese components producers. 'In 1982, there were 57 technological cooperations and 17 joint ventures involving major automotive components. These cooperative arrangements had allowed the industry to make the quantum leap from churning out labour intensive replacement parts to complex, state of the art original equipment manufacturing processes' (King 1986: 8).

At present, it could be argued that South Korea and its motor vehicle industry stands as the exception – the only Third World country to genuinely develop a motor vehicle industry geared primarily to export markets. The country has followed a combination of the first two strategies that we noted as open to Third World countries in developing their motor vehicle industries. Other countries, however, have had less control over the development of their motor vehicle industry – and less incorporation of state-of-the-art technology that Jones and Womack saw as so important for the nascent vehicle industries of Third World countries.

Export Incentives for Car Multinationals

The analysis of locational shifts in the world motor car industry during the 1960s and early 1970s tended to be dominated by the increasing significance of economies of scale. During the late 1970s and 1980s, the ability to attain and successfully incorporate state-of-the-art technology has become a much more significant underlying factor. However, in Latin America, the period of expansion in the motor car sector was very much

during the 1960s and early 1970s. In that period, Latin America offered the continental perspective of economic growth, expanding markets, and considerable capital inflow – three factors that attracted multinational vehicle corporations to invest in large plants in the larger countries and thus benefit from significant economies of scale (Gwynne 1978a).

However, the late 1970s and 1980s have, in general, brought a dismal development period to Latin America. Stagnant economies, declining markets and considerable capital outflow mean that the previous favourable trends have been totally reversed. Latin American governments have been faced with the primary need of expanding exports in order to register large trade surpluses that can go some way to paying the huge annual debt repayments that the debt crisis has effectively signified. With declining internal markets for motor cars, governments have turned to the vehicle multinationals to assist in the national need to increase exports by reorienting their spare capacity to international markets. In order to encourage them, they have been prepared to give considerable export incentives to the multinationals. This is the general background to the third strategy of promoting vehicle exports from Third World countries. However, for most Latin American countries, the vehicle industry was always too high cost for any serious possibility of a reorientation towards international markets (Gwynne 1978). Such reorientation has basically been restricted to two countries, Brazil and Mexico, both of which provide contrasting scenarios in the late 1980s.

Recent export trends in Brazil

The Brazilian government had begun to require export commitments from its vehicle multinationals as far back as 1972 with the negotiation of the first of the Special Fiscal Benefits for Exports (BEFIEX) programmes with Ford. One of the major privileges that car multinationals received from the scheme was the reduction in the very high levels of local content that they previously had to comply with – from 99 to 85 per cent. Under BEFIEX, vehicle exporters were also eligible for a number of special tax incentives and exemptions from restrictions on imports. Reductions of between 70 and 90 per cent of the Industrial Products Tax on imported equipment and up to 50 per cent of the tax on imported raw materials, components and intermediate products were offered.

> The pressure which forced firms to take up the BEFIEX programme was the control of the Brazilian Council for Industrial Development over the authorization of investment and its ability to offer attractive incentives to the manufacturers. The initial agreement with Ford was signed when the company wished to expand in Brazil through the introduction of the Maverick. In 1973 Volkswagen, worried about the impact of the Maverick on its market share, entered the **BEFIEX programme in order to introduce a new** model (Jenkins 1987a: 193).

By 1978 almost all the car multinationals in Brazil had signed BEFIEX agreements. In addition, firms were able to benefit from the general fiscal incentives for manufactured exports introduced in the late 1960s and early 1970s. The most important of these were the exemption from the state sales tax in 1967 and the introduction of a tax credit for the industrial products tax in 1969. The total value of incentives received by the industry was 62 per cent of the value of exports in 1971 and 67 per cent in 1975 (Jenkins 1987). Meanwhile, the traditional investment incentives available to the car industry, apart from those related to an export commitment, were all withdrawn in 1974. According to Mericle (1984: 28), 'the message to the automobile producers was clear; any major future expansion was contingent on a commitment to export'.

As a result, Brazil had already begun to record a rapid growth in vehicle exports during the late 1970s and early 1980s. Vehicle exports rose gradually from 13 528 in 1972 to 70 026 in 1977 but then increased rapidly to reach 213 266 in 1981. This 1981 export figure represented 27.3 per cent of all vehicles manufactured in Brazil in that year. The majority of these vehicles were exported to other Third World countries, not only in Latin America but also in Africa and the Middle East; Volkswagen was particularly prominent as an exporter to Third World countries.

However, exports of finished vehicles to other less developed countries proved highly volatile.

Whereas 1981 proved a highly successful year with 213 266 vehicles worth US$1227 million being exported, the following year saw increasing problems of debt and recession in the Third World and a concomitant drop in Brazil's vehicle exports to 173 254 vehicles, worth nearly one-third less (US$887 million). Nevertheless, the Brazilian government did benefit in the early 1980s from the buoyant exports of Brazil's four vehicle multinationals (Volkswagen, General Motors, Ford, Fiat). In 1981 Brazil's exports signified a large trade surplus on the motor industry account of over US$1.5 billion.

During the early 1980s, the Brazilian motor vehicle industry was undoubtedly the largest in the Third World, producing an average of nearly 1 million vehicles a year. Its large market, that reaches to over 1 million vehicles a year during times of economic prosperity, has been a major attraction to the automobile multinationals. The only multinational to be allowed in after the 1950s, Fiat, certainly saw it that way. After closing down its plants in Argentina, Chile and Colombia in 1982, a difficult loss-making year for its worldwide operations, Vittorio Ghidela, the head of Fiat's world operations, said: 'The key country in the South American car business will continue to be Brazil and we are determined to stay there, even if the losses continue' (Gwynne 1985).

However, the late 1980s must inevitably have brought second thoughts from the top executives of vehicle multinationals. The problems of Brazil's debt crisis, the mismanagement of the economy and economic stagnation have severely reduced Brazil's internal market for cars – from nearly 1 million vehicles per annum in the late 1970s to 330 000 in 1987. Almost all these cars are powered by alcohol engines, a technological development that has been rendered idiosyncratic and inappropriate for export by the reduction in the oil price during the 1980s. It seems that Brazil's severe economic problems will continue until at least the mid-1990s with the corollary that the domestic vehicle market will remain at only one-third of its former level.

For the multinationals themselves, increasing exports has become a matter of survival for their Brazilian subsidiaries. In April 1987, an agreement was struck between the government and the three Brazilian vehicle subsidiaries (in November 1986, Ford and Volkswagen merged their Brazilian operations to form Autolatina). The vehicle subsidiaries were worried about their increasing losses in Brazil (due to price controls) as well as their increasingly low capacity utilization. Under the deal, the government conceded regular price rises every 30 to 40 days to combat double digit monthly inflation. In return, the manufacturers undertook to invest about US$1 billion by the end of 1989 in order to raise export sales to US$7.4 and thus leave a US$4.5 billion trade surplus on the motor vehicle account after imports. However, the agreement has subsequently been the focus of much conflict between the multinationals and the government; in 1987, Autolatina took the government to court for breaching the terms of the agreement.

It seems unlikely, therefore, that the planned US$1 billion of investment will be forthcoming. Such investment is, however, vital both for the multinationals and Brazil. The technological level of the Brazilian motor vehicle industry is rapidly falling behind not only that of the developed world but also that of such East Asian countries as Korea and Malaysia. The year 1987, in fact, was the first year that Korea (790 000) produced more vehicles than Brazil (683 000). The Brazilian industry is increasingly relying on just two locational factors – low labour costs and cheap steel. However, such cost advantages will only have limited applicability in the future unless considerable new investment is made in process technology.

In the meantime, the three vehicle companies have been moderately successful at increasing their vehicle exports. In 1987, an estimated 353 000 vehicles were exported or 51.6 per cent of total production, making 1987 the first year in which production for export was greater than that for internal demand. In contrast to the early 1980s, the majority of these exports now go to the developed world. Fiat uses its Brazilian subsidiary as a supplier of small cars to the European market. Autolatina and GM orient their exports more to the North American market. In particular, the Volkswagen Fox (made in Brazil as the Voyage) has been particulary successful at the

low end of the United States market; indeed, the success of the Brazilian-made Fox relative to the US-made Golfs and Jettas in the US market was one reason why Volkswagen closed its Pennsylvania plant at the end of 1988 (see Fig. 10.2).

However, most Brazilian vehicle exports to developed world markets are now at the lower, cheaper end of the vehicle range. Although this continues to be a market niche for Brazilian exports in the late 1980s, competition from Korea is already making this a highly competitive market segment. In the meantime, the considerable export incentives and subsidies from the Brazilian government combined with the necessity for multinationals to find new markets in the face of a collapsing home market has temporarily made Brazil a major Third World exporter of vehicles. For such a short-term trend to become long term, however, major new investments are required, particularly in process technology and organizational methods.

Recent export trends in Mexico

One reason why it was believed that the product life cycle model would not apply to the motor vehicle industry was due to the importance of transport costs in the sector's cost structure. However, on that basis, Mexico, located the other side of the Rio Grande from the world's most dominant economy, should enjoy considerable locational advantages. Furthermore, the Mexican government has attempted to promote both vehicle and components exports ever since 1969 when an agreement was signed between Mexico's Industrial Ministry and the leading multinationals producing there. Under this agreement, the multinationals would have to steadily increase their vehicle and component exports, with the long-term aim of fully compensating their imports by exports (Bennett and Sharpe 1985: 164). In 1977, this was set for 1982.

However, the oil boom of the late 1970s and early 1980s rendered this policy complicated as the multinationals found it difficult to keep up with the rapid increase in internal demand during this period. The onset of the debt crisis in 1982, the ensuing recession and severe drop in the oil price has, however, changed the feasibility of the policy. After Mexico's vehicle exports (mainly components) climbed slowly between 1972 and 1982 (from US$52.5 million to US$531 million), they increased more than five fold in the following five years to US$2763 million in 1987 (see Table 10.3).

Vehicle parts rather than finished vehicles have constituted the majority of exports in Mexico's vehicle sector since the early 1970s (see Table 10.3). Indeed, even in 1985, the export of vehicle parts constituted approximately 90 per cent of the sector's exports. Mexico, therefore, provides a major contrast with Brazil, because the multinationals have primarily used it as a source for parts and components, particularly engines and gearboxes, rather than finished vehicles. One important reason for this is that the three North American companies operating in Mexico (General Motors, Ford and Chrysler) have used their Mexican bases in order to export parts back to Detroit or to other plants in their worldwide operations (as well as to comply with Mexican government regulations). Table 10.4 shows the extent of new investment by the US automobile corporations in Mexico during the 1970s and 1980s. One point to note is that the capacity of engine plants has been much greater than that of assembly plants.

The older assembly plants based either in Mexico City or within a radius of 150 kilometres of the metropolis have been mainly geared to the national market (see Fig. 10.3). The small pre-1960s plants within Mexico City have subsequently changed their function to the production of either commercial vehicles or components. The second stage plants of the 1960s, spatially more decentralized, have been mainly geared towards producing cars for the domestic market. However, the plants of Chrysler (in Toluca) and Nissan (in Cuernavaca) have been successfully reoriented towards producing for export. In 1987, Chrysler exported about 63 000 cars (38.5 per cent of total Mexican car exports) and Nissan about 16 000 (10 per cent of car exports).

The other three plants of the 1960s generation had only limited exports. However, in the case of General Motors and Ford, this was largely because exports now emanate from specially designed plants in the north of Mexico (see Table 10.4 and Fig. 10.3). Ford's new US$500 million assembly plant in Hermosillo, opened in November 1986 and building the Tracer model for the North American market, provides a clear example of a major Mexican assembly plant being primar-

Table 10.3 Performance of Mexican vehicle exports, 1972–88

Year	No. of export vehicles	% Share of production	Value (US$ million)			Trade balance (US$ million)
			Vehicles	Parts	Total	
1972	2 212	1.0	5.7	46.8	52.5	−225.7
1973	20 141	7.0	40.4	80.2	120.6	−231.3
1974	19 117	5.4	44.7	104.9	148.9	−356.1
1975	2 938	0.9	8.7	113.3	122.0	−628.3
1976	4 172	1.3	18.4	173.9	192.3	−526.4
1977	11 743	4.2	30.0	223.5	253.5	−385.4
1978	25 828	6.7	67.9	266.0	333.9	−559.1
1979	24 756	5.5	116.8	260.0	376.8	−1 049.5
1980	18 245	3.7	128.6	275.8	404.4	−1 498.8
1981	14 428	2.4	107.3	263.0	370.3	−2 148.3
1982	15 819	3.4	81.2	449.8	531.0	−816.5
1983	22 456	7.9	113.3	551.1	664.4	+314.4
1984	33 635	9.5	180.8	733.0	913.8	+280.3
1985	58 423	12.9	115.3	1 013.9	1 129.2	+421.7
1986	72 429	21.4	314.0	806.8	1 120.8	+782.5
1987	163 073	41.4	1 127.6	1 635.5	2 763.1	+2 290.1
1988	173 147	33.9				

(*Sources*: Asociación Mexicana de la Industria Automotriz (1988) *La Industria Automotriz de Mexico en Cifras*; Jenkins (1987a))

Table 10.4   Investments of US car corporations in Mexico, 1970–86

Corporation	Location	Product	Capacity	Investment (US$ million)
Ford	Chihuahua	Engine	500 000	445
Ford	Hermosillo	Assembly	130 000	500
Ford	Saltillo	Aluminium cylinder heads	860 000	n.d.
GM	Ramos Arizpe	Engine	400 000	300
GM	Ramos Arizpe	Assembly	100 000	
Chrysler	Ramos Arizpe	Engine	400 000	125

(*Source*: Adapted from Jenkins 1987a: 219)

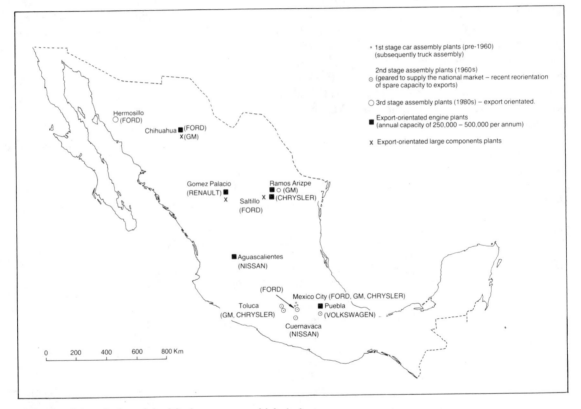

10.3   Spatial evolution of the Mexican motor vehicle industry.

ily geared to the US market. Both the product and the process technology were designed by Ford's Japanese partner, Mazda, and thus represents one of the first technologically advanced plants in Mexico. The plant has a capacity for 130 000 vehicles per annum but in 1987 only 60 000 were produced, mainly for the United States.

In contrast, the engine plants were constructed with a view to producing for the world market from the outset and thus they were not constrained by the limited size of the domestic market. It was thus possible to take advantage of economies of scale and construct plants with capacities around the minimum efficient scale. The capacity of Ford's engine plant at Chihuahua and the engine plants of General Motors and Chrysler at Ramos

Arizpe, near Monterrey, 'compare favourably with most estimates of the scale of plant necessary to take advantage of scale economies' (Jenkins 1987a: 218). Furthermore, these plants are equipped with modern technology and new machinery. 'The General Motors engine plant in Ramos Arizpe uses automatic transfer machines and is comparable in terms of its technological level to equivalent plants in the United States. Labour productivity is three times as high as the average productivity in previously existing engine plants in Mexico' (Jenkins 1987a: 218).

Meanwhile, the US producers in Mexico benefit from labour rates nearly one-tenth the US level – in approximate terms, a labour rate of $1 per hour in Mexico as opposed to $10 per hour in the United States, in 1986 (Gardner 1987). High labour productivity levels (due to new machinery), low labour costs and low transport costs to the US market are thus making a Mexican location attractive to the US producers. The fact that fiscal incentives have been used by the Mexican government to persuade the multinationals to come and that these incentives can be worth 'almost half the value of exports' (Jenkins 1987a: 216) means that the Mexican location has also become a highly profitable one.

The potential advantages of Mexican proximity to the United States for components and engine production had also been recognized by the non-US firms operating in Mexico. In the last decade Volkswagen has built a large four-cylinder engine plant (400 000 per annum capacity) near its Puebla base, Nissan has completed an engine and stamping plants in Aguascalientes with an annual capacity of 350 000 engines and Renault has built sizeable engine (250 000 per annum capacity) and suspensions (300 000 per annum capacity) plants in the northern location of Gomez Palacio, near Torreón. These plants used to be closely linked to production in the United States – indeed, in 1987, Nissan exported 70 000 engines from its plant at Aguascalientes to the Nissan assembly plant in Smyrna, Tennessee (1987 production of 177 334). However, since the closure of the Volkswagen and Renault car plants in the United States, Mexican engine production is now principally geared to European and world markets. As with plants of the US corporations, these plants enjoy maximum

benefits from economies of scale and employ the latest technology in order to achieve high labour productivity. As a result, Mexican engines are being supplied to the world network of all three multinationals as well as giving a potential cost-saving boost to local assembly.

However, Mexico's future as a manufacturer of vehicles may still be limited due to the lack of new technology in the assembly sector (apart from Ford's Hermosillo plant and GM's plant in Ramos Arizpe). As with Brazil, the multinationals set up plants in Mexico principally for access to the internal market. During the years of the oil boom, production of finished vehicles for the internal market increased rapidly reaching 581 000 in 1981. By 1986, however, production for the internal market had declined to 258 000. In that year, one of the six multinationals producing in Mexico, Renault, closed down its assembly plant at Hidalgo. The Mexican vehicle market is now divided up between Nissan (28.3 per cent in 1987), Volkswagen (22.8 per cent), General Motors (16.5 per cent), Chrysler (16.1 per cent in its only plant outside the United States) and Ford (13.7 per cent). However, with some exceptions, Mexican assembly plants have not been extensively modernized. Technology is labour intensive but the low wage rates of Mexico are often not sufficient compensation in terms of international competition. According to the head of Nissan's Mexican operations in 1987, Mr Shoichi Amemeiya, 'the costs of producing a Nissan vehicle in Mexico, in spite of lower labour costs, is only 10 per cent less than in the US and slightly more expensive than in Japan' (Johns 1987). In Nissan's case, such relatively high costs of production occur despite low wage rates, the incorporation of quality circles and the employment of 700 Japanese staff in Nissan Mexicana. Mr Shoichi Amemiya attributed the latter to the following: 'If you train and motivate [Mexican workers] they can be very good workers – with the quality of good soldiers but not sergeants or petty officers. Something extra is needed to cope with technological change' (Johns 1987).

The Mexican motor vehicle industry thus makes an interesting contrast to both Brazil and Korea. It has traditionally been a major exporter of components rather than the finished vehicle itself. However, in the late 1980s, it is gradually turning into a significant exporter of finished vehicles. Compared to Brazil, there has been considerably more investment during the 1980s, investment furthermore in technologically advanced plant. However, the majority of Mexico's exports in the motor vehicle sector still correspond to the components sector. In contrast to both Korea and Brazil, vehicle exports continue to be secondary to those of components. Recent investment plans by the leading multinationals (now further benefiting from Mexico's debt–equity scheme) and component manufacturers point to this continuing specialization. External financing from the World Bank and Japan's Import–Export Bank are also focusing on components for further expansion. Meanwhile, GM and Chrysler in particular are increasing the number of components plants along the Mexican border where they benefit from duty exemptions (see Ch. 7).

TECHNOLOGICAL DIVERGENCE: THIRD WORLD AS MARGINAL PRODUCER

At the beginning of this chapter, the spatial development of the motor car industry in the Third World was placed within the context of its technological future, and, in particular, two views of this future. One view of the future saw motor car production being geared to achieving maximum economies of scale and reducing costs; low labour-cost locations in the Third World seemed theoretically attractive to multinational producers within this perspective. A rival view of the future saw changing production processes and work practices, combined with increasing use of computer-aided manufacturing as keeping most car manufacturing in the developed countries.

Our survey of recent corporate development has demonstrated that the latter view seems to have been the more correct forecast for the 1980s. The analysis of the Third World motor car industry demonstrated that only three less developed countries have managed to develop car industries with a strong export performance. However, the reasons behind the export success of these countries are different.

The explanation for the original growth of the car industry in Brazil lies in that country's large market and the interest of US and European multinationals in producing for that market. The recent export growth in the car sector is closely linked to subsequent attempts by government to make the multinationals export. However, future growth of the Brazilian industry would now seem difficult if the explanation of Volkswagen's worldwide sales director, Werner Schmidt, behind the decision to merge Volkswagen and Ford in Brazil and Argentina into one company, Autolatina, is taken seriously: 'We think it will take so long for the Brazilian economy to recover, it is best not to wait another 20 years before taking some action' (Gooding 1986). With the Brazilian market likely to be declining for the next decade, the future growth of Brazil's car sector now relies squarely on exports. However, to achieve sustained export growth into the 1990s, considerable investment in new process technology will be required.

Massive investment in motor vehicle plants has only been taking place in the other two countries, Mexico and Korea, during the late 1980s. In Korea, it seems that strategies of linkage with Japanese multinationals have been particularly significant, particularly in the case of Hyundai. The other two vehicle corporations of Korea, Daewoo and Kia, have, however, registered links with Japanese vehicle technology through their North American partners, General Motors and Ford respectively. Furthermore, they have theoretically benefited from direct access to the US market through the distribution networks of GM and Ford. If the successful linking with both Japanese technology and 'world car' corporations of the United States can explain Korean success, Mexican success is inevitably linked to its spatial proximity to the US market. Three US, two European and one Japanese corporation have heavily invested in export-oriented plant in Mexico as a result – mainly in component production but recently in vehicle assembly as well. Again, links with Japanese multinationals seem to be increasing through the US multinationals – with Mazda via Ford, Isuzu via GM and Mitsubishi via Chrysler.

The motor vehicle industry remains strongly market oriented. The most dramatic locational shift in the industry, that of Japanese productive growth, has been caused by technological advances in product design and production process rather than any consideration of labour costs. As a result, the product life cycle would appear to have little relevance for the industry and its locational future. The motor vehicle is not a standardized product with a standardized technology. Rather, it is an industry continually open to change in product design, process technology and organizational methods and most particularly in the 1980s. According to the MIT report, only the location of standardized parts such as starters, lighting and suspensions would shift to Third World countries in the future due to the attraction of lower labour costs.

Therefore, in terms of the expansion of the industry into Third World countries, the future looks difficult. From the argument that has been presented, it appears that the motor vehicle industry may grow in large markets (such as Brazil), technologically dynamic countries with their own diversified multinationals (Korea) or in countries located near to core country markets (Mexico). Unfortunately, apart from Mexico, there is no Third World country adjacent to a core country. In Europe, the nearest comparison has been Spain which the multinationals (General Motors, Ford, Volkswagen, Peugeot and Renault) have identified as the low-cost producer of small cars for the European market. Third World countries may be able to maintain assembly operations but a genuine development of an export-oriented industry seems difficult, particularly for small countries with small markets. Even for large markets, such as India and China, future growth in vehicle production will be limited unless exports can rapidly increase. At present, however, the world motor vehicle industry is characterized by spatial retrenchment, increasing its concentration in the industrial market economies of North America, Europe and Japan. In global terms, the Third World seems set to be a marginal producer of cars, at least into the foreseeable future. However, if the motor vehicle industry is to expand in Third World countries, it cannot pretend to rely on the locational attractions of low labour costs alone. As in South Korea, the emphasis must always be on improving technological sophistication, not only in terms of product design but also as regards the manufacturing processes employed.

—PART IV—

CONTINENTAL PERSPECTIVES

11

LATIN AMERICA: THE HERITAGE OF INWARD-ORIENTED INDUSTRIALIZATION

In the following three chapters, the aim is to examine Third World industrialization from a continental perspective. The purpose in not to attempt a comprehensive survey, but rather to explore continental themes of industrialization. In this chapter on Latin America, the aim is to examine the impact of a largely inward-oriented process of industialization.

THE ORIGINS AND NATURE OF INWARD ORIENTATION

The origins of inward orientation in Latin American manufacturing can be firmly traced back to the Depression and crisis in world trade that developed so rapidly between 1929 and 1933. Before 1929, Latin American economies had been characterized by free trade, but the world trade crisis caused Latin American governments to radically rethink their philosophies of political economy. Latin American exports declined from an average of about US$5000 million in 1928–29 to US$1500 million in 1933, causing grave problems with balance of payments and foreign exchange shortages.

Latin American governments found themselves able to finance decreasing amounts of imported manufactured goods from the industrial countries. As a result various measures were taken to conserve and ration decreased foreign exchange resources. Tariffs were raised by most countries, import quotas were enforced and restrictions placed on the use of foreign exchange. An array of policies was developed out of the crisis, and an administrative machinery established to carry them out. In general terms, Latin America changed from a set of free-trade economies to one of highly protected economies, Tariffs, quotas and exchange controls provided protection from foreign competitors by making the entry of foreign goods expensive or impossible. Latin American entrepreneurs, observing the scarcity of goods and the level of protection, began to produce or increase the domestic production of goods previously imported.

Such a strategy of industrial development behind high protective tariffs continued to be followed in most Latin American countries after the adverse effects of the Depression had diminished. It was noted that all major industrial countries had industrialized behind high protective tariffs. It was further argued that a country needed to develop a mature industrial structure before it could become involved in the free trading of industrial goods. As a result, protective policies promoted a wide rather than a specialized range of industries. More and more industrial sectors came to be protected due to the infant industry argument: the idea that national firms need to learn new product and process technologies slowly and without the threat of international competition reducing their profits or indeed causing losses. At a time of rapid growth in both national populations and labour markets, protection towards industry was also favoured for reasons of employment.

Due to such perceived advantages of protection for industrial development, protective policies were maintained after the Second World War and in the 1950s became formalized in the policy known as 'import substitution industrialization' (ISI). Adherents of the policy, which included the influential United Nations Economic Commission for Latin America, came to envisage the policy in essentially four stages of industial development. The first stage concentrated on the production of basic non-durable consumer goods such as textiles, foodstuffs and pharmaceuticals. This was to be followed by a second stage in which specialization would turn to more complex products, known as consumer durables, such as cookers, radios, televisions and motor vehicles. Both the technology and parts for these products had to be imported at the outset, although it was hoped, that in time, the domestic generation of technology and a national supply of components would take over. This provided the link with the third and fourth stages of the model. The third stage promoted intermediate industries. On the one hand, this signified the development of large-scale 'feedstock' plants manufacturing steel, petrochemicals, aluminium and so on. On the other hand, it necessitated the development of a wide range of parts and component plants, supplying the consumer goods industries. The final stage of the policy planned to develop domestic technology through the capital goods industry, responsible for manufacturing machinery and plant.

Characteristics of Inward Orientation

As ISI progressed through the 1950s and 1960s, it became clear that the policy was more suitable for large than for small countries. Industries in the smaller countries of Latin America came to be characterized by high costs and consequently high prices because their markets were too small.

High costs and high prices made possible by high protective tariffs were due to a wide variety of factors, but one key structural problem was the lack of economies of scale in producing for small markets, particularly in the critical second

and third stages of the import substitution process. It has already been noted in Chapter 8, that as production increases in any operation, unit costs normally decline as fixed costs (plant and technology, for example) are spread over more and more units. The decline in units costs with increased production slackens and evens out at some stage (known as the minimum efficient scale) before perhaps rising as output increases still further. Figure 11.1 shows the notional relationship between output of a vehicle assembly operation and per unit costs in Latin America. The minimum efficient scale is reached at approximately 200 000 vehicles per annum but there is a low per unit cost penalty for annual output between 100 000 and 200 000.

The example of the motor vehicle industry can demonstrate the relationship between economies of scale and actual production levels in Latin America. Table 11.1 shows vehicle output in each producing country by firm for 1977, about twenty years after import substitution legislation had started to attract assembly firms to most Latin American countries; these assembly firms were either subsidiaries of the multinational vehicle corporations or national firms holding the licence of one of these corporations. From Table 11.1, it is evident that the assembly plant economies illustrated in Fig. 11.1 were only achieved by firms

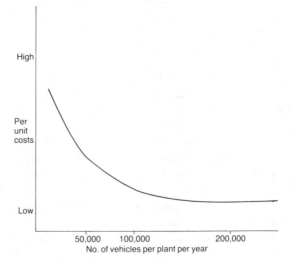

11.1   Notional relationship between output of a vehicle assembly operation and per unit costs in Latin America.

Table 11.1 Distribution of motor vehicle production by country and firm in Latin America, 1977

	Argentina	Brazil	Chile	Colombia	Mexico	Peru	Venezuela	Total	%
Chrysler	23 434	21 970	—	8 275	57 956	7 169	32 430	151 234	9.1
Fiat	47 837	77 963	3 120	4 128	—	—	4 889	137 937	8.3
Ford	56 795	130 197	—	—	50 503	—	61 665	299 160	17.9
General Motors	20 897	153 836	2 124	—	34 638	—	32 281	243 776	14.6
Renault	34 744	—	2 568	17 353	27 559	—	5 153	87 377	5.2
Volkswagen	—	472 192	—	—	52 143	6 075	5 340	535 750	32.1
Others	51 649	63 084	5 277	—	58 014	11 980	21 539	211 543	12.8
TOTAL	235 356	919 242	13 089	29 756	280 813	25 224	163 297	166 677	100.0
Percentage	14.1	55.2	0.8	1.8	16.8	1.5	9.8	100.0	

operating in Brazil (Volkswagen, General Motors, Ford and Fiat). Other countries had firms whose annual level of production was below 100 000 and therefore incurred significant cost penalties. As a result, high-cost cars were being produced and sold to national consumers. A detailed cost analysis of the Chilean motor vehicle industry in 1969 demonstrated that cars were produced at up to three times the cost in the vehicle's country of origin (Gwynne 1978b). Cars in both Argentina and Venezuela (Gwynne 1979a) were being sold at double international levels in the late 1970s.

Such high prices and high costs were not solely the result of a lack of sufficient economies of scale in the assembly of vehicles. In order to promote certain stage three industries, many governments instituted schemes whereby assembly firms had to purchase increasing quantities of nationally produced components. The Brazilian decree of 1956 forced assemblers to increase the proportion of domestically produced components to 99 per cent by weight for cars by 1961. The Argentine decree of 1959 made any firm importing more than 10 per cent of the value of a car after 1964 pay stiff customs penalties, while the Mexican and Chilean decrees of 1962 required about 60 per cent of the direct costs of vehicles to be accounted for through national production by 1964 and 1968 respectively.

However, components production can require an even greater level of production than vehicle assembly in order to achieve maximum economies of scale. Modern engine and transmission plants attain maximum economies of scale at annual production levels of 500 000 per annum (although cost penalties are not too great once 100 000 per annum levels are reached). As by the late 1970s only Brazilian assembly firms could offer such a level of demand, much of the Latin American motor vehicle industry has been characterized by small-scale plants manufacturing high-cost components for assemblers producing at high cost due to low economies of scale and selling to a restricted local market, itself limited in extent due to the high prices of the finished vehicle. Such characteristics were particularly harmful during periods of recession when falling demand could start a downward spiral of lower economies of scale, higher costs, higher prices and further reductions in demand.

Developing in the 1960s and 1970s, the motor vehicle industry was critical in the process of ISI. As an assembly industry, it produced one of the more sophisticated goods of the second stage. However, in terms of government planning, its critical role was to develop a variety of components industries which, through backward linkage, would create additonal demand for the national production of such basic goods as steel, alloys, aluminium, plastics and glass. Its eventual high cost in the smaller countries of Latin America caused scepticism about the applicability of import substitution for the efficient production of more sophisticated products and for the ability of ISI to advance further than stage one without the aid of very high tariffs.

For smaller countries, one possible solution to the restrictions of low demand and low economies of scale was for countries to group together and form, through a process of economic integration, a much larger market. The Central American

Common Market (CACM) created in 1960 and consisting of Guatemala, El Salvador, Nicaragua, Costa Rica and Honduras gave manufacturers a market of 10 million, up to ten times larger than previous national markets. In 1969, five Andean countries (Chile, Bolivia, Peru, Ecuador and Colombia) formed the Andean Pact. The main motivator in its formation was Chile whose industrial development through import substitution has been severely constrained by small market size. The prospect of an enlarged market of 70 million attracted all five countries and later Venezuela in 1973.

One of the key industrial programmes of the Andean Pact concerned the manufacture of cars – the Andean Group Automobile Programme, passed finally in 1977 after Chile had left (Gwynne 1980, Jenkins 1987a: 198–204, 229–36). The scheme was not a success, partly due to the complicated machinery set up in order to dis-

tribute benefits as equally as possible through the five participating countries. Seven car and two four-wheel drive plants were supposed to be allocated among the five countries, which had a combined market of only 170 000 cars in the late 1970s. However, the lack of any rationalization meant that the basic problem of small production runs did not improve. In the early 1980s, no model in the Andean Group had a production run greater than 10 000 apart from GM's Malibu Sedan in Venezuela (Jenkins 1987a: 234); this was a North American model geared to Venezuela's cheap petrol policy for motorists, and therefore inappropriate to be exported to other Andean countries. The Andean Group's ambitious plans for components production in general and engine manufacture in particular also met with little success, with only one engine plant (out of eleven planned) being built (Jenkins 1987a). On the whole, very little automotive trade

Table 11.2 Latin America: Growth rates of the population and the manufacturing product, 1950–78

	Population	Manufacturing product			
	1950–78	1950–65	1965–73	1973–78	1950–78
Large countries	3.1	7.3	10.4	6.3	8.0
Brazil	3.0	7.3	12.0	6.3	8.5
Mexico	3.3	7.2	8.1	6.3	7.3
Andean Pact (incl. Chile)	3.0	6.8	5.6	4.1	6.0
Bolivia	2.4	2.0	5.6	8.3	4.2
Chile	2.1	5.5	3.4	1.4	3.7
Colombia	3.2	6.2	7.7	5.4	6.5
Ecuador	3.2	5.3	7.1	11.9	7.0
Peru	2.8	7.8	6.6	1.8	6.4
Venezuela	3.5	9.5	5.0	7.6	7.9
CACM[a] (incl. Panama)	3.0	7.4	7.4	5.3	7.0
Costa Rica	3.2	7.9	9.4	8.1	8.3
El Salvador	3.1	7.2	5.8	5.2	6.4
Guatemala	2.8	5.4	7.7	6.2	6.2
Honduras	3.2	8.3	6.4	6.3	7.4
Nicaragua	3.0	9.5	6.9	3.6	7.6
Panama	2.9	10.1	8.1	0.2	7.7
River Plate countries	1.6	4.6	5.6	−0.4	4.0
Argentina	1.6	4.8	5.9	−1.0	4.1
Paraguay	2.7	3.3	6.0	7.2	4.8
Uruguay	1.4	2.7	0.9	5.9	2.7
Latin America	2.8	6.3	8.2	4.5	6.5

[a] Central American Common Market.

(*Source*: United Nations Economic Commission for Latin America)

was generated between the Andean Group countries.

What then has been the differential impact of ISI policies on large and small countries and what have schemes of economic integration achieved for the smaller countries? The manufacturing growth rates presented in Table 11.2 demonstrate the influence of import substitution and economic integration policies on industrial development. The large countries, where ISI policies had the advantage of supplying large national markets, recorded much higher manufacturing growth rates than other countries, particularly in the 1965–73 period when average growth rates of 12 per cent in Brazil and 8 per cent in Mexico were achieved. The industrial achievements of the CACM countries from a low base are reflected in the 7.4 per cent average annual growth rate from 1950 to 1973, while the limited success of the Andean Group is demonstrated by the relatively low growth rate of 4.1 per cent between 1973 and 1978.

Meanwhile, the failure of ISI policies to provide industrial growth outside large countries or schemes of economic integration is most clearly seen in the River Plate countries where industrial decline was recorded between 1973 and 1978. Arguably, the import substitution process was

Table 11.3 Latin-America: Population, total and manufacturing gross domestic product, level of industrialization, industrial weight within the region and *per capita* manufacturing GDP, 1978

	Population (thousands of inhabitants)	GDP (millions of 1970$)	Manufacturing GDP (millions of 1970$)	Level of industrialization (manuf'g GDP as % GDP)	Industrial weight within the region (%)	*Per capita* manufacturing GDP (1970 prices in US$)
Large countries	184 898	170 140	48 172	28	62.4	261
Brazil	119 477	101 056	30 327	30	39.3	254
Mexico	65 421	69 084	17 845	26	23.1	273
Andean Pact (incl. Chile)	83 394	66 662	13 132	20	17.0	158
Bolivia	5 848	2 072	325	16	0.4	56
Chile	10 843	10 335	2 451	24	3.2	226
Colombia	28 424	19 162	3 384	18	4.4	119
Ecuador	7 798	4 434	905	20	1.2	116
Peru	17 148	10 323	2 554	25	3.3	149
Venezuela	13 333	20 336	3 513	17	4.5	264
CACM (incl. Panama)	21 002	12 279	2 198	18	2.8	105
Costa Rica	2 111	2 031	461	23	0.6	218
El Salvador	4 524	2 238	436	19	0.6	96
Guatemala	6 623	3 783	617	16	0.8	93
Honduras	3 362	1 166		16	0.2	55
Nicaragua	2 559	1 195	238	20	0.3	93
Panama	1 823	1 866	261	14	0.3	143
River Plate countries	32 490	43 042	13 761	32	17.8	424
Argentina	26 395	38 011	12 512	33	16.2	474
Paraguay	2 888	1 553	250	16	0.3	87
Uruguay	3 207	3 478	999	29	1.3	312
Total Latin America	321 784	292 123	77 263	26	100.0	240

(*Source*: United Nations Economic Commission for Latin America)

'completed' earlier in Argentina and Uruguay, but with the high costs of national industry preventing exports and further domestic expansion, such 'completion' brought industrial stagnation. Argentine industry declined by 1 per cent a year between 1973 and 1978 causing *per capita* manufacturing product to fall from US$531 in 1973 to US$474 in 1978. In this way, the industrial weight of the River Plate in Latin America fell from 35 per cent in 1950 to only 18 per cent in 1978 (see Table 11.3).

Meanwhile, the two larger countries that had forged a more competitive industrial structure from import substitution, Brazil and Mexico, had increased their combined industrial weight in Latin America from 43 per cent in 1950 to 62 per cent in 1978. This record of rapid relative industrial growth within Latin America demonstrates the close links between market size and industrial success in import substitution, particularly when the more technologically demanding levels of industrialization are reached. However, economic integration had little relative impact on the industrialization of small countries. The industrial weighting of the twelve smaller countries involved in regional schemes of economic integration fell slightly from 22 per cent in 1950 to 20 per cent in 1978.

Industrial Structure and Technology under Import Substitution

Import substitution has brought certain structural changes in manufacturing. As would be expected from the model, industries producing non-durable consumer goods, such as clothing, have declined in relative importance as the industries producing intermediate goods, consumer durables and capital goods have developed. In 1950, non-durable consumer goods represented almost two-thirds of total manufacturing production, as opposed to 40 per cent by the late 1970s. At the same time, the relative importance of intermediate products in manufacturing output rose from less than 25 per cent to over one-third, and of consumer durable/capital goods from 11 per cent to over one-quarter.

There were major structural differences among Latin American countries according to market size. Table 11.4 demonstrates that by the mid-1970s the process of import substitution was much more complete in the large than in the smaller countries. Manufacturers of intermediate and consumer durable/capital goods accounted for 37 and 28 per cent respectively of total value-added in the larger countries (including Argentina) by 1975, as against 35 and 17 per cent in medium-sized countries and only 26 and 9 per cent in small countries.

The production of intermediate goods has expanded significantly in medium-sized countries (Venezuela and Chile for example) but less so in small countries. Production of basic metals is almost entirely restricted to the larger countries and the one medium-sized country, Venezuela, that benefits from considerable comparative advantages (in the form of cheap raw materials and power) in both steel and aluminium production.

Table 11.4 Latin America: Structure of industrial production by size of country, 1950 and 1975 (Percentage of value-added in the manufacturing sector)

		Non-durable consumer manufactures	Intermediate manufactures	Consumer durable and capital manufactures	Total manufactures
Large countries	1950	64	24	12	100
	1975	35	37	28	100
Medium-sized countries	1950	66	28	6	100
	1975	48	35	17	100
Small countries	1950	85	14	1	100
	1975	65	26	9	100

(*Source*: United Nations Economic Commission for Latin America)

By the late 1970s, 94 and 100 per cent of Latin American steel and aluminium production, respectively, corresponded to Argentina, Brazil, Mexico and Venezuela.

At the continental scale, the most pronounced concentration of industrial growth in the larger countries has occurred in the consumer durable/capital goods sectors. By the early 1980s, over 90 per cent of Latin American car production took place in Brazil, Mexico and Argentina. A similar level of concentration occurs in the capital goods sector generally, with Brazil having the technologically most advanced and broadest machinery sector. In a recent report on newly industrializing countries, the OECD (1988: 61) was moved to comment: 'The Brazilian economy has acquired the advantage of a better "articulation" between its industrial sectors than is the case of the other Latin American countries, since the capital goods sector covers a significant part of Brazil's industrial needs'.

This concentration, at a continental level, of the capital goods industry in the larger countries in general and Brazil in particular is linked with the internal generation of new technology under policies of import substitution (see Ch. 8). Much of the process of modernization and technological change which takes place in Latin America consists of the imitation of products and processes that have already been developed in more advanced countries. At this stage of purchasing technological designs, there are few differences among Latin American countries. It is at the next stage, the adaptation and improvement of imported technology to meet local circumstances, that the larger countries have considerable advantages over other countries. Argentina, Brazil and Mexico have large numbers of highly trained professional and technical personnel both to generate national technological knowledge and to adapt imported technology to local conditions (Katz 1987).

There have been contrasts in the policies of government towards technological development in the three countries. Argentinian governments have not strongly intervened in new technological developments, unless they are closely linked to military purposes. Thus, in the dynamic, numerically controlled machine tool (NCMT) sector (see Ch. 9), little assistance has been provided by government for Argentine manufacturers, in contrast to the experience in Korea and, indeed, Brazil.

> The Argentine experience in the production of NCMTs has been undertaken so far without any specific government policy, except tariff protection, which is given to any local production, and some credit facilities . . . it is doubtful that the government will be able to put into practice a firm and product-specific policy in this segment of the machine tool industry (Chudnovsky 1988: 730).

Government involvement in the generation of technology in Mexico is also not sector specific, outside of the sectors that are reserved for state ownership (oil, petrochemicals, mining, nuclear energy) or have majority state control (steel). The Mexican government promotes local technological development through joint ventures between Mexican private firms and foreign companies (as in the case of computers) and through a close monitoring of technology transfer.

> Mexican legislation requires all contracts involving technological transfer to be registered with the government, which then examines them to ensure that Mexican companies obtain fair access to advanced technology at minimum cost. In this general context, it has been estimated that the Mexican government finances fully 90 per cent of all R & D expenditure, and that, of the remainder, 4 per cent comes from the Mexican private sector and 6 per cent from foreign enterprises established in Mexico (OECD 1988: 54).

Brazil, however, has followed a policy more similar to the Japanese model of developing technology (see Ch. 8). On the one hand, the import of new technological designs is welcomed but the domestic adaptation and improvement of these designs are vigorously promoted, often through sector-specific programmes. The results of such a policy are reflected in the development of the national computer industry where a government body, the *Secretaria Especial de Informática* (SEI), has supervised its growth. The SEI has divided the industry into mainframe and smaller computers. Its policy towards mainframe computers has been to leave it to the multinationals, notably IBM and Burroughs, as long as they increase both their manufacturing capacity in Brazil and level of exports.

The SEI's policy towards the manufacture of smaller computers has been radically different. The government reserved this growth area for Brazilian manufacturers in 1978. Four companies from the private sector were allowed to join COBRA – *Computadores e Sistemas Brasileiros* (a government-controlled company). The SEI allowed these companies to begin by buying technology abroad but approval of new projects depended on their use of Brazilian expertise and locally produced components. In this way, the SEI stressed the need for these companies to adapt and improve technological designs, and to integrate their products into the Brazilian market and supply network. Subsequently, the five Brazilian companies extended their range from mini-computers to micro-computers, and were joined in this latter field by a number of new companies. Between 1979 and 1983, computer sales of local firms increased from US$190 million to US$687 million, by which time they were similar in scale to the sales of the multinationals in the Brazilian market (Evans 1986: 796). The implications for the generation of computer technology from within Brazil have been considerable.

Evans (1986: 797–8) makes the point that the SEI sectoral programme came to favour the micro sector much more than that of the mini-computer, due to the relative ease of global technology transfer, greater competition and market expansion within Brazil in the micro sector. Indeed, in 1984, the SEI had to authorize a new round of licensing in order to import 32-bit 'supermini' technology, because of the complete lack of this technology within Brazilian firms (Evans 1986: 798).

Using the example of the computer industry, the Brazilian policy towards the generation of local technology in manufacturing can be seen as enlightened due to the balance it has achieved between an openness to international innovation on the one hand, and the promotion of local initiative on the other.

The Brazilian computer strategy requires continued access to international technology just as it requires nationalist protection of efforts to develop indigenous technology. To see the Brazilian computer industry as one which is developing without reliance on international technology would be a fundamental mistake (Evans 1986: 799).

However, the balanced policy has been successful in creating a locally controlled manufacturing capacity in a technologically complex industry, with significant growth in R&D employment, product innovation and exports.

As local firms grew, the number of people they employed in R&D grew even faster. By 1983 there were roughly 1200 R&D jobs in the computer industry that would not have been there if transnationals had been allowed to totally dominate the industry (Evans 1986: 796).
The increasing ability of local firms to export is testimony to the effectiveness of local product innovation. Exports of information processing products by local firms grew from $147 000 in 1982, to over $1 million in 1983 and to over $18 million in 1984 (Evans 1986: 800).

Investment in research and development has had a significant impact on the rate of industrial growth in Brazil over the last two decades. Away from the computer sector, there has been rapid growth in other technologically advanced sectors, most notably that of machinery, The OECD (1988: 65) noted that recent industrial development in Brazil has 'resulted in the emergence of a fairly diversified capital goods sector, able to satisfy most heavy equipment orders placed by the iron and steel, cement and oil industries and also by hydroelectric power stations'. It has been argued that the concentration of Latin American technology in Brazil and, to a lesser extent, in Mexico and Argentina, may indicate a future role for these countries as suppliers of technologically sophisticated manufactures and new innovations (through licensing arrangements and direct investment) to neighbouring countries. There seems little evidence of this occurring as yet. Indeed, Brazil's exports to other Latin American countries notably declined in relative terms during the early 1980s – from 19 per cent of the total in 1981 to 11 per cent in 1984.

The Triple Alliance

The process of ISI in Latin America has been engineered through a distinctive institutional structure, known as the triple alliance or an alliance between state firms, national private enterprise and multinational corporations. The balance between these three institutional categories varies from country to country. Furthermore, the balance between these categories in any country has been continually changing. Within the framework of inward orientation in larger countries, national private enterprises were seen to be losing ground in the 1970s to both public enterprises and multinational corporations. More recently, in the late 1980s, with the increasing popularity of privatization policies, national private firms have been expanding slightly in relative terms.

It has been seen as the role of the state enterprise to invest in those intermediate and capital goods sectors that continued industrial expansion seemed to require. Governments developed these enterprises because of inadequate domestic capital markets which meant that only the state could provide the necessary capital for such large investments. Furthermore, as some of the investment was of a strategic nature (power, communications, steel), governments wished to exclude the participation of the multinationals. In Brazil, the state is massively present in such activities as oil (Petrobras), electricity (Eletrobras), mining (CVRD) and steel (Siderbras). Between 1959 and 1988, the number of state-owned companies increased from 45 to 176, coming to employ an estimated 650 000 workers and valued at US$42 billion in 1988. Of Brazil's 500 biggest corporations, 66 are government controlled, and responsible for about 60 per cent of total assets (Gould 1988: 59–60).

State firms have also been established in the extractive industries and in the further processing and refining of the minerals concerned. State firms in this case have developed due to a national wish for greater control over the crucial resources of the country – resources that can be crucial for exports, taxes, the state budget, employment and the exchange rate. Thus, Mexican oil is controlled by PEMEX, Venezuelan oil by PETROVEN, and copper in Chile by the world's largest copper producer, CODELCO.

In contrast to the state enterprise, the national private firm is characterized by great diversity in terms of size, technological level and forms of organization. In most large and medium-sized countries, large national conglomerates have developed with a wide variety of manufacturing interests and often important tertiary functions in such areas as banking, insurance, finance, tourism, commerce and the media. In Brazil, some of the largest private companies are based around construction (Mendes Junior, Camargo Correa, Norberto Odebrecht) and capital goods (Romi, Acos Villares). In Chile, the largest private conglomerates are now wide ranging but based around the production and export of natural resources, such as Angelini (fish meal, cellulose, timber, petrol stations, insurance), Matte (paper, cellulose, timber, construction materials) and Luksic (copper products, timber, beer, soft drinks, food products, tourism).

At the other end of the size range, large numbers of small enterprises are at work filling the demand gaps left by, or providing low-cost competition for, the large state, national and international companies. Due to labour-intensive methods and low capital inputs, these enterprises generate a much higher proportion of employment than their production levels would indicate. In 1970, the 135 000 small firms of Brazil, while accounting for only 21 per cent of the total value of production, employed as much as 44 per cent of the total manufacturing manpower (Tyler 1981). The organization of most of these small firms is simple, based around a single entrepreneur or family, and many are highly susceptible to changes in the macroeconomy or the policy shifts of the large companies. As a result, they have to be very adaptable and flexible in order to survive.

In terms of their relationship with multinational companies, it is often pointed out that the latter predominate in the technologically more dynamic sectors, leaving the national private firms to specialize in the more traditional industries. The 2700 largest private firms in Brazil, for example, account for 75 per cent of production in the nondurable consumer good sector but only 33 and 45 per cent in the intermediate and metal goods/machinery sectors respectively.

Throughout Latin America, the majority of firms producing in the food, beverages, textiles, footwear, clothing, leather, cement, furniture and ceramic sectors are of national origin (Gereffi and Evans 1981). Some new sectors have tended to be reserved for national firms, as with the motor vehicle components industry and, in Brazil, national firms have figured prominently in the plastics, paper, machinery and micro-computer industries. However, even within the same manufacturing sectors, national firms tend to be more labour intensive, technologically more backward and less efficient than their multinational rivals. In Willmore's study (1986) of 282 pairs of foreign-owned and private national Brazilian firms, matched by both sales and four-digit manufacturing sector, he found:

> ... that foreign firms utilize quite capital intensive techniques of production compared to their local counterparts, and capital intensity tends to increase the importance of scale economies. Foreign firms also have significantly higher ratios of value-added to output ... [and] ... have high levels of labor productivity compared to local firms of a similar size operating in the same industry (Willmore 1986: 497–8).

Not only are multinational companies characterized by a greater use of modern technology than their national counterparts in the same sector, but they have also tended to become the most significant operators in the more dynamic and technologically innovative sectors. This has been intimately linked to policies of import substitution, which favoured the domestic production of foreign technological packages, controlled by multinationals, for national consumption. Thus in Brazil, which accounts for about a half of continental foreign direct investment in manufacturing, about three-quarters of this investment was channelled into technologically dynamic sectors during the late 1970s – chemicals, vehicles, machine tools, pharmaceuticals, communications, electrical and medical industries (Cunningham 1981); all these sectors were, however, producing principally for the domestic market during the 1970s. By the late 1970s, multinational enterprise controlled 56 per cent of total assets in the transport sector, 51 per cent in the electrical and over 35 per cent in the machinery sector – precisely the three sectors that recorded the highest growth rates during the 1970s.

The multinational enterprise in Latin America has historically been of West European and US origin but Japanese interests have been increasing recently. The role of multinational enterprise as an agent of Latin American industrialization is crucial, not least because no other continent has received such a major contribution from foreign companies in their process of industrialization. The United States, Japan and the countries of Europe have largely industrialized through national agents, whether state or private; Korea and even Taiwan could be said to be following this path (see Ch. 12). Other Third World countries are presently industrializing with the assistance of multinational enterprise, but Latin American countries have, through policies of import substitution, already developed complex and diverse industrial structures alongside significant foreign investment.

In Chapter 9, it was noted that the flavour and structure of multinational enterprise in Latin America had changed since the Second World War and the nationalization of international mining interests in such countries as Mexico (1936), Chile (1971) and Venezuela (1976). Foreign investment in manufacturing has become much more important than that in primary activities (mining and plantation agriculture). Furthermore, it has become spatially concentrated in those countries that had reached the latter stages of ISI: Mexico and Brazil. By the late 1970s, nearly 70 per cent of direct foreign investment in Latin American manufacturing was channelled into those two countries (Gereffi and Evans 1981). Under import substitution, the majority of foreign investment in Latin America was from the United States; in the mid-1970s, for example, US foreign investment still accounted for over 50 per cent of the total in the large countries, and between 70 and 80 per cent in the medium-sized and smaller countries.

The pattern of industrialization in Latin America between the 1930s and 1970s was undoubtedly inward orientated. We have briefly examined the policies of inward orientation and the structures, technologies and organizations that evolved from these policies. However, there is some evidence to suggest that the 1980s have witnessed a gradual change in orientation to a more outward-looking approach.

TOWARDS A NEW PHASE OF OUTWARD ORIENTATION?

The possibility of identifying the beginnings of a new outward-oriented phase in Latin American industrialization in the 1980s seems to rest on two factors, one general and one rather more specific. The first is provided by the example of the industrial success of certain developing countries in East Asia; despite contrasts in state involvement and the role of foreign investment between the various countries, the one common theme has been that of outward orientation (see Ch. 6 and 12).

The second factor is that of the debt crisis. In Chapter 4, we examined the problem of the debt crisis in Latin America, and noted that the decade of the 1980s has brought tremendous capital constraints to almost all Latin American countries compared with the decade of the 1970s. High world interest rates during the 1980s have meant that the large external debts inherited from the 1970s have become a grave economic burden. However, it has also been recognized that the amelioration of the debt crisis can be partially solved by high balance of trade surpluses, with the value of exports being substantially larger than that of imports. One way to achieve these balance of trade surpluses is to promote exports and, due to the low prices of primary products during the 1980s, particularly manufactured exports.

Within Latin America, there are at least three countries whose conversion to outward orientation essentially predates the debt crisis – Brazil, Chile and Uruguay (World Bank 1987: 83). The beginnings of Brazil's shift from an inward- to a more outward-oriented mode of industrial development can be traced to 1972 and the beginnings of the BEFIEX (Special Fiscal Benefits for Exports) system, which created joint programmes between the government and exporting firms. In exchange for lower import tariffs and duties, firms undertook to reach a predetermined export target. This enabled firms to import modern equipment and parts more easily as long as they increased their exports in a corresponding fashion. Between 1972 and end-1984, 294 programmes were approved, involving export pledges from firms of US$85 billion against US$18.7 billion in imports. By the end of 1984, the concrete achievement was one of US$17.3 billion of exports as against US$4.7 billion of imports (OECD 1988: 64), which meant that the BEFIEX system had not only provided a significant boost to manufactured exports but had also provided a net foreign exchange gain of US$12.6 billion.

The BEFIEX programmes have been particularly significant in boosting exports in the motor vehicles sector (see Ch. 10), footwear, textiles, railway equipment, iron and steel, machinery and pulp. Consumer goods have generally been channelled toward the markets of the developed world, while capital goods have been directed more towards the developing countries. Between 1973 and 1982, Brazilian exports of manufactures grew at an annual rate of 22.8 per cent (OECD 1988: 64); in 1982, manufactured exports accounted for about 40 per cent of Brazil's total exports (World Bank 1985: 193).

Subsequently, and partially due to the debt crisis, manufactured exports to the developing (and particularly Latin American) countries have declined. It has taken time for Brazil to counterbalance this declining trade with increased exports of manufactures to the developed world (see Ch. 10 for the case of the motor vehicle industry). As a result, between 1982 and 1986, manufactured exports from Brazil increased by only 20 per cent (from approximately US$7.5 to US$9.0 billion); most of this growth has been accounted for by the increasing exports of manufactured goods to the United States.

To what extent, then, has Brazil changed the orientation of its industrial strategy? An interim assessment would say that, outside the promotion of exports, there are distinct limits to the opening up of the Brazilian economy. The export ratio for manufacturing, although rising steadily from 1.8 per cent in 1968 to 6.3 per cent in 1982, is still modest (OECD 1988: 64). Meanwhile, the share of industrial imports in apparent consumption (as measured by output + imports − exports) of industrial goods, which had risen from 6.8 per cent in 1965 to 17.8 per cent in 1974 (with BEFIEX-inspired liberalization) had slipped back to 8.9 per cent by 1982 (with the onset of recession and the debt crisis). With this type of reaction to the early 1980s crises, the Interamerican Development Bank (1985) commented that Brazil had, in fact, pursued a coherent import substitution programme. The statement was justified by the behaviour of the capital goods imports/gross fixed investment ratio, which fell from 8.7 per cent in 1970–78 to 5.6 per cent in 1979–81, and to 5 per cent in 1982–84. The trend for intermediate goods was similar, with ratios of 8.9, 6.6 and 4.8 per cent respectively. Economic nationalism remains a very potent force in Brazil and has effectively restricted further outward orientation and liberalization of the economy during the macro-economic crises of the 1980s:

> But adopting free trade in Brazil is not a question of simply reversing an inward-looking trade policy. Brazil has grown into an industrial power largely because of four decades of protectionism, state support of local industry and import substitution. Protection has created a politically powerful constituency that opposes liberalisation. The nationalists say that Brazilian capitalism would not survive if it had to compete, unprotected, with unshackled transnationals. They say that Brazil must earn a trade surplus exceeding US$12 billion every year just to service its debt repayments. Increasing imports could destroy carefully hoarded foreign reserves before any of the benefits of trade liberalisation appear (Gould 1988: 51–53).

The opening up of the Brazilian economy has therefore been a rather one-sided affair, limited to exports. Trade liberalization has certainly not gone as far as it has done in Chile (see Ch. 6). Furthermore, in Chile, liberalization has extended to other areas of the economy, such as foreign investment and privatization. Although Brazil has begun a process of privatization, by 1988 it still only applied to 'private sector companies temporarily under government care' (Gould 1988: 59). Liberalization of foreign investment and foreign capital transactions in Chile further led to schemes of debt–equity swaps, which have both boosted foreign investment and reduced the external debt (see Ch. 4).

Again, in relative terms, Brazilian debt–equity swaps have been rather limited.

In extending the analysis from the outward-oriented countries of Brazil, Chile and Uruguay to the inward-oriented countries of Latin America (World Bank 1987: 83), one is invariably met by greater economic nationalism and less pragmatism than in the case of Brazil. In some countries (such as Mexico) there are some signs of movement towards a more outward-oriented approach, but in others (such as Peru) the reverse is the case. The case of Mexico is interesting because the policies of the administration of President Miguel de la Madrid (1982–88) demonstrate the growing recognition of the need for more liberal trade policies in a country strongly characterized by inward-oriented manufacturing and economic nationalism. With severe problems of massive debt repayments and stagnant exports (unlike Brazil), the Mexican emphasis in the 1980s has been on attempting to diversify and rapidly expand exports.

The first concrete steps to promote exports took place in 1985 with the DIMEX plan. Its aim was to liberalize imports of goods so that exporting firms could have access to cheaper inputs than those supplied by local industry and hence reduce their costs. Under the plan, firms could freely import up to 30 per cent of the value of their exports. The plan was followed by a major devaluation of the Mexican peso, by an exemption on prior licensing of a range of imports and by tariffs supplanting quantitative restrictions as the primary means of protection (OECD 1988: 57). Tariffs started to be reduced in the following year (1986), and by the end of 1988, the maximum tariff was down to 30 per cent. In 1986, Mexico became a member of GATT.

Trade liberalization has had a rapid and significant impact on Mexican exports. By 1986, non-oil exports were greater than oil exports, and between 1985 and 1987, the value of non-oil exports effectively doubled. The impact on manufactured exports has been particularly dramatic; their share of total exports jumped from 16 per cent in 1982 to 45 per cent in 1987 (Graham 1987: 7). The most dramatic growth has occurred in the motor vehicle sector (see Ch. 10). Much of the growth has been accounted for by trade with Mexico's northern neighbour – in 1987, the US economy absorbed 66 per cent of Mexican exports and provided 65 per cent of imports. The Mexican economy remains beset by severe macroeconomic problems, yet its gradual but significant process of trade liberalization during the last half of the 1980s seems to be giving the national economy an engine of growth that otherwise it would have lacked.

Overall, then, there is a shift to greater outward orientation in Latin America. However, outside of Chile and, to a lesser extent, Uruguay, the process is at best slow and uneven. In Brazil, severe import restrictions remain, while in Mexico foreign investment has normally to be tied to joint venture agreements with Mexican firms. In other countries, moves to liberalization are evident, but the short-term problems of restructuring can often dampen the political initiatives taken.

INWARD ORIENTATION AND SPATIAL CONCENTRATION

The spatial emphasis so far has concerned contrasts in industrial development *between* countries. However, it is worth while dropping down the spatial scale of analysis to consider the relationship between industrialization and the spatial development of industry *within* Latin American countries. This is best done within the historical framework of the inward orientation of Latin American industry. In this section it is argued that the inward orientation of Latin American manufacturing since the 1930s has been intimately linked with the spatial concentration of manufacturing value-added and employment in the primate cities of Latin American countries. For example, within Chile, the concentration of manufacturing employment in the primary city, Santiago, increased from 43 per cent to 57 per cent of the national total between 1928 and 1979.

One important reason behind such increasing concentration is that the 'new' import-substituting industries are consistently drawn to the primate city. In 1967, according to the Chilean census of that year, the four 'newest', and most rapidly-growing, import-substituting sectors of pharmaceuticals, electrical durable goods, plastics and professional and scientific equipment had over 90 per cent of their Chilean employment generated in Santiago. With modern industries attracted to the primate city, the process of concentration continues to increase. In the two most advanced industrial nations of Brazil and Mexico well over 50 per cent of their respective manufacturing production and employment is located in the São Paulo and Mexico City agglomerations. Two-thirds of Argentina's industrial employment is located in the Buenos Aires metropolitan areas, 75 per cent of Venezuelan value-added is generated from the Valencia–Caracas axial belt (see Fig. 11.2) and 70 per cent of Peruvian manufacturing employment is centred in Lima/Callao. In the smaller, less industrialized countries where only the first stage of ISI has been completed, spatial concentration of industry in the primate city is greater still, e.g. El Salvador.

How can such pronounced concentration of manufacturing employment and value-added be understood? As industrial entrepreneurs in the triple alliance compete for domestic markets and attempt to find export markets through offering cheaper products, locational costs and accessibility to markets are dominant considerations. Such considerations normally reveal the advantages of the primate city.

The introduction of the railway in the nineteenth century created national transport networks that radiated out from the capital and/or primate city. As a result, Buenos Aires in Argentina, Montevideo in Uruguay, São Paulo and Rio in Brazil, Santiago-Valparaíso in Chile, Lima-Callao in Peru and Caracas-La Guaira in Venezuela adopted pivotal roles in the transport development of their countries. As a result, the most accessible point in each country was not the geographical centre but a point near or on the coast. As countries began to embark on policies of ISI, the large coastal city (or city at the centre of the nation's transport system) provided the most advantageous location for the development of three significant industrial types:

1. Consumer-good industries that supply the whole of the national market from one or two plants.
2. Industries in which various raw materials from

the hinterland of a country are processed and combined together in one place. This is because the primate city will be the only city linked to the various sources of the raw materials.

3. Industries that have an element of imported raw materials and/or components in their productive structure.

These industrial types have been particularly prominent in the process of ISI. The original idea of ISI was to substitute imports of a product through the creation of a small number of national plants (Type 1). As the process of ISI continued, plants producing consumer durable products were established. These plants needed to import machinery and components, at least initially, for their manufacturing process (Type 3). Later the manufacture of intermediate products was encouraged, combining either raw materials from the country's hinterland or from abroad (Types 2 and 3).

At the same time, the major metropolitan city provides the optimal location for industries whose market is that city. In order to identify the importance of this type of industry, it is useful to assess the market size of the principal towns of Latin America. In terms of populations alone, the concentration within the primate city can be very high (see Table 11.5). Five countries (Mexico, Argentina, Uruguay, Panama and Chile) have over 20 per cent of their national population concentrated in the primate city. A further five countries (Costa Rica, Nicaragua, Paraguay, Peru and Venezuela) have between 15 and 20 per cent of their population thus concentrated.

Of course, population concentrations cannot be directly compared with levels of industrial demand, given that the income levels of the populations concerned radically affect that demand. However, it is a well documented fact that high-income groups are attracted to the major city in Latin American countries and that as a result the average income per family is much larger in these cities than in smaller cities. Data from Mexico showed that 500 000 plus cities recorded virtually double the monthly family income level of towns with populations between 10 000 and 150 000 inhabitants in the early 1970s

Table 11.5 Primacy in Latin America, 1979

Country	Population of primate city as % of population of country	Population of second city as % of population of country
Uruguay	40.4	n.d.
Argentina	36.5	3.0
Chile	33.5	5.6
Panama	23.2	7.9
Mexico	20.7	3.5
Peru	19.1	1.7
Venezuela	19.1	5.9
Paraguay	19.0	n.d.
Costa Rica	18.2	n.d.
Nicaragua	16.0	n.d.
Ecuador	12.8	9.2
Bolivia	12.7	4.6
Colombia	11.0	4.4
Guatemala	10.3	n.d.
Honduras	9.7	4.8
El Salvador	7.6	n.d.
Brazil	6.1	4.1

(*Source*: Gwynne 1982)

(Ternent 1976). This is not to say that income distribution is considerably skewed in the large city. Rather it emphasizes that the concentration of demand in the big cities is made up of high average incomes as well as large populations.

It could be argued that, although incomes are higher in the big cities, costs are also higher – a factor that would serve to reduce industrial demand. Unfortunately there are very few data on the relationship between city size and costs in Latin America. It would appear that housing costs are higher in the bigger cities as are, due to greater journey-to-work distances, transport costs. However, an interesting retail survey at the end of the 1960s in Chile demonstrated that retail costs were not neccessarily higher in the big cities than in cities further down the urban hierarchy. Indeed the relationship between city size and the retail index could be described as an inverted U-shaped curve, with the lowest average price indices occurring at both ends of the city-size range (Gwynne 1978c: 139). Although such evidence is only partial to the overall cost structure of large cities, it does imply that the higher relative incomes enjoyed in the larger cities are not necessarily reduced in comparative terms by higher costs.

Cheaper labour costs at other locations could

attract industrial entrepreneurs away from the primate city. It has often been assumed that labour costs in the primate city are higher than the national average and considerably in excess of those prevalent in the peripheries of Latin American countries. However, a comparison of the Chilean 1967 Industrial Census (all firms over five employees) and the 1978 Industrial Survey (all firms over fifty employees) reveals a different spatial distribution and structure of labour costs (see Table 11.6). In terms of both white- and blue-collar workers, the Chilean primate city of Santiago had both average salaries and wage rates below or near the national average on both occasions. It should be borne in mind that between

Table 11.6 The changing rank of Chilean provinces between 1967 and 1978 in terms of salaries and wages

Province	Ranking in terms of provincial average for white-collar salaries in manufacturing		Ranking in terms of provincial average for blue-collar wages in manufacturing	
	1967	1978	1967	1978
Tarapacá	9	4	6	3
Antofagasta	6	5	2	6
Atacama	1	12	1	2
Coquimbo	19	16	9	18
Aconcagua	17	15	14	13
Valparaíso	5	6	4	5
Santiago	7	7	10	8
O'Higgins	2	1	7	1
Colchagua	10	8	11	7
Curicó	22	14	21	20
Talca	18	10	13	9
Linares	8	21	15	12
Ñuble	15	13	19	10
Concepción	4	9	3	4
Arauco	21	2	24	14
Bío-Bío	3	3	5	15
Malleco	13	17	20	21
Cautín	20	22	18	22
Valdivia	16	18	17	16
Osorno	11	11	12	11
Llanquihué	14	19	16	17
Chiloé	23	24	22	24
Aysén	24	23	23	23
Magallanes	12	20	8	19

(*Source*: Gwynne 1982)

1967 and 1978, Chilean industry underwent major structural changes, first undergoing Marxist policies of state control and then experiencing monetarist policies stressing comparative advantages. Despite such major shifts in industrial policy and direction during the period, the pattern of provincial ranking of industrial salaries and wages remained remarkably stable.

Those provinces dominated by export industries tended to have salary and wage rates higher than those of the primate city. The average ranking of the copper-exporting provinces of O'Higgins, Atacama and Antofagasta in terms of both white- and blue-collar workers was high in both years, while the timber- and cellulose-exporting provinces of Bío-Bío, Arauco and Ñuble improved their combined average ranking substantially during the period (from thirteen to six in terms of white-collar workers). As export industries are linked to world rather than national markets, there is greater elasticity in wage and salary rates in regions dominated by such industries. However, more significant for the location of consumer goods industries was the fact that Chile's second and third industrial conurbations of Valparaíso and Concepción generally had higher average salaries and wages in manufacturing than Santiago on both occasions. The major industrial decentralization schemes of Chile, located in Arica and Iquique in the province of Tarapacá, also had higher salaries and wages than the primate city. Thus, in Chile, the most attractive alternative locations for industrial entrepreneurs had higher average labour costs than those prevalent in Santiago. Meanwhile, Santiago could offer a wider range of labour skills and training than these alternative locations.

Industrial entrepreneurs may choose a metropolitan location due to what are known as the economies of agglomeration. Agglomeration economies are generally divided into economies of localization and economies of urbanization. Localization economies are those gained by firms in a single industry (or set of closely related industries) at a single location, economies accruing to the individual production units through the overall enlarged output of the industry as a whole at the location. Urbanization economies apply to all firms in all industries at a single location and represent those external economies passed on to enterprises as a result of savings from the large-scale operation of the agglomeration as a whole.

Localization economies may at first glance appear to have limited applicability in large Latin American cities. However, there is growing evidence of the spatial concentration of some industries in certain cities – such as the Brazilian motor vehicle industry in the Greater São Paulo conurbation. Furthermore, there is evidence of subcontracting linkages within industries in large cities. Complex networks of production have evolved in which a modern factory may commission a small, family enterprise to undertake part of its production such as in the assembly of refrigerators, the upholstery of buses or dressmaking. Even when the modern factory is located in a peripheral region, such subcontracting linkages may be concentrated in the primate city – as with the early development of the Chilean motor vehicle industry. In 1968, when the majority of Chilean motor vehicles were assembled in the northern port of Arica and when over 50 per cent of parts by value had to be Chilean-made, 89 per cent of the 300 parts-producing plants that had been created in Chile were nevertheless located in Santiago; only 8 per cent of the plants had decided to locate near the assembly plants in Arica (Gwynne 1978d). The metalworking and other small firms that ventured into components production in Santiago were generally not new firms but existing companies that were intent on adding a further line of production to their organization. The concentration of this small-scale manufacturing economy in the primate city is one of the principal elements of localization economies in Latin America and can effectively reduce costs for the large-scale firm located there.

Urbanization economies can also have powerful attractions for industrial decision makers. The effect of economies of massed reserves and large-scale purchasing is to reduce the per unit cost of inputs and reduce the amounts of non-productive capital in the production process in comparison with similar cities. Furthermore, the nature of urban systems in Latin America provides the primate city with a greater variety and quality of services. An example of this is banking. São Paulo has become the financial hub of Brazil; in 1988, it was estimated that as much as two-thirds of Brazil's banking activity was based in the state of São Paulo (Gould 1989). A major concentration of banking functions is found in Mexico where the Federal District accounted for 68 per cent of the total capital stock and reserves in the national banking system and 93 per cent of the long-term deposits in the early 1970s (Garza and Schteingart 1978). Furthermore, the banks of the Federal District granted 76 per cent of the national total of mortgage loans and handled 68 per cent of the country's investments in stocks and bonds during this period.

Finally, the infrastructure of primate cities, with an international airport, central railway system and spare power capacity has many advantages over the comparable infrastructure of smaller cities. In many Latin American countries, there have been cases of small towns lacking the necessary power capacity to cope with the operation of new high-energy industries at peak times; the consequent stoppages can have severe cost penalties for industries using continuous casting or other such processes. An example from Chile is interesting in this respect. In 1969, the Chilean company, Manufacturas de Cobre (MADECO), decided to locate a plant making copper telephone cables in the northern port of Antofagasta. Despite the fact that Antofagasta was the fourth city of Chile and despite its proximity to the Chuquicamata copper mine, an enormous user of electricity, the MADECO plant suffered for seven years from cuts in electricity supply at peak periods of demand. As MADECO had smelters which used a continuous casting process, where temperature is kept constant to produce the required type of refined copper, a cut in electricity meant the total loss of copper being refined and a period of no production as the smelters cooled, were cleaned out and prepared again for production.

However, it has frequently been pointed out that the considerable infrastructure that the capital city possesses has normally been heavily subsidized by national funds and that the entrepreneur in the primate city does not pay the real costs for such services. For example, in

Mexico, the price of electricity is the same in Mexico City as in all other parts of the country despite the fact that the bulk of electricity consumed by the city is generated at the hydroelectric complexes of Malpase and Infiernillo, 1000 and 600 km (621 and 373 miles) away respectively. The considerable cost of transmission is not directly passed on to the entrepreneurial consumer.

Processes of industrial decentralization

The large primate city does, however, have some disadvantages for the location of industry in Latin America. The cost of land is normally higher and tends to dissuade land-intensive industries. The increasing congestion of many large Latin American cities makes transportation more difficult both for people and products. The costs of housing, health, recreation and labour can also be higher in the major city.

The potentially high costs of locating or even maintaining an industry in the primate city can be found in the Venezuelan capital, Caracas. In 1976, the Caracas agglomeration had a population of 2 600 000, crowded into an elongated but narrow basin whose east–west axis measures 16 km (10 miles) from Catia to Petare but whose north–south dimensions rarely exceeded 3 km (2 miles). To the north, the steep Cordillera de la Costa prevents any expansion and indeed the area has been designated as a national park. To the east and west, high land similarly excludes development. It is only in the south where five valleys penetrate hills of more moderate but still significant elevation that outward expansion of the city can still occur – an area that because of high costs of construction, land and transport, is becoming an exclusive residential zone for the middle classes.

The unavailability of flat land for industry after 1966, the concomitant high land prices and congestion have acted as powerful decentralizing forces for Venezuelan manufacturing. In no sector is this better represented than in the motor vehicle assembly industry where the use of large areas of cheap flat land is at a premium. As Fig. 11.2 demonstrates, nine vehicle assembly plants are now located outside Caracas in the axial belt stretching from Las Tejerías to Valencia and

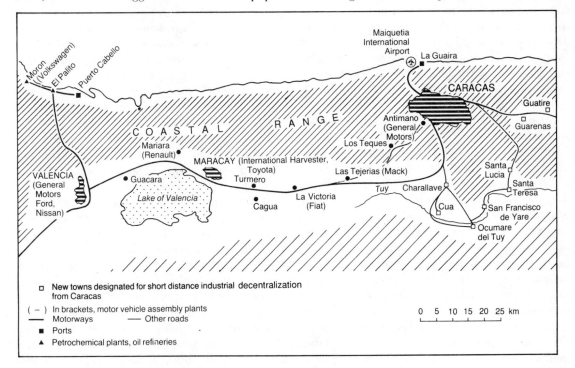

11.2 The Venezuelan axial belt.

Morón. Only the original General Motors plant remains in the Caracas agglomeration, in the southern industrial suburb of Antimano.

The movement of assembly plants into the axial belt effectively began with the introduction of Ford as a new producer in 1963 and that company's decision to locate its new plant at a green field site on the outskirts of Valencia. Within four years Ford had become the major vehicle manufacturer of Venezuela, overtaking the two other US producers, Chrysler and General Motors, in the process. Chrysler and General Motors found it difficult to react to Ford's increases in market share, partly because of the restrictions their plant site put on productive expansion. This was felt most acutely by Chrysler which had a site near central Caracas, in which further expansion was impossible. As a result, Chrysler decided to sell its plant in Caracas, followed Ford's locational decision and located a new plant on a site in Valencia with ample room for expansion. The selling of the Caracas plant almost covered the costs of the land and new plant in Valencia. As a result, the production of Chrysler vehicles was able to expand and by 1973 Chrysler had pushed General Motors into third place in terms of production. This position lasted until 1979 when General Motors bought out the Chrysler plant and started producing its own vehicles there. Since then, General Motors has been concentrating production at the ex-Chrysler plant in Valencia and using the Antimano plant for more specialized activities.

Industrial decentralization has therefore been occurring in Venezuela but mainly in the form of movement along the Caracas–Valencia axial belt. The well-established towns of Valencia and Maracay have been the main recipients of new and relocating industrial plants. Small towns, however, such as La Victoria, and even large villages, such as Mariara, have attracted significant industrial enterprises. Meanwhile, government planners have been intent on promoting the short-distance movement of industry out of Caracas, both southwards to a collection of new towns in the middle Tuy valley, and eastwards to a large planned town, Ciudad Fajardo, that will be a binodal agglomeration combining the settlements of Guarenas and Guatiré (see Fig. 11.2). Nevertheless, in 1974, 47 per cent of Venezuela's 300 000 manufacturing workers were employed in the Caracas agglomeration (including the port of La Guaira). Increasing numbers were working in flatted factories such as those in La Urbina built in the far east of the Caracas basin near Petare. Meanwhile, only 90 000 manufacturing workers (30 per cent of the total) were employed in the other settlements of Venezuela's axial belt in 1974.

This process of industrial decentralization from Caracas into the axial belt has been encouraged further outwards by the industrial decentralization policy of 1974. Few benefits can be achieved by any but high priority industry in Caracas (Area A) or the Caracas–Valencia–Puerto Cabello axis (Area B) (see Fig. 11.3). Benefits in the form of favourable credits and profit tax reductions can be acquired for most industrial plants locating in Marginal Area B (non-industrial areas to the south of the Puerto Cabello–Valencia–Caracas–Guatiré axis) and Areas C and D. The basic idea has been to extend the industrial belt both eastward (to include Barcelona and Cumaná) and westwards (to include Barquisimeto and San Felipe). Industries whose development has been closely controlled by the state (motor vehicles, aluminium) have been prominent in the process.

Such decentralization policies seek to expand upon the well-known resource growth pole of Ciudad Guayana in eastern Venezuela. This famous experiment in regional development based on abundant mineral and energy resources has been planned and organized by a semi-autonomous government body (the CVG) since its beginnings in 1958. Generously funded by Venezuelan oil money in the 1970s, the CVG has created an iron and steel complex, massive hydroelectric potential and the first fully integrated aluminium industry in the Third World with all three stages present – extraction of bauxite, production of alumina and the refining of aluminium. A small number of steel- and aluminium-using industries have been attracted to the frontier towns of Ciudad Guayana and Ciudad Bolívar, but it is interesting to note that most of the national consumption of CVG steel

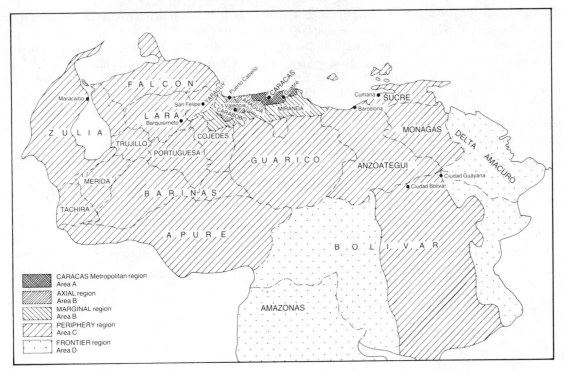

11.3   Spatial divisions of Venezuela's industrial decentralization programme.

and aluminium is still located in Venezuela's axial belt.

Short-distance industrial decentralization from the primate city and government encouragement of the phenomenon are common to other Latin American countries. In Mexico, short–distance industrial movement has been prevalent along the Mexico City–Puebla axis. At the same time, Mexican governments have encouraged short-distance decentralization by establishing large industrial estates at Queretaro and Irapuato, by creating new industrial cities at Ciudad Sahagún and Cuernavaca and by planning an industrial zone of the west, south of Guadalajara, and including the towns of Octlán and La Barca. As a result most of the effective industrial decentralization of Mexico has been confined to the Mesa Central where 70 per cent of Mexican industrial production is generated.

The twentieth-century development of Latin America's major industrial agglomeration, São Paulo, has been characterized by the steady onion-like growth of industrial zones around the original centre. The 'municipio' of São Paulo still represents the largest concentration of industry in Brazil with 24 per cent of all industrial workers in Brazil and over half of all employment in the electrical and plastics industries. Surrounding and including the 'municipio' is Greater São Paulo, reflecting industrial decentralization in the 1950s and 1960s when the ABC towns of Santo André, São Bernardo do Campo and São Caetano do Sul became attractive for a wide range of industries but particularly that of motor vehicles. The original vehicle plants of Ford, Mercedes Benz, Saab-Scania, Toyota and Volkswagen are concentrated in Brazil's vehicle capital of São Bernardo with General Motor's plant in neighbouring São Caetano. São Paulo state was responsible in 1988 for over 80 per cent of national vehicle production by value and for about 80 per cent of Brazilian vehicle exports (US$2.5 billion out of a total of US$3.1 billion) (Gould 1989: 37).

In the 1960s and 1970s, however, new industries have located in and older industries moved out to the smaller inland towns of São Paulo state. It is these towns of between 200 000 and 500 000 inhabitants where industrial productivity is highest in São Paulo state (Townroe and Keen 1984). São Paulo's industrial engine has moved out along three axes (see Fig. 11.4). One axis can be observed to the north-east along the Paraiba valley, incorporating the towns of São José dos Campos and Taubaté. This has been the preferred decentralizing direction for the motor vehicle industry, with General Motors locating a plant at São José and Volkswagen at Taubaté during the 1970s. São José has also become the main location for the Brazilian armaments industry, responsible for about 60 per cent of production and centred around the state firms of

Engesa (tanks and armoured vehicles), Embraer (aircraft) and Avibras (missiles) (Gould 1989: 38–41). A second axis can be identified to the north-west along the Paulista railway line, incorporating such towns as Campinas, Piracicaba and Americana, where engineering and textiles stand out in a wide range of industry. Finally, to the west, a third axis is evident, including such towns as Sorocaba, where non-metallic minerals, food processing and textiles are the major sectors.

The spatial association of industrization with the primate city has had the corollary that towns further down the national urban hierarchy and distant from the primate city have attracted little industry. In particular, the inward-looking,

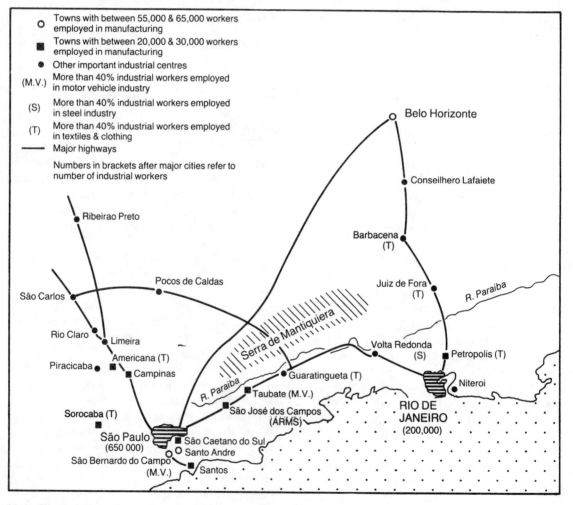

11.4   The industrial core of Brazil in the early 1980s.

consumer-good industries were strongly attracted to the large city and avoided the smaller provincial towns. The need to be near the major internal market and to have easy contacts with foreign technology and companies were always vital considerations for these industries. As a result, manufacturing has had relatively little impact on the occupational structures of small- and medium-sized towns distant from the primate city. Table 11.7 demonstrates this relationship for the Chilean urban hierarchy in 1970, one of the last years of the ISI model. Santiago and the port-industrial town of Concepción had approximately one-quarter of their substantial workforces in the manufacturing sector. Medium- and small-sized towns away from Santiago had only about one in eight of their workers employed in manufacturing. The attraction of industry for a location near the primate city can be gauged from the differential performance of medium- and small-sized towns located near Santiago. San Bernardo, Puente Alto and Peñaflor had up to 35 per cent of their workforce involved in manufacturing (see Fig. 11.5).

Such short-distance decentralization has become most associated with the larger, more dynamic industrial countries of Brazil and Mexico, where import substitution industrializ-ation has progressed furthest and has created a highly diversified, closely interlinked urban–industrial structure. Within a national framework of rapid economic growth, both multinational and domestic industrial firms aim to expand production continually and to diversify into new, often related, areas. Successful multinational and domestic firms can therefore become involved in a large number of locational decisions, such as those of plant expansion, new plant creation and relocation of old plant. Many of these locational decisions take place within the specific spatial framework of the primate city and its environs as this is not only where the majority of industrial firms are based but also where the fastest-growing firms are developing. In this sense, short-distance decentralization can best be envisaged as an intensification of the process of industrial concentration and as an expansion of the industrial core beyond the boundaries of the primate city to a wider functional region beyond.

Until recently, Latin American industrialization has been characterized by inward orientation. In the first section of this chapter, it was demonstrated that such a policy assisted the manufacturing development of the larger countries much more than the case of the smaller countries, particularly in terms of the maturity of

Table 11.7 Manufacturing workers as a percentage of the total non-agricultural workforce for urban areas in Chile, 1970

	Total non-agricultural workforce (A)	Manufacturing workforce (B)	(B) as % of (A)
Santiago	848 606	199 729	23.5
Concepción	113 014	28 727	25.4
Antofagasta (north)	33 516	3 499	10.4
Temuco (south)	30 431	4 442	14.6
Rancagua (central valley)	24 682	2 389	9.7
Chillán (central valley)	23 691	3 035	12.8
Puerto Montt (south)	19 074	2 444	12.8
Los Angeles (south)	14 765	1 819	12.3
Coquimbo (north)	12 564	1 251	10.0
Curicó (central valley)	12 172	1 353	11.1
Small towns in Santiago province			
San Bernardo	31 504	7 069	22.4
Puente Alto	21 600	6 622	30.7
Peñaflor	8 638	3 050	35.3

(Source: Instituto Nacional de Estadisticas 1973)

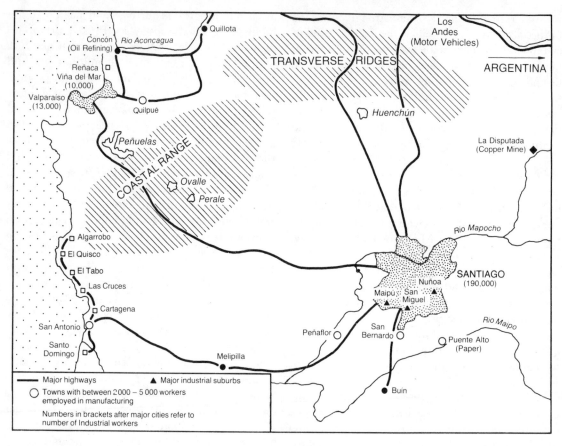

11.5 Chile's central region, 1980.

the industrial structures that evolved and the technological levels achieved. In the last section of the chapter, the close links between inward orientation and the spatial centralization of industry have been explored. However, as the focus is switched from the eastern to the western side of the Pacific, a more outward orientation of industry can be observed.

12

EAST ASIA: THE
HERITAGE OF
OUTWARD
ORIENTATION

It was noted in the last chapter that the effect of the 1930s Depression had a major impact on the reorientation of the Latin American economies from being outwardly to much more inwardly oriented. The modern inward orientation of Latin American economies very much originated in government reactions to the crises in world trade of the 1930s. Subsequent change and reorientation of national economies have been difficult due partly to inertia and nationalism. Indeed, it could be argued (see Ch. 8) that the short-term costs of trade liberalization have prevented a major outward reorientation of the economy, except in the case of Chile, and perhaps Uruguay and Mexico if the present process of trade liberalization continues (see Ch. 11).

In East Asia, however, the Depression did not have such an effect, mainly because most countries were linked to colonial powers whether European or, as in the case of Taiwan and Korea, Japan. Japan maintained itself as a major industrial exporter during the 1930s, although its industrial growth during the decade was also based on the build-up of heavy industry and military armaments. Meanwhile, Japan's outward-oriented approach to economic development in general, and industrial growth in particular, can be traced to the last quarter of the nineteenth and early twentieth centuries, a period in the recent history of the world economy that was characterized by the importance given to free trade as a motor for national economic growth (see Ch. 2).

However, it should be pointed out at the outset that East Asian industrialization is not characterized by a continent-wide similarity in policy adoption as was the case in Latin America after the Depression. Indeed, East Asia may be seen to contain the extremes of inward and outward orientation. On the one hand, there are countries whose process of industrialization has been almost completely oriented towards a protected home market (China, Vietnam). On the other hand, there are countries whose industrial growth has been dominated by supplying the varied and ever-changing array of world markets with an evolving range of manufactured goods (Hong Kong, Singapore). In between these extremes, there is almost every shade of industrial policy in terms of relative orientation to external and internal markets.

Besides containing the extremes of modern industrial policy, it must be emphasized that Asia also contains the most successful industrial economy of the twentieth century, Japan. The industrial success of Japan is of great significance for East Asian industrialization in two ways. First, it must be remembered that less than one hundred years ago, Japan was a good example of a less developed country – densely populated, impoverished in terms of resources and with the great majority of the population working in agriculture. Japan thus gives a 'model type' of how many Asian countries can transform themselves from peasant economies to highly successful manufacturing economies in a relatively short space of time.

Secondly, the Japanese manufacturing economy, which grew at an average annual rate of 13.6 per cent in the 1960s, 6.5 per cent in the 1970s and 7.8 per cent in the first half of the 1980s, can be envisaged as a massive economic pole whose growth has generated a whole series of linkages with other Asian countries and particularly with those in or adjacent to the Pacific rim. These linkages have long taken the principal form of resource supply, but increasingly they **are shifting to the supply of components, sub-assemblies** and even completely assembled products. The industrial pre-eminence of Japan in Asia is demonstrated by the data in Table 12.1 In 1984, Japan recorded an index of manufacturing value-added *per capita* of US$3439, nearly three times that of Hong Kong and six times that of Korea. However, in terms of the value of manufactured exports *per capita*, the Japanese

index was considerably behind that of both Singapore and Hong Kong. This demonstrates that Japanese manufacturing success has not been over-reliant on manufacturing exports and has been oriented as much to serving the expanding local market. Because of the manufacturing pre-eminence of Japan in Asia, this chapter will begin by briefly describing the most salient points of its manufacturing development before attempting an analysis of the most relevant aspects of the Japanese model.

It could be argued that the Japanese model, with manufacturing growth oriented towards both increasing domestic demand and export expansion, has by necessity, not been followed by **Singapore and Hong Kong, where manufacturing** growth has been intimately linked to international markets; the extent of this orientation is revealed in Table 12.1, where Singapore and Hong Kong record very high *per capita* indices for manufactured exports – between three and four times greater than the Japanese index. The Japanese model seems to be more closely followed by Korea, and for this reason the present chapter will

Table 12.1 *Per capita* indices of manufacturing value-added and exports for various East Asian countries, 1984

Country	1 Value-added in manufacturing (US$ millions)	2 Population (millions)	(a) Index 1/2	3 Value of manuf'd exports ($ millions)	(b) Index 3/2
Japan	412 667	120.0	3439	166 637	1388
Singapore	3 854	2.5	1542	13 952	5581
Hong Kong	6 944*	5.4	1286	25 769	4772
Korea	26 650	40.1	665	26 616	664
Malaysia	6 770	15.3	443	4 430	290
Thailand	8 325	50.0	167	2 595	52
Philippines	8 644	53.4	162	2 749	52
China	143 822	1 029.2	140	13 404	13
Indonesia	13 165	158.9	83	2 408	15

* 1983 values.

Ranking of countries based on the *per capita* values for manufacturing value-added.

(a) *per capita* values for manufacturing value-added (US$)
(b) *per capita* values for manufactured exports (US$)

(*Source*: World Bank 1987 and 1986: various tables)

continue by analysing this country's pattern of manufacturing expansion and comparing it with that of Taiwan. If Korea and Taiwan could be termed the 'first generation' of countries to attempt to follow the broad pattern of the Japanese model, a 'second generation' of countries may be identified in the economies of Malaysia, Thailand and the Philippines (see Table 12.1 for the intermediate nature of their manufacturing indices). Beyond these countries are those that have adopted very different policies to those of Japan, generally much less intent on expanding exports; Table 12.1 reveals the very low *per capita* export figures for manufacturing in China and Indonesia.

THE JAPANESE CASE STUDY

In the context of East Asian industrialization, why is it important to investigate the case of Japan? The principal reason must be that one hundred years ago, Japan was *definitely* what we would term now a less developed country – poor, densely populated, with a stagnant economy steeped in rural traditionalism and without any notable natural resources. Now, given its significant trade surplus with the United States in manufactured goods, it is probably the most dynamic and economically most powerful country in the world. It has achieved this quite dramatic transformation through the process of industrialization. As a result, it can be argued that the Japanese case study can be seen as a model for less developed countries in general and Asian countries in particular to follow if they too have the ambition to transform their economies in less than a century.

Having said that, it is difficult none the less to define exactly what are the essential points of the Japanese model. So far in this book, we have referred to three elements of the Japanese model as being independently important. First, we have noted the significance that the attainment of increasing economies of scale have had in the industrial development of Japan (Ch. 8). In terms of more recent technological change, attention has been drawn to what has been termed the 'just-in-time' system of manufacturing (Ch. 10), which allows for the combined advantages of economies of scale, quality control, low inventories and improved labour relations while providing a framework for technological advance with maximum participation of the workforce. Thirdly, on the corporate level, Chapter 10 has pointed to the advantages of the 'keiretsu' system in which groups of companies are linked around the central focus of a bank and with the constituent companies investing in each other's enterprises; this system was regarded as providing the framework for technological and managerial assistance between the constituent companies of a group and concentrating competition between rather than within groups.

However, beyond these three elements of success, it is more difficult to pinpoint key reasons for Japanese expertise in manufacturing and it becomes necessary to look at some of the cultural and historical underpinnings of Japanese society. Furthermore, throughout its recent history, Japan has modelled its development on other societies (Lehmann 1982: 288). In crude terms, this model could be described as one that attempts to extricate and emphasize the vital ingredients of Western capitalist success. Although this model has undergone a significant degree of indigenization, the external model has nevertheless existed. This case study will therefore attempt to trace the broad pattern of the historical development of Japanese industry and give some idea of the types of phases that present Third World countries may have to face if they are to industrialize successfully.

Japan's industrial expansion can be said to fall into a number of distinct phases of growth. Firstly, mention must be made of the feudal rule of the Tokugawa family from the early seventeenth century until 1868. Nakamura (1966: 16) has attributed a positive role to the Tokugawa performance, suggesting that much of the groundwork for the development of industry was laid during this period, when Japan was not as backward and feudal as was once thought. In the 1850s Japan was reasonably productive for a traditional economy and possessed several features that made it more responsive than most traditional economies to economic stimuli (Crawcour 1965: 44). These included a high potential for saving, a well-developed system of national markets, an emerging national communications network, a comparatively well-educated and economically motivated population, national unity and independence from foreign domination.

In 1868, in response to a number of internal and external pressures, the Tokugawa regime yielded power to the restored imperial dynasty. The Meiji restoration was to see a series of revolutionary changes (Patrick and Rosovsky 1976: 7). Like most modernizing nations, Japan had to pass through a period of transition (1868–88). The old society and economic order was discarded, frontiers were opened to foreign commerce and the new rulers began the task of building a modern country on the basis of an industrialized economy. They felt that in order to maintain Japan's independence it was necessary to catch up with the West (Frank 1975: 32), and for both military and economic motives industrialization was the means adopted to achieve this aim (Sen 1984: 128).

Initially, the traditional agricultural resources were exploited in order to generate exports and revenues for the government. At this stage, there were no other significant sources of revenue to tap, and, in spite of the onus placed on the agricultural sector in the early stages of industrialization, it nevertheless continued to expand (Lehmann 1982: 192). The government used its funds to establish pilot factories to demonstrate that industrial investment was possible and could pay off (Moulder 1977: 177). It was hoped that private capital would thus be more forthcoming. In addition, in the 1870s, the government began to promote railway construction. After two decades of conditioning, Japan reached what could be called the 'take-off' stage in industrialization in about 1888 (Hone 1965: 183). In the 1880s and 1890s, the Meiji government switched emphasis to subsidizing private industry, and above all heavy industry, railway construction and shipping. The government had begun to experiment with the establishment of national banks as early as the 1870s, but in 1900 the Industrial Bank of Japan was founded to provide long-term low-interest loans to investors in modern industry.

The importance from an early stage of an outward-oriented approach to economic growth and industrialization must be emphasized. In the beginning, this meant importing manufactured goods and exporting primary products, but there followed a gradual shift in the structure of trade. Thus, in the first couple of decades of the Meiji period, just under half of Japan's imports consisted of finished manufactured goods; by 1911, however, they represented less than a quarter. In terms of exports, in the initial stages about 50 per cent were raw materials (including foodstuffs) – these decreased to 20 per cent by 1911; meanwhile, exports of finished manufactured goods rose from 2 per cent in the early 1870s to over 30 per cent by 1911 (Lehmann 1982: 181). As Japan became absorbed into the world economy, it emerged not merely as a client to the major industrial powers but indeed as a major competitor. By 1900 the share of agricultural employment had fallen to 66 per cent, capital formation was 13 per cent of GNP, and modern factory output accounted for 6 per cent of domestic production. Such a level of industrializaion certainly helped the Japanese military in defeating the Russian Empire in 1905.

The next phase of Japan's model of industrial expansion lasted from 1905 until the Great Depression and included the development boom of the first World War and the years of adjustment during the 1920s. On average the economy continued to expand rapidly at a real annual growth rate of about 3.5 per cent. Cotton textiles became the most important industry, and by 1914 finished textile products made in Japan were competitive throughout the world and especially in Asia and Africa. The most striking characteristic of Japanese expansion was its strength after the First World War (Shionoya 1968: 78). While European countries showed industrial decline or stagnation as a result of war destruction, Japan continued to expand even more quickly than before and this period very much sees Japan catching up with the European countries (Shionoya 1968: 78). During the First World War boom, the investment ratio had reached 17.7 per cent. By 1931, less than half of the labour force remained in agriculture and factory production had risen to 19 per cent of domestic production.

Unlike many other countries, Japanese industrial expansion was particularly strong in the 1930s with GNP expanding at over 5 per cent a year. During this period, in response to the militarist ambitions of the government, the industrial structure shifted decisively to new leading sectors, namely the chemical, metal and machinery industries, and large industrial units came to dominate the economic scene. A military–industrial complex associated with heavy industry was thus imposed on the existing textile base. The internationalization of the economy increased throughout this period so that by the time of Pearl Harbour, Japan was a relatively advanced economic power, both a major exporter of manufacturing products and a major importer of raw materials. The labour force in agriculture had declined to nearly 40 per cent, capital formation had topped 20 per cent and factory output had achieved 30 per cent of domestic production (Patrick and Rosovsky 1976: 8–9).

Japanese postwar industrial expansion can be divided into a number of phases. The phase of postwar reconstruction has been seen, in retrospect, as particularly important, with considerable assistance offered by the United States (see Ch. 2). Recovery was very rapid, although occurring against a backcloth of high rates of inflation and monetary expansion, severe food shortages and, initially, declining production. In accordance with the policy of the US occupation authorities, there was a reduction in the concentration of business power and the establishment of more competitive markets. This involved the dissolution of the large family-owned and family-controlled 'zaibatsu' conglomerates which had characterized the modern industrial sector before the end of the war. By the end of 1947, forty-two conglomerates were dissolved (Haitani 1976: 119). In addition, cartels and monopolies were eliminated and a Fair Trade Commission was established to monitor and enforce new rules of competition in business. Most efforts for industrial reform occurred in the first two years of occupation, but thereafter policy shifted to industrial recovery.

The Korean War provided a boost to Japan's economy in 1950. This conflict lasted for roughly three years and caused a vast American military build-up in East Asia with Japan becoming the focal point of that effort. Japan became a giant supply base serving the American war effort. Thus the first postwar boom developed. Huge sums of money flooded into Japan, and the government targeted five basic industries as strategic – steel, shipbuilding, coal, power and fertilizers. These received special government assistance in the form of duty-free equipment imports, accelerated depreciation benefits, loans from government banks and raw material quotas (Rapp 1976: 38). The Ministry of International Trade and Industry (MITI) was the chief architect of Japan's postwar industrial policy, which gave government aid in terms of depreciation allowances, technical support and loans for industry in the early 1950s.

The Allied occupation of Japan ended in 1952 and Japan once again became an independent nation. According to Shinohara (1968: 278), a second phase of postwar expansion occurred between 1952 and 1955. The period was characterized by a slowing down of industrial expansion and of private fixed investment and by a stabilization of inflation. Restrictions on 'zaibatsu' conglomerates were relaxed and many of these companies reformed or merged around major banks, becoming known as 'keiretsu'. Figure 12.1 reveals how the DKB 'keiretsu' had been reformed by the early 1980s; a wide variety of sectoral interests (finance, insurance, retailing, trade, chemicals, steel, metals, rubber, paper, electrical goods, motor vehicles, optical goods, engineering and machinery, services and construction were now loosely tied together around the central focus of the Dai-Ichi Kangyo Bank).

The period from 1955 to 1961 marked the adoption of a 'Five Year Plan for Self-Support', designed to guide and direct industrial activities. The plan was prompted by the belief that the $2 billion received in aid from the United States after the war, and perhaps another billion a year during the Korean conflict, were inappropriate ways of stimulating industrial expansion. The idea was now that autonomous, self-supporting policies were superior (Okita 1980). This period also saw an investment boom, highly oriented towards the production of capital goods, as well as consumer durables. Private fixed investment increased 4.5 times in these six years. Production expanded in every sector and technical innovation occurred in many fields of industry. The pattern of excess demand, evident in the earlier postwar

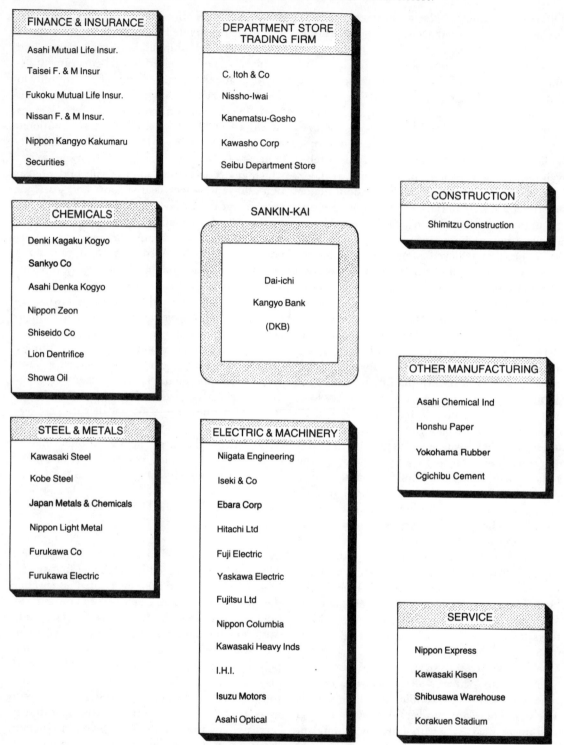

FINANCE & INSURANCE

Asahi Mutual Life Insur.

Taisei F. & M Insur

Fukoku Mutual Life Insur.

Nissan F. & M Insur.

Nippon Kangyo Kakumaru

Securities

DEPARTMENT STORE TRADING FIRM

C. Itoh & Co

Nissho-Iwai

Kanematsu-Gosho

Kawasho Corp

Seibu Department Store

CONSTRUCTION

Shimitzu Construction

CHEMICALS

Denki Kagaku Kogyo

Sankyo Co

Asahi Denka Kogyo

Nippon Zeon

Shiseido Co

Lion Dentrifice

Showa Oil

SANKIN-KAI

Dai-ichi

Kangyo Bank

(DKB)

OTHER MANUFACTURING

Asahi Chemical Ind

Honshu Paper

Yokohama Rubber

Cgichibu Cement

STEEL & METALS

Kawasaki Steel

Kobe Steel

Japan Metals & Chemicals

Nippon Light Metal

Furukawa Co

Furukawa Electric

ELECTRIC & MACHINERY

Niigata Engineering

Iseki & Co

Ebara Corp

Hitachi Ltd

Fuji Electric

Yaskawa Electric

Fujitsu Ltd

Nippon Columbia

Kawasaki Heavy Inds

I.H.I.

Isuzu Motors

Asahi Optical

SERVICE

Nippon Express

Kawasaki Kisen

Shibusawa Warehouse

Korakuen Stadium

12.1   The structure of the DKB 'keiretsu' in the early 1980s.

period, was now replaced by a pattern of excess capacity. Indeed the period 1961–65 was characterized by Shinohara (1968: 287) as one of excess capacity and investment stagnation as an aftermath of the preceding investment boom. Nevertheless, there was substantial growth recorded in heavy industry and consumer durables and Japanese economic growth was more than double that of the United States.

During the last half of the 1960s, Japanese growth was so dramatic that it managed to double its industrial capital stock in only five years (1965–70), a feat never before accomplished by an advanced industrial country. Japan now had one of the strongest international balance of payments and was a considerable lender to other countries in international money markets. Frank (1975: 4) noted that during this period 'it become apparent that Japan's international competitive position had greatly strengthened across a broad range of industrial products and that the country had unequivocally moved into the position of structural surplus on trade account'

Even in the 1970s, when growth rates around the world were stagnant, Japan still maintained a fairly respectable 4.8 per cent average growth rate between 1970 and 1980. The country's heavy and chemical industries continued to grow and motor vehicles, televisions, audio systems, washing machines and other consumer electronics became the high expansion industries. Initially these products had served as substitutes for imports in the large and growing domestic market, but during the 1970s they became large exports. Exports grew at least twice as rapidly as world trade, making Japan an increasingly weighty factor in the world economy. Many American industries have been severely affected by the growing competition from Japan's efficient and productive plants, most particularly during the 1980s.

During the 1970s and 1980s, investment has shifted away from labour-intensive sectors, as Fig. 12.2 reveals in graphical form. To a lesser extent, investment has also shifted out of raw-material-intensive industry, such as steel, aluminium and chemicals – particularly since the oil price rises of the early 1980s. Instead investment has shifted into microelectronics, high technology and

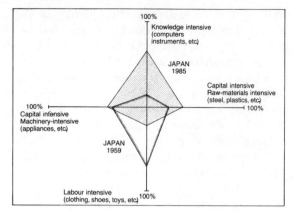

12.2 The changing profile of Japanese industry between 1959 and 1985.

knowledge-intensive industries. In 1981, the Japanese government launched a ten-year programme to build a fifth-generation computer system with the aim of becoming the world's leading supplier of advanced computer systems.

After the high economic growth rates of the 1970s and early 1980s, the late 1980s seemed to herald distinctly slower growth, particularly after the significant appreciation of the yen against the dollar in the mid-1980s. However, by the end of 1987, the expected slowdown had not occurred:

> Japan stayed on its independent course, shifting with agility from the world of the low, undervalued yen to the harsher terrain of the high yen. Corporate earnings for the second quarter of 1987 were up by nearly 30 per cent. By August [1987], unemployment was down to 2.8 per cent and industrial production was running at an annual growth rate of 5 per cent. Despite a 45 per cent appreciation of the yen, not a single notable bankruptcy was recorded in the export sector. In short, it has been a year of stunning adjustment (Rapoport 1987b: 1).

Implications of the Japanese case study

The Japanese case study undoubtedly has implications for all Third World countries. One hundred years ago, Japan was only beginning its path towards industrialization. Now it is the most successful industrial economy on the planet. The implications of Japanese growth are perhaps most relevant for the countries of Asia, and, within Asia, for those countries of the Pacific rim. Up to now the Japanese model has merely been described. Now we will consider the various explanations of Japan's industrial success and their relevance for the present industrializing countries of Asia.

A factor commonly associated with the rapid expansion of industry in Japan is its late entry into modern economic growth and its economic backwardness at the initial stages of growth. This argument is closely associated with that of Gerschenkron that we discussed in Chapter 5. As a latecomer Japan had the advantage of learning from the greatest number of previously industrialized nations. Watanabe (1968: 121–2) described Japan's rapid industrialization process as 'an imitative development with a special emphasis on the absorption of imported technology'.

However, the important point to stress is that while late entry provided the need to be open to new innovations and inventions from all parts of the industrialized world, Japanese success stemmed from the ability to distil the essence of the various product, process and organizational innovations from industrialized countries and develop a unique synthesis of the most relevant factors behind continued industrial growth. The 'just-in-time' system that we referred to in Chapter 10 can be envisaged as being based on the most salient points of modern capitalist growth, and most particularly the need to provide the framework for continued technological change. Japan showed that late entry is only an advantage as long as an adaptable and flexible form of technological development emerges in the country in question.

The dual structure of the Japanese economy is often assigned an important role in the country's industrial expansion. This refers to the contrast between modern and traditional sectors within the same country. Modern, efficient, large-scale enterprises exist alongside small, labour-intensive production units within the same industrial sectors (Watanabe 1968). Interactions between the two sectors in terms of subcontracting, absorption and transmission of cyclical fluctuations and behaviour of capital and labour markets are very important. The close contacts between large and small enterprises and the self-interest which the former had in keeping the latter alive (such as in the provision of cheap components for assembly) has meant that growth in the large-scale sector was transmitted fairly rapidly to the small-scale one. Such dual structures are in evidence in most Third World countries and provide the possibility of transmitting growth to the small business sector. The essence of the dual structure in Japan concerns the nature of long-term cooperation and technical assistance that exists between the large enterprise and its small supply firms.

To what extent has foreign trade been a major mechanism by which Japan secured the means of industrial expansion? It will be remembered from earlier in this chapter that even in 1911, one-third of Japan's total exports corresponded to manufactures. Manufactured exports came to have a steadily expanding share of total exports during the following thirty years, a trend that was re-emphasised after the Second World War. Certainly the expansion of industrial exports has contributed greatly to advancing productivity in Japan and provided a means of paying for indispensable imports of raw materials, energy, capital equipment and technology. However, it should be noted that the domestic market has traditionally absorbed the major share of key export products. Every Japanese export industry has achieved significant overseas penetration only after a large domestic market base had emerged. In terms of Japan's growth up until 1938, Lockwood (1954: 364) noted that 'the fortunes of the export trade made the difference between prosperity and depression in Japan...it was the domestic market that was the chief stimulus to growth'. In terms of the two decades after the Second World War, most authors have thought that Japan was much less dependent on foreign trade. They tended to see a pattern of industrial growth based on a repetition of import substitution, expansion of domestic demand and exports applied to newly-emerging modern industries. However, during the following two decades (1965–85), this model was instrumental in causing Japanese exports to grow at twice the rate of world trade, thus making Japan more and more significant on the world stage as an exporter of manufactured goods.

The role of government in Japan's industrial expansion has been a matter of some dispute. The image of a centrally directed 'Japan Incorporated' in which the government, in close consultation with business, allocates resources among productive activities is certainly overemphasized. Admittedly government has given the highest priority to industrial development and structural problems generated by economic growth, but it has aimed more to guide business decision making rather than to control it. The main stimulus to growth has been from the private sector, both in terms of business initiative and private demand. Thus, the government adopted a supportive role to provide an environment conducive to industrial expansion by protectionism, preventing excessive competition and by making funds available through the banking system at low interest rates. Its intervention (developing infant industries and the structural adjustment of declining industries) accelerated trends already set in motion by private market forces. In addition to macroeconomic policies aimed at full employment and price stability, the government adopted a coordinated set of macroeconomic policies designed to accelerate structural change in favour of promising high-growth sectors. The Japanese model of government actively encouraging industrial expansion but leaving the actual business initiatives to the private sector has had an impact on the governments of many Asian countries eager to industrialize and expand manufacturing exports.

The critical role of government in the framework of industrial strategy alongside the Japanese interpretation of the most salient points of Western capitalist success has led to the idea that a key factor in Japaese industrial expansion has been the cultivation of the right industries at the right time, and particularly since the Second World War. Japan has moved sequentially from light, technically unsophisticated industries to more capital-intensive and technologically advanced industries. What initially was an *ad hoc* imitation of Western economic development became a structural policy of dynamic comparative advantage under which industries were developed in response to local demand and in anticipation of future competitiveness in the world economy. As these industries became internationally competitive, they were left on their own to provide their contribution to growth and development (Frank 1975: 42).

Government has also been prominent in channelling resources towards education. Ever since Japan opened up to Western commerce and trade in the Meiji period and adopted the slogan 'Wakon Yoksai' (Japanese Spirit, Western Technology), enormous resources have been devoted to education. This has meant that the labour force is highly educated and receptive to change. Furthermore, it has built upon the character of the Japanese people, that has itself been a major element in Japan's rapid industrialization. The propensity to save and invest in future expansion is strong at both the individual and corporate level. Individuals usually deposit their savings in city banks and commercial banks, which in turn channel funds into investment loans to business. Partly as a result, Japan's industrial investment levels have far surpassed those of the other industrialized countries (Baranson 1981: 10). Moreover, Japan's industrialization is generally presented as being exceptional in that Japan generated its own capital, and was not dependent on foreign loans (Lehmann 1982: 173).

Kuznets (1968) argued that the interplay between the social, political and economic aspects in the process of Japan's industrial expansion was vital. Borrowed technology, dual structure and foreign trade, he maintained were all mechanisms in the industrialization process but they were far from sufficient. 'What made them sufficient was the underlying capacity of Japan's social and political system to respond to the challenges that the crisis constituted; and to respond in such a way that technology would be borrowed, exports expanded or modern components adapted' (Kuznets 1968). It is interesting to point out that foreign explanations of Japanese industrial success cite factors such as permanent employment, close business/government interaction, quality circles, large trading firms, long-range investment horizons and superior industrial engineering. In contrast, the Japanese view their strengths as the product more of hard work and careful planning than any brilliant technology worthy of foreign emulation (McMillan 1985: 7). Putting it simplistically, while foreign observers stress the economic, the Japanese concentrate on the cultural and social – the idea of a society of consensus, where strong corporate loyalties can be traced back to the concept of 'ie-ism' from the Edo period (1603–1868) – the 'ie' or merchant company exercised full authority over its members and expected to receive complete loyalty, but in return members of the 'ie' were guaranteed security for life. In the modern corporate landscape of Japan, similar cultural values still pertain:

> Every Japanese worker feels part of the company he works for; each knows how well the company is doing, what the profits for last year were and what percentage of the market the company controls. The concept all workers agree on is the better the company does the greater the rewards they will receive. The family idea remains a strong one throughout all the firms. Ask a Japanese man what he does for a living and he will tell you the company he works for, not the job he does. The family mentality is maintained throughout the company and as one senior manager was heard to comment, 'all workers must have the minds of managers' – indicating the desire for continual improvement for the benefit of all. The ideas of collectivism, 'ie-ism' and consensus born in earlier Japanese history still underpin the society and industrial development of the present day (Allan 1985: 19).

The success of Japanese industrialization can therefore be explained not only in terms of the 'economic' theory of Gerschenkron but also in terms of the 'social and cultural' ideas of Parsons (see Ch. 5).

Whether the determining factors behind Japanese industrial success are economic or cultural, the Japanese example has had and continues to have a profound effect on other Asian countries and particularly those of the Pacific rim. This effect can be seen in two ways. First, the Japanese economy has provided a powerful growth pole in the Pacific rim of East Asia, stimulating resource and component linkages with other East Asian countries; most recently linkages in terms of the imports of assembled manufactured goods have been of increasing sig-

nificance. Secondly, Japan has provided a model of how densely-populated, resource-poor countries in East Asia can achieve rapid economic growth through concentrating on industrialization. The precise interpretation of the salient features of Japanese industrial success may vary from country to country but, none the less, there have been many attempts to follow the broad outline of the Japanese model. It is to these 'model followers' that we now turn our attention.

FIRST GENERATION FOLLOWERS?

Japanese influence and the industrialization of Korea and Taiwan

> To the extent that any country has been the model for Korea in its industrialisation it is Japan. Explanations are easy to find; geographical propinquity; recent experience; familiarity with the language, particularly in its written form; recognition that the Japanese have already adapted Western technology to Eastern social and political mores; and, surely a necessary part of the explanation, Japanese success in their own endeavours (Enos and Park 1988: 217).

In their recent book on manufacturing technology in Korea, Enos and Park stress the importance of the Japanese model on recent Korean development. One of the factors they stress is that of 'recent experience' which refers to the fact that from before the First World War until 1945, Korea constituted part of the Japanese empire. During this time, Japan introduced a modern administration, monetary system, railway network and education system into Korea. Under Japanese rule, Korea did become a secondary manufacturing centre within the empire; for example, the manufacturing share of GDP rose from 1 to 15 per cent between 1910 and 1940 (Harris 1986: 33). However, it was a highly dependent form of industrialization with most of the capital employed in manufacturing being Japanese and most of the technicians coming from Japan. By 1940, there were an estimated 700 000 Japanese in Korea or about 17 per cent of the labour force.

The end to the Second World War thus brought the removal not only of the ruling order but also of a whole swathe of the business and technical class. Further economic instability naturally associated the partition of the country between the heavy industrial north and the light industrial south. For the south, occupied by the Americans, the end of the Japanese imperial trading system brought the loss of external markets and access to resources. As a result, the number of industrial establishments was halved and employment fell by 40 per cent (Harris 1986: 34).

The postwar American occupation did introduce one interesting policy, whose subsequent relevance to manufacturing growth is much debated – the reform of the land-holding system. 'The Americans expropriated Japanese holdings, and pressed the new Korean administration to purchase all large Korean landed estates on specially favourable terms. By this means, the landowner class was eliminated. No free market in land was permitted to develop thereafter, and the maximum size of holding was limited to three hectares' (Harris 1986: 34). As a result, the Korean landscape became characterized by large numbers of smallholders, who, it could be argued, provided an extensive market for domestically produced manufactured goods.

However, between 1950 and 1953, Korea, both north and south, became the scene of a horrific war that left 1.3 million people killed and brought economic ruin. After the war, the South Korean economy was mainly supported by massive American military and civil aid. However, by the late 1950s, a reasonable recovery was in progress. Manufacturing was in the vanguard of recovery with annual growth rates fluctuating between 8 and 20 per cent. Manufacturing enterprises benefited, on the one hand, from protection against imports and, on the other, from favourable export credits.

The role of the military in Korea's industrial development became even more significant after 1961 when the eighteen-year dictatorship of General Park began. A strongly export-oriented industrial policy evolved with the Korean currency being halved in value, restrictions on external trade being eased (so that exporters acquired virtual freedom to import provided they exported) and tax incentives to export being increased. As North American military aid declined through the

1960s, the economy switched its emphasis to increasing manufactured exports relatively smoothly. Korea entered on a new phase of industrialization in the late 1960s and early 1970s when the government shifted emphasis to the development of heavy, intermediate (feedstock) industries – steel, non-ferrous metals, chemicals, petrochemicals, machinery and shipbuilding.

As the Korean government forged industrial expansion through both import substitution and the stimulation of exports, the similarity between Korean and Japanese patterns of industralization became evident. The most significant aspects of the Japanese model that the Koreans have identified and adopted would seem to be the crucial role of government in the industrialization process, a firm belief in new technology and the maximising of economies of scale, and the idea that successful industrialization basically concerns going through a whole series of different phases. This attitude is clearly revealed in the Korean petrochemical industry.

First of all, Korea, like Japan earlier, had no obvious comparative advantage in the production of petrochemicals, an industry intensive in its use of capital, natural resources and technology – in all three of which Korea was lacking in the 1960s. Nevertheless, the government pursued the creation of a petrochemical complex in Korea quite relentlessly. Some extracts from Enos and Park's case study of the Korean petrochemical industry clearly reveal this:

> The Korean government invited an American consulting firm, Arthur D. Little Co., and the Fluor Corporation to make marketing and engineering feasibility studies for a petrochemical industy in Korea. The first reports submitted in 1966, indicated only a moderate increase in the demand for petrochemical products in the early 1970s and concluded that the domestic market was far too small to support plants capable of producing at low unit costs, relative to plants abroad.
>
> However, the Korean government had made different forecasts, yielding higher estimates of demand for petrochemicals, high enough to make new plants economically feasible. These demand estimates suggested that a petrochemical complex changing 66 000 metric tons per year of ethylene would be appropriate. To exploit economies of

large-scale production, the Korean government chose an even more ambitious programme for inclusion in the Second Five-Year Economic Development Plan (1967–71), one which resulted in the petrochemical complex (at Ulsan) changing 150 000 MT/Y of ethylene.

It took almost two years to complete the financial arrangements with foreign investors and international banks. During this period demand grew, justifying the ambitious programme. In 1970 the Korean government issued a Law for the Promotion of the Petrochemical Industry, which offered five years of full tax holiday (for the foreign firms that invested half of the equity capital and provided the technology). The incentive was supplemented by a guaranteed return on the invested capital. In 1975 the second petrochemical complex at Yeocheon was authorised without these special incentives.

What stimulated the establishment of the petrochemical industry in Korea was the expansion in demand for intermediate and basic materials brought about by the expansion of production of final goods. It is thus a classic case of import substitution; of chemicals for identical goods manufactured abroad and incorporated into domestic production at a later stage – i.e. import substitution of intermediate products (Enos and Park 1988: 48–50).

The above evidence demonstrates the Korean government's firm commitment to new phases of industrial growth despite the almost complete absence of comparative advantage and despite contrary advice from international consultants. However, the policy worked because the phasing was correctly timed. Demand for petrochemical products in Korea escalated during the 1970s, and the plants coming on stream had a ready market locally.

The continued expansion of Korea's petrochemical industry during the 1970s (Enos and Park 1988: 50–2) took place regardless of significant increases in world oil prices and the consequent increases in both feedstock and energy costs. As in Japan, the reaction was to promote more investment. Between 1976 and 1979, investment as a share of gross product increased from 25 per cent to 35 per cent, and about 80 per cent of the investment went into the energy-intensive heavy industrial and chemical sectors (Harris 1986: 36). Such dramatic increases in investment

and a concomitant expansion in foreign borrowing did have critical consequences in the early 1980s, with higher world oil prices, increasing world interest rates and stagnant world trade (see Ch. 3 and 4). South Korea not only underwent a political crisis (Park was murdered in October 1979) but also a debt crisis as South Korea became the third largest debtor in the world (after Brazil and Mexico); the external debt was still as high as US$58 billion in 1985.

The crisis of 1979/80 served to change the direction of Korea's industrial path, partly due to external forces (the IMF and US government) and partly due to internal pressures. Government withdrew from its policy of promoting heavy industry, regardless of comparative advantage and investible funds. A gradual process of trade liberalization began in terms of tariff reform and the reduction of non-tariff barriers; this was largely carried out to keep the markets of developed countries open for Korean manufactured exports. Korea's large conglomerates or 'chaebol' (Hyundai, Daewoo, Goldstar, Samsung, for example) began to switch their investment plans from heavy to light industry – motor cars, electrical and electronic goods, office machinery.

In many ways, such a shift (although a response to a crisis) can be seen as copying the Japanese example of changing the emphasis of future industrial growth from heavy to light industry. Japan had decidedly shifted the emphasis of future growth in the late 1960s/early 1970s; Korea was having to make a similar shift only a decade later. As with Japan, the shift was to high-technology and information-intensive industries. However, for this to occur, it was necessary to rapidly build up its infrastructure of qualified scientific personnel and intensify its research and development (R&D) activities. The OECD (1988: 37) commented that during the 1980s, 'Korea has moved the fastest in increasing its R&D/GNP ratio, and that it has made striking progress in expanding the output of its educational institutions, notably in engineering education'. New developments in R&D in such sectors as engineering and electronics are being achieved as far as possible through indigenous agencies.

Trade liberalization and the shift in investment to lighter, more technologically advanced industry has certainly had an impact on the balance of trade. After five years of trade deficits, Korea recorded a trade surplus of US$4.6 billion in 1986. Korea's continued dependence on its special relationship with the United States is, however, demonstrated by its US$7.3 billion trade surplus with that country. In other words, South Korea still maintains a large trade deficit with the rest of the world and particularly Japan (approximately US$5 billion and mainly composed of machinery and capital goods).

Direct Japanese influence in Korea dated from 1907 to 1945; in Taiwan, it dated back even further to 1895 (Allen 1981: 50). While Korea had received some industrial investment from Japan (partly due to the processing of raw materials from Japan's possessions in Manchuria), Taiwan was to receive relatively little. Indeed, Japan saw Taiwan primarily as a source of agricultural products for its empire. Nevertheless, significant infrastructure was built in order to serve this aim – railways and roads as well as health and educational facilities. 'The Japanese also transferred to Taiwan their own belief in the importance of education, and of an educational system geared to mass literacy and practical skill formation' (Corbridge 1986: 181). Apart from improving literacy and health, the Japanese occupation considerably increased the production and productivity of Taiwanese agriculture, most notably through the expansion of irrigation and the introduction of fertilizers. Industrial production related directly to agriculture also became significant, most notably sugar refining and rice milling.

The post-1945 period was particularly difficult, as Taiwan lost its administration, its overseas markets and became part of China until 1949, when it became the refuge of China's republican forces, the Kuomintang. About 1 million refugees arrived in Taiwan and effectively came to constitute a new ruling order, administration, business class and army. A radical land reform followed which had the result of producing a rural landscape of large numbers of small farms. Its impact on subsequent industrial development has been stressed by many observers: 'The Taiwanese land reforms and the associated cooperative movements had the effect of institutionalizing a pattern of rural demand which was at once supportive of low-level agrotechnologies and which could be met largely by local production in a decentralised industrial strategy' (Corbridge 1986: 182). Throughout the 1950s, there was a continued emphasis on expanding production and productivity in the agricultural sector.

It was not until the late 1950s that the Taipei government began to promote seriously the manufacturing sector. The success of nearby Hong Kong has long been credited with providing the stimulus. After years of an overvalued exchange rate (in order to keep manufactured imports cheap), the Taiwan dollar was devalued by more than a half at the end of the 1950s. Tariffs remained high and non-tariff barriers elaborate. From the early 1960s, however, the growth of manufacturing output and exports was rapid. As we noted in Chapter 7, Taiwan provides a good example of the product life cycle model working to the advantage of a less developed country. During the 1960s Taiwan's annual manufacturing growth rate fluctuated between 8 and 24 per cent as textile and clothing exports began to boom. During the 1970s fast growth in the assembly and export of such standardized electronic products as radios and televisions meant that electronic products overtook textiles as Taiwan's major export category. This was linked to the fact that Taiwan permitted much greater possibilities for foreign investment than Korea during this time.

However, with Taiwan's Sixth Plan (1973–76), the Taipei government could be seen following the Japanese and Korean experience by assisting in the development of five heavy industrial sectors – steel, aluminium, shipbuilding, petrochemicals and synthetic fibres – although, in contrast to both Japan and Korea, most of the enterprises in these sectors came to be controlled by the state. Subsequently, in the early 1980s, the Taiwanese government followed its Korean counterpart in presiding over a further switch in emphasis and stressed the production of technologically sophisticated electronic products – micro-computers, terminals, video and telecommunication equipment. In the late 1980s, even more dramatic shifts were being considered:

The Government has set as its goal an industrial structure radically different from the one that has over the past two decades carried Taiwan's economy to its current heights. That means higher technology, increased spending on R & D, forays into new areas such as biotechnology, and an end to protection of local industries through tariffs and the like (King 1987: 4).

The industrialization of both Taiwan and Korea has been strongly influenced by Japan. Firstly, both countries formerly constituted Japanese colonies. There were many problems associated with Japanese colonialism, but, in terms of subsequent industrial development, the importance placed on infrastructure (railways, roads, ports) and human development (education, health) should not be underestimated. Secondly, the rapid industrialization of both countries since the late 1950s has been based on national interpretations of the Japanese model. It should be stressed that for South Korea to industrialize always had a strong military rationale – in order to defend itself better against North Korea after that country's invasion of 1950. As a result, the military government of General Park exerted extraordinary powers over the pattern of industrial growth:

> In the sixties and seventies, the state dominated the entire process of rapid economic growth. Between a fifth and a quarter of the gross national product was government spending: public investment was about 40 per cent of the national total, and public savings were between a fifth and a third of the whole. The government had appropriated the five leading commercial banks in the early sixties and, with the Bank of Korea and direct public-sector activites, the state controlled two-thirds of national investment. . . On top of this, by means of political patronage, discriminatory tax, credit and pricing policies, medals and awards, orders, bribery, bullying, and monthly conferences between Ministers and businessmen, the wishes of the state shaped the whole development process (Harris 1986: 41–2).

In retrospect, the strong government involvement in industry under Park had both positive and negative points. As we noted earlier with relation to Korea's petrochemical industry, it managed to create successful and efficient modern industries

in sectors where Korea had no comparative advantage. On the other hand, it did allow for a more cavalier attitude to accounting. During the late 1970s many public corporations built up major deficits, foreign borrowing increased dramatically and, as a result, Korea was hit by a major debt crisis in the first half of the 1980s.

Meanwhile, the state has been less overpowering in Taiwan, despite the existence of state enterprises in the intermediate sectors. The military burden has been significant in Taiwan as well, but it was not translated into such an overpowering state influence in the industrial economy and the rise to power of a relatively small number of very large and multifunctional private corporations. The Taiwanese model has been more strongly influenced by Hong Kong and very much relied on a wide range of private sector enterprise rather than on the public sector and a small number of massive and privileged domestic corporations. As much as 90 per cent of provincial manufacturing output in Taiwan comes from small- and medium-sized companies and nearly 70 per cent of jobs are in units employing ten or fewer workers; 57 per cent of Taiwanese value-added comes from units employing 300 workers or fewer.

This is not to say that the public sector has not been significant in Taiwanese development. It has maintained a strong role in the provision of infrastructure and education and made significant contributions to Taiwan's heavy industrial programme of the 1970s. However, widespread foreign borrowing did not occur, which has meant no debt crisis in the 1980s; indeed, by 1987, Taiwan had as much as US$69 billion of foreign reserves. Thus Taiwan has recorded continued high growth rates during the decade so that in 1987, Taiwan's *per capita* GNP index went over the US$5000 mark, twice that of South Korea.

One major contrast between Taiwan and Korea has been in government attitude towards direct foreign investment (DFI), particularly in the recent high-technology phase of development. The Taiwanese government has attempted to attract foreign investment as long as the enterprises export (normally at least 50 per cent of production) and rely on local suppliers for over one-half of their components. Between 1973 and 1980 DFI accounted for about 10 per cent of total investment made in Taiwan's manufacturing industry, but it reached much higher levels in the high-technology sectors – 50 per cent in electronics and 25 per cent in machinery. According to the OECD (1988: 41), at the end of 1981 total accumulated investment by developed countries in Taiwan amounted to US$2.3 billion. The equivalent figure for Korea (with a population double that of Taiwan) was US$1.6 billion. This reflects the Korean policy of not permitting direct foreign ownership of enterprises, preferring instead joint ventures. Foreign firms tend to provide the technological expertise and knowledge in joint ventures, but are generally not permitted to hold more than 50 per cent of the equity. This policy has been adopted by the Korean government to maximize technology transfer, in the sense of promoting the indigenous ability (of the Korean half) to understand, adapt and improve upon imported technologies.

Direct foreign investment, then, has been attracted much more to manufacturing plant in Taiwan than in Korea, particularly during the 1980s. Partly as a result of this DFI and partly due to the lack of external debt, Taiwan has tended to suffer from the problems of achieving too much success in promoting manufactured exports. During the late 1980s, manufactured exports constituted one-half of GNP, and even Taiwan's trade surplus (US$20 billion in 1987) constituted about 20 per cent of GNP. Compared with the Japanese model, Taiwan has come to rely too much on exports and not sufficiently on developing domestic demand. In this sense, Korea has more closely approximated the Japanese model with industrial growth being more evenly distributed between domestic and export markets. Finally, as a point of economic history and referring back to Chapter 5, Taiwan and Korea differed in terms of their chronology of agricultural and industrial development; industrialization came after agricultural development in Taiwan, but before it in Korea.

Having explored the differences between the Korean and Taiwanese patterns of industrialization, one is nevertheless struck by the common factors and the similarity of these with those of Japan's industrial growth. First, both countries have taken the maximum advantages from late entry into world industrial markets. Both made their first manufacturing strides in sectors where low labour costs were a distinct advantage, that is in textiles and footwear. However, after establishing a firm base in these sectors, there have been concerted attempts in both countries to move to more technologically demanding sectors – labour-intensive electronics, capital-intensive heavy industry, information-intensive manufacturing in a broad, overlapping order. The phasing of industrial development has been as obvious in these two countries as it has been in Japan. The emphasis on achieving the latest technology and the maximum economies of scale has been apparent. The ability to generate technology autonomously has been less apparent than in Japan, and in Taiwan the reliance on imported technology may present serious problems in the future. Technological adaptation and generation in Korea, dominated by government, more closely follows the Japanese model:

> Japan's lead, in terms of years over Korea, varies from a decade or so in the absorption of operating techniques to a longer period in mastering the 'core' technology. . . . In Korea, the process of absorption was approached systematically, the government assuring itself that the contracts negotiated with the foreign suppliers contained clauses relating to the acquisition of patents, designs and know-how; to the training, both abroad and on the site, of Korean engineers and managers; to the speedy replacement of expatriates; and to access to improvements in the products and processes. . . . Looking at the speed with which the different stages in the process of absorption were carried out, we find a similar pattern in the two countries (Enos and Park 1988: 228–9).

As with Japan, Korea and Taiwan present the impression of having a hard-working and dedicated workforce with an enormous capacity for saving. Indeed, in Taiwan, the savings ratio is too high; at 40 per cent in 1987, it was about double the investment rate (King 1987: 2). Balanced growth in the economy would call for these two rates to begin converging, most feasibly through an increase in domestic consumption (and hence a reduction in saving) – remarkably however, increasing consumption is proving very difficult in Taiwan.

So far this section has attempted to compare the industrial development of what could be termed the first generation of Asian imitators of the Japanese model. The previous, 'direct' experience of Japanese administration probably made both societies conducive to the aims and achievement of rapid economic growth. Radical land reforms in both Taiwan and Korea introduced the possibility for close links between agricultural and industrial development. As with Japan, the role of the military and the role of the state in industrial development were important though in rather different ways. As in Japan, again, their industrial success lies firmly in their ability to take advantage of late entry into world industrial markets and subsequently to phase in new industrial products which rapidly became successfully traded in world markets. If a short summary is required, the success of the three countries has lain in their ability to continually take advantage of their changing position in the evolving world economy.

Industrialization in the East Asia city states

I have concentrated on the cases of Korea and Taiwan in East Asia because they constitute countries where, for example, the linkages between agricultural and industrial development are apparent and the spatial tension between urban and rural development can be perceived. In terms of these basic characteristics, they represent similar historical patterns of development to Japan on the one hand; and on the other hand, they started from similar backgrounds to those presently faced by the majority of other East Asian countries.

The other two Asian countries put into the category of successful newly industrializing countries are Hong Kong and Singapore. However, these countries very much represent the conditions of city states, with limited territory and agriculture. Their economic base has by necessity depended on successful trade and, as Table 12.1 demonstrates, they have the highest *per capita* values of manufactured exports in the world –

Singapore's values are four times as high as those of Japan and over eight times those of Korea.

Having noted this overriding similarity of the free-trading city states, it must be emphasized that there have been differences in their industrial strategies: 'If Hong Kong could be seen as a working model of the neoclassical thesis, Singapore is an example of the social democratic one, with the predominant state capitalism of mixed economies, replete with consistent Keynesian policies' (Harris 1986: 60). Whereas government direction in Hong Kong's industrial growth has been relatively small, the government of Singapore has intervened strongly in the direction of industrial activity, selecting sectors of labour-intensive manufacture in the 1960s and subsequently shifting to increasingly more capital- and knowledge-intensive sectors. In this sense, the process of Singapore's industrial growth has been much more in line with that of Korea and Taiwan – with the state exercising a strong influence on the process and direction of industrial investment within a free-market framework.

> The central body for the planning and promotion of industrial development is the Economic Development Board, which maps its priorities in response to changing international and domestic conditions. The Board is active in promoting both indigenous and foreign investment in line with these priorities, by administering selective tax incentives and grant and loan schemes. More than half of the very high national savings are channelled into public institutions – the Post Office Saving Bank and the Central Provident Fund, the latter being fed by the compulsory employee and employer contribution (OECD 1988: 45).

Contrasts between Singapore and Hong Kong also occur in terms of the prevailing size of firm, with the former characterized more by giant companies and the latter by a mass of small companies. In this regard, then, Singapore provides greater similarity with Korea and Hong Kong with Taiwan. This contrast is linked to the different patterns of foreign investment. In Singapore, the predominant pattern has been that of fully and majority foreign-owned enterprises, with the reliance on foreign investment strengthening during the 1970s and 1980s. For example, the stock of direct foreign investment increased from US$0.6 billion in 1973 to an astounding US$7.3 billion in 1983 – at the time, three times that of Taiwan and about four times that of both Korea and Hong Kong; unlike Korea, Singapore relied much more on foreign investment rather than foreign borrowing during the 1970s and early 1980s.

Another significant difference relates to the political future of both city states. Hong Kong will be reincorporated back into China by the end of the century, while the future independence of Singapore seems relatively assured. I have already noted (in Ch. 7) the increasing tendency of Hong Kong's industrial entrepreneurs to establish labour-intensive plants in the surrounding

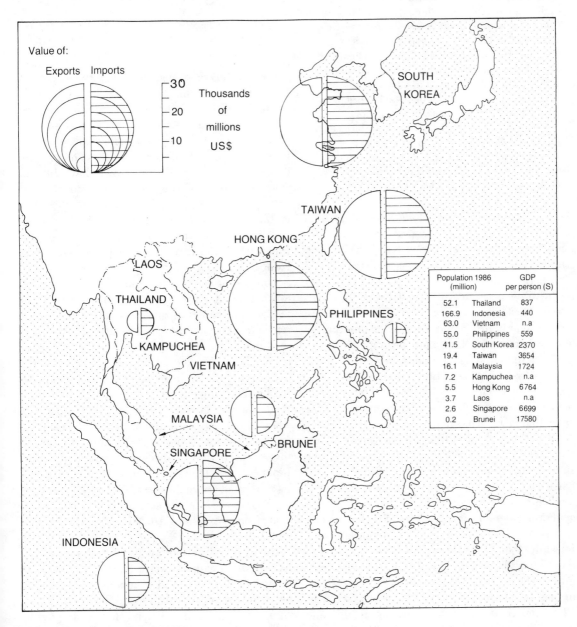

Population 1986 (million)		GDP per person (S)
52.1	Thailand	837
166.9	Indonesia	440
63.0	Vietnam	n.a
55.0	Philippines	559
41.5	South Korea	2370
19.4	Taiwan	3654
16.1	Malaysia	1724
7.2	Kampuchea	n.a
5.5	Hong Kong	6764
3.7	Laos	n.a
2.6	Singapore	6699
0.2	Brunei	17580

12.3   Trade in East Asia in 1985.

region of China and most notably the county of Dongguan. At the same time, however, Chinese investment in Hong Kong itself is rapidly increasing. In June 1988, the *Far Eastern Economic Review* (published in Hong Kong) noted:

> During the past two years, China has emerged as the major foreign investor in Hong Kong. Although Chinese holdings are shielded by myriad official and unofficial companies, the best estimates put investment through the 2000 or so companies with substantial Chinese backing at about US$10 billion – compared with US investment of about US$6 billion. . . . Chinese investment in Hong Kong is a microcosm of the changes that have occurred in China since 1979. . . . As China's open-door policy began to take hold, China's presence in Hong Kong evolved from a small group of long-established state-controlled companies to a mixed bag of organisations representing national, provincial, municipal, cooperative and private interests (*Far Eastern Economic Review* 23/6/88: 64–5).

Cross-investment between Hong Kong and China is becoming so complicated and apparently difficult to disentangle that Hong Kong firms using Chinese investment are investing in firms back in China (in order to benefit from the privileges given to overseas investors in China). It is apparent, then, that Hong Kong's economic future will be dominated by an increasing interaction and linkage with China and, most particularly, with the surrounding Cantonese region.

Industrialization in South Korea, Taiwan, Singapore and Hong Kong has undoubtedly benefited from the theoretical advantages of late entry that Gerschenkron postulated three decades ago (see Ch. 5). Apart from Hong Kong, the importance that Gerschenkron attributed to active state involvement in the industrialization process has been vindicated; the theoretical advantages of late entry (receiving the latest technology and generating significant economies of scale) are further points that make the Gerschenkronian thesis relevant today. However, the success of industrialization in the four countries has also been intimately linked to their achievements in trading in highly competitive world markets (see Fig. 12.3) and their ability to phase in steadily the production of more sophisticated industrial sec-

tors, points not emphasized or developed by Gerschenkron's analysis. The success of the Japanese model made such factors important. However, the crucial question in terms of the wider issue of Third World industrialization must be – can these models of industrial growth be passed on to further generations of industrializing countries?

PROSPECTS FOR FURTHER GENERATIONS OF INDUSTRIALIZING COUNTRIES IN EAST ASIA

Although I have argued that the influence of the Japanese model has permeated the industrial strategies of the first generation of industrializing countries in East Asia, it has also been emphasized that the process of industrialization has been affecting very different countries and that the precise patterns of industrial growth have differed from country to country. This geographical proviso becomes even more evident as the focus is shifted to those East Asian countries attempting to follow in one way or another the examples of Japan, Korea, Taiwan, Singapore and Hong Kong.

One Asian country that presently seems to be making great efforts to follow the East Asian models of industrialization is Thailand. Some relevant aspects of how this country is fitting into the broader pattern of Asian industrialization are revealed in Table 12.2. First, the table demonstrates that investment in manufacturing has been booming in the mid-1980s, approximately doubling between 1985 and 1987. Second, whereas domestic investment has climbed slowly, foreign investment has nearly quadrupled in the three-year period. However, investments from Japanese and Taiwanese sources have increased by a factor of approximately 18 and 10 respectively; thus, in 1987, 59 per cent of inward investment came from two other East Asian countries, Japan and Taiwan.

Enterprises from both countries were investing heavily in Thailand in order to shift labour-intensive assembly and component production away from domestic locations to the cheap labour sites of Thailand. Sharp, for example, is decentralizing production of microwave ovens,

Table 12.2 Sources of foreign investment capital from applications approved in the mid-1980s in Thailand (in million baht*)

Source of Investment	1985		1986		1987 (Jan-Sept)	
	Amount	%	Amount	%	Amount	%
Japan	169	9.0	1 675	53.4	2 347	43.2
Taiwan	111	5.9	46	1.5	860	15.8
United States	737	39.1	143	4.6	377	7.0
Hong Kong	163	8.7	230	7.3	210	3.9
United Kingdom	45	2.4	291	9.3	72	1.3
India	12	0.6	27	0.9	36	0.7
Singapore	37	2.0	97	3.1	27	0.5
Australia	13	0.7	16	0.5	27	0.5
West Germany	11	0.6	121	3.9	24	0.5
Netherlands	21	1.1	37	1.2	14	0.3
Malaysia	97	5.1	130	4.1	12	0.2
South Korea	12	0.6	4	0.1	1	0.0
Others	456	24.2	322	10.3	1 419	26.2
Total foreign investment	1 884	100.0	3 139	100.0	5 427	100.0
Domestic investment	5 537		6 064		7 495	
TOTAL INVESTMENT	7 421		9 203		12 992	

* 1987 exchange rate – 26 baht/US$.

(*Source*: Adapted from Dalby 1987: 2)

refrigerators, washing machines and audio products to Thailand, and similar investments are being made by Toshiba, Sony and Matsushita. These Japanese corporations are drawn by the low relative cost of labour in Thailand; assembly line workers in the Toshiba assembly plant in Thailand earn about 73 baht (£1.50) for a nine-hour day (Housego 1988: 12), less than one-twentieth of the equivalent wage rate in Japan and one-sixth of the average Taiwanese rate (Dalby 1987: 2). Alongside the assembly plants, Japanese component firms are establishing subsidiaries. For example, doors and other stamped metal parts for Sharp microwave ovens are made by the little-known Japanese component firm, San El Kinzoku. Recently the latter has located a small component plant in Thailand near to Sharp's assembly plant. Due to the influx of Japanese and Taiwanese investment, the United States has dropped from being the major foreign investor in 1985 to a poor third in 1987, only a little ahead of Hong Kong. Even from such relatively crude data, then, it can be said that Thailand's industrialization is benefiting from capital and technological linkages with enterprises from Japan and the first generation of industrializing countries in Asia.

Thailand's strategy of industrialization is gradually coming round to copy that of Taiwan and Korea. Until 1977, Thailand's industrial policy was undoubtedly based on import substitution, with little incentive to export manufactured goods, tariffs of up to 600 per cent (on imported cars) and a reliance on primary good exports. A relatively high-cost and inefficient industrial structure prevailed. Between 1977 and 1983, Thailand attempted to copy Korea by establishing costly capital-intensive projects in oil refining, chemicals, motor vehicles and machinery (Housego 1988: 12), backed by tariff protection. However, there was still little incentive to export as the baht tended to remain fixed in parity to the dollar. As the dollar rose in the early 1980s, so the baht became increasingly overvalued and exporting unprofitable.

To give an idea of the loss of competitiveness that this policy cost the Thai economy, the Thailand Development Research Institute has compared Thai and Korean exchange rate management. While the baht barely changed against the dollar between 1955 and 1984, the Korean won depreciated by an average of 10 per cent a year (Housego 1988: 12).

Thailand eventually devalued the baht by 15 per cent against the dollar in November 1984 and has linked the baht to a basket of international currencies since October 1985. After 35 years of an overvalued currency, the depreciation of the baht has considerably helped exporters – in a similar way that an undervalued exchange rate had assisted in the industrialization of Japan, Korea and Taiwan. Manufactured exports have grown by an average of 40 per cent in both 1986 and 1987. Most of these increases are in the well-defined labour-intensive sectors that have started off the export drives of all the successful NICs; in 1987, for example, Thailands's footwear and garment exports increased by 73 per cent, and leather and plastic luggage by 208 per cent and 173 per cent respectively. Foreign investment in manufacturing has boomed and particularly in export-oriented projects. Although the Thai government produced a foreign investment statute that was distinctly unfavourable to foreign enterprise in 1972, the terms have steadily become more advantageous for foreign companies in subsequent years. Furthermore, with the value of agricultural exports declining, manufactured goods have overtaken agricultural products as Thailand's main source of export earnings. In 1987, Thailand recorded GDP growth of 7 per cent, but the growth rate of the industrial sector itself was higher than this.

In the fact that Thailand's industrial strategy is export oriented and based on boosting private enterprise and in the fact that government has become involved in heavy industrial and infrastructural developments, Thailand's recent manufacturing growth has certain similarities with the industrial patterns of the better established Asian countries discussed earlier. Thailand is still at an early stage of its manufacturing development, but is undoubtedly benefiting at the moment from closer links with enterprises from other Asian countries. The government has also attempted to provide a macroeconomic framework similar to that of Korea and Taiwan, with an undervalued exchange rate, incentive for domestic saving, attractions for foreign investors

and some government involvement in the industrial process – though, in this latter case, certainly less than in Korea.

Housego (1988: 12) in his survey of Asia's Pacific rim sees the full integration of the Chinese business community into Thai society as being a significant explanatory factor behind the recent record of economic growth. In contrast, he sees Malaysia's New Economic Policy (1970–90) as having the emphasis on 'helping the Malays to the extent that the Chinese feel discriminated against'. Nevertheless, as Table 12.1 indicates, Malaysia stands out as the 'next' country after Korea in terms of manufacturing success in East Asia in 1984 – at least according to the indicators of *per capita* value-added in manufacturing and the *per capita* value of manufactured exports. As with Korea, a very strong role has been given to government in promoting industrialization, with large investments in such heavy industries as cement, steel, sponge iron, pulp and paper. The Malaysian government has also been noted for its promotion of the 'Malaysia car' – the production of a domestically developed car known as the Proton Saga when production started in 1985. Unfortunately annual production has varied between only 20 000 and 30 000 cars, meaning low economies of scale, high domestic prices, low levels of internal demand and negligible exports. Whereas the Hyundai Pony of Korea has been able to enter strongly both American and European markets, the 'Malaysia car' has been confined to a limited internal market. In the late 1980s, there is evidence that a more export-oriented policy is being developed and that attempts are being made to attract Japanese investment and technology; for example, the Proton car project has benefited from technological and investment links with Mitsubishi (see Ch. 10). In the meantime, industrial growth in Malaysia contrasts strongly with that of Korea; in the latter, strong government involvement in manufacturing has been allied to an overt export orientation in policy, while in the former, strong government intervention has produced industrial structures more similar to the Latin American experience – high-cost import-substituting plants, where both trading growth and technological evolution have been disappointing.

Perhaps one reason for Malaysia's lack of success in manufactured exports has been the perception of its low priority in a country richly endowed with basic natural resources – oil, natural gas, rubber, timber, tin, palm oil and cocoa. Until the serious decline in commodity prices in the early 1980s, the Malaysian economy seemed to function reasonably well while depending on the export of a wide variety of primary products. However, with declining commodity prices, and particularly that of oil, in the 1980s, the problems of trade deficits came to have serious economic consequences. Similar trends can be identified in Indonesia where, as in many oil-exporting countries, surplus oil funds were invested in manufacturing plant, but mainly oriented towards the domestic market. As with Malaysia, Indonesia is now turning more overtly to an export-oriented strategy for manufacturing, combined with attempts to attract Japanese, Taiwanese and Korean enterprises to establish assembly and component plants in their country.

At present, it seems that the prospects for other East Asian countries to industrialize can be broadly framed within the mutual coexistence of both negative and positive factors. On the positive side, there is the possibility to follow the broad patterns of industrial development set by such countries as Japan, Korea and Taiwan. Furthermore, these countries not only provide a model to follow but also constitute significant East Asian growth poles. Linkages from the more to the less industrialized countries of East Asia can come in the form of investment, subcontracting of parts production and decentralized assembly. Certain countries, such as Thailand, already seem to be taking considerable advantage of these investment, production and technological linkages. On the negative side, the less industrialized countries have the problem of entering highly competitive world markets in which the influence of East Asian countries is already significant; late entry could therefore becoming harder. Secondly, the form of linkages with the East Asian growth poles may not be conducive to long-term industrial growth if they remain at the level of simple assembly and subcontracting. The vital ability to generate technological change internally may be more difficult in the next generation of industrializing countries than it has been, for example, in Japan, Singapore and Korea.

THIRD WORLD INDUSTRIALIZATION IN AN INTERNATIONAL FRAMEWORK

This book has placed the question of Third World industrialization into an international framework in order to evaluate better the need for manufacturing growth. During the decade of the 1980s, the validity of an industrializing strategy has been demonstrated most forcibly. The decade has witnessed a world economy characterized by low prices for primary products relative to prices for manufactured products (see Ch. 3). Therefore, because manufactured products maintained their prices much better in international trade than primary products, those Third World countries promoting industrial exports performed much better in world trade than Third World primary-producing countries. Furthermore, the decade of the 1980s has witnessed high interest rates that have seriously affected the borrowing countries of the Third World and particularly those that borrowed heavily (relative to their economies) during the 1970s. However, during the 1980s, the industrializing countries of the Third World have tended to reduce the impact of their inherited debt burden more successfully than non-industrializing countries, particularly if they have adopted an outward-oriented approach.

The record of the 1980s has seemingly vindicated further the verdict of the last two centuries of economic history – that the economic development of poor countries must inevitably be based on industrialization. Industrialization can create rapid growth in GDP, concomitant growth in employment, and provide the basis for technological advance and an increasingly skilled workforce.

The geographical approach has, however, emphasized the great variety of conditions in the industrializing countries of East Asia and Latin America and that the success of each newly industrializing country can be explained by different combinations of factors. As a result, and returning to the theories of industrialization set out in Chapter 5, industrial success can be explained in terms of both economic *and* sociocultural parameters. Furthermore, the advantages attributed by Gerschenkron to late entry can still be seen to pertain, although with additional factors evident and again varying between countries.

THE CASE FOR OUTWARD ORIENTATION

The major theme of this book has concerned the relative advantages of inward and outward strategies of industrialization, also referred to as import substitution versus export promotion. This author once supported the theoretical advantages of import substitution approaches as expounded by such as Hirschman (1968), but case studies on the motor vehicle and television industries in Latin America (Gwynne 1978b, 1978d, 1980b) revealed the severe practical problems that can arise from these inward-orientated approaches. As a result I tend to agree with other supporters-turned-critic such as Schmitz (1984: 3) that import substitution policies have seven major failings in terms of a long-term process of industrialization:

1. *Intrinsic problems of government interference* Excessive administrative regulations have given rise to bureaucratization, corruption, uncertainty and delays. These have discouraged both productive private investment and foreign trade initiatives (see Ch. 6).

2. *Bias against exports* The existence of import restrictions led to a higher exchange rate than would have prevailed under a free trade regime, reducing the relative gains obtained from exporting.

3. *Bias against agriculture* The protection of local industry raised the prices of manufactured goods relative to agricultural products in the home market and the overvalued exchange rate reduced the domestic currency receipts for agricultural exports.

4. *Underutilization of installed capacity* Since import controls did not apply equally to capital goods and since credit for installing machinery was relatively cheap, factories were over-equipped with imported machinery. At the same time, protection in domestic product markets made it possible to earn good profits even at low capacity utilization.

5. *Underutilization of labour* Imported capital goods could be obtained relatively cheaply due to the combined effect of overvalued exchange rates, low import restrictions for such goods and subsidized financing conditions. ISI thus became characterized by the location of capital-intensive plant within countries characterized by labour markets with large numbers of underemployed and low-skilled workers.

6. *Import intensity of ISI* Although consumer good imports were reduced substantially, this was achieved at the expense of increased imports of equipment and materials, resulting in an even more rigid dependence on foreign supplies, particularly in Latin America (see Ch. 11).

7. *The slowing down of ISI* Although initially industry can grow faster than domestic demand for manufactures, Third World countries soon run out of import substitution possibilities. After that growth rates can only be maintained by a growth in domestic demand or in exports. However, by then, the structure and inefficiency of industry stand in the way of conquering export markets.

Industrial strategies based on import substitution and inward orientation are thus not appropriate for the long-term development of industry. Many countries, including Korea and Taiwan, have often started off with ISI policies, but have rapidly shifted to export-oriented policies – normally through a series of devaluations. Policies of devaluation and the liberalization of trade can immediately rectify the bias against exports and the bias against agriculture mentioned above. Furthermore, governments can begin to liberalize the economy more widely and reduce the restrictions on imports and other regulations concerning manufacturing (local content, foreign investment); as a result, private initiative may flourish to a much greater extent.

Manufacturers in the less developed country can be encouraged to become more oriented towards export markets in which the developing country's comparative advantage of low labour costs is stressed. Industrialization should become more labour intensive as a result. Manufacturers now have to operate within the wider context of international markets, and find it necessary to maximize the utilization of their installed capacity. As they now have the potential to sell to a wide variety of international markets, the growth of their production is no longer restricted to the level of demand of the local market, and therefore there need be no slowing down of production. Indeed, if exports of manufactures increase dramatically, the manufacturer in the less developed country will have to invest further in imported machinery in order to increase capacity; however, now, because of booming product exports, the import of new machinery should not have negative implications for the balance of payments. The change to policies of export promotion can therefore considerably reduce the constraints placed on the economy by industrial strategies based on import substitution.

According to Corbo, Krueger and Ossa (1985: 4), these policies of export promotion should be successful as long as:

1. The economic authorities provide a stable macroeconomic framework.
2. The level of the real exchange rate is appropriate and stable over time.
3. Exporters operate under a regime very close to free trade. For this purpose, trade raw materials have to be priced close to world prices, while non-tradable services have to be supplied at prices and terms not too different from those facing main competitors.
4. Financial markets guarantee that the export-oriented sector receives timely financing at domestically competitive rates.
5. Discrimination against savings is lifted.

In terms of the analysis developed in this book, outward orientation facilitates greater links between manufacturers in the less developed economy and the world economy in a series of crucial areas – trade, technology, investment, management systems and training. In Chapter 6 we pointed to the advantages of trade liberalization for Third World countries, but also demonstrated the political difficulties consequent upon attempts to liberalize trade. Trade between developed and developing countries can partly be envisaged in terms of the product life cycle model, energized most often by multinational companies but also through trade between domestic corporations and companies of developed and developing countries respectively. Trade between developed and developing countries can be in the form of finished goods, subassemblies and components, provided that the product or part is sufficiently standardized (see Ch. 7).

Three spatial relationships have been seen to exist: between a developed industrial country and an adjacent less developed country (such as between the United States and Mexico); between a developed industrial country and a newly industrializing country (NIC) (such as between Japan and Taiwan); between a NIC and the adjacent area of a less developed country (Hong Kong–Dongguan) or a 'second generation' industrializing country (Taiwan–Thailand) (see Chs 7 and 12).

The fact that the benefits from rapid manufacturing growth in the NICs permeate throughout society can be seen from the evidence of increases in real wages – as much as 4.8 per cent per annum in Taiwan between 1979 and 1984 (OECD 1988: 70). 'Rising wage costs in the NICs have resulted in the displacement of certain very labour-intensive operations, such as semiconductor assembly, to lower-cost countries like Malaysia and the Philippines. This shift has coincided with the move of the Asian NICs to promote more sophisticated electronic activities' (OECD 1988: 74). The comparative cost advantages that less developed countries have in terms of wage rates is presently causing considerable shifts of industry not only from developed countries but also from the 'first generation' NICs.

The manufactured exports of the NICs are strongly oriented towards the developed countries, a trend that seems likely to continue. Brazil attempted to diversify its exports to Third World countries during the late 1970s, but after the early 1980s recession, which particularly hit Third World countries, has subsequently reoriented its trade growth back to the industrialized countries. However, as a result, the success of export-oriented policies in the industrializing countries of the Third World now rely heavily on the openness of markets in the developed world. Protectionist measures in developed countries, although rarely excluding products, make export growth a difficult and, undoubtedly, a long-term process (see Ch. 7).

Outward orientation, then, can facilitate the long-term expansion of manufactured exports for developing countries. However, it has been argued in this book that outward orientation brings even greater advantages in terms of the generation of new technology (see Ch. 8). Perhaps the central problem for many less developed countries is their small domestic markets. Meanwhile, technological change over the last century has twinned increasing economies of scale with rapid reductions in per unit costs. As a result, the structural problem of the size of the domestic market can prove critical. However, operating in terms of international markets allows for increasing the economies of scale of production and, more recently, introducing continuous flow technology and automation. This leads to one of the biggest contrasts between national manufacturing firms in inward- and outward-oriented trade regimes at present. In the former regimes, discontinuous technology can often prevail in medium and large manufacturing firms, whereas in the latter, most of the larger and many medium-sized firms operate with continuous flow technology. It is the national firm in the outward-oriented country, then, that can enter into the favourable spiral of lowering per unit costs, increasing sales, expanding profits and investment and can install even more sophisticated technology.

One example of such a firm would be the Korean car manufacturer, Hyundai (see Ch. 10), a company that only started car manufacturing in 1974, and had only achieved an annual production figure of 78 000 by 1982 (and only a 50 per cent utilization of capacity) after a distinctly fluctuating performance in terms of both profit and production. In 1983, however, Hyundai launched a major investment and modernization programme in order to increase annual capacity from 150 000 to 300 000. Substantial loans were provided by government to design a new model (the Excel) and invest in new machinery, mainly from Japan. Technological links with the Japanese motor vehicle firm, Mitsubishi, became important, assisting in the laying out of the expanded plant at Ulsan and designing the production system. Furthermore, Mitsubishi provided under licence the fuel efficient engine, the front-wheel drive and the gearbox. As a result, Mitsubishi took a 15 per cent stake in Hyundai Motors.

However, the decision to expand capacity, in spite of the low utilization of existing capacity in 1982, was taken in terms of a wholehearted outward-oriented approach. Capacity was expanded and modernized in order to link in as strongly as possible with international markets, most particularly North America. Hyundai decided to make a major sales drive in Canada before the US market and started exports in 1984. The Japanese influence in production design, the use of Japanese technology combined with the high-quality but cheap labour at the Ulsan plant (1984 hourly wage rate of only US$1.3) produced a cheap, high-quality vehicle that found a large niche at the bottom of the Canadian 'new car' market − sales of 50 000 in 1984 and 80 000 in 1985. In the following year, the launch came in

the United States and even more dramatic sales figures were recorded − 168 882 in 1986 and 263 000 in 1987. In 1985, Hyundai had begun further expanding plant capacity from 300 000 to 700 000 in order to meet future export demand. In 1987, Hyundai Motors was producing 700 000 vehicles a year with virtually 100 per cent utilization of capacity and exports have accounted for over 70 per cent of production.

The success of Hyundai has been intimately linked with the outward-oriented approach of the Korean government and the concomitant fostering of private initiative. In the case of Hyundai the enterpreneurial drive and substantial risk-facing has been provided by Chung Ju Yung and his extended family of two brothers and seven sons (Housego 1988: 8). However, the significant components of success, in retrospect, have been the ability to combine increasing economies of scale, the use of modern machinery and highly skilled but cheap labour to manufacture a product of considerable appeal (on grounds of both price and quality) in international markets. The importance of highly skilled technologists and engineers should also not be underestimated.

An essential condition for the NICs to make further progress in their high-tech endeavours is to increase their R&D potential. Korea has moved the farthest in this area, having increased its R&D/GNP ratio from 0.57 per cent in 1980 to 1.06 per cent in 1983 (compared to 2.03 per cent [of GDP] in that year for the Netherlands, a median country in the OECD ranking). Korea is reported to be aiming at doubling its R&D spending between 1985 and 1990. . . . In the Asian NICs, engineering education has increased at a particularly rapid rate. By 1980 Korea was producing more than twice as many university-level engineering graduates as West Germany; and at levels below first university degree as many engineering students were graduating from Korean institutions as in the United Kingdom, West Germany and Sweden combined (OECD 1988: 71).

Such impressive educational provision and concern with applied research and development partly explains the verdict of such Pacific rim commentators as Housego (1988: 6) that 'there are few things so impressive in the track record of the NICs as their ability to absorb foreign technology'.

The Hyundai example further illustrates the increasing complexity and variety of foreign investment. In retrospect, Mitsubishi's 15 per cent investment in Hyundai Motors has been most valuable for the latter – providing modern components (engine, gearbox, front-wheel drive) and assistance with process technology, plant design and quality control. At the same time, Mitsubishi's relatively low stake has meant relatively few risks on its part. The OECD sees this type of multinational behaviour (licensing and joint ventures) becoming a more generalized phenomenon among the multinationals of developed countries in the future:

> OECD-based multinational enterprises may find the newer forms of partnership increasingly attractive as a strategy for acting on the input side [technology] and also, through marketing agreements, exercising control over markets, while avoiding the costs and risks associated with direct investment (OECD 1988: 81).

These arrangements are also seen as favourable to the companies of newly industrializing countries as they will probably need close participation with OECD country firms (such as Hyundai with Mitsubishi) in order to move upward into new technologies.

> As innovation accelerates internationally, there may be increasing scope for new forms of partnership reflecting the aspirations both of the foreign firms and of the NICs, e.g. joint ventures, licensing, technical assistance, marketing agreements. NICs which possess relatively abundant technological and management capacities may increasingly find such arrangements an advantageous route to technology transfer (OECD 1988: 76).

With considerable competition now existing between multinationals from different world regions (North America, Western Europe, Japan) and the increasing complexity of their relationships with productive plant in less developed countries, the results of foreign investment can be generally seen as more favourable to the developing country recipient in the last quarter of the twentieth century, particularly if the developing country in question can exert some form of bargaining power

(large market, good record of export-oriented growth) (see Ch. 9). The Hyundai case study provides a further complicating twist to traditional views of multinationals, as it provides a good example of the Third World multinational. Hyundai Motors now has an assembly plant operating in Canada and the construction wing of Hyundai has become a major contractor in the Middle East.

Some industrial sectors, such as that of motor vehicles (see Ch. 10), have become dominated by multinational corporations with global networks and a considerable amount of intra-firm trade (in both components and finished vehicles), capital flow and technological transfer at the global scale. In terms of their relationships with outside suppliers, these networks are following the Japanese example and becoming increasingly cooperative rather than competitive. More transfer of technology, training and management assistance now occur between the assembly firm and component firms in order to achieve long-term improvements in component quality as well as low costs. Again, outward orientation can favour these changes in management practice. Korea, for example, is presently attempting to move from a highly authoritarian relationship between management and worker to the Japanese ideal of worker participation in order to facilitate 'just-in-time' production systems and quality circles.

An international approach, therefore, not only assists Third World industrialization in terms of increasing trade, but also provides the means to keep on expanding manufactured exports. Outward orientation can be closely linked to the introduction and utilization of new technologies, the incorporation of new systems of management and labour relations and innovative relationships with foreign investment and multinational corporations. However, one must be careful not to turn outward-oriented industrialization into a new panacea of development. As this book has shown, outward orientation and concomitant trade liberalization can be linked with major problems, particularly in the short term (see Ch. 6). In the final section of this chapter, I will attempt to review briefly the future and relevance of outward-oriented industrialization to the contrasting regions of the Third World.

THE FUTURE FOR INDUSTRY IN THE THIRD WORLD

Africa

The empirical analysis in this book has tended to concentrate on what could be loosely described as the Pacific rim, that is East Asia and Latin America. In moving away from this relatively dynamic area in terms of modern economic growth, one must be wary of offering prescriptions seen as appropriate in these regions to other regions of the Third World.

This proviso seems particularly appropriate in terms of Africa. In Chapter 1, the relative paucity of modern industry in Africa was duly noted. Only two African countries were classified as having recent manufacturing growth linked to exports (Morocco and Tunisia) and only one country had witnessed the substantial investment of surplus oil revenues to stimulate recent industrialization (Nigeria). Otherwise, five more African countries had a manufacturing product greater than that in agriculture (South Africa, Botswana, Zimbabwe, Egypt and Zambia). However, Botswana's classification was due to its very low agricultural product as its manufacturing product was only 8 per cent of GDP in 1985.

Most writers on African industrialization (such as Hawkins 1986) analyse only what they describe as the sub-Saharan region. This tends to mean all African countries south of a mid-line through the Sahara, excluding South Africa. Such a classification immediately eliminates Morocco, Tunisia, Egypt and South Africa from the analysis. The main reason seems to be the difficulties of generalizing about industrial trends not only in sub-Saharan Africa but also in such diverse countries as Morocco, Tunisia, Egypt and South Africa. Within sub-Saharan Africa, it should also be noted that 60 per cent of manufacturing value-added comes from five countries – Nigeria, Zimbabwe, Ivory Coast, Ghana and Kenya (Hawkins 1986: 280).

In all of sub-Saharan Africa (as well as Egypt and South Africa), industrial policies since the 1950s have been dominated by the strategy of import substitution. In the analysis of Latin American industrialization, the problems that small markets and government protection have on the process of industrialization have already been stressed. In African countries, the experience of import substitution industrialization has been even worse and, in particular, has adversely affected the vital agricultural sector. 'The agricultural sector suffered from negative protection to the extent that almost all the locally manufactured items the farmers buy are protected' (Hawkins 1986: 283). Furthermore, the problems of government planning of import substitution in poor countries were immense. 'The consequence – reliance on a large, centrally planned and administered public sector – is that the greatest possible claim is placed on the scarcest possible resource. That is administrative talent, with its complementary requirements in expert knowledge, experience, and discipline' (Galbraith 1979: 92).

Despite the fact that away from Morocco and Tunisia, there have been few genuine attempts at export-led industrialization in Africa, there do seem to be some real advantages in the strategy. According to Hawkins (1986: 285), export-oriented growth strategies have been shown 'to be more labor-intensive than production for domestic consumption, with the unskilled labor component estimated to range between 50 to 100 per cent higher than in import-substituting industries'. However, even if African governments responded with outward-oriented trade policies (see Ch. 6), there would still be many problems with export-led industrialization, not least inadequate access to technology and limited entrepreneurial capacities.

One variant on the export-led model is resource-based industrialization. However, as was emphasized in Chapter 3, the 1980s have witnessed significant decreases in almost all primary product prices. In the case of Zambia, heavily reliant on copper mining and the refining of copper, such resource-based industrialization has proved disastrous during the 1980s (see Ch. 3). However, according to Hawkins (1986: 287), resource-based industrialization has been successful in the Ivory Coast, Malawi and Zimbabwe; 'in each case, industrialization has been partially encouraged by protectionist strategies and agriculture has played a critical role either as the primary foreign exchange earner or as creator of a market for the outputs of domestic industry while simultaneously earning foreign exchange from raw material or semi-processed exports'.

A third industrial strategy, specific to Africa, has been put forward by Adelman (1984). The strategy is based on the underlying assumption that a domestic mass market will develop as a result of increased agricultural productivity. Hence the strategy is called agricultural-demand-led industrialization (ADLI).

> The ADLI strategy consists of building a domestic mass-consumption market by improving the productivity of agriculture and letting farmers share in the fruits of the improved productivity. Even though this strategy is, to some extent, motivated by a certain amount of export pessimism, the ADLI strategy is not to be viewed as an old style import-substitution strategy which operates by biasing the system of incentives in favour of domestic 'infant' industries.
>
> The emphasis of the ADLI strategy should be on improving the productivity of small- and medium-scale agriculture. . . . Small- and medium-scale agriculture has larger linkage effects with domestic industry than does large-scale agriculture while having at least as high a productivity level. Smaller farms are labour intensive and use domestic implements and machinery. . .small farmers have a larger marginal propensity to consume, and a larger marginal share of their consumption is devoted to locally produced textiles, clothing, footwear and simple consumer durables such as refrigerators, bicycles, sewing machines and simple electronics. Also, they tend to invest heavily in the buildup of human capital, devoting a large share of their incremental income to education (Adelman 1984: 944–5).

The ADLI strategy seems appropriate for poorer countries with limited prospects for export growth in manufactures over the short term. For the countries of sub-Saharan Africa, with limited textile, clothing, footwear and other labour-intensive industries, an industrial strategy geared to local agricultural demand is therefore appealing for two reasons. First, for countries with food shortages and static agricultural production on the one hand and rapid population growth on the other, it gives the correct overall development emphasis on expanding agricultural production as the major imperative. Secondly, modest manufactur-

ing growth directed towards the needs of local farmers has been the initial strategy for industrial growth for many East Asian countries that have subsequently become successful NICs; agriculture-led growth provides the origins for small-scale manufacturing enterprises that subsequently may be able to take more dramatic leaps into international markets.

The ADLI strategy seems particularly appropriate in Africa where the development imperative must be to increase food production. Between the early 1960s (1961–65 average) and 1983, food production per head in Africa declined dismally – by as much as 23 per cent (*The Economist* 2/2/85: 94). In contrast, food production per head increased by over 15 per cent for the same period in both Latin America and Asia. Industrialization in both these continents need not, in general, be so closely wedded to the agricultural sector. Indeed, the analysis provided in this book becomes much more appropriate to them (while it is less so in Africa, apart from the North African states).

Asia

In turning to Asia, it is interesting to note that the outward-oriented policies of East Asia have not been followed in the rest of Asia. In the Middle East and Persian Gulf areas, industrialization since the early 1970s has been intimately linked to oil. The great boom in oil revenues during the 1970s and early 1980s generally led to great increases in domestic demand that provided the basis for major growth in import-substituting industries; Saudi manufacturing growth, for example, averaged about 7 per cent a year between 1973 and 1986. Data for other countries in the region tend to be very patchy indeed. However, there was one type of export-oriented policy adopted towards industry, often described as one of 'sowing the oil' – investing the surplus oil revenues in government-controlled, capital-intensive projects that used oil as feedstock (petrochemicals) or as a source of cheap energy (aluminium, steel). In Chapter 7, it was argued that these types of projects could be seen as fitting into the energy-cost version of the product life cycle, because the lower energy costs of oil-rich countries provided locational attractions to energy-intensive industries. However, as yet, it seems that these projects have only had a limited impact on export figures – in 1986, only 9 per cent of Saudi exports were classified as industrial (World Bank 1988: 245).

In the populous countries of South Asia, India (1986 population of 781.4 million), Pakistan (99.2 million) and Bangladesh (103.2 million), industrial policies have been firmly inward oriented since Independence. Manufacturing growth rates have been moderate but certainly not impressive; for example, between 1965 and 1980, they averaged 4.4 per cent a year in India, 5.3 per cent in Pakistan and 6.8 per cent in Bangladesh (see Table 1.1). During the 1980s, modest attempts have been made to promote manufactured exports but success has been somewhat limited; between 1980 and 1986, the manufacturing sector grew by an average of 9.3 per cent a year in Pakistan, 8.2 per cent in India and only 2.1 per cent in Bangladesh.

In India, the origins of an inward-oriented industrial policy can be dated to the Second Five Year Plan (1956–61). Government was to play an important role in the process of industrialization and the main priority was to develop the heavy industrial sector. The government took full control of seventeen large firms and had influence on most other large firms in the capital- and intermediate-goods industries through the complex systems of licensing (for example, for new plant and plant expansion) that evolved. Small industrial enterprises (providing the consumer goods for the domestic market) were not prone to such government control. Domestic industrial production received considerable protection in the form of high tariffs and tight quotas on imports, particularly for consumer goods. There was little incentive to export.

An interesting comparison can be made between the Korean and Indian policies towards industrialization. Both have had strong government intervention in their industrial development, with concomitant problems of indifferent decision making, corruption and political criteria overriding technical, economic criteria. The question must be why one process of industrialization has been so much more successful than the other. The fundamental answer seems to lie in the outward orientation of the Korean and the inward orientation of the Indian strategy and the differential impact that this has had on industrial growth. Four clear points can be made.

First, there is the question of indifferent decision making. The outward-oriented approach of the Koreans allowed political decisions to be constantly reviewed in terms of international markets and competition. When decisions were seen to have untenable consequences, they tended to be quickly changed. In India, however, there was no such international arbiter of bad decisions, because of the closed nature of the economy. Bad investment decisions were not changed and were lived with – normally at public expense.

Secondly, the fact that Korean firms have had to operate in international markets from an early stage has also created the imperative for them to be competitive in those markets. Such an imperative has not, however, occurred within Indian state firms, and, as a result, lack of competition has fostered high costs. It has been estimated that Indian steel is around 50 per cent dearer than the world-market price (*The Economist* 25/2/89; 102). With such basic 'feedstock' industries producing such internationally expensive products, downstream goods (using Indian steel, for example) also become internationally uncompetitive.

Thirdly, and as was stressed in Chapter 8, outward orientation provides the ability and incentive to 'keep up' with technological change at the world scale. In the Korean case, this has meant the production of goods that are not only technologically sophisticated but also of high quality. The inward orientation of Indian industrialization, despite large numbers of trained scientists and engineers, has tended to produce the reverse in the manufacture of goods – low levels of technological sophistication and low quality control; again this seriously hampers export prospects.

Finally, one must mention the contrasting attitudes to foreign investment. Both countries have strongly favoured the development of domestic corporations. In the Korean case, domestic corporations have been promoted alongside foreign investment, normally in the form of joint ventures. In the Indian case, however, foreign investment has been more resolutely excluded, at least until recently. One example here is the case of motor vehicles. Since the 1950s, successive Indian governments have studiously avoided giving multinational vehicle corporations access to their market. As a result, domestic demand tended to be met by the production of models based on the old Morris Oxford and Fiat 1100 by two local producers, Hindustan and Premier Motors respectively. The Indian market was thus supplied by cars of 1950s technology, both inappropriate to the domestic market (expensive and with high petrol consumption) and impossible to export.

It was not until 1982 that the first multinational was let in when the Indian government chose Suzuki as the partner for a public-sector company, Maruti, which had a large purpose-built factory established outside Delhi (Elliott 1986). Suzuki was only allowed a 26 per cent stake in the company, but installed its corporate products and production methods. In 1986, it started producing its basic Third-World 800 cc model with various alternatives (car, van, pick-up), with the capacity for manufacturing 85 000 vehicles a year. Full capacity was rapidly achieved and, by 1987, Suzuki Maruti had 50 per cent of a 190 000 vehicle market. Hindustan and Premier Motors have reacted by forging links with Isuzu and Nissan respectively. In the meantime, Indian permission to allow multinational entry in the motor car sector has caused a five-fold increase in both production and sales during the 1980s, and provided the possibility for future exports, now that internationally saleable models are being produced.

The issue in South Asia, then, is not so much the problem of government intervention itself in industrial development but its historical alliance with an inward-orientated approach. Future industrialization in India, Pakistan and Bangladesh must be based on liberalizing their trading structures, in spite of the short-term problems of such a policy as outlined in Chapter 6. If these countries of South Asia can achieve such reforms, they may be incorporated into the 'second generation' of newly industrializing countries of East Asia that presently includes Thailand,

Malaysia, Indonesia and the Philippines.

As was pointed out in Chapter 12, both OECD-country and NIC firms are switching labour-intensive production from the 'first generation' NICs to 'second generation' NICs as wage rates increase in the former. The role of the 'first generation' city states, Singapore and Hong Kong, may be critical in this process. Already about 40 per cent of Singapore's trade is with non-oil Asian developing countries (including re-exports). Firms based in Singapore (both multinational and local) may establish labour-intensive 'offshore' plants to produce finished products or components in neighbouring Malaysia and Indonesia.

A potentially much more significant relationship is emerging between Hong Kong and China (see Ch. 7), a relationship that should steadily increase both before and after the re-incorporation of Hong Kong into China in 1997. The closer relationship has been permitted due to the process of economic reform in China that started in 1978/9. The process of economic reform has concerned changing the centrally planned economic system to make it more responsive to technological change, markets and consumer demand. White (1984: 8) saw the reforming strategy as containing four sets of measures. First, the national planning system was to be streamlined, taking on a narrower range of macroeconomic functions. Second, planners were to make greater use of 'economic levers' such as credit, taxation and subsidy to achieve their objectives in place of mandatory targets on enterprises. Third, 'natural' economic linkages were to be allowed greater scope in defining relations between enterprises, and particularly in a regional context. Fourth, the managers of enterprises were to be granted greater decision-making autonomy and their performance 'verified' by increasing involvement in competitive markets.

Chinese economic reforms have certainly been evolutionary rather than revolutionary, particularly in the industrial sector. By the late 1980s, the Chinese industrial structure is still dominated by central planning, although with some possiblities for local initiative. This is demonstrated by the contracted responsibility system, under which factory workers negotiate a contract with the government, defining targets for profit, tax and growth, and are then left to bear the brunt of any additional losses or to reap direct benefits from higher-than-expected profits. However, the system has major problems because it is still the centrally planned contract that constitutes the bulk of production. This central planning can radically misinterpret markets. For example, in 1986, China made 35 million watches and 10 million bicycles that it could not sell (50 per cent and 25 per cent of production respectively) (Dodwell 1987b). Modified central planning through the contracted responsibility system has worked well in agriculture, because the demands are relatively simple – to increase production. In industry, the simple increasing of production, is not always appropriate.

There is a serious problem of lack of information for the decision makers at enterprise level, locked into the wider strategies of central planning. Anecdotal evidence provided by Dodwell (1987b) very much reinforces this point:

> The manager of a factory in Wuxi in Jiangsu that made shirts for export had no idea of the export price for his shirts, no idea of how such a price would compare with the price of a similar shirt made in a factory in Korea or Taiwan, no idea of where they were sold, or of their reputation for style or quality. He is typical of all small-to-medium exporting companies in China that are asked by an import–export corporation to supply a particular number of products by a certain date, and are paid in local currency for the work. Whether the goods are being sold at a loss, or whether the factory is missing out on a share of substantial profits in foreign exchange is an issue that passes him by.

The role of Hong Kong entrepreneurs in the Pearl River delta region of China must be put into this context. They are much more aware of international market opportunities than either central and regional planners or the decision makers of individual enterprises. This provides one of the main reasons for the rapid industrial growth experienced in the Pearl River delta region over the last decade.

It is therefore very difficult to predict the future of industrial growth in China. It is, however, unlikely to become an export-oriented country,

simply because of the massive size of its internal market (1054 million in 1986) and the inheritance of central planning that emphasizes production totals rather than quality and design. This perspective can presently be empirically justified by data from China's leading industrial province, Jiangsu (Yangtze delta region); despite its preeminence as leading provincial producer within China since 1984, only 3 per cent of Jiangsu's production is exported, mainly corresponding to textiles (Thomson 1987: 15). Furthermore, it seems that although China is gradually opening up to foreign investment via major joint ventures, it seems determined to keep Japanese influence as small as possible. This is made evident by recent decisions in the motor vehicle industry, where joint venture agreements have been signed with European rather than Japanese firms – Volkswagen in cars and Fiat in trucks. However, by restricting links with the major growth pole of East Asia, the Chinese government will be effectively reducing the export potential of the country.

However, in restricted geographical areas, such as Guandong province, with strong links to Hong Kong enterprises, export performance should expand rapidly and, indeed, be encouraged by a central government continually worried about balance of payments problems. The main threat to the Hong Kong/Guandong province relationship will probably come because the success of the latter will create grave inequalities within China. Already the population of Guandong province (62 million) has the highest average *per capita* income in China, and some of the more industrialized localities have urban salaries about 50 per cent above the national average (Dodwell 1987a). However, the political repression of 1989, which might have heralded a reversal in economic policy, has not seemed to have had a substantial impact on restricting economic growth in Guandong province (Economist 1989b: 45–6).

THE PACIFIC RIM: FOCUS OF MANUFACTURING GROWTH INTO THE TWENTY-FIRST CENTURY?

The two continental regions that have been focused upon in this book have been Latin

America and East Asia. There have been distinct industrial policy differences between the two regions, with inward orientation prevailing in the former and outward orientation in the latter. However, for most countries in the two regions, there is one common geographical theme – direct access to the Pacific (the countries of eastern South America being the exceptions).

The Pacific is now bordered by the two most powerful industrial economies in the world, Japan and the United States. This book has argued how important these massive centres of demand have been for the newly industrializing countries of East Asia and Latin America. In East Asia, the influence of both Japan and the United States has been significant in terms of technology transfer, trade, offshore production and subcontracting. In Latin America, the influence of the United States has been paramount in these areas, although Japanese investment has also begun to increase rapidly in Mexico during the 1980s.

The Pacific rim has also been the scene for the growing relationship between some of the 'first generation' NICs (Korea, Taiwan, Hong Kong, Singapore) and the 'second generation' (Thailand, Malaysia and the Philippines for example). This has led to the growing complexity of relationships on a Pacific-wide basis – for example, Japanese firms subcontracting the manufacture of subassemblies to firms in the 'first generation' NICs, who in turn subcontract out labour-intensive component production to firms in the 'second generation' NICs, with the final product destined principally for the North American market. The subcontracting out of sub-assembly and component production by Japanese firms, and their decisions to promote 'offshore production' have increased substantially during the late 1980s with the high value of the yen against the US dollar.

In East Asia, therefore, there is considerable evidence of certain production shifting from Japan to the 'first generation' NICs and then from these latter countries to 'second generation' NICs. This process is likely to continue into the 1990s and, indeed, into the twenty-first century. Three factors stand out.

First, there is the question of changes in OECD trading attitudes towards the 'first generation' NICs, known formally as 'graduation' policies. In broad terms, 'graduation' policies involve 'the gradual withdrawal from LDCs, as they become more developed, of special concessions and differential treatment within the world trading system and their gradual acceptance of GATT obligations and of conformity with the principle of an open multilateral trade regime' (O'Neill 1984). As special trading concessions are withdrawn by OECD countries on imports from 'first generation' NICs, the exporting firms of 'second generation' NICs should theoretically be permitted greater and relatively favoured access to OECD markets. This could be one powerful stimulus to the shifting of manufacturing production from 'first' to 'second' generation NICs.

The increasing wage differential between first and second generation NICs is perhaps the main reason for both OECD and NIC firms to shift production between them. Between 1979 and 1984, average real wages increased by 6.6 per cent a year in Taiwan, 6.5 per cent in Singapore and 4.1 per cent in Korea (OECD 1988: 70). These increases have been a powerful factor behind the seeking of cheaper labour-cost locations in East Asia for labour-intensive assembly and component production.

A third and related factor giving opportunities for industrial expansion in 'second generation' NICs is the adoption in most of the 'first generation' NICs of the Japanese model of moving up market to more sophisticated areas of production as wage costs rise and domestic technological generation improves. As the emphasis in the 'first generation' NICs changes from labour-intensive to more capital- and information-intensive industries, this again leaves opportunities for 'second generation' NICs within international markets.

In Latin America, however, there has been no such relationship between the 'first generation' NICs (Mexico, Brazil) and a second generation of industrializing countries. This can be mainly explained by the relatively closed nature of the 'first generation' economies, particularly as regards imports. This closure to the imports of other developing countries of Latin America has tended to increase rather than decrease during the 1980s as the debt crisis has hit these countries particularly hard, demanding a large trade surplus at all costs (see Ch. 4). Furthermore, 'the structural problems of the Latin American NICs – Mexico and Brazil – are very different from those of their Asian counterparts. They are big economies with the constraints inherent in the existence of very great income differentials and social tensions and possessing a large public sector beset with serious problems of efficiency' (OECD 1988: 84). These constraints have effectively ruled out any substantial trade liberalization at least in the form of imports from other Latin American countries.

Indeed, the three factors that are assisting in shifting industry from 'first' to 'second' generation NICs in East Asia do not seem to be operating in Latin America. First, average wages (in US dollar terms) have been declining rather than increasing in both Brazil and Mexico during the 1980s. Secondly, OECD countries in general and the United States in particular have been and seem likely to continue to be relatively amenable to permit increasing imports from Brazil and Mexico, due to the severe debt problems of these two countries and their imperative need to have large trade surpluses in order to keep up with debt repayments. Thirdly, the industrialization policies of both Brazil and Mexico, due to the heritage of import substitution policies, have been to stimulate domestic production in as many sectors as possible and then to retain production in these sectors. The gradual shift of industrial emphasis to more sophisticated manufacturing sectors, although it occurs, is also not associated with the letting-go of the more traditional, labour-intensive sectors. These latter are maintained as well, often with critical government support. Because of the non-operation of these three factors, there is then little evidence in Latin America of manufacturing industry shifting location from the 'first generation' NICs of Brazil and Mexico to a new group of industrializing countries. The manufacturing growth impulses of both countries are kept as far as possible within the spatial limits of the national economies themselves.

What then are the perspectives for outward-oriented industrialization in the smaller Latin American countries that not only have had a poor record in import-substitution industrialization but also have a lack of access to the economies of the more successful industrializing countries of Latin America? If the success of Chile's outward-oriented model can be drawn upon (see Ch. 6), two factors emerge. First, the need to regard the basic principles of comparative advantage (see Ch. 3). Many smaller Latin American countries such as Chile have both small populations and a large and varied resource base (in contrast to the countries of East Asia). Outward-oriented policies should attempt to develop the wider resource base and to promote industries that are linked to these sectors. For example, Chile now has major forestry resources, and thus its industrial policies should concentrate upon promoting linked manufacturing sectors, such as timber products, cellulose and paper. Certainly this is a policy with considerable short-term potential, which could lead into other specialized but related sectors subsequently – forest product machinery, for example. Secondly, a more generally resource-based strategy may be seen as more tenable in the twenty-first century, particularly within the international trading system of the Pacific rim, where East Asian countries in contrast to Latin American are, by necessity, major importers of resources. This would be particularly appropriate in terms of renewable resources, such as that of forestry.

The Pacific rim seems likely to be a major focus of new industrial growth into the twenty-first century. It contains not only the two most powerful market economies in the world, but also the most vibrant of the newly industrializing countries. It has been the focus of major innovations in the last third of the twentieth century, through the emergence of flexible manufacturing systems and 'just-in-time' approaches to worker participation and quality control – what some American and European writers have referred to in an annoyingly 'North Atlantic-centred' way as 'post-Fordist'. The recent rapid growth in the Pacific rim and the likelihood of its continuation reminds all economic observers of the constant changes in economic combinations and their often dramatic implications for the location of economic activity. Within the broad framework of outward orientation, there seem to be considerable opportunities within the Pacific rim for economic and industrial growth. As the OECD staidly but optimistically put it:

> The mutual influence and permeability of contemporary societies, resulting largely from the rapid development and diffusion of new technologies, is such that no given international stratification of economies can be taken as established. There seems to exist, across a considerable range of national societies, a broad continuum from which, through either incremental progress or an alteration in the international environment giving rise to new pressures and stimuli, new 'NICs' can emerge (OECD 1988: 87–8).

REFERENCES

Abernathy W 1987 *The Productivity Dilemma: Roadblock to innovation in the automobile industry.* Johns Hopkins University Press.

Ablin E, Katz J 1987 From infant industry to technology exports: the Argentine experience in the international sale of industrial plants and engineering work, In Katz J (ed) *Technology Generation in Latin American Manufacturing Industries.* Macmillan, pp. 446–80.

Adelman I 1984 Beyond export-led growth, *World Development,* **12**: 937–49.

Allan D 1985 Japan: A state of development. Unpublished dissertation, Department of Geography, University of Birmingham.

Allen G C 1981 *A Short Economic History of Modern Japan.* Macmillan.

Altshuler A *et al.* 1984 *The Future of the Automobile: the report of MIT's international automobile program.* Allen & Unwin.

Amin S 1977 *Imperialism and Unequal Development.* Harvester.

Anell L, Nygren B 1980 *The Developing Countries and the World Economic Order.* Methuen.

Associación Mexicana de la Industria Automotriz 1988 *La Industria Automotriz de Mexico en Cifras.*

Auty R 1983 MNCs and regional revenue retention in a vertically integrated industry: bauxite/aluminium in the Caribbean, *Regional Studies* **17**: 3–17.

Auty R 1984 The product life-cycle and the global location of the petrochemical industry after the second oil shock, *Economic Geography* 60: 325–38.

Balassa B *et al.* 1982 *Development Strategies in Semi-Industrial Economies.* Johns Hopkins University Press.

Baldwin R E 1966 *Economic Development and Growth.* John Wiley.

Banco Central de Chile 1984 *Indicadores Economicos y Sociales.*

Banco Central de Chile 1985 *Indicadores de Comercio Exterior, Diciembre 1984.*

Banco Central de Chile 1986 *Indicadores de Comercio Exterior, Diciembre 1985.*

Banco Central de Chile 1987 *Indicadores de Comercio Exterior, Diciembre 1986.*

Baran P A 1973 *The Political Economy of Growth.* Penguin.

Baranson J 1981 *The Japanese Challenge to U.S. Industry.* Lexington.

Bardón A, Carrasco C, Vial A 1985 *Una Década de Cambios Economicos: la experiencia chilena, 1973–1983.* Ed. Andres Bello.

Barnet R, Muller R 1974 *Global Reach: the power of the multinational corporations.* Simon & Schuster.

Becker D 1984 Development, democracy and dependency in Latin America: a post-imperialist view, *Third World Quarterly* **6**: 411–31.

Bennett D C, Sharpe K E 1985 *Transnational Corporations versus the State: the political economy of the Mexican auto industry.* Princeton University Press.

Berry B J L, Conkling E C, Ray D M 1976 *The geography of economic systems.* Prentice-Hall.

Bloomfield G T 1981 The changing spatial organisation of multinational corporations in the world automotive industry. In Hamilton F E I, Linge G J R (eds) *Spatial Analysis, Industry and the Industrial Environment.* Wiley, vol. 2, pp. 357–94.

Boltho A 1975 *Japan: an economic survey.* Oxford University Press.

Bromley R, Gerry C (eds) 1979 *Casual Work and Poverty in Third World Cities*. John Wiley.

Brooke M S, Remmers H L 1973 *The Strategy of Multinational Enterprise*. Longman.

Buckley P, Casson M (1976) *The Future of Multinational Enterprise*. Macmillan.

Cable V, Persaud B (eds) 1987 *Developing with Foreign Investment*. Routledge.

Caves R E 1982 *Multinational Enterprise and Economic Analysis*. Cambridge University Press.

Chenery H B 1977 Transitional growth and world industrialisation. In Ohlin B *et al.* (eds) *The International Allocation of Economic Activity*. Macmillan.

Chenery H, Robinson S, Syrquin M 1986 *Industrialization and Growth: a comparative study*. Oxford University Press.

Choksi A M, Papageorgiou D (eds) 1986 *Economic Liberalization in Developing Countries*. Basil Blackwell.

Chudnovsky D 1988 The diffusion and production of numerically controlled machine tools with special reference to Argentina, *World Development* **16**: 723–32.

Cline W R 1982 Can the East Asian model of development be generalised? *World Development* **10**, 2.

Congdon T 1985 *Economic Liberalism in the Cone of Latin America*. Trade Policy Research Centre.

Congdon T 1988 *The Debt Threat*. Basil Blackwell.

Corbo V 1985 Reforms and macroeconomic adjustments in Chile during 1974–84, *World Development* **13**: 893–916.

Corbo V, Krueger A O, Ossa F 1985 *Export-Oriented Development Strategies: the success of five newly industrializing countries*. Westview.

Corbridge S 1986 *Capitalist World Development*. Macmillan.

Crawcour E S 1965 The Tokugawa heritage. In Lockwood W W (ed) *The State and Economic Enterprise in Japan*. Princeton University Press.

Cunningham S M 1981 Multinational enterprise in Brazil: locational patterns and implications for regional development, *Professional Geographer* **33**: 48.

Dalby S 1987 Thailand, *Financial Times Survey*, 2/12/87.

Dawnay I, Coone T 1986 Ford and VW to merge in Brazil and Argentina, *Financial Times* 25 November: 1.

de Jonquieres G 1987 Out of volume and into value-added, *Financial Times Japanese Industry Survey*, December 7: 5.

Dicken P 1986 *Global Shift: Industrial change in a turbulent world*. Harper & Row.

Dickenson J P 1978 *Brazil*. Dawson.

Dodwell D 1987a The richest county in China, *Financial Times* 18 July: 1.

Dodwell D 1987b Industry: a labyrinth of obstacles to market forces, *Financial Times China Survey* 18 December: 8.

Dunning J 1983 Changes in the level and structure of international production: the last one hundred years. In Casson M (ed) *The Growth of International Business*. Allen & Unwin.

Economist (The) 1984 A boom that is not animal, vegetable or mineral, 11 August: b1–2.

Economist (The) 1985a In praise of peasants, 2 February: 94–5.

Economist (The) 1985b Another turn of the wheel: a survey of the world's motor industry, 2 March.

Economist (The) 1987 International debt: a lesson from Chile, 7 March: 87–90.

Economist (The) 1989a India by design, 25 February: 101–2.

Economist (The) 1989b Amid the sourness, a portion of China that is still sweet, 19 August: 45–6.

Economist Intelligence Unit (EIU) 1983 *Foreign Outsourcing by US Auto Manufacturers*. EIU, Special Report No. 151.

Edwards S, Edwards A C 1987 *Monetarism and Liberalization: the Chilean experiment*. Ballinger.

Edwards S, Teitel S (eds) 1986 Growth, reform, and adjustment: Latin America's trade and macroeconomic policies in the 1970s and 1980s, *Economic Development and Cultural Change* **34**, 3, Special Issue.

Elliott J 1986 India: a 1950s comeback, *Financial Times Motor Industry Survey* 14 October: 9.

Ellsworth P T 1965 *The International Economy*. Macmillan.

Enos J L 1984 Government intervention in the transfer of technology; the case of South Korea, *IDS Bulletin* **15**: 26–31.

Enos J L, Park W H 1988 *The Adoption and Diffusion of Imported Technology: the case of Korea*. Routledge.

Evans P B 1986 State, capital, and the transformation of dependence: the Brazilian computer case, *World Development* **14**: 791–808.

Far Eastern Economic Review 1988 The China syndrome, 23 June: 64–5.

Fieldhouse D K 1971 *The Colonial Empires: a comparative survey from the eighteenth century*. Weidenfeld & Nicolson.

Financial Times reports:
15/3/88: 6 – Latin American debt crisis
30/11/87: 1 – Latin Americans act to reduce burden of debt servicing by half.
31/12/87: 2 – Banks give Mexican debt plan a cautious welcome.

17/3/88: 3 – Bolivia to buy back debt at 11% of face value.

Ffrench-Davis R 1980 Liberalización de las importaciones: la experiencia chilena en 1973–79, *Estudios Cieplan* **4**: 39–78.

Ffrench-Davis R, Tironi E (eds) 1982 *Latin America and the New International Economic Order*. Macmillan.

Ford M 1988 The motor industry in South Korea: reacting to trends at home and abroad, *Financial Times*, October 20: 10.

Frank A G 1969 *Capitalism and Underdevelopment in Latin America*. Monthly Review Press.

Frank A G 1982 Asia's exclusive models, *Far Eastern Economic Review* 22–3.

Frank I (ed) 1975 *The Japanese Economy in International Perspective*. Johns Hopkins University Press.

Franko L G 1976 *The European Multinationals*. Harper & Row.

Fransman, M 1985 Conceptualising technical change in the Third World in the 1980s; an interpretative survey, *Journal of Development Studies* **21**: 572–652.

Fransman, M 1986 International competitiveness, technical change and the state: the machine tool industry in Taiwan and Japan, *World Development* **14**: 1375–96.

Galbraith J 1967 *The New Industrial State*. Penguin.

Galbraith J 1979 *The Nature of Mass Poverty*. Penguin.

Gardner D 1986 Mexico: aiming for exports, *Financial Times Motor Industry Survey* 14 October: 8.

Gardner D 1987 The rich pickings in America's backyard, *Financial Times* 31 July: 14.

Garza G, Schteingart M 1978 Mexico City: the emerging metropolis, *Latin American Urban Research* **6**: 51–86.

Gereffi G, Evans P 1981 Transnational corporations, dependent development and state policy in the semiperiphery: a comparison of Brazil and Mexico, *Latin American Research Review* **16**: 31–64.

Germani G 1965 *Politica y sociedad en una epoca de transición*. Paidos.

Gerschenkron A 1962 *Economic Backwardness in History Perspective*.. Harvard University Press.

Gilbert A 1974 Industrial location theory: its relevance to an industrialising nation. In Hoyle B S (ed) *Spatial Aspects of Development*. John Wiley, pp. 271–90.

Gooding K 1979 The car majors embark on a revolutionary change of course, *Financial Times* 14 August: 12.

Gooding K 1986 Accelerating on road to change, *Financial Times Motor Industry Survey* 14 October: 1 & 12.

Gooding K 1987 South Korea's Hyundai gears up for the big league, *Financial Times* 20 February: 16.

Gould B 1988 Brazil, *South* 93: 49–61.

Gould B 1989 The state of São Paulo, *South* **101**: 35–45.

Graham R 1987 Mexico, *Financial Times Survey* 10 December.

Griffith-Jones S 1982 Transnational finance and Latin American national development, *IDS Discussion Paper 175*, University of Sussex.

Gwynne R N 1976 *Economic development and structural change: the Chilean case, 1970–73*. Department of Geography, University of Birmingham, Occasional Publication No. 2.

Gwynne R N 1978a The motor vehicle industry in Latin America, *Bank of London and South America Review* **12**: 426 37.

Gwynne R N 1978b Government planning and the location of the motor vehicle industry in Chile, *Tijdschrift voor Econ. en Soc. Geografie* **69**: 130–40.

Gwynne R N 1978c City size and retail prices in less developed countries, *Area* **10**: 136 40.

Gwynne R N 1978d Industrial development in the periphery: the motor vehicle industry in Chile, *Bulletin of the Society for Latin American Studies* **29**: 47 69.

Gwynne R N 1979a The Venezuelan automobile industry, *Business Venezuela* **64**: 24–28.

Gwynne R N 1979b Oligopolistic reaction, *Area* **11**: 315–19.

Gwynne R N 1980 The Andean group automobile programme: an interim assessment, *Bank of London and South America Review* **14**: 160–8.

Gwynne R N 1982 Location theory and the centralization of industry in Latin America, *Tijdschrift voor Econ. en Soc. Geografie* **73**: 80–93.

Gwynne R N 1985 *Industrialisation and Urbanisation in Latin America*. Croom Helm.

Haitani K 1976 *The Japanese Economic System*. Lexington.

Hamilton F E I 1984 Industrial restructuring: an inter-national problem, *Geoforum* **15**: 349–64.

Hamilton F E I 1986 The multinationals: spectre or spearhead? In Dixon C J, Drakakis-Smith D, Watts H D (eds) *Multinational Corporations and the Third World*. Croom Helm, pp. 1–24.

Harris N 1986 *The End of the Third World: newly industrialising countries and the decline of an ideology*. I. B. Tauris.

Hawkins A M 1986 Can Africa industrialize. In Berg R J *et al*. *Strategies for African development*. University of California Press, pp. 279–307.

Hirschman A O 1968 The political economy of import-substituting industrialization in Latin American countries, *Quarterly Journal of Economics* 82: 1–32.

Hone Y 1965 Modern entrepreneurship in Meiji Japan. In Lockwood W W (ed) *The State and Economic Enterprise in Japan*. Princeton University Press.

Housego D 1988 New world in the making: Asia's Pacific Rim, *Financial Times Report, 30 June.*

Hughes H, Parry T (eds) 1987 *Explaining the Success of Industrialization in East Asia.* Cambridge University Press.

Interamerican Development Bank (IADB) 1985 *Economic and Social Progress in Latin America.*

Isard W 1956 *Location and Space Economy* MIT Press.

Jacobsson S 1984 Industrial policy for the machine tool industries of South Korea and Taiwan, *IDS Bulletin* **15**: 44 9.

Jacobsson S 1985 Technical change and industrial policy: the case of computer numerically controlled lathes in Argentina, Korea and Taiwan, *World Development* **13**.

Jacobsson S 1986 *Electronics and Industrial Policy: the case of computer controlled lathes.* Allen & Uwin.

Jenkins R O 1987a *Transnational Corporations and the Latin American automobile industry.* Macmillan.

Jenkins R O 1987b *Transnational Corporations and Uneven Development.* Methuen.

Johns R 1987 The Mexican motor industry: compensating for home slump, *Financial Times*, December 10.

Johnston R J 1984 The world is our oyster, *Transactions of the Institute of British Geographers* **9**: 443–59.

Johnston R J (ed) 1985 *The Future of Geography.* Methuen.

Jones D, Graves A 1986 The race for pole position – revolution in the car industry, *Marxism Today* **30**: 28–32.

Jones D, Womack J 1985 Developing countries and the future of the automobile industry, *World Development*, **13**: 393–407.

Kaplinsky R 1984 The international context for industrialisation in the coming decade, *Journal of Development Studies* **21**: 75–96.

Katz J 1982 Technological change and development in Latin America, In Ffrench-Davis R, Tironi E (eds) *Latin America and the new international economic order.* Macmillan, pp. 192–211.

Katz J 1987 Domestic technology generation in LDCs: a review of research findings, In Katz J (ed) *Technology Generation in Latin American Manufacturing Industries.* Macmillan, pp. 13–55.

Kemp T 1983 *Industrialisation in the non-western world.* Longman.

Kidron M, Segal R 1984 *The state of the world atlas.* Pan.

Kim K S 1985 Lessons from South Korea's experience with industrialization. In Corbo V *et al.* (eds) *Export-oriented development strategies.* Westview, pp. 57–78.

Kindleberger C 1969 *American Business Abroad.* Yale University Press.

King R 1986 South Korea: exporting to major world markets, *Financial Times Motor Industry Survey* 14 October: 8.

King R 1987 Taiwan, *Financial Times Survey*, 12 November.

Kirkpatrick C N, Nixson F I (eds) 1983 *The Industrialisation of the Less Developed Countries.* Manchester University Press.

Kitching G 1982 *Development and Underdevelopment in Historical Perspective.* Methuen.

Knickerbocker F T 1973 *Oligopolistic Reaction and the Multinational Enterprise.* Harvard University Press.

Krueger A O 1983 *Trade and employment in Developing Countries.* University of Chicago Press.

Krueger A O 1985a The experience and lessons of Asia's super exporters. In Corbo V *et al.* (eds) *Export-Oriented development Strategies.* Westview, pp. 187–212.

Krueger A O 1985b Importance of general policies to promote economic growth, *World Economy* **8**: 93–108.

Kuznets S 1968 Notes on Japan's economic growth. In Klein L, Ohkawa K (eds) *Economic growth: the Japanese experience since the Meiji era.* Irwin, pp. 385–422.

Lall S, Streeten P 1977 *Foreign Investment, Transnationals and Developing Countries.* Macmillan.

Landes D S 1969 *The Unbound Prometheus.* Cambridge University Press.

Lehmann J P 1982 *The Roots of Modern Japan.* Macmillan.

Lewis W A 1955 *The Theory of Economic Growth.* Allen & Unwin.

Liedholm C, Mean D C 1986 Small-scale industry. In Berg R J *et al. Strategies for African Development.* University of California Press, pp. 308–30.

Little I M D, Scitovsky T, Scott M F 1970 *Industry and Trade in some Developing Countries.* Oxford University Press.

Lloyd P, Dicken P 1977 *Location in Space: a theoretical approach to economic geography.* Harper & Row.

Lockwood W W 1954 *The Economic development of Japan: Growth and structural change, 1868–1938.* Oxford University Press.

Maddison A 1982 *Phases of Capitalist Development.* Oxford University Press.

Manners G 1986 Multinationals and the exploitation of non-renewable resources. In Dixon C J, Drakakis-Smith D, Watts H D (eds) *Multinational Corporations and the Third World.* Croom Helm, pp. 25–38.

Mcmillan C J 1985 *The Japanese Industrial System.* De Gruyter.

Mendez C 1979 *Chilean Economic Policy*. Central Bank of Chile. Santiago.

Mericle K 1984 The political economy of the Brazilian motor vehicle industry. In Kronish R, Mericle K (eds) *The Political Economy of the Latin American Motor Vehicle Industry*. MIT Press.

Mill J S 1848 *Principles of Political Economy*. P. F. Collier (1900).

Morley S A 1982 *Labor Markets and Inequitable Growth: the case of authoritarian capitalism in Brazil*. Cambridge University Press.

Moser C O N 1978 Informal sector of petty commodity production: dualism or dependence in urban development?, *World Development* **6**:

Moulder F V 1977 *Japan, China and the Modern World Economy*. Cambridge University Press.

Mountjoy A B 1962 *Industrialisation and Developing Countries*. Hutchinson.

Nakamura J I 1966 *Agricultural production and the economic development of Japan, 1873–1922*. Princeton University Press.

Newfarmer R (ed) 1985 *Profits, Progress, Poverty: Studies of international industries in Latin America*. Notre Dame University Press.

Nicoll A 1988 The Latin American debt crisis, *Financial Times* 15 march: 6.

Ohkawa K, Ranis G (eds) 1985 *Japan and the Developing Countries: a comparative analysis*. Basil Blackwell.

Okita S 1980 *The developing economies and Japan*. University of Tokyo Press.

O'Neill H 1984 NICs, MICs, HICs and LICs: some elements in the political economy of graduation and differentiation, *World Development* **12**: 7.

Organisation for Economic Cooperation and Development (OECD) 1988 *The Newly Industrialising Countries: Challenge and opportunity for OECD industries*.

Pack H 1987 *Productivity, Technology, and Industrial Development*. Oxford University Press.

Parsons T, Shils E (eds) 1951 *Towards a General theory of Action*. Harvard University Press.

Patrick H, Rosovsky H (eds) 1976 *Asia's new Giant: How the Japanese economy works*. Brookings.

Poznanski K 1986 Patterns of technology imports: interregional comparison, *World Development* **14**: 743–56.

Prebisch R 1950 *The Economic development of Latin America and its Principal Problems*. UNECLA.

Rapoport C 1987a Japanese digital audio tape sales short of target, *Financial Times* 13 July: 7.

Rapoport C 1987b Japanese industry, *Financial Times Survey* 7 December.

Rapp W V 1976 Firm size and Japan's export structure. In Patrick H (ed) *Japanese Industrialization and its Social Consequences*. University of California Press, pp. 201–48.

Ricardo D 1817 *On the Principles of Political Economy and Taxation*. Penguin (1971).

Rosenstein-Rodan P N 1962 Notes on the theory of the 'Big Push'. In Ellis H S (ed) *Economic Development for Latin America*. Macmillan.

Rostow W W 1960 *The Stages of Economic Growth*. Cambridge University Press.

Roxborough I 1979 *Theories of Underdevelopment*. Macmillan.

Rugman A M 1981 *Inside the Multinational: The economics of internal markets*. Croom Helm.

Sainmont H 1979 *La pequeña y mediana industria chilena*. UNIDO.

Salter W E G 1960 *Productivity and Technical Change*. Cambridge University Press.

Schmitz H 1982 *Manufacturing in the Backyard: Case studies on accumulation and employment in small-scale Brazilian industry*. Frances Pinter.

Schmitz H 1984 Industrialization strategies in less developed countries: some lessons of historical experience, *Journal of Development Studies* **21**: 1–21.

Schumpeter J A 1934 *The Theory of Economic Development*. Harvard University Press.

Schumpeter J A 1939 *Business Cycles*. McGraw-Hill.

Schumpeter J A 1943 *Capitalism, Socialism and Democracy*. Allen and Unwin.

Sciberras E, Payne B 1985 *Technical Change and International Competitiveness: a study of the machine tool industry*. Longman.

Scott A M 1979 Who are the self-employed?, In Bromley R, Gerry C (eds) *Casual Work and Poverty in Third World Cities*. John Wiley.

Sen G 1984 *The Military Origins of Industrialisation and International trade Rivalry*. Pinter.

Shinohara M 1968 Patterns and some structural changes in Japan's postwar industrial growth. In Klein L, Ohkawa K (eds) *Economic growth: the Japanese experience since the Meiji era*. Irwin, pp. 278–302.

Shionoya Y 1968 Patterns of Industrial Development. In Klein L, Ohkawa K (eds) *Economic Growth: The Japanese experience since the Meiji era*. Irwin, pp. 69–109.

Sigmund P E 1980 *Multinationals in Latin America*. University of Wisconsin Press.

Skinner A (ed) 1979 *Adam Smith: the wealth of nations*. Penguin.

Smith C H 1980 *Japanese Technology Transfer to Brazil.* UMI Research Press.

Smith R H T 1964 Toward a measure of complementarity, *Economic Geography* **40**: 1–8.

Soon T T 1983 South East Asia. In Storey D J (ed) *The Small Firm: an international survey.* Croom Helm, pp. 218–247.

Sunkel O 1973 Transnational capitalism and national disintegration in Latin America, *Social and Economic Studies* **22**: 132–76.

Ternent J A S 1976 Urban concentration and dispersal: urban policies in Latin America. In Gilbert A (ed) *Development Planning and Spatial Structure.* John Wiley, pp. 169–85.

Thomson R 1987 Jiangsu, *Financial Times Survey* 8 September.

Tipton H 1979 Numerical control, *Engineer's Digest* 69–74.

Todaro M 1978 *Economic Development in the Third World.* Longman.

Townroe P M, Keen D 1984 Polarization reversal in the state of São Paulo, *Regional Studies* **18**: 45–54.

Trebilcock C 1981 *The Industrialization of the Continental Powers, 1780–1914.* Longman.

Tsing S C 1985 Foreign trade and investment as boosters for take-off: the experience of Taiwan. In Corbo V *et al.* (eds) *Export-oriented Development Strategies.* Westview, pp. 27–56.

Tussie D (ed) *Latin America in the World Economy.* Gower.

Tyler W G 1981 *The Brazilian Industrial Economy.* Heath.

Ullman E 1956 The role of transportation and the bases for interaction. In Thomas W L (ed) *Man's Role in Changing the Face of the Earth.* University of Chicago Press, pp. 862–80.

United Nations Economic Commission for Latin America (UNECLA) 1979 *Analysis and Prospects of Latin American Industrial Development.* CEPAL.

US Academy of Sciences 1983 *The Competitive State of the US Machine Tool Industry.* National Academy Press.

Vaitsos C 1974 *Inter-Country Income Distribution and Transnational Enterprises.* Clarendon Press.

Vernon R 1966 International investment and international trade in the product cycle, *Quarterly Journal of Economics* **80**: 190–207.

Vernon R 1977 *Storm over the Multinationals: the real issues.* Macmillan.

Vernon R 1979 The product life cycle hypothesis in a new international environment, *Oxford Bulletin of Economics and Statistics* **41**: 255–67.

Wallerstein I 1974 *The Modern World System.* Academic Press.

Wallerstein I 1979 *The Capitalist World Economy.* Cambridge University Press.

Wallerstein I 1984 *The Politics of the World Economy.* Cambridge University Press.

Warren B 1973 Imperialism and capitalist industrialization, *New Left Review* **81**.

Warren B 1980 *Imperialism: Pioneer of Capitalism.* Verso.

Watanabe S 1983 *Market Structure, Industrial Organisation and Technological Development: the case of the Japanese electronics-based NC machine tool industry.* ILO.

Watanabe T 1968 Industrialization, technological progress and dual structure. In Klein L, Ohkawa K (eds) *Economic Growth: the Japanese experience since the Meiji era.* Irwin, pp. 110–34.

Watts H D 1987 *Industrial Geography.* Longman.

Weiss J 1988 *Industry in Developing Countries.* Routledge.

White G 1984 State and market in socialist development: the case of Chinese industrial planning, *IDS Bulletin* **15**: 4–10.

Whitehead L 1987 Latin American debt; an international relations perspective. Paper delivered at the Annual Conference of the British International Studies Association, Aberystwyth.

Willmore L N 1986 The comparative performance of foreign and domestic firms in Brazil, *World Development* **14**: 489–502.

Wolf M 1982 Timing and sequencing of trade liberalization in developing countries, *Asian Development Review* **4**: 1–24.

Wood A 1984 When the bottom goes out of copper, *Geographical Magazine* **56**: 16–20.

World Bank 1981 *World Development Report 1981.* Oxford University Press.

World Bank 1983 *World Development Report 1983.* Oxford University Press.

World Bank 1984 *World Development Report 1984.* Oxford University Press.

World Bank 1985 *World Development Report 1985.* Oxford University Press.

World Bank 1986 *World Development Report 1986.* Oxford University Press.

World Bank 1987 *World Development Report 1987.* Oxford University Press.

World Bank 1988 *World Development Report 1988.* Oxford University Press.

—— I N D E X ——